Venezuela's Bolivarian Democracy

Participation, Politics, and Culture under Chávez

David Smilde and Daniel Hellinger, editors

Duke University Press
Durham and London
2011

© 2011 Duke University Press
All rights reserved
Printed in the United States of America on acid-free paper ∞
Typeset in Charis and TheSans by Tseng Information Systems, Inc.
Library of Congress Cataloging-in-Publication Data appear on the
last printed page of this book.

We dedicate this book to all Venezuelans
working to create participatory democracy.

Contents

Venezuela's Bolivarian Democracy

Julia Buxton

Venezuela during the Chávez period (from 1998 to the present) provides rich insights that can inform conceptual understanding across a range of different scholarly disciplines. From social science to the liberal arts, from economics to international relations, the Bolivarian experience of radical change in economic, social, energy, and foreign policy challenges many contemporary assumptions and paradigms. Moreover, the experience of conflict and polarization that characterized the development and application of the Bolivarian process fundamentally transformed Venezuelan society and culture. Consequently the country is an interesting laboratory for exploring the impacts of major political upheaval on identities, loyalties, and values.

The Bolivarian Revolution may also provide helpful lessons for the international donor and development community. In 1999 Hugo Chávez inherited a country characterized by profound inequalities in the distribution of wealth, land, housing, education, employment, and security. His regime sought to reverse this through novel policy and organizational initiatives to distribute and redistribute public goods in favor of those located outside mainstream political and economic activity in the informal sector. Community participation, social capital development, stakeholder engagement, and gender mainstreaming were central elements of programs that were intended to recast citizenship and promote inclusion. These are all stressed in the donor and development literature, but they are rarely applied in practice. Venezuela provides a rare opportunity to study the implementation of such major projects of social transformation, their successes and failures in application, their impact on communities, and whether they reached their stated goals.

Opportunities Lost

Despite the contextual and conceptual importance of the Bolivarian Revolution, there is a marked reluctance to bring empirical depth to discussion and analysis of Venezuela during the Chávez period. Commentary in the media, academic, and policy circles has been polarized, disarmingly subjective, and narrowly focused on high politics. There are a number of factors that account for this, in particular the lack of quality analysis of the *popular* experience of the Bolivarian Revolution. Actually, more subtle and informed interpretations may be found in entertainment programming than news, as Acosta-Alzuru's chapter shows.

The Bolivarian process and Chávez's foreign policies challenged the fundamentals of liberal peace theory and its twin tenets of free markets and liberal democracy. As international initiatives to expand and consolidate this post–cold war vision were given fresh impetus by the events of September 11, 2001, Venezuela moved against the orthodoxy of policy. Located in a hemisphere dominated by the United States, this was a dramatic move, particularly as national and energy security moved to the forefront of U.S. strategic imperatives. The Chávez period was one of rupture, constant change, and displacement. Old elites and system beneficiaries were replaced by new actors and constituencies with different interests, identities, cultures, and priorities, and traditional lobby mechanisms were supplanted by new and typically informal networks of influence and access.

This context proved deleterious for meaningful engagement with, and qualitative analysis of, developments in the country. There was a marked reluctance within academic and policy circles to break with the analytical framework of liberal democracy. Venezuela's failure to conform to procedural benchmarks led to the swift categorization of the Bolivarian process and its initiatives as authoritarian (Diamond 2008; Dominguez and Jones 2007; Legler, Lean, and Boniface 2007; Ottaway 2003; Shifter 2007), in turn delegitimizing and discrediting the participatory initiatives and the validity of new social and organizational forms emerging in the country. Exploring Venezuela through the prism of authoritarianism also led to a disproportionate focus on high politics and state institutions even though these had effectively ceased to be the primary mechanisms for the articulation of interests, representation, and government oversight. But the assumption that the diminution of the competency and authority of these organs translated into the negation of all forms of bargaining, exchange, and accountability was fundamentally wrong. Politics in Venezuela had assumed new dimensions and dynamics, but these could not be captured through the authoritarian framework of analysis.

The tendency to negatively evaluate the Bolivarian process against the universal standards of liberal democracy was also reflected in the opinions of government officials, particularly in the United States (Reich 2005). These opinions reinforced and were reinforced by highly negative assessments of economic and political freedom in Venezuela produced by nongovernmental and quasi-governmental organizations, such as the National Endowment for Democracy, Freedom House, and Transparency International. These organizations created a cycle of opinion formation and information exchange among critics who were inadequately positioned to understand the drivers of the government's popularity because of the rigidity of their approaches and their failure to engage with the popular experience.

A consuming focus on the figure of President Chávez in the academic and policy literature further obscured the dynamics of change at the grassroots level, while marginalizing the complexity of the process of social change (Marcano and Barrera Tyszka 2007). Efforts to understand the Bolivarian process through the lens of populism and to squeeze the revolution into established analytical categories rarely engaged with the social and cultural changes set in motion or broke with the democracy-authoritarianism dichotomy (Reid 2007; Sylvia and Danopoulos 2003; Weyland 2003b), while the predominance of orthodox economists and a related focus on the economic determinants of voting behavior exacerbated the lack of engagement with the impacts of the Bolivarian Revolution on Venezuelan society (Penfold-Bencerra 2007; F. Rodríguez 2008; Weyland 2003a). With collective and individual actions reduced to economic transactions, the capacity to anticipate the future, understand the popular experience, and assess consequences was ameliorated. Econometric analysis of the rationality, fiscal or otherwise, of the missions, for example, provided no insight into the popular experience of participation in these projects, the type of associative experience they afforded, their role in building social capital, or their contribution to the legitimacy and popularity of the government.

Even within development organizations, there was a profound reluctance to examine the Venezuelan case, despite the fact that the administration designed and delivered a host of initiatives to help the poor. And so, for example, while USAID and the UK Department for International Development enthusiastically supported micro-credit schemes for the poor, mainstreaming of gender in anti-poverty initiatives, community empowerment, and stakeholder engagement in social-policy initiatives (all of which were central to the Bolivarian model), they saw the Venezuelan experience as irrelevant on the grounds that the country was unequal and not impoverished. The Bolivarian model of democracy was not regarded by the liberal, peace-oriented development community as one that could be endorsed. Thus, opportunities to identify best practices, success, and constraints in devising transformative social projects in the context of institutional sclerosis and social deprivation were squandered or dismissed out of hand due to subjective biases that failed to disentangle Chávez the individual from the policies enacted.

As David Smilde notes in the introduction to this volume, the Bolivarian Revolution has received much attention in the international media. On the whole, this has cultivated negative impressions of the Bolivarian experience by maintaining a focus on Chávez and approaching governance in the country through the rubric of authoritarianism. An over-reliance on wire services and a failure to undertake investigative reporting and a strongly pro-opposition bias in sourcing, have served to marginalize popular views and experiences.

Ultimately, much of what has been written about Venezuela during the Bolivarian Revolution has not been based on "facts on the ground," robust and rigorous analysis, or objective assessment of the Chávez government and its functioning. Instead, there has been a profusion of media articles, conference papers, think-tank reports, and political statements based on assumption and speculation, not interviews or fieldwork with relevant stakeholders or actors. These have served to shed darkness where there is a need for light, they have misled audiences, and in countries like the United States, Colombia, and the UK they have birthed counterproductive interventions.

The Need for New Approaches

This volume is important in four fundamental respects. First, it breaks with the notion that Venezuela should be analyzed or assessed as a liberal democracy. It defines Venezuela as a state-sponsored participatory democracy and as a result, it is positioned to explore new dimensions in debates on citizenship, civil society, and the meaning of democracy. Second, the book redresses the distortions and imbalances created by the traditional focus on liberal democracy, formal institutions, and high politics by addressing grassroots interests, communities, informal mechanisms, and public culture in line with its analytical focus on state-sponsored participatory democracy. These are all fundamental to an understanding of the multiple and complex changes that have occurred in Venezuela during the Chávez period. In particular, the volume breaks with the temptation to analyze participatory and mobilizational initiatives through formal organizations, such as political parties, interest groups, and trades unions. The contributions in the volume identify new trends, actors, and tendencies, and in doing so they reveal a host of new organizational realities in the country. Third, the contributors support their assessments with empirical information and detailed fieldwork. The results are illuminating. They challenge many of the basic assumptions about social and political engagement in the country, in turn identifying possible future trajectories. The shift back to qualitative research in many of the chapters marks a welcome break from the purportedly logical assumptions of economists and from the crude, elite-focused moldings of the populist school. It grounds analysis in the popular experience and in doing so highlights the manifold challenges and opportunities faced by the Chávez government.

Following Venezuela's democratization in 1958, there was interest in the psephology and political culture of the country. But academic inquiry was incrementally hijacked by narrow institutionalist approaches that focused on formal structures and in particular on pacts and political parties. This detracted attention from the growing informal sphere of social, cultural, political, and economic life. Venezuelan academics were as culpable as their North American counterparts in neglecting the history and dynamics of the "other" Venezuela. It is only now, through efforts to understand the meaning, roots, and appeal of Chavismo through engagement with the informal, that the history of the marginalized majority is being researched and written. As demonstrated by the contributions to this volume, it is a rich and multilayered history that feeds into our understanding of contemporary reality, one that questions both the classification of Chavismo as an authoritarian project and depictions of Chávez as all powerful, unconstrained, and unaccountable. Instead, the analysis presented in these chapters points to a mesh of formal and informal constraints, limitations, and pressures that bind the administration and indicate elements of its fragility and vulnerability. The authors portray a dynamic, reflexive, and vibrant civil society, a participatory reality that counters the populist and econometric assumptions of an inarticulate and irrational mass. Herein lies the fourth significant advance made by this book. The chapters in this volume reintegrate the Bolivarian process back into the specific social, political, and cultural context of Venezuela's evolution. In addressing changes to popular culture, public discourse, and social identity, the chapters root assessment of transformation against the legacy of the illiberal Punto Fijo democracy. This makes it possible to gauge the scope, depth, and sustainability of the process and also to identify patterns of continuity with the *status quo ante*. This approach is infinitely more instructive and valuable than assessments predicated on illusory norms.

Lessons to Be Learned

This volume provides a number of important insights that merit wide dissemination so scholarship and commentary on Venezuela can progress from the current polarized stalemate and the perennial emphasis on benchmarks of democratic quality.

The first of these is the heterogeneity of Venezuelan society. In highlighting how participation, sentiment, and experience differ across communities, sectors, barrios, states, and regions, the chapters demonstrate the limitations of generic accounts and the importance of nuanced, focused, and context-specific analysis. Contemporary Venezuela emerges as a highly fluid and diverse polity, characterized by multiple and crosscutting cleavages, identities, and loyalties. Interrelated with this, each chapter presents a rich account of pluralism and tolerance. This cuts across crude pro- and anti-Chávez schemas, demonstrating a proliferation of values and opinions within what are otherwise perceived as static, homogenous, and conflicting camps. As demonstrated in Smilde's introduction and in particular the contributions by Daniel Hellinger and Alejandro Velasco, we find, for example, that among those who identify as *chavistas* there is a dynamic profusion of (sometimes antagonistic) ideologies and aspirations, which in turn points to the challenges the government faces in sustaining a broad-based alliance, responding to popular demands, and consolidating new participatory forms and representative mechanisms such as the PSUV (Partido Socialista Unico de Venezuela). Hellinger's analysis of political values further demonstrates the importance of grounded research. His findings confront established assumptions about the political opinions and perspectives of barrio residents. Hellinger's work and also the contribution by Kirk Hawkins, Guillermo Rosas, and Michael Johnson show barrio residents—who are typically portrayed as unwaveringly loyal to Chávez (and by default illiberal)—to be highly pluralist, diverse, and autonomous, with loyalties driven by a variety of factors. This research is all the more insightful when set against the backdrop of the PSUVs' defeat in large and politically important barrios such as Petare and Sucre in the regional elections of November 2008.

In comparison with the Punto Fijo period (1958–1998), associational life in Venezuela has undoubtedly been strengthened as a result of both the government's participatory initiatives and the context of conflict. The legitimacy of political participation, political engagement, and political institutions has been strengthened as well. As poll surveys demonstrate, Chávez himself remained remarkably popular through the end of 2009, a decade after assuming power; confidence in the National Assembly and politicians improved strongly after the nadir of the 1980s and 1990s; and Venezuelans had a high level of confidence in democratic forms and their own democratic and electoral systems, as indicated by the Latinobarómetro surveys of 2006, 2007, and 2008.[1] This raises important questions as to the most appropriate analytical tools and benchmarks through which the Bolivarian process should be evaluated. The utility of measurements based on the procedural mechanisms of liberal democracy is clearly questionable, and as Hellinger's chapter on political attitudes in the barrios notes, so is the view that liberal democracy is a universally popular aspiration. Sections of Venezuelan society have repeatedly endorsed the Bolivarian vision of a participatory democracy based on horizontal linkages and with a strong social-welfare component. To dismiss Bolivarianism as authoritarian in this context is to deny plurality in democratic forms and also the legitimacy of endogenous democratic models.

Certainly it is the case that if Chávez's Venezuela is to be judged by the procedural benchmarks of liberal democracy, there is a deficit of checks and balances on government, the rule of law is weak, the military is not apolitical, and executive power is pronounced. But this leads to a number of related considerations. It has never been the case that liberal democracy was consolidated in Venezuela. During the Punto Fijo period, the country had a model of illiberal democracy that delimited participation, restricted access to power, privileged a minority, and politicized all state institutions. The rule of law was historically weak, and corruption and human rights abuses were pronounced. To present the Bolivarian process as some form of democratic regression or authoritarian aberration in this historical context is misleading. It denies the structural legacies of Puntofijismo and negates the progress that has been made in extending social and political inclusion in a historical context characterized by disaffection with political parties, politicians, and institutions.

The procedural mechanics of liberal democracy and the concept of contractual sovereignty are themselves characterized by manifold flaws in application and implementation, even in those countries that uphold themselves as the most advanced democracies in the world. Bolivarianism does not eschew liberal democratic mechanisms. For example, great stress has been placed on election processes, constitutionalism, and the legitimacy of formal institutions such as the National Assembly and the electoral administration. But the overriding objective has been to create a higher form of participatory democracy that engages all citizens on a routine and regular basis. Without understanding the aims and objectives of participatory democracy, it is difficult to engage with the initiatives developed and delivered by the government and to measure their success and legitimacy. More problematically, it is difficult to judge (and criticize) Venezuela for its failure to meet illusionary yardsticks of good governance and democracy set by, for example, Transparency International or Freedom House, to which the Chávez administration does not aspire, and which few countries actually meet in practice. Venezuela is but one of a number of countries where the universalist, modernizing assumptions and democratic classifications of liberals should rightfully be challenged on the basis that they do not engage with or measure popular understanding of real existing democracy and its practice.

Compounding the image of Venezuela as a politically complex country that defies facile generalization, it is also evident that political values and opinions are multifaceted. While on the one hand, there is popular support for new participatory mechanisms, at the same time, Venezuelan voters have shown themselves to be guarded in endorsing major structural changes that would allow the Bolivarian model to be institutionalized. Concurring with the findings of Latinobarómetro, Hellinger's survey and Velasco's analysis show that Venezuelans are reluctant to dispense with the trappings of liberal democracy, a factor that may have contributed to President Chávez's defeat in the constitutional reform referendum of December 2007 and the subsequent quashing of his ambitions to introduce a new geometry of power in the country. These nuances in opinion merit more sustained and detailed analysis.

Problematically, as Hellinger, Margarita López Maya and Luis Lander, and Velasco outline, there are continuing questions over the meaning and precise contours of the government's participatory vision, further complicating discussions on the nature and future of democracy in Venezuela. By way of contrast to critical commentaries that point to Bolivarianism as a well-articulated authoritarian strategy, the contributions in this volume flag ideological and organizational uncertainty at the highest level of the Venezuelan government. The administration has yet to articulate a comprehensive vision of its participatory model or elucidate how this will work alongside or in place of existing institutional mechanisms such as the National Assembly, ministries, and state governors. The administration's approach to governance has also too often proved inimical to participatory processes. This has been evident in the repeated use of decree powers by Chávez, the promotion of centrally determined candidates in local elections, and the ongoing tensions in the old MVR (Movimiento Quinta República) and subsequently the PSUV over the role of the pro-government party. The Chavistas finally convened an ideological congress in November 2009, but the direction and end goals of the revolution remain subject to flux, the necessities of alliance building, and pragmatism. Despite abjuring the formal trappings of liberal democracy, the government has, somewhat ironically, relied heavily on elections rather than popular consultation in order to legitimize its programs and policies. This may have come at the cost of developing and institutionalizing new participatory forms.

Linked with debates on the meaning of democracy, this volume also contributes to discourses on civil society. As outlined in the introduction, underpinning the liberal peace and liberal democracy is the notion of a vibrant and autonomous civil society birthed from free markets and political liberty. But in the contemporary Venezuelan experience, political inclusion and participation have been catalyzed by state support. In the populist and authoritarian schools, this has ipso facto been conflated with demagoguery and clientelism. However, the authors here point to a far more optimistic vision of the potentialities of state-sponsored social organization, though not without raising concerns as well.

Autonomous civil society is reified in the social science literature and in contemporary programs and strategies promoting democracy. Social organization supported and financed by the state is too quickly dismissed as fundamentally at odds with the independence and power-checking capacities that autonomy is seen to provide. But as this volume contends, assumptions about Venezuelan social organization, and conceptual schemas that seek to frame understanding of civil society, are not the same as existing and actual reality. Given gross inequities in the distribution of resources, opportunities, and capacities, it is necessary to question how marginalized and excluded groups can take organizational form and gain traction if not through state assistance. State neglect of financial support for associational opportunities for the poorest serves only to institutionalize grotesque inequities in access and participation. In countries such as Venezuela, these inequalities are reinforced by external funding programs, for example, the National Endowment for Democracy, that channel resources to those who have access to program managers, who can complete funding application forms, and who share the interests of the United States in the region, which is to say the old elite. In sum, autonomous civil society is an ideal type that rarely exists in practice and whose democratic tendencies should not be taken for granted. More crucially, as a number of the chapters in this volume highlight, state funding should not be automatically conflated with depreciated autonomy or inevitable harmony with the administration.

The contributions by López Maya and Lander, María Pilar García-Guadilla, Naomi Schiller, Sujatha Fernandes, Velasco, and David Smilde and Coraly Pagan certainly highlight the dilemmas faced by state-sponsored organizations and the complex evaluations that have to be made by actors seeking to position themselves favorably with the administration. Decisions on linkages and maximization of access are forged within a highly unstable context characterized by a perennial turnover of personnel and a high level of reliance on personal contacts and informal networks. While this raises issues of co-optation, it is through the rich discussion of contingent autonomy that this volume portrays the density of Venezuelan civil society, the complexity of contemporary social relations, and the multiple spaces for negotiation.

The chapters by Luis Duno Gottberg, Elizabeth Gackstetter Nichols, and Smilde and Pagan remind us that opponents of the government have also had to adjust to evolving participatory opportunities and limitations on the promotion of their influence and interests. The capacity to articulate critical positions was severely eroded following the collapse of the historically dominant parties and their subsequent decision not to participate in electoral processes. As the organizational impetus passed to the media, the Catholic Church, the private sector and the national intelligentsia, opponents of the government forged new spaces for dissent outside of formal institutions, exploiting principles of freedom of speech and organization to discredit and delegitimize the government. A reading of Duno Gottberg's chapter reinforces Smilde's introductory remarks that civil society is not necessarily progressive or democratic, while both of Hellinger's chapters—on Aporrea.org and on community-level participation— point to the potential for this antagonism to be channeled through the new participatory framework. Taken together, these chapters reinforce a vision of sweeping social and cultural change and experimentation across all sectors with new organizational forms that have been driven by conflict, revolution, and legacies of the pre-Chávez period. These may not prove enduring, but the chapters make it clear that the changes cannot be simply rolled back. Political inclusion and participation have expanded exponentially in the country, with important ramifications for the future of the Chávez government and the post-Chávez political landscape.

In providing a legal framework for social organization, and in some cases financing participatory initiatives, the Chávez administration may have created serious long-term constraints on its own power. Whether these organizations are part of the unofficial structure of governance—such as the MTAs (Mesas Técnicas de Agua), the CTUs (Comités de Tierras Urbanas), the missions, and the communal councils—or not (as with the community media organizations), they demonstrate a marked tendency toward independence and defense of constituency interests, which is in turn premised on the networks and functions of accountability that bind them to their own communities and social bases (Antillano 2005). The participatory initiatives consequently emerge as vectors of democracy. These complicated transactional realities, often obscured by analytical and classificatory schemes putting the focus on authoritarianism and high politics, are captured in a number of the chapters presented here.

In this context, another valuable contribution of this volume is in writing the long-neglected history of organization and activism among the traditional elite—as discussed by Smilde and Pagan and by Nichols—and in reclaiming barrio histories from Chavismo. It is commonly assumed that associational life in the barrios was negligible until the ascent to power of the Chávez government. This feeds into populist accounts that look to Chavismo as a top-down model of social incorporation and subsequent demobilization, and also into a Bolivarian narrative that posits barrio organization as a product of the revolution and its defense. The reality, marginalized in established scholarship on Venezuela, is that self-organization and activism has a vibrant history in the most deprived and marginalized neighborhoods of the country. It is certainly the case that the Chávez government provided unprecedented financial support and official access to these groups and associations, but the idea that Chávez inherited a tabula rasa of organizations among the poor that it subsequently set about molding is quite wrong.

Without knowledge of these informal traditions and associational forms, it is difficult to engage with the constraints faced by the Chávez government or to understand the myriad of networks that embed accountability and structure legitimacy. Loyalties and identities are evidently crafted by both proximate, localized concerns and broader macro-ideological allegiances, but it should not be assumed that the latter inevitably trumps the former. Community activism is structured by rational and immediate interests, and where these are countered or negated by national policy, they will be defended. Recognition of and re-engagement with the diverse histories of community organization point to a stronger capacity for autonomy and dissent than is commonly assumed, particularly given the spur to organizational coherence that has been provided by political conflict and material support from the state.

Bolivarianism in Context

As in any revolutionary process, the Chávez government's agenda faced strong resistance from the historical status quo—resistance that was notoriously supported and condoned by the United States and some European and South American countries. Despite the noisy, destabilizing, and frequently unconstitutional and undemocratic interventions on the part of the administration's opponents, Chávez and the Bolivarian Revolution prevailed. In a region where progressive ideologies have been violently suppressed, where edgings toward European social democracy have been quashed as communist infiltration, and where the demands of the "barbarous" majority have been brutally sidelined, Bolivarianism marked a revolutionary rupture from traditional domestic and regional alignments of power and ideology. That this was achieved within the bounds of electoral democracy and through constant recourse to popular consultation (including five referenda between 1999 and 2008) makes this process of change all the more significant.

Despite the emphasis on revolution and change, in locating itself within the Venezuelan historical context this book is also positioned to highlight issues of continuity. Many of the chapters express concern that the Chávez administration is making the same mistakes as the Punto Fijo period. Elements of this continuity are evident in, for example, the discussion on the sustainability of the government's oil-financed social programs in the contribution by López Maya and Lander. Here the Chávez government appears guilty of replicating misguided Punto Fijo strategies of over-reliance on oil export revenues to finance state-led development strategies. An additional aspect of continuity lies in the patterns of exclusion and inclusion. Contributions in this volume demonstrate that the Bolivarian model, like the Punto Fijo system, is structured around networks of privileged access and loyalty. The distinction between the two regimes is predicated on the displacement of traditional Punto Fijo beneficiaries with a new constituency of favorites. The dynamics of zero-sum politics and conflict between groups who are in or out have consequently persisted. Politicization, corruption, and favoritism emerge as serious challenges for the Chávez administration, just as they were during the Punto Fijo period, with ultimately debilitating implications. And just as previous presidents relied on decree powers to push through major programs, so Chávez has fallen back on enabling authorities in order to drive through his project of revolutionary change. The manner and execution of executive authority, based as it is on a high concentration of powers, has therefore not been adequately addressed by the Chávez government, despite its commitment to creating a new participatory democracy and despite the generous financial resources it directs toward communal councils.

As highlighted in a number of the chapters, organizational approaches persist that emphasize penetration and control of independent social organizations. This was a key characteristic of party political activity during the Punto Fijo period, and it is one that has been perpetuated by the Chávez government. Linked with this, and as discussed by Hellinger, the Chávez administration has found it difficult to build a political organization dedicated to the promotion of consultative processes. As during the Punto Fijo period, machine politics and related issues of candidate favoritism, parachuting of central-party-favored candidates and sidelining of local candidates have continued during the Bolivarian process, hindering the development and institutionalization of new mobilization and organizational forms at the community level.

A final element of continuity that merits highlighting relates to institutionalism. A fundamental problem during the Punto Fijo period was that the country's elites failed to develop functioning, meritocratic institutions capable of delivering public goods in a neutral and universal manner. The chapters by López Maya and Lander and by García-Guadilla demonstrate that consolidation of policy initiatives and institutionalization of processes have not been priorities for the Chávez administration. This failure in turn has serious implications for the government's ability to ensure the sustainability of its antipoverty and participatory initiatives. As the formal and informal continue to rub alongside each other in a broader context of policy fluctuation and new patterns of favoritism, the potential for adequately monitoring, evaluating, improving, and maintaining projects will diminish. That said, this should not negate the analytical value of exploring the impacts of these programs.

Flux and Motion

This volume repeatedly emphasizes the difficulties of tracking and assessing social and political change in Venezuela. All authors are keenly aware of the rapidly evolving context and the challenges that this poses for evaluating initiatives and the sustainability of new social forms. This recognition of flux and evolution allows this volume to engage with the dynamism of the Bolivarian process, and in doing so, the authors highlight the rigidity of the authoritarian/liberal democracy schema.

The Chávez government of 2009 was a manifestly different proposition from that which initially took power in 1999. When first elected, Chávez cited the British prime minister Tony Blair as a role model, and he endorsed models of "third way socialism," as espoused by Anthony Giddens in his 1998 publication *The Third Way: Renewal of Social Democracy* (according to Gott 2000, 196). Over the following decade, the Chávez government became progressively more radicalized on the back of rising oil export revenues and as it identified and consolidated its core constituency of support and insulated itself from domestic and international pressures from opponents. In many respects, it could be argued that Venezuela arrived at "twenty-first-century socialism" by default, not design (Buxton 2008).

In this environment of dramatic shifts and lurches, new spaces for access and participation opened up and in some cases closed, there was constant innovation and revision, and networks of influence shifted. It is impossible to capture these dynamics unless new analytical tools are developed through which the evolution of Venezuelan politics can be assessed, and without engaging with the multiple and often hidden spaces of activism and participation. This volume has demonstrated the tensions inherent in the creation and generation of new transactional forms in the country and the need to break with sclerotic conceptual frameworks in order to understand how these operate. In doing so, it presents contemporary social and political relations in Venezuela as complex, multilayered, and shifting. It also points readers to possible future trends as Venezuela has entered a period of major change in the macroeconomic environment and as the governance style has narrowed around the authority of President Chávez. Even if those factors that facilitated the initial laying out of the participatory project and the radical, if ad hoc, experimentation with popular mobilization have withered, this volume reminds us that the loyalties, values, and aspirations of ordinary Venezuelans should not be assumed or taken for granted by either the government or its critics.

Note

1. See the annual Latinobarómetro reports for 2006, 2007, and 2008, http://www .latinobarometro.org.

Participation, Politics, and Culture

Emerging Fragments of Venezuela's Bolivarian Democracy

David Smilde

Hugo Chávez's rise to and consolidation of power in Venezuela over the last decade has set into motion perhaps the most controversial political processes in contemporary Latin America. The structure of the Venezuelan government was transformed by the constitution of 1999. The structure of the economy has been transformed by a far-reaching renationalization. Popular participation has become an integral part of state policy. And, of course, Venezuela's role in regional geopolitics has moved from faithful ally of the United States to outspoken critic and competitor.

These processes have correspondingly transformed public discourse. Throughout the 1980s and 1990s political scientists were interested in Venezuela as a case study of an elite-pact "second wave" democracy, which never broke down and seemed to be surviving the neoliberal era (e.g., McCoy et al. 1995); however, other scholarly disciplines and the international media were more interested in the Central American and the Southern Cone countries that were making halting and conflictive transitions from dictatorship to pluralist democracy.

The relative lack of social-historical scholarship on Venezuela was one of the reasons that Chávez's rise to power at the end of the 1990s took so many by surprise. An overwhelming focus on the central institutions of the democratic state and organized political actors such as parties and unions left scholars and journalists under-appreciative of the extent of discontent and the burgeoning forms of alternative participation growing within Venezuelan society.[1] Now the Chávez period has dramatically increased interest in Venezuela. International journalists cover the Venezuelan government's increasing international profile and file human interest stories on aspects of the Chávez Revolution.

Progressive blogs, web pages, and listserv discussion groups exchange alternative information and organize support initiatives. And renewed scholarly interest has diversified research on Venezuela, complementing the traditional focus on the central institutions of the state with ground-level research on the relational contexts in which politics occurs in everyday social life. This book brings together some of the fruits of this newly diversified interest with chapters representing six different disciplines and multiple methodological approaches. The common thread within this diversity is that each chapter seeks to understand actually existing democracy in contemporary Venezuela through empirical research on political phenomena outside of the central institutions of the state.

The collaborators share a concern that the liberal-democratic concepts through which Venezuelan, indeed Latin American, democracy are generally studied have become normative measuring sticks used to evaluate actually existing processes rather than to analyze them on their own terms. As such, the concrete dynamics and logics of actually existing conditions remain in the shadows and elude our understanding. The goal here is not to reject normative considerations per se, but to pursue constructive and critical empirical engagement rather than deductive judgment.

Each chapter shares a focus on phenomena outside of the central institutions of the state. This comes not from a desire to look beyond politics, but from a conviction that political discourse and exchange occur not only in ministries, congresses, and parties but also within and at the intersections of the multiple networks that make up what is often referred to as civil society. Especially when studying a government that has declared its intention to increase the participation of its citizens in multiple ways, it is essential that our scholarly analyses of democracy move beyond so-called big politics. The central institutions of the state are not unimportant—indeed most of the chapters in this volume will make reference to them. But if we want to understand the nature, direction, and future of Venezuela's actually existing democracy, we need to examine how collective life is created and re-created through participation in the myriad institutions, spaces, and contexts that make up Venezuelan society. Indeed, as I will suggest below, the most tangible effects of the revolution might not be the concrete institutions and actors the government creates, but the development of new discourses, identities, networks, and forms of association.

From Punto Fijo to Bolivarian Democracy

We need to start by reviewing the series of social and political changes that ripened conditions for the emergence of Bolivarian democracy, as well as its basic outlines. This is a story that has been told in more detail elsewhere, but some basic orientation is in order.[2]

The democratic regime that ruled Venezuela from 1958 to 1999 was based on the "Pact of Punto Fijo"—named for the home of President Rafael Caldera where it was hammered out—whose overriding goal was to maximize political stability. It pursued this goal not only by excluding elements of the radical Left (for example, the Communist Party), but through a relatively restricted form of representative democracy in which participation was limited to elections in which citizens chose the president and party that would then, in turn, choose the rest of the government officials—from senators and representatives to local mayors and union leaders. These parties were autocratic and hierarchical, and they developed pacts and commissions through which organized political and economic interests were guaranteed a disproportional voice in policy making. They also did considerable grassroots work in organizing the lower classes into clientelistic party networks, providing favors and benefits for votes and support (Ray 1969).

The most important factor in the Punto Fijo regime's legitimacy was the provision of economic well-being and promotion of societal development. Indeed, using its vast oil wealth, the state was able to attend simultaneously to the demands of private capital for accumulation and to the majority's demands for social and economic well-being (Crisp, Levine, and Rey 1995; E. Lander 1995; Salamanca 1997; Neuhouser 1992; Navarro 1995; Karl 1995). Annual growth in the gross domestic product averaged 5 percent from 1958 to 1980. Immunization drives and modernization of health care dramatically increased life expectancy, lowered infant mortality, and led to a threefold increase in population between 1950 and 1990. A country that was 50 percent rural and 50 percent illiterate in 1950 was almost 90 percent urban and 90 percent literate by 1990 (Salamanca 1997). In effect, during this modern period Venezuela went from a poor, unhealthy, and uneducated population to a relatively prosperous nation in full demographic transition.[3]

Considering that Venezuela maintained political and economic stability through a period in which democracies in Chile, Brazil, Argentina, and a number of other Latin American countries broke down, the achievements of this model were remarkable. Indeed through the end of the 1980s, political scientists considered Venezuela to be a model of democratic stability. Summarizing this literature, Steve Ellner (2003, 8–9) says that scholars attributed this stability to seven basic aspects:

1. A two-party system with minimal ideological differentiation.
2. Political leaders committed to democracy who avoided ultranationalist rhetoric.
3. A mature political leadership that, learning from past experiences, discarded sectarian attitudes and formed interparty agreements.
4. Major parties of multi-class composition with a predominately middle-class leadership.
5. An emphasis on party discipline within the two main parties.
6. A political system sufficiently open to provide attractive opportunities for junior coalition partners and other small parties.
7. Parties that were highly institutionalized rather than vehicles for ambitious leaders.

Venezuelan modernity began to unravel in the early 1980s as a drop in oil prices and rising debt burden created a fiscal crisis. While the currency was first devalued in 1983, successive governments postponed structural change as long as possible, until in 1989, under the guidance of the International Monetary Fund (IMF), a severe structural adjustment package was implemented, followed by another round in 1996. The economic figures after 1980 are sobering. Through the 1980s and 1990s, the percentage of the government's budget that went to paying interest on foreign debt steadily increased. Per capita growth for the decade of the 1980s was −3.2 percent. In the 1990s it was −0.3 percent.

Each of the seven strengths of Punto Fijo democracy listed above has to do with the central structures of the state or political elites and leadership. However, the real story of change and transition in the 1980s and 1990s was developing outside of these institutions, among those who bore the effects of this economic decline. While most political scientists continued to view Venezuela as an exceptional example of democratic stability in the region, a few did see the implications of a deteriorating socioeconomic base. Terry Karl, for example, warned that "the long-term viability of this form of pacted democracy and its value as a model for other countries may become clear only when the oil money begins to disappear" (1986, 219). Daniel Hellinger wrote that though the Left was showing little strength electorally, this masked "the steady erosion of mass confidence in the present 'democratic' regime. The Venezuelan state is likely to find itself increasingly caught up in reviving class struggle as the decade proceeds" (1984, 56; see also 1991).

The economic decline of the 1980s and 1990s, however, had consequences that went beyond class polarization. It spurred a fundamental realignment in social-class identity and political cleavages. In effect, Venezuela moved from a modern conflict between Right and Left, to a postmodern clash between those with a place in organized, formal society and those without (Castells 1997). The former work in jobs with benefits and legal protections, have legally recognized property, and enjoy municipal services such as water, telephone, and police protection; the latter lack formal employment, live in barrios and rural areas not fully recognized by the state, and do not enjoy full access to the benefits of modern citizenship: job security and protections, professional health care, municipal services, and professional police protection.[4]

Between 1981 and 1997 unemployment almost doubled. Even more revealing is the decline of formal employment and remuneration. While at the end of the 1970s more than twice as many workers were employed in the formal sector as in the informal, by the end of the 1990s the formal and informal sectors were roughly equivalent. By 1997 real wages for all citizens were, on average, 37 percent of what they were a decade earlier and the poor disproportionately bore the brunt of this decline. Whereas in 1981 the poorest 40 percent of Venezuela's population and the richest 10 percent earned roughly the same percentage of Venezuela's overall wealth, by 1997 the bottom 40 percent earned less than half of what the top 10 percent earned (*Statistical Abstract of Latin America*; Ocampo and Martín 2003, 236).

It is important to note that despite this vertiginous economic decline, human development indicators measuring health, education, and consumption of information continued their upward march throughout the 1980s and 1990s. And as often happens, an increasingly literate, educated, and informed population demanded more voice in their government (E. Lander 1995; Crisp, Levine, and Rey 1995; Karl 1995; Navarro 1995). The stated intention of the designers of the Punto Fijo regime was for it to transition toward increasing the participation of citizens as societal development progressed. Unsurprisingly, however, democratizing reforms by those with privileged positions of power were slow in coming and limited in scope. An effort to modify the constitution or write a new one, for example, was repeatedly offered as a campaign promise but never actually made it onto the government's agenda once in office. The two main parties—the social-democratic party, Democratic Action (AD), and the social-Christian party, the Independent Political Electoral Organizing Committee (COPEI)—responded to the challenge by taking a pragmatic turn. Looking inward, they resisted reform, sought to conserve their power, and in the process sacrificed efforts at ideological leadership (E. Lander 1995; Crisp, Levine, and Rey 1995; Karl 1995; Navarro 1995). A continual flow of corruption scandals combined with recurring efforts at neoliberal reform generated among the populace an image of professional politicians as focused on their own well-being and unconcerned with the plight of the average citizen (Roberts 2003).

The response of the citizenry to this economic decline and failure of political reform could hardly be clearer. In February 1989 President Carlos Andrés Pérez, elected just months before on a center-left, social-democratic platform, pushed through a dramatic package of neoliberal reforms designed in collaboration with the IMF. Those most affected responded with three days of looting and riots in which hundreds were killed and hundreds of millions of dollars of property damage was inflicted (López Maya 1997). The *Caracazo*, as the popular uprising has come to be known, marked a turning point for Punto Fijo democracy, inititiating its progressive delegitimization (Ugalde et al. 1994). While in the 1988 elections the two main political parties together captured over 90 percent of the vote, in the 1993 elections that total dropped to 45 percent, according to the National Electoral Council (Consejo Nacional Electoral, or CNE). By the elections in 1998 it would plummet to 11 percent.[5] 1992 saw two coup attempts against the government of Andrés Pérez—the first led by Chávez. And in 1993 Andrés Pérez was impeached on corruption charges, giving way to an interim government. In December 1993, Rafael Caldera became the first elected president not to be affiliated with one of the two main parties. Four years later, the leading candidate for the 1998 elections was Irene Sáez, a former Miss Universe running as a political outsider.[6]

The decline of Venezuela's development model took a heavy toll on cross-class party mobilization, as well as social-democratic discourse through the 1980s and 1990s, leading the institutionalized, electoral Left to move to the right and become indistinguishable from it, as happened throughout Latin America. Indeed the first package of neoliberal reforms was pushed through not by COPEI but by AD in 1989. The second attempt at structural reform was engineered by the longtime leftist leader Teodoro Petkoff. Eventually the interests of the two traditional political parties became so indistinguishable that in the elections of 1998 they eventually supported the same candidate in opposition to Chávez. This is the setting in which Chávez and the Bolivarian Movement emerged as an electoral force in 1998: a context in which the majority were experiencing ever-decreasing socioeconomic prospects and enjoying virtually no political representation, but were increasingly literate and informed.

The Rise of Bolivarian Democracy

The Bolivarian Revolutionary Movement-200 (MBR-200) led by Chávez began in the 1980s as a clandestine group of young officers dedicated to the internal reform of the armed forces (López Maya 2003).[7] In the view of the MBR-200, the original heroism and ideals of Simón Bolívar as well as his continental project for democracy were betrayed by the Venezuelan oligarchy who adopted foreign development models for the country (MBR-200, n.d., 1). This betrayal reached its apex with the onset of democracy and the Punto Fijo Pact. The MBR-200 rejected liberal, representative government in favor of more participatory, direct forms of government, based upon varying sources and influences. On the one hand, Bolívar's conception of democracy was heavily influenced by Rousseau's notion of a general will that emerges from the collectivity and overcomes individualism. According to this Romantic perspective, true democracy is achieved when the disjuncture between the individual will and the collective will is overcome, making representative structures superfluous—in contrast to the assumption of irreducible pluralism that is the basis of the liberal conception. This emphasis on the mobilization and participation of citizens is coupled with an emphasis on executive power and strong leadership that interprets the will of the people (see Wiarda 2001b, 2002).

The other main component of the MBR-200's rejection of liberal democracy comes from the thought of Venezuela's revolutionary Left. Chávez was deeply influenced by his brother Adán Chávez, who long participated in Venezuela's guerrilla movement and later dissident groups (López Maya 2003; Ellner 2008). In the Southern Cone countries the Left was repressed in the context of authoritarian dictatorship and therefore came to value liberal-democratic structures as providing a space in which to organize. However, in Venezuela the Left was marginalized in the context of representative democracy and therefore came to view it as a form of class dictatorship through which the dominant classes were able to perpetuate their power (Daniel Levine 1973). Hence, the revolutionary Left did not transition toward participating in electoral democracy (as the Movimiento al Socialismo did in Bolivia; see Ellner 1988) and maintained a traditional Marxist distrust of representative democracy.

When the coup of 1992 failed, the leaders of the MBR-200 wound up in jail. However, the two years they spent in jail gave them the space and time to develop their ideology and plans. Once out of prison, they began to develop a nationwide "civic-military" movement based on popular organizations like the "Bolivarian Circles" (Hawkins and Hansen 2006). For the next four years Chávez and the MBR-200 worked on grassroots mobilization. When in 1997

Chávez announced his candidacy for the 1998 presidential elections he was a marginal figure with popularity in the single digits. But his candidacy surged in 1998 as Venezuela's economy declined and the party system continued to self-destruct (López Maya 2003).

Chávez was elected in 1998 on the promise of a more participatory form of democracy, and his government immediately organized a referendum calling for a constitutional assembly to work in this direction. The 1999 constitution indeed contains a number of instruments designed to increase democratic participation and government responsiveness such as referenda, the participation of civil society in the nomination processes of public officials, and incentives for local organizations that can make demands of the government. The government has symbolically and materially supported movements that were only incipient in late Punto Fijo democracy, such as the Urban Land Committees (which work for the normalization of property titles and rights in informal squatter settlements; see "Urban Land Committees" by García-Guadilla, chapter 3, this volume); Technical Water Committees (which work to establish regular water service to their neighborhoods; López Maya 2008), and community media outlets (see the chapters "Catia Sees You" by Schiller, and "Radio Bemba in an Age of Electronic Media" by Fernandes). Its social policy increasingly works through missions by which health and education services as well as wholesale food items are brought to people in residential locations (see "The Misiones of the Chávez Government" by Hawkins, Rosas, and Johnson, chapter 7, this volume). Finally, the government's domestic economic policy has focused on socializing production through cooperatives—profit-making enterprises owned by their employees. These were given preference in government contracts, as well as access to preferential loans (see "Participatory Democracy in Venezuela" by López Maya and Lander, chapter 2, this volume).

As we will see in the empirical chapters, the Chávez government has clearly succeeded in mobilizing and incorporating people—many of whom had never before participated in an extra-household initiative—and this is one reason for its enormous popularity. While this is clearly a victory for the socialist rejection of civic autonomy and efforts to politically mobilize civil society, there is no clear indication that the classic pitfalls pointed out by liberal political theory have been overcome. For example, according to liberal political theory, Venezuelan participatory democracy will fall to the "iron law of oligarchy," whereby this mass mobilization will channel into the development of a centralizing, corporatist government in which power will increasingly flow away from people and toward the executive branch (Michels 1915; Wiarda 2001a). The authors in this volume do not resolve this dilemma but empirically examine it in order to provide readers elements with which to draw their own conclusions.

During its first two years, including the constitutional assembly, the Chávez government enjoyed a broad consensus around the push to deepen political democracy and enjoyed high levels of approval. However, in the course of 2001, a move toward extending democratic changes into social and economic realms generated increasing opposition (López Maya 2005; see figures in Smilde 2008a). The two-and-a-half-year period from December 2001 to August 2004 saw an intense and protracted struggle between the Chávez government and opposition political and economic forces.[8] Passage, near the end of 2001, of forty-nine reform laws radicalizing the government's efforts at change created a sense of urgency among the opposition and the first nationwide work stoppage in December. In April 2002 an oil strike and march resulted in violence near the presidential palace, which led to a coup, a thirty-six-hour interim government, and a countercoup two days later. Attempts at reconciliation were largely unsuccessful and, over the next two years, opposition efforts focused on a recall referendum to oust Chávez, while government efforts focused on avoiding it. The deadlock over a referendum led the opposition to initiate another national work stoppage in December 2002 that lasted two months and a shutdown of oil exports initiated by managers of the state oil company and union leaders associated with the parties of the Punto Fijo era. Here again the government ended up on top, in the process regaining control over the government's primary source of revenue by mobilizing loyal and retired workers, soliciting help from abroad, and firing about half of the state oil company's thirty thousand employees. Throughout 2003 and 2004 attempts to exercise the right to a recall referendum were scuttled by errors and technicalities leading to frequent conflict in the streets. This period of conflict ended when the opposition successfully gained a recall referendum in June 2004 but lost its momentum in the run-up to it, resulting in a resounding victory for the Chávez government in August.

The tension, acrimony, and miscommunication characterizing this period can be understood by looking at the political actors involved, as well as some of the conditions of inequality in Venezuela's major urban centers. The largest segment of the Chávez coalition has come from within the masses of impoverished Venezuelans existing on the margins of formal citizenship (Roberts 2003). These supporters are not strongly ideological. Rather, their support is based upon a perception, and in most cases a lived experience, that for the first time they have a government that prioritizes their plight and fights for their interests. Chávez himself is a symbolic vehicle for the sentiments of this sector. He looks, talks, and thinks like his supporters in the popular sectors, and his track record of electoral and economic successes is a source of great pride for them.

The Chávez coalition also includes a new emerging political elite consisting of the state employees involved in innovative projects, as well as members of the growing number of popular organizations and movements whose ideas and projects are supported by the government (López Maya 2003; Valencia Ramírez 2007). This process has provided social and political space for leftist activists and professionals long marginalized from public administration, and it has generated a new layer of government employees who serve as liaisons to communities, as well as community leaders with the networks to procure resources for neighborhood committees, community councils, and other groupings. These same people often subordinate community responsibilities to political mobilization, as their networks, livelihood, and future are integrally tied into the viability of the Chávez government (Smilde 2008b; also several chapters in this book highlight this tendency).

The opposition coalition, on the other hand, consists mainly of those who have (or at least had) a solid place in formal society. This includes not only traditionally conservative sectors associated with the Catholic Church, industry, commerce, and construction, but also the reformed Left, including the academic and media establishment, and organized labor—a large portion of which consists of unionized, white-collar state employees (Roberts 2003; López Maya 2005). Their critical discourse focuses on threats to liberal democracy such as declining freedom of the press; politicization of education, the state oil company, and other public institutions; threats to private property; increasing exclusion from the benefits of the state; and supposed government incompetence. A long series of missteps and political defeats from 1998–2006 left the opposition movement weakened and regrouping by 2007. Their persistent overconfidence and miscalculation during this period can be understood as a consequence of two factors: the decline in opposition political parties after 1998 and the geography of inequality in Venezuela.

The implosion of the two main political parties in the late 1990s left opponents to the Bolivarian government without adequate political representation. In this vacuum the role of political mediation and representation was taken up by the Catholic Church (see "Christianity and Politics in Venezuela's Bolivarian Democracy" by Smilde and Pagan, chapter 12, this volume); the mass media (see "Venezuela's Telenovela" by Acosta-Alzuru and "The Color of Mobs" by Duno Gottberg); sectors of the armed forces (Norden 2003; Trinkunas 2004);

and aspiring political leaders with minimal organizations (López Maya 2005). In each case, rather than moderating and transforming constituents' political demands into realistic and effective proposals, these types of institutions and leaders tended to radicalize them as they jockeyed for position and used discourses typical of their traditional roles. As a result, the opposition movement has consistently done a good job of mobilizing its base, but not of grabbing the center. One can add to this the fact that most members of the middle and upper classes have never set foot in a popular barrio and have only a diffuse sense of the inequality that surrounds them. As a result they underestimate the social urgency behind Chávez's popularity.

It would be a misinterpretation to think that "polarization" meant the entire population has divided into pro- and anti-Chávez camps. Indeed, the percentage of the population that identifies with neither the Chávez government nor its opposition generally ranges from one-third to one-half (Datanalisis 2008b). This mass in the middle supports or opposes the government according to its perception of the government's performance, and this is what explains the success of the Chávez government in elections—not the uncritical messianism so often reported in the press. The number of people who positively evaluate the work of the Chávez government is routinely twenty to thirty points higher than the number of people who consider themselves pro-Chávez (Datanalisis 2008a).

The shift from deepening democracy in the first couple of years of the Chávez government toward extending it to the social and economic realms has been accompanied by a progressive centralization of political and economic power in the executive branch. While the key concept of the Chávez government in its first years was *participatory democracy*, this has progressively ceded its centrality to *twenty-first-century socialism*. While this is frequently thought of as a dramatic political shift, it is better thought of as a progressive working out of a leftist interpretation of the Romantic tradition of democracy embodied by Bolívar. Eighteenth-century Romantic ideas of the fusion of individual and collective interests in an emergent, democratic general will were influential in Bolivar's political thought, as well as Karl Marx's later elaborations of socialism (Donald Levine 1995). The acute conflict after 2002 was interpreted by the Chávez government as evidence that simply mobilizing the masses was not enough. Chávez's supporters in turn sought to further empower him as the one who could interpret the sentiment of "el pueblo" as the general will; and they saw this as more important than institutions of representative democracy. This underlying consistency is the reason we use the term *Bolivarian democracy* in this book.

Beyond Civil Society

Having reviewed the outlines of the political conjuncture in which the case studies in this book take place, we need also to locate the Venezuelan experience in debates on participation and civil society. The idea of civil society underwent a dual renaissance in the 1980s and 1990s in scholarship on Latin America. On the one hand, it became central to rethinking and reformulation on the left after the defeat of the armed struggles of the 1960s and 1970s. On the other hand, it became the centerpiece of neoliberal thought in the 1990s, looking for an alternative to the developmentalist state. A comprehensive discussion of civil society will not be possible here, but an outline of the main issues will help us understand the case studies that follow.[9]

While derided in many versions of Marxism, the concept of civil society came to play a central role in the Latin American Left of the 1980s and 1990s (Dagnino 1998; Petkoff 2005). The defeat of armed struggles in the 1960s and 1970s and the accompanying rise of authoritarianism challenged leftist intellectuals to rethink their understanding of societal conflict as well as their strategies for affecting change. The work of the twentieth-century Italian theorist Antonio Gramsci was key to this rethinking. First, Gramsci's critique of the economic determinism of classic Marxism made sense of the failure of revolution by pointing to sociocultural formations. In Gramsci's analysis, civil society provided trenches of stability that protected bourgeois society even when the economy was in crisis and the state was weak, and this explained the durable character of existing capitalist regimes (Cohen and Arato 1992, 143). Instead of an economic reductionism, Gramsci provided a tripartite system in which economy, politics, and civil society were on an equal footing. Key to the distinction between state and civil society was his portrayal of an equivalence of material and cultural forces through his concept of hegemony. The power of bourgeois society was exercised not only through the coercive capacities of the state, but also through the inculcation of consent through civil society. This consent is a cultural phenomenon inculcated by religion, popular culture, and other forms of association.

While the multidimensionality of Gramscian theory and the concept of hegemony provided a more robust understanding of the social authoritarianism of Latin American societies, it also pointed in a new direction in the struggle for change. In Gramscian theory the emphasis was no longer on the attempt to take over the state but on the war of position, the development of alternative sources of power struggling for political space. Here democratization became the key metaphor instead of revolution; and pluralism, diversity, and flexibility became central assumptions (Dagnino 1998). Especially in the Southern Cone countries, civil society became the main response to authoritarian regimes as people sought to organize in free spaces of association and work together to overcome marginalization. Central to this response was the idea that not only did these movements achieve institutional changes but the very struggle itself would give subordinate and marginalized peoples an identity as political subjects. In the transition from authoritarianism to democracy in places like Brazil, Chile, and Nicaragua, religious groups, women's associations, student movements, neighborhood associations, and other groups played a key role. In other countries with formally democratic regimes controlled by an elite-pact, like Colombia, Venezuela, and Mexico, civil-society groups worked to open democratic regimes to include marginalized populations and issues (Dagnino 1998; Roberts 1998).

In the 1990s, the part played by civil society in the decline of Eastern-bloc socialist regimes, combined with the decline of welfare states in the West, led neoliberal scholars to reemphasize the role of nongovernmental associations as service providers and mediators between citizen and government. Whereas previous versions of modernization theory sought to limit the participation of citizens to the act of voting in order to maintain order and facilitate the extension of state control over territories and populations (Huntington 1968), neoliberal scholars came to see civil society as the key to open democracies and civilian well-being in a time of reduced state protections (Seligman 1992; Wiarda 2001a, 106).

The idea of society as a realm of social interaction not determined by political organization was a centerpiece of liberal social theory from the very beginning (Taylor 1995), and neoliberal scholars returned it to a place of prominence. John Locke saw pre-political or nonpolitical forms of association as guided by natural law and thereby tending toward progress and well-being when left unfettered. In his view, society forms before government but sets up the latter as a necessary evil for purposes of security. Freed of the interference of political organization, both the economy and the public sphere will be self-regulating and productive of well-being. Later liberal theorists like Bentham and Mill, despite numerous differences, focused their attention on political organization and the threat it posed to otherwise virtuous society. In contemporary Anglophone political science this tradition has led to an almost exclusive focus on the institutions of the state as the realm of association that needs to be problematized, critiqued, and engineered. Forms of association outside of the state are referred to as "civil society" and considered unproblematically positive.

Given these historic trends and the seeming convergence of Left and Right, in the 1990s the idea of civil society reached a level of positive consensus rarely seen in academics or activism. It was not just an analytic concept but a normative one; not just a model of but a model for. It was seen as the key to increased civic participation and the provision of well-being in the new reality of democracy and reduced states.

Scholars have increasingly pointed out the class inequality that has developed in civic participation during the neoliberal period. In his book *Deepening Democracy?* Kenneth Roberts (1998) looks at the efforts of the Left in Chile and Peru over the past several decades and argues that the transition in leftist activism toward civic participation has not provided a very good substitute for the classic forms of leftist organizing through workers' movements and mass political parties articulated with a social-welfare state. He argues that the social and economic fragmentation characteristic of neoliberal contexts makes collective action extraordinarily difficult among the lower classes. As work progressively moves from the industrial workplace to the informal economy, unions, parties, and other forms of interest aggregation have declined, and people are increasingly atomized. Thus while in economic terms neoliberal reforms have meant, for the majority, a decline in economic well-being, in political terms it has made it extraordinarily difficult for the poor majority to come together into civil associations or social movements to represent their interests. As a result, the growth of NGOs and civil associations tends to have a strong class bias, in which people in the middle and upper-middle classes who have more economic resources, more education, and more organizational experience are more equipped to represent their interests through associations than the poor majority. Thus, concludes Roberts, the autonomous civil society that develops in neoliberal contexts tends to reaffirm existing class inequalities rather than address them.

A recent ethnography by Javier Auyero and Debra Swistun (2009) demonstrates some of these difficulties in the failure of a community to address the environmental contamination of a squatter's settlement outside of Buenos Aires. Villa Inflamable was a small squatter's settlement that developed unplanned over thirty years in response to the direct and indirect employment provided by a growing petrochemical industrial district. Of course, while the latter provided residents with employment opportunities, it also progressively contaminated their water, soil, and air. However, the social-structural location of Villa Inflamable's residents prevents them from engaging in collective action. First, most residents have their home as their only asset and are employed directly or indirectly by the petrochemical industry. They cannot simply pick up and leave and are dependent on the government or industry to provide some sort of solution. However, the mismatch in resources is extreme, and the government and industry effectively deflect residents' claims with denials of responsibility, purposeful confusions regarding the nature of the problem, vague promises of future benefits, and selective distribution of charity programs and benefits. As a result, rather than unified in their struggle, residents of Villa Inflamable are atomized, confused, and passive.

Villa Inflamable's story reveals the most common result of injustice in any context, not just in the neoliberal era. Collective organization and mobilization generally do not occur in all the situations in which they could be beneficial, because of preexisting social atomization, because of organizational chaos, or because there are powerful actors that have an interest in keeping things the way they are and the resources to do so. But if part of the justification of the neoliberal reduction of the state was precisely that civil society would pick up the slack—bringing to light injustice and addressing the effects of economic restructuring—the processes revealed in the case of Villa Inflamable clearly suggest some problems with this logic. Withdrawal of the state in contexts of radical inequality merely perpetuates that inequality.

The second line of research that calls into question reigning assumptions regarding civil society suggests that state engagement of civil society does not necessarily generate a comprehensive passivity. Some of these studies effectively demonstrate agency in contexts that are normally thought of as dictatorial or clientelistic and thereby suggest we move beyond residual theorizations of illiberal contexts. In his study of Peronism in Argentina, Javier Auyero (2000) argues that we need to get beyond the "metonymic prison" of clientelism as an endpoint critique and instead look at the phenomena from the perspective of the client. Doing so allows us to see the subtle mechanisms through which poor people use clientelistic relationships to address their needs at the same time that they facilitate the rule of the powerful.

In a study of Cuba, Sujatha Fernandes (2006) analyzes "artistic public spheres" in contemporary Cuba, arguing that they provide forums of vigorous democratic debate in a context of restricted political liberties.[10] The historical sociologist Carlos Forment (2003) has likewise pushed beyond stereotypical notions of Latin America's undemocratic heritage. In the first volume of his historical investigation of civil society in Latin America, he puts forth copious evidence of a robust civil sphere in Latin America throughout the eighteenth and nineteenth centuries, including independent newspapers, discussion groups, and associations. This robust democratic culture remained at the social level, however, because these groups took an authoritarian state for granted. The point of these studies is not to argue that these political contexts are desirable.

Instead Forment wants to convince scholars that participation when state and society are tightly linked is a problem worthy of empirical research.

Other studies have looked at more desirable situations. Gianpaolo Baiocchi (2005) argues that classic emphasis on the autonomy of civil society from the state makes the effectiveness of participatory budgeting in Porto Alegre impossible to understand. Here civil society acts collaboratively with the municipal government rather than independently from it. He argues that it is precisely the interconnections between civil society and the state and the dialogue and debate that flow through them that permit democratic accountability.

Of course, Gramscian thinking about counter-hegemonic projects looks at corporatist mobilization of civil society as a solution to passivity and fatalism, and this points to a tension in appropriations of his thought (Cohen and Arato 1992). Some in the Latin American Left have focused on the progression from autonomous civil organizations resisting authoritarianism to organic projects of social and moral education and reform once power is obtained. Others have emphasized diversity and pluralism as structural features of modern society and see autonomy from the state as an enduring necessity (see Dagnino 1998 for a discussion).

The last trend I would like to review has questioned the automatic association of civil participation and democratic deepening. First, scholars have pointed out the problem of democratic accountability. Civil associations are not necessarily internally democratic and might not have any larger constituency other than their funding agencies. This funding often comes from private industry or international donor agencies, which have their own set of interests that do not necessarily align with the people these civil associations presumably serve (see Jelin 1999).

Roberts also focuses on the problems of political aggregation that arise in getting all sorts of different associations to work together on the large-scale projects that are necessary for social and economic transformation. A bustle of women's groups, environmental groups, human rights groups, and religious groups each working on their own projects is great for democratic vitality. But such groups have limited abilities to engage in the concerted action needed for larger projects of social and economic transformation such as land reform, expansion of educational opportunity, or a new social-security regime. Many of them explicitly do not want to collaborate with other groups, or have particular objections to collaboration—think, for example, of evangelicals collaborating with progressive women's groups, or human rights groups collaborating with neighborhood anticrime initiatives. And those that are willing might not have the resources to carry out larger projects.

Scholars have also challenged the idea that voluntary organizations neces-sarily generate tolerance, understanding, and justice. In their study of Italy and Spain in the twentieth century, Riley and Fernandez (2006) argue that state en-gagement of society generates participation. But the participation they are re-ferring to is the frequently violent mass mobilization characteristic of fascism. And with reference to the case of Peru, the sociologist Luis Pásara (1991) has provocatively pointed out that the Romantic idealization of Latin America's new social actors tends to leave out skinheads, neo-Nazis, guerrillas, drug traf-fickers, and crime networks. Indeed, in the case of Peru, the most impressive case of mobilization following the Velasco regime was the bloody Maoist insur-gency Sendero Luminoso (McClintoch 2001; see also Blee 2002 for her treat-ment of organized racism in the United States).

Angelina Snodgrass Godoy's (2006) study of lynching in post–civil war Guatemala provides a chilling example of such "uncivil society." Lynch mobs grow out of communities, show initiative, and act autonomously from the state. Yet their actions can hardly be seen to deepen democracy. Functioning outside of due process, their popular character provides them with no special vocation for justice. They take aim at the ostracized as well as the criminal, the envied as well as the corrupt, and political rivals as well as community trouble-makers. Snodgrass Godoy concludes that formal political inclusion in a context of socioeconomic exclusion and neoliberal reduction of the state produces not a democratic civil society but a volatile cocktail for violence. People indeed participate—but in unexpected ways such as lynching, crime and drug dealing (for a similar argument on Venezuela, see Smilde 2007).

The common denominator of these critiques is a questioning of the liberal portrait of abstract, unencumbered individuals ready to join movements and organizations that aggregate demands. Instead these portraits focus on indi-viduals existing in concrete sociohistorical contexts embedded in cultural dis-courses and identities, and on structures of social, economic, and political power.

Thus the causal sequence underlying the liberal perspective can be ques-tioned in multiple ways. Autonomy can lead to participation in certain condi-tions, but to passivity in others. Likewise, state engagement of society can lead to participation in certain conditions, but passivity in others. Also, participa-tion does not necessarily lead to anything we would recognize as democratiza-tion. It can just as likely lead to violence, discrimination, and further inequality or simply be irrelevant. In *The Illusion of Civil Society*, Jon Shefner concludes bluntly: "The concept of civil society has run its course. Civil society analysis interferes with our understanding of what kinds of conflicts exist, who the constituents of varied groups embroiled in these conflict are, and the differential results of varied strategies and struggles" (2008, 207). Shefner argues that we need to return to specificity, to the examination of particular conflicts in concrete times and places. Of course this does not mean we have to set aside our concepts and perspectives for historicist detail. Rather, we need to look at how, where, and when participation takes place and with whom.

Participation, Politics, and Culture

An alternative has emerged that works against some of the reifications and normativity that run through the civil society approach. Instead of seeking to detect whether civil associations have autonomy vis-à-vis the state and ending there, this alternative perspective seeks to understand types of relationship or forms of communication involved in concrete examples of participation and does not assume that any given form of participation is virtuous. The withdrawal of the state may not provide an open and even playing field; instead, relationships and forms of communication inevitably involve unequal power and unequal resources and are shot through with conflict and negotiation. Furthermore, instead of a common-sense, interest-based view of collective action, this perspective assumes that the actions of collectivities are inevitably cultural in the sense that they embody visions of citizenship, democracy, social obligation, and the future. This alternative focus on politics and culture also leads to a broader view of what participation includes, from an exclusive focus on coherent bounded actors like nongovernmental associations and social movements, to an expanded focus that includes networks, relational contexts, discursive spaces, cultural constructions, and meaningful discourses.

Careful ethnographic work in multiple contexts has sought to examine and characterize the relationships that make up what we think of as civil society and democratic life. In his work on religious groups grappling with welfare reform in the United States during the 1990s, Paul Lichterman (2005) has pushed beyond simplistic conceptualizations of civil society in terms of social capital. He suggests that we think instead of the multiplier effects of civic participation in terms of a social spiral in which people and groups from dissimilar social contexts come to communicate in open-ended ways. Lichterman shows that simply working on behalf of the disadvantaged does not necessarily generate this social spiral. Indeed, in most of the cases he reviewed, no lasting networks, discourses, or understandings were generated. Rather, such phenomena only appeared in cases in which there was open-ended, face-to-face contact and a decided effort at two-way communication. Robert Fishman (2004) has made a similar argument in his work on the labor movement in Spain. He shows that the contacts union organizers develop with intellectuals impacts the nature of their democratic discourse. Those union organizers with such contacts establish broader concepts of democracy and are able to place their local struggles in national and global context. Those that do not have such contacts frame their struggle in more local and instrumental terms.

In her work on the Brazilian student movement in the 1980s and 1990s, Ann Mische (2008) develops a fourfold schema of political communication organized by two distinctions: an emphasis on ideas versus actions and an orientation toward collaboration versus competition. She calls an emphasis on ideas and an orientation toward collaboration "exploratory dialogue," which she associates with Habermas's (1989) concept of the public sphere. Here political leaders seek to build consensus through open dialogue about the common good. She calls an emphasis on ideas and an orientation toward competition "discursive positioning" and associates it with Gramsci's concept of civil society. Here political leaders function as "organic intellectuals" who propose moral and intellectual reforms. She calls an emphasis on actions and orientation toward collaboration "reflective problem solving," related to John Dewey's concept of the democratic community. Here skilled leaders facilitate joint learning and problem solving. Finally, she calls an emphasis on actions and orientation toward competition "tactical maneuver," associated with Machiavelli's ideas on leadership. Here skilled leaders seek to command and control in order to achieve their ends.

Mische's point in making these distinctions is to argue that each of these styles of communication has a characteristic set of strengths and weaknesses and that all have important roles in democratic politics at different moments. While "exploratory dialogue" and "reflective problem solving" fit nicely with the classic liberal version of civil society and indeed are generative of new ideas and social networks, they can become paralyzed and ineffective when confronted with contentious political arenas. While "discursive positioning" and "tactical maneuver" are normally what we consider partisan and can lead to cynical, ossified political positions, they also provide straightforward appreciation of the political nature of democracy. Mische's main achievement is in portraying these as forms of communication rather than as distorted versions of one another, or as descriptions of layers of society (for example, civil society versus political parties), or of types of leader. This is the type of analysis our authors seek to employ with their case studies of participation politics and culture in the Venezuelan context.

All of this and other work on participation in Latin America (e.g., S. Alvarez, Dagnino, and Escobar 1998b) have led to post-structural understandings of culture and power. One basic element of the post-structuralist concept of culture is the idea of cultural and material practices being inextricably bound up together. On the one hand, culture is political because it is constitutive of social and political power. Hence, many Latin American social movements focus on the resignification of participation, citizenship, and democracy itself. Put differently, they are seeking to resignify and thereby redefine social and political power. On the other hand, the political needs to be expanded as well. Sonia Alvarez, Evelina Dagnino, and Arturo Escobar say, "In exploring the political in social movements, we must view politics as more than just a set of specific activities (voting, campaigning, lobbying) that occur in clearly delimited institutional spaces such as parliaments and parties; it must also be seen to encompass power struggles enacted in a wide range of spaces culturally defined as private, social, economic, cultural, and so on" (1998b, 11).

Thus we need to look for politics not only in the central institutions of the state but also in social spaces and cultural discourses. This is the reason that this book includes chapters on classic forms of participation such as social movements, NGOs, and state-sponsored mobilization, and also on religion, poetry, and mass media.

But this approach means not only that we look for politics in different spaces, but also that we push beyond the focus on coherent, bounded actors to try to understand social and cultural power and influence better (Rubin 2004). Alvarez, Dagnino, and Escobar emphasize the way social movements develop interpersonal networks extending beyond themselves to other organizations and the state. They suggest the term "social movement webs" to try to understand the way social movements' resignifications, demands, and practices "circulate in weblike, capillary fashion . . . in larger institutional and cultural arenas" (1998a, 16).

Jeffrey Rubin has suggested an even more decentered way of thinking about the influence of participation. Rubin (2004) uses an approach he calls "seeing and not seeing." In it he combines the traditional political science focus on bounded, coherent actors with a post-structural emphasis on the discourses, meanings, and representations out of which they are made: "This means acknowledging the existence, force, and cohesiveness of political actors, though simultaneously recognizing something else at play in them, the mixture of fragments and pieces . . . [that] enable[s] us to understand where political actors or forces come from and how they change, indeed what they are and what multiple capacities they have" (109). Understanding these fragments and pieces—

new discourses, identities, and social articulations—is central to understanding how the efforts of bounded social actors actually concatenate into everyday democratic politics.

Emerging Fragments of Venezuela's Bolivarian Democracy

This emerging perspective on participation is especially important for understanding Venezuela. During the Chávez years, political polarization and conflict have themselves pushed scholars studying Venezuela toward abstract, normative portraits that replace empirical research with praise or condemnation. The scholars gathered together in this volume seek instead to provide portraits of interaction and communication in concrete cases that will allow us first to understand what is happening before rushing to judgment. Work that emphasizes the cultural dimensions of politics and the political dimensions of culture is also opportune. Chávez and his movement rose to power using a Manichean critique of the previous regime and its institutions, supported by elements from multiple ideological discourses. While Chávez's discourse is centered on nationalist myths of heroic figures from the nineteenth century, such as Simón Bolívar, it also includes elements from panindigenous and Afro-Venezuelan ideologies, socialism, neofascist thought, and liberationist Catholicism, as well as evangelical Protestantism. And the processes of transformation generated by the Chávez government have also relied on cultural politics, engaging in symbolic work that seeks the redefinition of citizenship, democracy, the nation, and even the economy. Finally, the conflict generated by these processes has taken place within religious institutions and practices, the media, and popular culture, as well as political institutions.

Engaging in empirical study of the present is fraught with difficulty in any context, but the torrid pace of change in Venezuela represents a particular challenge. Groups, initiatives, and policies gain prominence and disappear faster than our ability to research and analyze them. The chapters discussed below all study moving targets, but through conceptually informed empirical portraits they try to address some of the issues and dilemmas that will likely run through the future trajectory of Venezuela's Bolivarian democracy. Following Rubin (2006), I think these "fragments" may be as important in the long run as the new social and political actors and institutions. The fragments analyzed in the chapters that follow include ignored spaces and hidden histories and the uncovering of transitions in citizenship as new citizens are created and existing citizens are marginalized, new forms of favoritism and corruption, resignifications of the word *democracy*, paradoxes of state-sponsored participatory democracy, and new discourses of race, class, and reconciliation bred through conflict.

Public Recognition of Ignored Spaces and Hidden Histories

As informal barrios have become a central focus of the state's social policy, they have gained an unprecedented public visibility. Part of the government's social policy with respect to local forms of participation has been for these groups to document their own local histories. Sujatha Fernandes's and Naomi Schiller's chapters show how community media are providing space for critical discussion of non-elite and unofficial realities and histories. Spaces that were formerly portrayed in the media only as social problems are being portrayed and discussed by their own inhabitants not just in face-to-face conversations but through electronic media. Documenting and writing local histories has also become a central part of the work of the CTUs (urban land committees) as they seek to normalize their neighborhoods. Coraly Pagan and I show how evangelical Protestants, who have long worked and organized in the shadows of formal society and official power, are being thrust into the spotlight, with President Chávez adopting their concepts and praising their efforts. Of course, we cannot assume these histories begin with the Chávez government. Alejandro Velasco documents the trajectory of alternative histories in the Western Caracas barrio 23 de Enero and focuses on how they challenge the official Bolivarian myth of a passive, disarticulated public heroically mobilized by the Bolivarian movement. He suggests instead a narrative in which the Bolivarian movement grew out of and depended upon decades of popular activism.

Transitions in Citizenship as New Citizens Are Created
and Existing Citizens Are Marginalized

One can certainly debate whether or not the Venezuelan transition amounts to anything more than a move from one form of limited democracy to another or whether it is destined to repeat the errors of populisms past. But it is indisputably clear that Venezuelan society is undergoing an extensive change of political elites. There is a corresponding change in citizenship as formerly marginalized sectors of society become the central focus of the government and are receiving full benefits of modern citizenship: municipal services, formal employment, national identification, social protections, and public education. For all its defects and whatever its outcome, the Chávez government clearly represents an original attempt to address the new inequality of Latin American society in which the distinction between formal and informal has replaced the distinction between Right and Left.

This transition presents multiple problems as formerly marginalized people and groups suddenly find themselves tied to the center of power. Velasco shows some of the ironies in this as radicals from 23 de Enero, a Chávez stronghold, need to affirm that they are "still rebels." María Pilar García-Guadilla discusses the issues of incorporation confronting the long-marginalized CTUs that are now expected to give unqualified support to the president. Fernandes and Schiller present similar dilemmas in the ascendancy of community media and speculate on whether and how they contest the government. Pagan and I tell of the conflict produced by the increasing marginalization of the Catholic hierarchy from power and the dilemmas and conflicts created by the new ascendancy of evangelical Protestants. Margarita López Maya and Luis Lander highlight the importance of the national campaign for identification. Dismissed by Chávez opponents as an attempt to stack the voter rolls in the government's favor, they portray it as a central aspect of new citizenship.

Several chapters focus on the dismay and frustration of formerly dominant social sectors at the new ascendancy of formerly marginal peoples and ways of being. In Carolina Acosta-Alzuru's review of the telenovela *Cosita Rica*, the character Olegario reveals the way dominant social sectors view Chávez and the newly ascendant political class. Equally, Luis Duno Gottberg's review of media images of Chávez's supporters demonstrates the civilization/barbarism dualism through which dominant social sectors see their opponents. The conflict between media producers in Schiller's piece on community television demonstrates the way the traditional journalists employed in the private sector see newly ascendant media opinion makers as illegitimate. Daniel Hellinger's chapter on Chavista discourse on the website Aporrea.org demonstrates that the Chavista movement is far from united on the value of highly personalized leadership, the kind of political party needed to advance Bolivarianism, the role of internal dissenters, and a number of other internal issues. Elizabeth Gackstetter Nichols's piece on poetry circles also reveals the frustration that openly politicized use of artistic forms, like poetry, produces among people raised on the notion of autonomous, nonpolitical civil society.

New Forms of Favoritism and Corruption

Venezuela has long been a country where elected leaders of a petro-state reward supporters and punish opponents. While this used to happen in the context of a two-party contest, it currently happens between those who support the revolutionary government and those who oppose it. Hawkins, Rosas, and Johnson's analysis of the missions examines the evidence for systematic distribution of state benefits. However, they question whether this is best viewed as clientelism or as the result of a charismatic populist interaction, in which those who support the Chávez project are favored and those who are favored support the Chávez project without, thus far, the need for any strings attached. My piece with Pagan on Catholicism and evangelicalism shows the Catholic Church falling out of favor with a government that holds the purse strings and evangelical Protestant churches being rewarded for their support with government financial support. This works both ways. Acosta-Alzuru broaches the way the government has clamped down on the private media in the case of Venevision and its telenovela *Cosita Rica*.

Resignifications of Democracy

The neoliberal era marked a bifurcation of Venezuelan discourse on democracy. On the one hand, the original framing of democracy combined liberal and social-democratic discourses—in other words democracy "of the people" and "for the people," but during the neoliberal era, the state shed its commitment to the latter in favor of the former, and the discourse of liberal democracy became the undisputed idiom of public discussion. The popular sectors, on the other hand, never forgot decades of social-democratic discourse and saw the state's retreat as a betrayal. Chávez came to power prioritizing social democracy and articulating a long present but only marginally articulated discourse of participatory democracy—in other words, democracy "by the people." As López Maya and Lander argue in their chapter, the constitution of 1999 included a mixture of mechanisms of representative and direct democracy. Hellinger's two chapters, on activist debates on the web and mass attitudes about democracy, respectively, demonstrate that the current disdain for representative democracy and praise for participatory democracy is more pronounced among the cadre of organic intellectuals than among the people themselves. His analysis of public opinion shows important class differences but remarkably high approval for norms of tolerance associated with liberal democracy in both the barrios and middle-class *urbanizaciones*. This point of view provides an important context for the findings of Hawkins, Rosas, and Johnson regarding clientelism, as well as some of the attitudes revealed by Fernandes's chapter.

The Paradoxes of State-Sponsored Participatory Democracy

State efforts to mobilize popular sectors present a paradox. On the one hand, in conditions of radical inequality, relying on autochthonous, independent participation in civil society simply perpetuates this inequality. On the other hand, mobilizing popular sectors through the resources of the state undermines the autonomy that is at the heart of the role that civil society is supposed to play. The chapter on the CTUs by García-Guadilla demonstrates precisely this dynamic. The CTUs have received substantial support from the government, but their freedom of action seems tenuous. The contributions of Fernandes and Schiller on new forms of popular media also look at this dynamic but are relatively more optimistic with regard to the autonomy of this participation. López Maya and Lander take on these issues systematically in their look at the institutionalization of participatory democracy, the transformation of social policy, and the government's efforts at representative democracy. Whether the Chávez government controls the popular movements it has helped mobilize or whether it is being supported only as long as it facilitates them is an open question. In her study of the development of popular mobilization in Peru, Susan Stokes (1995) shows how the Velasco military regime in the late 1960s and early 1970s mobilized popular sectors with a discourse very similar to what we see now with the Chávez government. However, when the regime failed to follow through with its promises, mobilized popular sectors asserted themselves and became agents in the military government's downfall. Naomi Schiller, Dan Hellinger, and Alejandro Velasco suggest the same could happen in Venezuela.

New Discourses of Race, Class, and Reconciliation
Bred through Conflict

More Venezuelans are more conscious than ever of racial and economic tensions because the long-standing myths of "racial democracy" and of a peaceful nation free of class conflict—perhaps never believed by poor or dark-skinned Venezuelans—have been shattered by acute political conflict. Cities like Caracas have become spatially segregated as never before as members of the popular classes increasingly occupy public spaces and members of the upper-middle and upper classes increasingly spend their leisure time in shopping malls and other private spaces. The chapter by Duno Gottberg demonstrates the racialization of the political conflict. The character of Olegario in *Cosita Rica* clearly demonstrates the class-based disgust oriented toward Chávez. Fernandes's examination of Radio Negro Primero and its programming intended "only for black men and women," demonstrates an increasing recognition of racism and race-based organization. It also puts forward the question of reverse-discrimination versus classic liberal principles of universal inclusion.

Nevertheless, new discourses of reconciliation have appeared—such as the love affair between Juancho and La Chata in *Cosita Rica*. This discourse contrasts love with politicization and leads Venezuelans to the conclusion that if "we" get beyond politicization, "we all fit here." Pagan and I look at one case of a community media outlet's role during the coup in 2002. For professional and religious reasons the Jesuit radio network Fé y Alegría refused to participate in the media blackout organized by the interim Carmona government. The private media did not cover the protests and street uprisings and instead put cartoons and nature programs on the air. The role of community media in turning back the coup has taken on mythic proportions and, as can be seen in Fernandes's and Schiller's chapters, still provides the guiding sense of purpose and values for those involved in community media.

Interrogating Bolivarian Democracy

The chapters in this volume provide a nuanced set of empirical case studies looking at the achievements, dilemmas, opportunities, and conflicts of Venezuela's Bolivarian democracy. On the one hand they seek to move beyond the abstract normative critiques characteristic of traditional liberal political science and toward open-minded investigation of concrete social processes. On the other hand, they seek to examine the Romantic socialist concept of democracy being developed in Venezuela, while not assuming it is the only alternative. Only uncompromising interrogation of data and carefully constructed arguments will permit us to understand, sympathetically yet soberly, contemporary efforts to upset social hegemonies, while keeping in mind the sad realities of illiberal experiments past.

Notes

I would like to thank Kirk Hawkins, Paul Lichterman, Michael McCarthy, Naomi Schiller, and Jeff Rubin for their comments on this chapter. It also benefited from presentations at the 2007 meetings of the Latin American Studies Association in Montreal, the 2008 meeting of the Venezuelan Studies Section in Caracas, and the 2008 Georgia Workshop on Culture, Power, and History. Daniel C. Hellinger also contributed to and commented on this chapter.

1. This criticism mainly applies to English-language scholarship on Venezuela. Within Venezuela there have been important projects in social-historical scholarship, including the work on "survival strategies" in poverty (Cariola et al. 1989), and on popular protest (López Maya, Smilde, and Stephany 2002) from the Centro de Estudios del Desarrollo, as well as community psychology by the School of Social Psychology (Wiesenfeld and Sánchez 1995), both at the Universidad Central de Venezuela. Several important studies have also been produced by the Universidad Católica Ándres Bello (Cartaya and D'Elia 1991; Ugalde et al. 1994). Nevertheless, Venezuelan social-scientific scholarship has also traditionally been characterized by a primary focus on the central institutions of the state.

2. The most comprehensive and current treatment is Ellner 2008. See also McCoy and Meyers 2004; Ellner and Hellinger 2003; Ellner and Tinker Salas 2007.

3. "Demographic transition" refers to the process whereby a nation moves from the premodern situation of high fertility and mortality to the modern condition of low fertility and mortality.

4. For descriptions of this process in several Latin American contexts see the contributions in Fernandez Kelly and Shefner's collection (2006).

5. All these figures come from the website of the Consejo Nacional Electoral, http://www.cne.gov.ve.

6. It should be pointed out that she also had a master's degree in political science and was a highly successful two-term mayor of one of Caracas's municipalities. Most relevant here is that her lead in the polls evaporated when she accepted the support of COPEI.

7. Their name underlines the principal symbolic focus of their movement, with "200" referring to Bolivar's bicentennial birthday celebrated in 1983—the date they claim to have founded the movement (López Maya 2003).

8. These are events that have received ample attention elsewhere, so I will not go into detail here. See McCoy and Myers 2004; Ellner and Hellinger 2003; López Maya 2005; as well as Petkoff 2005.

9. The literature, of course, is large. Good starting points are Cohen and Arato 1992; Seligman 1992; Taylor 1995; Wiarda 2001a.

10. Eiko Ikegami (2005) makes a quite similar argument with respect to early modern Japan, speaking of "civility without civil society" in Japan during the seventeenth and eighteenth centuries. Here the samurai-warrior class tightly controlled any manifestations of political organization that could threaten its power. However, the development of aesthetic thought and artistic production provided a space in which people could have political discourse free from their duties within networks of state power. The development of this civic culture later led to processes of democratization. And see Lisa Wedeen (2008) for a similar argument regarding contemporary Yemen.

CHAPTER ONE

Defying the Iron Law of Oligarchy I

How Does "El Pueblo" Conceive Democracy?

Daniel Hellinger

The Venezuelan constitution declares in its preamble ("Exposition of Motives") that the Bolivarian Republic will have a government whose political organs "shall always be democratic, participatory, elective, decentralized, alternative, responsible and pluralist, with revocable mandates." In letter and spirit, the goal of the Constitutional Assembly of 1999 was to check the oligarchic tendencies that undermined the 1961 constitution and the regime of Punto Fijo (1958–1998). In liberal constitutions, a system of checks and balances is normally the mechanism intended to render inoperable the "iron law of oligarchy," as Robert Michels (1915) termed it, but the framers of the Venezuelan constitution regarded sole reliance on separation and division of powers to be inadequate to the task. The constitution depends instead on new participatory institutions to do the job. However, Bolivarian discourse is less than clear about whether participatory democracy is to supersede representative democracy, or if a balance is to be struck.

Most of this book consists of studies of innovative forms of participation in everyday life, with attention to how these practices may shape or be shaped by the public sphere. However, we know little about popular *conceptions* of democracy after the unhappy denouement of Punto Fijo. President Chávez often dismisses the Punto Fijo era entirely as just another episode in a pageant of oligarchic regimes that made up the "Fourth Republic" over nearly the entire history of Venezuela since independence. However, Punto Fijo was Venezuela's first extended experience with electoral democracy and constitutional alternation in government. While Punto Fijo might be in disrepute, can we say that this era left no imprint on Venezuelan political culture? Perhaps one reason why, as Chávez acknowledges, the Cuban model cannot be imported to Venezuela is that certain democratic principles associated with pluralist, representative democracy continue to influence popular conceptions of democracy today.

Are Venezuelans completely jaded about representative democracy, or is it more specifically the shortcomings of Punto Fijo that they reject? Do Venezuelans really understand democracy in the terms described in their constitution? To what extent are they practicing democracy as described therein? Here we look more closely at the way Venezuelans living in communities with a reputation for a high level of popular organization and participation view democracy today—in particular, how they *conceive* of democracy.

Many of the leaders of and participants in Bolivarian social movements and organizations are deeply mistrustful of politicians and of representative democracy (e.g., see chapter 8, my companion chapter on Chavista discourse on the Internet). They place their faith in the possibility of developing strong horizontal ties in civil society and the public sphere, in alternative economic development, and in a new political party (the Partido Socialista Unico de Venezuela—PSUV). They want institutions not merely to *represent* but more to *reflect* the popular will. In effect, they are challenging one of the most sacred notions about political life, Michel's "Iron Law of Oligarchy"—"Who says organization says oligarchy" (1915, 28). They are also challenging the pluralist response to Michels: elite competition waged within the boundaries of liberal constitutional rules (equal representation, checks and balances, civil liberties, periodic elections, etc.) alone makes democracy possible (e.g., Dahl 1971).

Given the experience with Punto Fijo (reviewed below) it would not surprise us that Venezuelans in general are skeptical about party competition as a sufficient guarantor of democracy. However, in placing more faith in horizontal networks and participation, they must overcome other well-known obstacles to achieving democracy without elites. Alternatively, at the least, they would have to create the kind of horizontal, participatory institutions by which an engaged citizenry can check elite power. The obstacles are formidable. Citizens in a large republic cannot assemble all in one location. Nor can all be heard at once, making access to media a crucial denominator of unequal power (as demonstrated in the chapters dealing with media, especially community broadcasting, in this book). Participatory democracy makes extraordinary demands on one's time. Chavistas hope that the networks of *consejos comunales* (communal councils), cooperatives, self-managed worker enterprises, popular media (e.g., community stations), and a new kind of democratic socialist party (the PSUV) can overcome these problems. Perhaps vertical systems of power cannot be abolished, but horizontal ties can be made to prevail over them.

I do not presume to judge the likelihood of success for the Bolivarian project.

Certainly we would be foolish to underestimate the challenges involved in making such a system work. Were Venezuelans to accomplish these goals, even imperfectly, they would be making history much in the way that the founders of the American (U.S.) Republic did in experimenting with mixed government and democracy (however limited) in the late eighteenth century. The prospects of success in forging genuine and innovative democratic institutions in Venezuela in the end may depend not so much on the quality of leadership demonstrated by Chávez, but on the determination of Venezuelans engaged in political activism to reconcile the competing principles of participation and representation.

This study represents a first attempt at examining popular conceptions of democracy and participation among ordinary Venezuelans living in communities known for their political activism—areas where participatory democracy ought to find the most widespread and enthusiastic endorsement. The context of debate about democracy in Venezuela provides background for both of my chapters in this book, explaining why many Venezuelans look to participation rather than to traditional forms of representation as the remedy for the defects of Punto Fijo democracy.

The Context of Debate about Democracy in 2006 and 2007

The question of how to ensure the autonomy of civil society from the petro-state has never been far removed from democratic discourse in Venezuela, from the earliest days of the struggle for democracy during the presidency of Eleazar López Contreras (1936–1941). Already, in the era when political parties first emerged (1935–1948), organizers of unions, peasant federations, and various middle-class organizations jealously defended their autonomy from parties and the state—a defense that ultimately failed (Battaglini 1993; Hellinger 2005; Ramos Rollon 1995).

Even before the rise and fall of the OPEC oil bonanza, Venezuelans were skeptical about parties and politicians (Martz and Baloyra 1979). Rather than viewing the economic hardships and corruption of the 1980s as having eroded a well-established liberal democracy, it makes more sense to view the period between 1974 and 1983 as exceptional, a period in which an economic boom and optimism about the future submerged deeper skepticism about the key institutions of polyarchy—political parties. Long before the Caracazo (1989), ordinary Venezuelans already felt unrepresented within their pluralist political order.

As López Maya and Lander indicate in their chapter, the 1980s and 1990s saw the emergence of diverse movements promoting a more profound conception of democracy. Of course, a more profound democracy might simply mean a more representative one. A common critique associated with social movements in the 1990s has it that party cabals (*cogollos*) substituted themselves for authentic representation of civil society. In the 1990s, middle-class groups, such as Queremos Elegir, promoted constitutional reforms calling for single-member (*uninominal*) representation at the district level, which was seen as an antidote to the enormous distance opened between representatives and the people by the highly disciplined system of proportional representation embedded in the 1961 constitution.

Many representatives in national and state legislatures, and in many social organizations (professional associations and unions, for example), were called parachutists (*paracaídas*)—politicians from other regions or sectors, imposed upon electors by a system that might best be compared to the *nomenklatura* systems of Eastern European communism. Although the Punto Fijo elite accepted some political reforms (e.g., direct election of governors), they stopped short of changes that would have undermined the list system of representation that was crucial to party discipline. Not only did this system cement the control of party cogollos over legislative bodies and internal party affairs, it assured that these political elites retained control over key institutions in civil society—unions, business confederations, student organizations, neighborhood associations, professional organizations, and the like.

Chávez capitalized on frustration with highly limited reforms by making the convocation of a constituent assembly to rewrite the constitution a central plank in his successful presidential campaign of 1998. The assembly would write a new Bolivarian constitution explicitly calling for a participatory and "protagonistic" democracy, but retaining many features of representative democracy. Always, however, there existed within Chavismo radical tendencies calling for the replacement of representative democracy with participatory democracy. Some of these calls came from radical Chavista politicians, such as Lina Ron, a National Assembly deputy, but others were from less prominent leaders of such organizations as peasant movements, neighborhood associations, and unions.

Decades of experience with stifling corporatist tendencies arising out of the nature of the petrostate experience (Karl 1997) opened Venezuelans to democratic innovation. This spirit animated debate and participation as the constituent assembly did its work of rewriting the national charter in 1999. The constitution established the trilogy of executive, legislative, and judicial branches of

government commonly found in liberal systems. The protagonistic and participatory features were to be institutionalized in several other provisions. Some
innovations, such as the recall mechanism and the ability to initiate and repeal
legislation through referendum, bear a resemblance to the reforms enacted in
many states in the U.S. during the progressive era. The Bolivarian Constitution goes even further, however, mandating participation of civil society in the
selection of the judiciary and appointment of the National Electoral Council,
established as a separate branch (*poder electoral*) of government in addition to
the three traditional branches—executive, legislative, and judicial. The constitution also provides for a fifth branch, citizens' power (*poder ciudadano*),
consisting of an ombudsman (*defensor del pueblo*), the general prosecutor (*fiscal general*), and the comptroller general (*contralor general*). These new institutions have in common the responsibility to represent and defend citizens in
their relations with the Venezuelan state. The constitution seeks to institutionalize popular influence over the judiciary, the poder electoral, and the poder
ciudadano by mandating consultation with and participation of social groups
in making appointments in these areas.

A measure of the voters' dissatisfaction with pluralist democracy was the
way that major presidential candidates in 1993 and 1998 eschewed the term
party even as they engaged in classic party-building activity—that is, as they
sought to organize their supporters to gain control over the state. Hence, although they fashioned themselves as anti-party, these so-called electoral movements still conformed to the classic definition of parties provided by Maurice
Duverger (1968, 1–2): they have had "as their primary goal the conquest of
power or a share in its exercise," and they have attempted "to draw their support
from a broad base . . . within the framework of society as a whole." Venezuelans
may eschew parties, but so far they have not been able to do without them.

The MVR (Fifth Republic Movement) was originally founded as an electoral
movement and assigned the task of generating votes for the December 1998
elections. It was to be a pragmatic vehicle for contesting an election; it was not
to be the embodiment of protagonistic democracy. Much to Chávez's dismay,
the MVR took on the characteristics of a traditional political party, attracting
professional politicians and carrying out functions of political aggregation in
place of the participatory and consultative processes specified in the Bolivarian Constitution. The president must himself bear some responsibility for this
development. For example, he chose to accelerate the social and economic aspects of his agenda in November 2001 via decree powers granted by the National Assembly, not through popular discussion and consultation with civil
society. The package of popular new laws decreed at the time was an example

of democracy *for* rather than *by* the people, but in his view there is no contradiction.[1]

Until the decision to accelerate the revolution in November 2001, the main accomplishment of the Chávez government had been to restructure Venezuela's political institutions. With the decrees of November, the political situation polarized further as the government moved into key economic and social areas for the first time. The most important and contentious changes were in oil policy, land reform, and rights to exploit coastal waters. The radicalization of the government's agenda brought about the departure of the head of the MVR, Luis Miquilena, a veteran leftist politician who had proved adept at playing the traditional political game in the new circumstances, but who was not eager at all to accelerate the revolutionary process. Under Miquilena, the MVR seemed to have fallen into emulating the politics of the despised Punto Fijo era. Chávez was so disgruntled with the state of the MVR and so determined to restore its vitality that he even briefly considered reestablishing the civic-military Bolivarian Revolutionary Movement (MBR) in place of MVR.

Miquilena's skills were well suited to winning elections and organizing support in the National Assembly, in which a formidable opposition bloc had emerged after the elections of July 2000. In fact, the government opted to go it alone without support from some of its coalition partners, making the decision to move forward without the adept Miquilena even more risky. The Chávez government came to rely mainly upon the support of several smaller leftist parties—most importantly Patria Para Todos (PPT), the Communist Party, and parts of the Movimiento al Socialismo (MAS), eventually reconstituted as PODEMOS ("We can"; PODEMOS would ultimately leave the coalition in 2007).

A new stage in radicalization was in part an outgrowth of the massive spontaneous mobilization that helped restore Chávez to power after the brief coup of April 11, 2002, and the subsequent victory in the face of the opposition's three-month *paro* (strike), including the shutdown of the oil sector, which ended in February 2003. Beginning in March 2003, Chávez launched a series of civic-military missions in health, education, urban land reform, and nutrition. New policies not only sought to change budgetary priorities and expand welfare, they also sought to involve citizens (often in partnership with the military) in various committees and popular organizations linked to the spending programs. These initiatives were not just a reward to supporters; they were linked to a mobilization strategy in anticipation of a possible recall referendum, which did in fact occur in August 2004. Much as the coup of April 2002 had been defeated by popular mobilization at the grassroots, the recall was won by grassroots Electoral Battle Units (UBEs), often led by community leaders with considerable disdain for all political parties. The MVR had failed to perform, and the tension between the grassroots base and political class only grew tauter as a result.

With local elections in October following hard upon the August 2004 recall, the need for unity among Chavista forces triumphed over grassroots resentment at the tendency to impose candidates via the old top-down processes and alliance bargaining. Although many leaders of UBEs called for primaries or some form of popular candidate selection, the candidates selected to run in the *oficialista* (pro-government) alliance kept their place on the ballot. The three elections that took place between the recall election of August 2004 and the presidential election of December 2006 were marked by high rates of abstention, peaking at 75 percent for the National Assembly election of 2005. The opposition's decision to boycott the assembly election no doubt contributed to the rate of abstention, but many Chavistas stayed home too. Less than 23 percent of the eligible electorate cast votes in support of Chavista candidates. Although the Chavista coalition swept the election, the outcome cast doubt on the commitment of Chávez voters to voting when survival of the regime was not at stake.

In declaring his candidacy for reelection to another six-year term in December 2006, Chávez called upon his supporters to mobilize 10 million votes on his behalf—a goal from which he retreated in July 2006. Still, the final result of the elections was a stunning majority enhanced by a very high turnout. This popular landslide (64 to 36 percent) must be understood in the context of repeated popular mobilizations in defense of the government, including a massive effort to locate and register poor voters and then get them to the polls on election day. No longer facing a national referendum on his rule, Chávez announced with customary boldness his plan to accelerate the revolution and the goal of a transition to "twenty-first-century socialism," terminology he adopted from the German sociologist Heinz Dietrich (1996) and first used in a speech to the World Social Forum in Porto Alegre, Brazil, in 2005.

In forceful terms, the president warned that he would exclude from government those parties that refused to dissolve themselves into the PSUV. He proclaimed in his speech on December 15, "The People voted this past December 3 for Chávez and not for the parties. These votes belong to [*son de*] Chávez; these votes do not belong to any party. Let us not fall into deceptions, these are the peoples' votes. . . . I want one party to govern with me, because every day there are more parties."[2]

Through the PSUV Chávez seemed to be aiming to resolve the contradictions among three different tasks: (1) mobilizing citizens for social and economic transformation; (2) linking citizens to government through the participatory institutions of twenty-first-century socialism; and (3) carrying out the political aggregation common to pluralist democracies. By its nature electoral politics inevitably raises questions about dividing the spoils of office, and coalition politics are never purely about ideological compromise. They also involve resolving conflicts about quotas of power. The processes of negotiation and compromise necessary to maintain a coalition would seem inevitably to clash with the idea of a participatory democracy in which representatives are mandated delegates, in which government responsiveness to the people is to be institutionalized through participatory, not just representative modalities.

With state and local elections approaching, and a referendum on presidential reelection not much further over the horizon, once again there loomed the prospect of a contraction between the need for a party to win elections and the ideological goal of building a participatory democracy. In early 2008 Chávez backed away from the threat to expel all other supportive parties from government. To some, the decision was a welcome sign of the president's flexibility and pragmatism, despite his missionary style of rule. To Chavista radicals, the political class had once again survived and remained a threat to the participatory revolution. The PSUV performed relatively well on the national level in the state and local elections of early 2009, but it could not deliver victory in some key urban states. New elections for the National Assembly in 2010 seemed likely to reinforce the side of the PSUV's split personality oriented toward electoral tasks.

Representation, Participation, or Both?

The term *representative* may be missing from the attributes of democracy listed in the 1999 constitution, but the terms *pluralist, responsible,* and *revocable mandate* are there, implying some type of intermediation between the people and state rather than direct democracy. The term *pluralism* has a somewhat ambiguous meaning here. In one sense it refers to ensuring a voice in government for all social sectors (defined by ethnicity, race, ideology, etc.). However, the overt commitment to pluralism in the constitution also seems to commit the regime to a philosophical tradition strongly associated with representative democracy.

As noted earlier, the 1999 constitution requires periodic elections and anticipates competition between incumbent and opposition political parties, a pluralist principle. Consistent with liberal norms, it establishes the three traditional branches of government—executive, legislative, and judicial. It also mandates consultation with social groups in making appointments to the judiciary, but even here it adopts a pluralist principle by assuming the existence of autonomous civil society. I do not mean to suggest that the constitution does not innovate or have a special participatory character. The constitution sets up a certain degree of antagonism between liberal and socialist principles. To work it requires a constant state of civic mobilization and participation, something that was embodied first in the Bolivarian Circles (workers' councils established by Chávez in 2001) and later in the consejos comunales.

Having superseded the problem of relying on a narrow majority and coalition government after the Chavistas swept the December 2005 National Assembly election, and flush with his landslide victory in the December 2006 election, Chávez decided to invigorate participation through constitutional reforms. One of the most important changes would have recognized a network of the consejos comunales as a sixth branch of government. Chávez did not ask for elimination of the traditional three branches of government associated with representative democracy, including the legislative. However, the rhetoric used by the president and his most enthusiastic supporters suggests at times that the new "geometry of the state" would replace representative democracy with participatory democracy. Certainly unanswered was the question of how the consejos, charged with developing spending priorities for local projects financed by the central government, would relate to existing state and local governments.

In 2007 Chávez launched several other initiatives that seemed to his critics at least to indicate a decisive move away from polyarchy. These included renationalization of several industries privatized by his predecessors and his decision not to renew the broadcasting license of an opposition television network, Radio Caracas Television (RCTV). However, even these moves left ambiguities. No other major private sector companies were slated for a state takeover.[3] RCTV was deeply compromised in attempts to overthrow the government between 2002 and 2004 and had flouted many of the restrictions in the media responsibility law, such as showing sexually suggestive programming during family hours. Moves to buy out majority shares of joint ventures in heavy oil were controversial, but this was a sector traditionally controlled by the state.

Another controversial move by the president was his request, quickly granted in early 2007, that the National Assembly grant him decree powers (ley habilitante—"enabling law") for eighteen months in eleven different policy areas. The ley habilitante was supposed to accelerate "endogenous development." The goal of such development is not merely to create a more sustainable economy and improve living conditions but also to foster a more "solidaristic" economic sector—cooperatives, micro-enterprises, enterprises self- or co-managed by workers—complementary of grassroots political democracy. About that same time the president announced his plans for the PSUV and demanded that all of his coalition partners disband their organizations. Some party leaders temporized, but few openly protested. However, some grassroots leaders and intellectuals were openly critical (see chapter 8, my companion chapter on Aporrea). Some argued that the president was trying to legislate participatory democracy from above and feared that the networks of councils, whose priorities would be funded directly by the national executive, would develop into new patronage networks beholden to the political class. Critics also asked why the president needed new decree powers, given that the Chavistas entirely controlled the National Assembly, thanks in part to the opposition's decision to boycott the election in December 2005.

The charismatic nature of the president's relationship to el pueblo often exposes a contradiction between the participatory philosophy of the constitution and the reality of power in the Bolivarian Revolution. Referendums, a key element of popular power in the charter, often take on a plebiscitary nature. This was never more evident than in the last weeks of the constitutional reform campaign of 2007. Sensing the danger of defeat, in the final month Chávez attempted to turn the vote into a referendum on presidency.

It hardly surprises that most of the political elites identified with the main parties of Chavismo, especially the MVR, rarely express disagreement with their leader in public, much less seriously debate the overall direction of the revolution. What about the intermediate cadres of the Bolivarian Revolution? What about the ordinary Venezuelans who have joined enthusiastically in the work of missions, communal councils, grassroots committees, popular radios, women's circles, radical union movements, and "electoral battle units"? What about the core supporters of Chávez who rescued him from the coup of April 2002 and repeatedly voted for him in earlier elections? Other chapters look more closely at the views of activists; here we look for answers by examining public opinion in some of the most active, organized barrios.

Research Strategy

In August 2006, with the aid of Venezuelan sociologist Luis Lander, I sought to capture public attitudes about democracy in their more complex and dynamic dimensions. I chose to focus our limited resources for research upon eleven barrios in Venezuela with a history of and reputation for activism. I designed a questionnaire to tap into popular conceptions of democracy in these barrios. The intention was to allow respondents to express their views of democracy, not simply to measure their attitudes against preconceived notions of *what* democracy is. These barrios were chosen because more than others they resemble the kind of organized, participatory communities that Chávez hopes will emerge throughout Venezuela. For purposes of comparison I drew a smaller sample from six middle-class urbanizaciones in the same three states.

The survey was taken in August 2006, just as the presidential campaign season was getting under way. The intention was to measure attitudes about democracy before any new spike of politicization that might result temporarily from a campaign or from a threatened opposition boycott (which did not in the end materialize). I did not anticipate that Chávez would announce his agenda to radically accelerate the development of participatory democracy, which took place immediately after the December 3 election. The survey allows us to gauge Venezuelan attitudes toward democracy in the period *before* Chávez launched his initiatives to accelerate the Bolivarian Revolution. It allows us to see how receptive Venezuelans in Chavista strongholds were to new participatory initiatives, such as the missions and *mesas técnicas* (committees of residents and government experts that work on improving living conditions, e.g., access to water and electricity). The survey sought to assess *how* they were thinking about democracy, not just *what* they were thinking about it.

My main hypothesis was that residents in barrios known for activism and organizations would prioritize criteria of democracy that included participation and social inclusion over liberal norms and representation. In contrast, I expected that middle-class residents would be most likely to embrace criteria of democracy more readily associated with pluralist or representative democracy. Data from the urbanizaciones also help us understand the degree to which citizens in opposition strongholds are hostile to Chavista initiatives, especially where alternative democratic institutions are concerned. To some extent, the data from the urbanizaciones provide a control group to gauge our evaluation of democratic norms in activist barrios. Unfortunately, we were unable, given limited resources, to survey residents in less organized barrios, another logical control group.

Surveys were conducted both house-to-house and through interception at markets and transit points. The surveys were carried out by IMEDIOPSA, an experienced, well-known research firm in Venezuela. Two samples were drawn simultaneously: one of 550 residents spread among eleven barrios in three different states; and one of 300 residents of six urbanizaciones spread among three different states. The stratified sample controlled for gender and age in each case. Were the two samples combined and treated as though they were a random sample of national opinion, they would yield an error range of + or −3.4 percent. For our sample of 550 barrio residents, the standard estimate of error would be + or −4.3. For our sample of 300 urbanización residents, the standard error would be + or −5.8.

I want to emphasize that combining the data from barrios and urbanizaciones does not yield a true national sample. The urbanizaciones are deliberately over-represented in order to have a large enough sample to draw reasonable conclusions about middle-class views of democracy. Although barrio conditions are more typical of the social and economic conditions prevailing in the country, these particular communities were chosen for their history of organizational activity, so the sample cannot be taken as representative of the national urban population.

To our knowledge, relatively little sociological investigation of the density of civil society in the barrios has been undertaken in recent years. One exception is Kirk Hawkins and David Hansen, whose research in July 2004 focused on members of the Bolivarian Circles. They concluded that circle members had "highly democratic goals and methods; however, their organizations embodied a charismatic mode of linkage to Chávez" (2006, 124). Kirk Hawkins, Guillermo Rosas, and Michael Johnson's contribution to this volume suggests that government patronage plays an important role in generating services and deploying missions in Venezuela. Our research is less focused on the impact of patronage or attitudes toward Chávez, but it also attempts to learn about democratic attitudes. We present here not a final analysis or even a full exploration of the data that we have, but some first indications of how Venezuelans in the forefront of the Bolivarian Revolution think about democracy. These indications also allow us to assess whether they see representative and liberal principles of democracy as compatible or conflicting with participatory democracy.

Confidence in Democracy

Most Venezuelans think of their country as a democracy. The 2007 Latinobarómetro survey of 1,200 Venezuelans, part of its more general annual survey of 20,234 Latin Americans, found Venezuelans second in the region, only slightly behind Uruguayans in their evaluation of democracy in their country.[4] In each case, 89 percent of those surveyed agreed, "Democracy may have problems, but it is the best system of government" (2007, 70). Seventy-six percent of

Venezuelan citizens felt confident that democracy could create "conditions for prosperity" (69). Using a combined index (ranging from 0 to 100) of questions about confidence in democracy, Latinobarómetro found that from its low point of 60 before the election of Chávez in 1998, the index of confidence in democracy rose to 70 in Venezuela in 2006. This score was, however, a drop-off from the high score of 76 reached in 2005. We might reasonably suppose that the decision of the opposition to boycott the December 2005 National Assembly elections contributed to the decline.

The respondents in our activist communities were asked, "Do you believe that there is democracy in Venezuela?" Table 1 presents the results—but we caution again that we must make our comparisons keeping in mind the *results are based on two samples of different size*, neither of which is a random sample of the entire population. The overall results do not differ greatly from the Latinobarómetro findings, but our results show the not surprising result that a much greater proportion of respondents in activist barrios believed that Venezuela is a democracy. Similarly, residents of activist barrios were much more likely to express approval of the functioning of the National Assembly (see table 2). Given the negative views of politicians and the performance overall of gov-

Table 1. Do you believe that there is democracy in Venezuela?

	Barrios	Urbanizaciones	Total
Yes	85% (423)	55% (138)	75% (561)
No	15% (74)	45% (112)	25% (186)
Missing	53	50	103

Table 2. Opinions about the National Assembly
N for barrios = 550; *N* for urbanizaciones = 300; *N* (total) = 850

	Barrios	Urbanizaciones	Total
How would you evaluate the performance of the National Assembly?			
Good	45.1% (248)	19.0% (57)	35.9% (305)
Fair	38.5% (212)	36.7% (110)	37.9% (322)
Poor	15.5% (85)	44.3% (133)	25.6% (218)
No answer. Don't know	0.9% (5)	0	0.6% (5)
Do you believe that the National Assembly is working efficiently for the benefit of the country?			
Yes	64.0% (352)	38.0% (114)	54.8% (466)
No	33.3% (183)	61.7% (185)	43.3% (368)
No answer. Don't know	2.7% (15)	.3% (1)	1.9% (16)

ernment (distinct from evaluations of Chávez himself), it should not be taken for granted that the National Assembly would enjoy such favorable opinion in the activist barrios. Not as many of our respondents were as dissatisfied as we might have expected.

Which Characteristics of Democracy Matter Most, Which Matter Least to Participants?

We asked respondents in these communities to select which three characteristics of democracy are most important to them from a list of nine. Respondents were asked subsequently to choose just one as most important to them. Finally, they were asked to pick one characteristic that they would eliminate as least important. Our hypothesis was that residents of barrios would be less likely than residents of urbanizaciones to select characteristics identifiable with polyarchy or liberal democracy, that is, procedural democracy, and more likely to stress characteristics linked to inclusiveness. Even allowing for a generalized distrust of parties in the electorate, one would expect that in the more affluent communities more respondents would choose, and fewer would eliminate, party competition as important. I hypothesized that party competition would be less valued in barrios for the same reason, and I anticipated that criteria related to inclusion and social equality would be more likely to be seen as important in the barrios. The results are reported in tables 3, 4, and 5.

Few observers of Venezuela would be surprised that in both kinds of community, competition among political parties was least often selected among the three most important characteristics of democracy, and that party competition was by far the most frequently chosen for elimination. Still, we should hesitate before concluding that Venezuelans have no use for parties. First, in response to a question about their political sympathies, we found that 51 percent of urbanización residents and 73 percent of barrio residents expressed "sympathy" for a political party ("none" was an explicit option on the menu of answers), a high rate of party identification in both types of activist communities.[5] Perhaps this finding means nothing more than "familiarity breeds contempt." Venezuelans may still feel that identification with a party is either useful or necessary for obtaining patronage. From a more optimistic perspective, perhaps they still believe parties are vehicles for political influence over the direction of their country.

Second, although party competition was the most frequently eliminated characteristic, fewer than half of barrio residents (where we might have ex-

Table 3. Which three do you believe to be the most important in defining what a democracy is?

(*N* for barrios = 550; *N* for urbanizaciones = 300)

	Barrios	Urbanizaciones	Total
That there be competition among distinct political parties	9.1% (50)	4.7% (14)	7.5% (64)
That the system of justice treat all citizens equally	43.8% (241)	52.3% (157)	46.8% (398)
That minorities have the same right to express views as the majority	24.9% (137)	22.0% (66)	23.9% (203)
That the media (TV, radio, the press) enjoy freedom of expression	23.3% (128)	47.0% (141)	31.6% (269)
That one can vote without worry ("votar limpiamente")	30.9% (170)	38.3% (115)	33.5% (285)
That a secure and trustworthy election system exist	37.5% (206)	31.7% (95)	35.4% (301)
That the government address the demands of the poor	36.9% (203)	21.7% (65)	31.5% (268)
That the state guarantee education and health for everyone	51.5% (283)	42.7% (128)	48.4% (411)
That all social sectors are included and enjoy the same rights	41.8% (230)	39.7% (119)	41.1% (349)

pected rejection to have been greatest) chose party competition for elimination from the list of characteristics.[6] Furthermore, a serendipitous discovery emerged during the research, revealing something surprising about the democratic condition in Venezuela. Whereas no one surveyed refused to answer the questions asking which characteristics were most important, more than a third of barrio residents and one in five urbanización residents refused to answer the question on eliminating a characteristic. This finding suggests that in activist communities, if not in general, Venezuelans are reluctant to dispense with parties, however much they mistrust the ones they have.

My hypothesis was that barrio residents would be more likely to rank highly criteria dealing with substantive equality and inclusiveness, while residents of urbanizaciones would be more likely to rank highly procedural rights identified with liberal democracy. Barrio residents did more frequently select (1) guaranteeing health and education, (2) including all social sectors in the system of rights, and (3) responding to the needs of the poor. It is notable that freedom of expression for media is chosen much less often in barrios, perhaps reflecting continuing anger at the role that the private media played in attempting to

Table 4. What characteristic of democracy is most important?

	Barrios	Urbanizaciones	Total
That there be competition among distinct political parties	1.5% (8)	1.0% (3)	1.3% (11)
That the system of justice treat all citizens equally	14.5% (80)	11.0% (33)	13.3% (113)
That minorities have the same right to express views as the majority	4.7% (26)	7.3% (22)	5.6% (48)
That the media (TV, radio, the press) enjoy freedom of expression	4.9% (27)	16.3% (49)	8.9% (76)
That one can vote without worry ("votar limpiamente")	8.5% (47)	14.3% (43)	10.6% (90)
That a secure and trustworthy election system exist	9.1% (50)	13.3% (40)	10.6% (90)
That the government address the demands of the poor	15.3% (84)	6.3% (19)	12.1% (103)
That the state guarantee education and health for everyone	25.8% (142)	13.3% (40)	21.4% (182)
That all social sectors are included and enjoy the same rights	15.6% (86)	17.0% (51)	16.1% (137)

*N.B. All those surveyed answered this question, in contrast with the relatively high rate of those not answering or saying they do not know for table 5.

overthrow the government in 2001–3, and their continued hostility toward the government that time.

On the other hand, one cannot say that respondents from the urbanizaciones value *only* procedural democracy. A high percentage (43) of respondents in these neighborhoods included guaranteed health and education in their rankings. Only 27 percent of respondents from urbanizaciones chose equal rights for all social sectors as the characteristic they would eliminate. Moreover, 60 percent in these more affluent communities opted to eliminate party competition from the list of characteristics of democracy, a higher percentage than those in the barrios.

In sum, in these relatively organized barrios, equality and inclusiveness were in general more frequently seen as important characteristics of democracy, more so overall than in the urbanizaciones, but procedural democracy seems to be valued as well. And in the urbanizaciones our respondents also seemed to value inclusiveness and equality, not just criteria identified with polyarchy. We might speculate that repulsion toward parties is more pronounced in the urbanizaciones because most residents could not abide the oficialista party

Table 5. What characteristic of democracy is least important?

	Barrios	Urbanizaciones	Total
That there be competition among distinct political parties	40.5% (22)	59.7% (179)	47.3% (402)
That the system of justice treat all citizens equally	2.7% (15)	1.7% (5)	2.4% (20)
That minorities have the same right to express views as the majority	2.7% (15)	2.0% (6)	2.5% (21)
That the media (TV, radio, the press) enjoy freedom of expression	13.3% (73)	5.7% (17)	10.6% (90)
That one can vote without worry ("votar limpiamente")	1.6% (9)	0.7% (2)	1.3% (11)
That a secure and trustworthy election system exist	0.7% (4)	0.3% (1)	0.6% (5)
That the government address the demands of the poor	1.3% (7)	1.7% (5)	1.4% (12)
That the state guarantee education and health for everyone	0.4% (2)	0% (0)	0.2% (2)
That all social sectors are included and enjoy the same rights	2.9% (16)	1.7% (5)	2.5% (21)
No answer, did not know*	33.8% (186)	26.7% (80)	31.3% (266)

*N.B. the contrast with table 4.

(the MVR at the time), but no opposition party had yet generated any enthusiasm or confidence that it would govern any better than the hegemonic parties displaced by Chávez in the 1998 election.

How Tolerant Are Venezuelans in the Context of Highly Polarized Politics?

Venezuelan politics since 1998 has been marked by a high degree of partisanship and social-class polarization. The period between 2001 and 2004 was a period of especially high tension. The opposition mounted huge mass demonstrations; a forty-eight-hour coup; *guarimbas* (highway blockades and other disruptive tactics); civic paros (an economically devastating work stoppage, including acts of sabotage) in the oil industry; and a pitched electoral battle to recall Chávez. Chavistas responded with their own massive marches and in some cases harassment of the opposition figures and institutions. Elite discourse on both sides remained characterized by a high degree of demonization. For all of these reasons, the natural hypothesis would be that Venezuelans would ex-

Table 6. Levels of tolerance in highly organized neighborhoods: At a public meeting in your community, who ought to participate?

	Always	Sometimes	Never
Among barrio residents			
Supporters of the government	84.9% (467)	10.2% (56)	4.9% (27)
Opponents of the government	75.3% (414)	16.9% (93)	7.8% (43)
Everyone	96.9% (533)	2.7% (15)	0.4% (2)
Among residents of urbanizaciones			
Supporters of the government	90.7% (272)	6.3% (19)	3.0% (9)
Opponents of the government	94.3% (283)	4.3% (13)	1.3% (4)
Everyone	98.7% (296)	1.3% (4)	0% (0)

Table 7. Tolerance of speech among supporters of the government, opponents, and "Ní-Ní": At a public meeting in your community, who ought to participate?

Who ought to participate?	Always	Sometimes	Never
Among supporters of the government			
Supporters of the government	91.2% (402)	6.3% (28)	2.5% (11)
Opponents of the government	77.8% (343)	15.0% (66)	7.3% (32)
Everyone	97.5% (430)	2.5% (11)	0
Among the "Ní-Ní"			
Supporters of the government	83.3% (255)	11.4% (35)	5.2% (16)
Opponents of the government	85.6% (262)	9.8% (30)	4.6% (14)
Everyone	98.0% (300)	1.6% (5)	0.3% (1)
Among opponents of the government			
Supporters of the government	79.6% (82)	11.7% (12)	8.7% (9)
Opponents of the government	89.3% (92)	9.7% (10)	1.0% (1)
Everyone	96.1% (300)	2.9% (5)	0.3% (1)

hibit little tolerance for dissenting opinions in their communities. What we see instead is an inspiring anomaly.

Respect for the liberal norm of free speech was evident in the degree of tolerance demonstrated among respondents in both types of neighborhoods. Among barrio residents, over 75 percent readily agreed that opponents of the government should be allowed to participate in community meetings; nearly 97 percent agreed that everyone is entitled to do so. Residents of urbanizaciones were slightly more willing to allow the other side to participate at a local meeting, but the difference was not great, and about the same high percentage of respondents in both types of neighborhood agreed that "everyone" is entitled to participate (see table 6). Similar results are obtained when answers are broken down by attitude toward the government (table 7).

Who Should Manage the Economy?

The Venezuelan labor movement is deeply divided over matters of internal organization and the desirability of several programs associated with endogenous development. For example, some labor leaders are deeply suspicious about the cooperative movement. Orlando Chirino—national organizer of the UNT (the pro-Chávez National Union of Workers) and leader of C-Cura (the United Autonomous Revolutionary Class tendency within the UNT)—once commented,

> Many people are using the cooperatives in a way that makes employment precarious, increasing [labor] flexibility, with subcontracts for a fixed period of time. Today the majority of cooperatives in the country are involved in this type of relation, where 4 or 5 people are owners of the cooperatives and make contracts with people for a limited time, with low wages and without trade union rights; they're like "small businesses." . . . This obviously contradicts what the government says about the construction of socialism. (Quoted in Gaudichaud 2006)

Others object to *cogestión*, whereby labor and capital jointly manage an enterprise. The most prominent use of cogestión has been in enterprises that have been renationalized by the government or expropriated because they were closed by their owners. In these cases, workers are to receive 49 percent of shares, the state retaining the rest in exchange for recapitalizing the enterprise. Often the state invests significant new capital. Profits from the co-managed enterprise are supposed to be used at some point in the future to buy out state shares and make the enterprise fully worker-owned and managed. While in some cases worker movements have occupied factories and demanded nationalization with cogestión, in others they have criticized cogestión. For example, workers at SIDEROCA, a co-managed metallurgical company, complained in 2005 that cogestión was nothing more than a cloak for bureaucracy and clientelism (Aporrea 2006).

Our survey respondents were asked to indicate in each of five cases a preference among four different models of enterprise governance: by professional management chosen internally (e.g., by private shareholders or by internal procedures in state-owned enterprises); by management appointed by the president (as in PDVSA and other basic industries owned by the state); by *cogestión*; or by *auto-gestión*. The five cases were:

— ALCASA: a state-owned aluminum enterprise in Ciudad Guayana, notorious for corruption and chronic losses, put under co-management in early 2005.

The government appointed Carlos Lanz, a sociologist and former guerrilla leader, to head the firm and implement the co-management scheme.

— PDVSA: Petróleos de Venezuela, the state oil company. Chávez appointed board members who were unacceptable to managers who had forged the "oil opening" of the 1990s, which set off the struggles that led to the short-lived coup of April 2002 and to the work stoppage of December 2002. Radical members within the petroleum-workers movement have argued that workers ought to exercise self-management of the firm given the crucial role they played in defeating the management-orchestrated work stoppage and sabotage of operations (Lebowitz 2003).

— POLAR: one of the best-known and largest private economic groups, best known for its popular "Polar" beer, but with holdings in diverse sectors.

— VENEPAL: a paper factory. In January 2005, the government invested $14 million to restart production in this factory that had been shut down since the work stoppage of December 2002, when workers occupied the plant. Its owners declared bankruptcy in July 2003.

— "A textile factory": a question intended to tap into a more generalized sentiment by referring to an important industrial sector, the site of frequent labor conflict.

We hypothesized that residents in our relatively organized barrios would be more likely than residents of our urbanizaciones to endorse principles of enterprise control associated with worker democracy. Also of interest, however, is whether a *majority* of barrio residents in these staunchly pro-Chávez areas favor democracy in the workplace—or if they continue to see enterprises as properly controlled by managers, accepting the traditional division of labor characteristic of capitalist and command economies alike. Certainly, twenty-first-century socialism would have to include some progress toward overcoming the division between manual and managerial labor. For all of the rhetoric about revolution and socialism, how much is workplace democracy on the minds of the Bolivarian masses?

As shown in table 8, the cogestión policy articulated by the Chávez administration was most often the choice among respondents from the barrios, but only in regard to ALCASA was it preferred by a majority. In the urbanizaciones, respondents were much more likely to choose the traditional form of management associated with capitalism, especially in the cases of PDVSA and POLAR. In both types of neighborhoods, few respondents opted for auto-gestión. Even pro-government respondents, from both types of neighborhoods, show little support for worker self-management (see column 3, table 8), though few would leave enterprises solely to traditional management either.

Table 8. Opinions about economic control: How do you think the following enterprises should be controlled?

How do you think the following enterprises should be controlled?	Barrios	Urbanizaciones	Pro-government
ALCASA (State-owned aluminum company in Ciudad Guayana)			
By their own efficient professionals	27.8% (153)	44.7% (134)	19.3% (85)
By professionals designated by the executive (country's president)	13.6% (75)	13.3% (40)	17.2% (76)
Through participation by professionals and workers (cogestión)	50.4% (277)	38.3% (115)	56.5% (249)
Only by workers (auto-gestión)	8.0% (44)	3.7% (11)	6.8% (30)
Petróleos de Venezuela (PDVSA, the state oil company)			
By their own efficient professionals	31.8% (175)	54.3% (163)	24.5% (108)
By professionals designated by the executive (country's president)	26.2% (144)	14.7% (44)	29.9% (47)
Through participation by professionals and workers (cogestión)	37.6% (207)	27.3% (82)	41.7% (88)
Only by workers (auto-gestión)	4.2% (23)	3.7% (11)	3.6% (16)
POLAR (Brewery; agribusiness network; owned by powerful family)			
By their own efficient professionals	39.9% (218)	58.3% (175)	31.5% (139)
By professionals designated by the executive (country's president)	12.0% (66)	8.0% (24)	15.4% (68)
Through participation by professionals and workers (cogestión)	41.3% (227)	30.7% (92)	46.5% (205)
Only by workers (auto-gestión)	6.9% (38)	3.0% (9)	6.3% (28)
VENEPAL (Paper company in midst of worker takeover at the time)			
By their own efficient professionals	29.5% (162)	43.3% (130)	20.9% (92)
By professionals designated by the executive (country's president)	12.9% (71)	16.0% (48)	16.6% (73)
Through participation by professionals and workers (cogestión)	46.7% (257)	35.3% (106)	51.9% (229)
Only by workers (auto-gestión)	10.7% (59)	5.3% (16)	10.4% (66)

Table 8. (*continued*)

How do you think the following enterprises should be controlled?	Barrios	Urbaniza-ciones	Pro-government
A textile factory (generic, referring to sector)			
By their own efficient professionals	24.4% (134)	41.3% (124)	18.1% (80)
By professionals designated by the Executive (country's president)	7.6% (42)	9.3% (28)	10.4% (69)
Through participation by professionals and workers (cogestión)	47.5% (261)	39.0% (119)	53.3% (235)
Only by workers (auto-gestión)	20.2% (111)	9.7% (29)	17.9% (79)

Our tables show that there is great variation in support for different options for control of enterprises—both by type of enterprise and by region (see table 9). The only generally consistent finding across region and enterprise is that auto-gestión was supported by only a very few respondents, with the exception of the pattern in the state of Bolívar, where 35.3 percent expressed support for auto-gestión—but for the textile sector, not ALCASA, one of the major industries in the state. Our respondents from Bolívar preferred one of the two more familiar management schemes for ALCASA. Overall, respondents from the Caracas barrios, who are much less likely to be employed in manufacturing, seem most likely to endorse cogestión. Caracas is the zone where worker participation schemes for POLAR and for textiles (most of which are privately owned) attract greatest support. Unfortunately, our survey does not include respondents from the states of the central valley from Caracas west to Barquisimeto, where one finds the greatest concentration of lighter manufacturing (textiles, paper, agro-industry, etc.).

More than half of the respondents in our urbanizaciones believed that PDVSA ought to be run "by their own efficient executives." This position mirrors, of course, that of the company meritocracy during the highly polarized conflicts between the government and company executives between 2001 and 2003. Perhaps more surprising is the small percentages of barrio residents receptive to worker participation in PDVSA—though they clearly prefer the president to choose executives, not the company's own managerial class. This preference of barrio residents probably reflects the unwillingness of any segment of Venezuelan society outside of the oil sector to vest control over an industry that generates such extraordinary profits, the lifeblood of the national economy.

Only in Zulia, a major oil producing region, do a majority of barrio residents

Table 9. Opinions about economic control, variations in barrios in different regions: How do you think the following enterprises should be controlled?

How do you think the following enterprises should be controlled?	State			Total
	Caracas	Zulia	Bolívar	
ALCASA (State-owned aluminum company in Ciudad Guayana)				
By their own efficient professionals	20.8%	20.7%	46.7%	27.8%
	(52)	(31)	(70)	(153)
By professionals designated by the executive (country's president)	10.0%	8.7%	24.7%	13.6%
	(25)	(13)	(37)	(75)
Through participation by professionals and workers (cogestión)	61.2%	59.3%	23.3%	50.4%
	(153)	(89)	(35)	(277)
Only by workers (auto-gestión)	8.0%	11.3%	4.7%	8.0%
	(20)	(17)	(7)	(44)
Petróleos de Venezuela (PDVSA, the state oil company)				
By their own efficient professionals	22.8%	30.7%	48.0%	31.8%
	(57)	(46)	(72)	(175)
By professionals designated by the executive (country's president)	27.6%	14.7%	35.3%	26.2%
	(69)	(22)	(53)	(144)
Through participation by professionals and workers (cogestión)	46.0%	48.7%	12.7%	37.6%
	(115)	(73)	(19)	(207)
Only by workers (auto-gestión)	3.6%	6.0%	0.7%	4.2%
	(9)	(9)	(5)	(23)
POLAR (Brewery; agribusiness network; owned by powerful family)				
By their own efficient professionals	26.0%	43.3%	58.7%	39.6%
	(65)	(65)	(88)	(218)
By professionals designated by the executive (country's president)	12.8%	6.0%	16.7%	12.0%
	(32)	(9)	(25)	(66)
Through participation by professionals and workers (cogestión)	55.2%	44.0%	15.3%	41.3%
	(138)	(66)	(23)	(277)
Only by workers (auto-gestión)	6.0%	6.7%	8.7%	6.9%
	(15)	(10)	(13)	(38)
VENEPAL (Paper company in midst of worker takeover at the time)				
By their own efficient professionals	21.2%	21.3%	51.3%	29.5%
	(53)	(32)	(77)	(162)
By professionals designated by the executive (country's president)	14.0%	7.3%	16.7%	12.9%
	(35)	(11)	(25)	(71)
Through participation by professionals and workers (cogestión)	53.6%	59.3%	22.7%	46.7%
	(134)	(89)	(34)	(257)
Only by workers (auto-gestión)	11.2%	12.0%	8.7%	10.7%
	(28)	(18)	(13)	(59)

Table 9. (*continued*)

How do you think the following enterprises should be controlled?	State			Total
	Caracas	Zulia	Bolívar	
A textile factory (generic, referring to sector)				
By their own efficient professionals	18.8%	21.3%	36.7%	24.4%
	(47)	(32)	(55)	(134)
By professionals designated by the executive (country's president)	6.8%	6.7%	10.0%	7.6%
	(17)	(10)	(15)	(42)
Through participation by professionals and workers (cogestión)	60.4%	56.7%	16.7%	47.5%
	(151)	(85)	(25)	(261)
Only by workers (auto-gestión)	14.0%	15.3%	35.3%	20.2%
	(35)	(23)	(53)	(111)

support worker participation (autogestión and cogestión) for PDVSA, but here one also finds a significant percentage (30.7 percent) supporting the notion of internal managerial control—something akin to what the old executive class of PDVSA called "meritocracy." This option also attracts some support in the barrios of Bolívar state. The most radical worker movements in the latter era of Punto Fijo were organized in Bolívar, especially in Ciudad Guayana. As noted earlier, the Chávez government appointed Lanz, a leader with a strong left-ist resume, to administer ALCASA, yet support for the government's preferred scheme for a transition to twenty-first-century socialism appears *not* to have garnered strong support in the region.

We must exercise caution in drawing conclusive estimates of support for Chavista labor and managerial policies in these regions. For any one of the three regions, our sample is small, yielding a much greater margin for error. Furthermore, we have sampled residents of barrios, not workers themselves. However, all of the barrios chosen for this analysis are known for their history of organization, which should have biased our samples in favor of participatory schemes.

How Aware Are Residents of Chavista Programs in Their Neighborhoods?

Given the relatively small size of the formal proletariat, *democracia protagónica* (protagonist democracy) relies heavily on democracy in the community. For this reason we wanted to assess the extent to which people were even aware of the work of misiones (the anti-poverty social programs) and the consejos (the communal councils) in their communities, and how they evaluated these programs. We asked respondents about a number of specific organizations associated with the Chavista political movements and government programs; and we also invited respondents to name organizations not on our list. We expected that a sizable majority of barrio residents would be aware of the misiones, and that the highest degree of awareness would be for those programs that had directly affected their quality of life.

In fact, nearly all (95 percent) barrio residents were aware of the prototypical Chavista mission, Barrio Adentro, operating in their community. On one level, this is hardly surprising, as the health clinics are a very visible and widely appreciated service. However, it is worth noting that our specific question was *not about the clinics themselves but about awareness of the mobilizational component* of the program—the neighborhood health care committees charged with going door-to-door to make residents aware of services, to carry out educational campaigns, and to identify problems.

By comparison, fewer than one in three respondents in the barrios were aware of the urban land committees (Comités de Tierras Urbanas—CTU), which were charged with carrying out a housing census and resolving property disputes in order to regularize home ownership in the barrios. Even fewer were aware of other committees, such as those dealing with water (19 percent), nutrition (9 percent) or energy (13 percent). Electoral battalion units (UBEs)—neighborhood Chavista activists responsible for the election campaign activity that many hoped would form the mass base of the new PSUV—were known to 27 percent of barrio residents. And 30 percent were aware of the Bolivarian Circles, even though they had been de-emphasized in favor of other organizations in recent years. More encouraging for the president's hope to restructure the geometry of the state in Venezuela is that two thirds of residents were aware of a consejo communal functioning in their community.

It is somewhat hazardous, given the size of our sample, to distinguish levels of organization in particular barrios, but the levels of awareness reported for Zulia are strikingly lower compared to those for the Caracas area and Bolívar. Zulia may differ for several reasons. First, the state has a distinct tradition reinforced by its history as an oil-producing region (though it has since been surpassed in production by eastern fields). Second, Zulia was in 2006 one of only two states, and by far the most important, where the governorship has been controlled by the opposition. The governor at the time, Manuel Rosales, was the main opposition presidential candidate, and he had developed his own populist programs to compete for support with Chávez. Third, urban residents of Zulia were deeply divided over the handling of workers who participated in the paro that nearly paralyzed the oil industry in December 2002.

Fourth, there also existed significant disillusionment with Chavismo among environmentalists and indigenous groups as a result of several development projects, especially around development of mining in the region. Whatever the explanation, government programs involving community participation seemed to have more shallow roots in Zulia, the most populous state in the country.

Not surprisingly, the misiones and committees associated with Bolivarianism in the barrios were less familiar to residents of the urbanizaciones. However, in the middle-class communities surveyed here (again, chosen for their reputation for activism), almost nine in ten (88 percent) of respondents were aware of a functioning neighborhood association (*asociación de vecinos*—AV). Somewhat more surprising, almost one in four respondents was aware of a functioning consejo comunal. Our surveys also found that residents of middle-class areas of Puerto Ordaz, in the industrial Ciudad Guayana, belonged to a myriad of community organizations that barely existed, if at all, in Caracas and Zulia. What these data suggest is that middle-class Venezuelans, though they are likely to greet the new geometry of the state with deep suspicion, are in fact quite capable of organizing themselves to participate and exert influence within a new state structure—especially given the financial incentives offered by the government to induce citizens to form consejos.

Given the resources and popularity of Barrio Adentro, it is unsurprising that barrio residents most favorably evaluated the work of the Health Committees. Nearly two-thirds (65 percent) said they function well, and only eight percent judged their work as "poor." However, among those familiar with their operation, respondents were generally evenly divided between judging them as "good" versus "fair," an indication, perhaps, that five years into their operations, residents were beginning to evaluate their effectiveness more critically. Concern about deterioration of the health clinics is often seen as one factor explaining the low turnout and defeat of the constitutional reform package of 2007. By early 2010 signs of discontent with the program had become more visible.

Of particular importance to the reform of state structures are citizen evaluations of the consejos. Of 363 barrio residents aware of these organizations in their communities, 56 percent judged them favorably. Here again there is significant regional variation, as barrio residents in Bolívar overwhelmingly judged their operation as only fair. Some of this variation may have to do with the quality of local leadership, much of which is associated with parties, held in low repute. Given lower awareness of the consejos in Zulia, and less favorable evaluations in Bolívar, it would seem that the viability of the Chávez reforms depends much upon improving awareness and satisfaction with the councils in areas of the country where they were less visible and valued in 2006.

Given the acute polarization in Venezuela over the Chávez record, one surprising finding is the positive evaluation of the *casas de alimentación* (nutrition centers) in the urbanizaciones. Nearly half of respondents rated this program as "good"; and only 11 percent rated it as "poor." In the two Caracas urbanizaciones, levels of approval were very high—95 percent in Cafetal and 79 percent in Montalban). Hence, although residents of middle-class neighborhoods may view the organs of participatory democracy with suspicion, they may be more favorably inclined toward government programs that strengthen the Venezuelan welfare state. (We caution that only 55 [110 combined] respondents were interviewed in each neighborhood.)

How Dense Is Bolivarian Civil Society in Organized Barrios?

What percentage of residents in these most active neighborhoods is actively participating in the organizational life of their community? Awareness of programs is one measure of the penetration of Chavista programs into these relatively organized communities, but direct, participatory democracy would demand high levels of civic engagement and commitment. Indeed, some say that participatory democracy is unrealistically predicated on an optimistic expectation of human capacity and political commitment to involvement. What levels of participation have been achieved, then, in these barrios, where we might expect experience and commitment to exceed the norm in Bolivarian Venezuela?

One preliminary benchmark we might use is awareness and participation in AVs in the urbanizaciones. Of urbanización residents, 88 percent were aware of an AV functioning in their community, but participation was much lower. The AVs attracted participation from only 27 percent of all respondents; and participants in an AV amounted to two-thirds of those of participating in any organization. (Only 4 percent mentioned participation in a consejo comunal.) Put differently, two-thirds (66 percent) of all respondents from these urbanizaciones, despite their reputation for relatively high levels of social organization, listed *no participation* in any organization.

In general, rates of participation in the barrios compare favorably to those in the middle-class zones. In fact, the rate of general nonparticipation in urbanizaciones was considerably higher than in the barrios, where only 44 percent indicated no participation in any organization. A higher percentage of barrio residents had been mobilized overall because of significant rates of participa-

Table 10. Participation in community organizations in the barrios: Number and percentage of respondents indicating participation in a community organization

Answer	Frequency	Percentage
Does not participate	239	43.7%
Family member participates, not individual	27	4.9%
Individual, no other family participation reported	126	22.9%
Individual and family participation	155	28.2%
Total for barrios	547 (3 missing)	
Percent and number of individuals reporting themselves as a leader ("dirigente")	64	22.8% of 281 participants; 11.7% of respondents
Participants in healthy committees of Barrio Adentro	131	46.7% of participants; 27.4% of respondents
Participants in Communal Councils	77	18.0% of all participants; 12.3% of respondents

tion in the misiones and other movements or organizations (e.g., a consejo, a barrio health committee, an urban land committee, or a UBE; see table 10). Among those identifying themselves as participants, more than one-fifth said they had assumed a leadership position, which translates into more than one of every nine residents taking a leadership role in these activist communities. However, the pattern shifts when we examine specifically participation in the consejos. The rate of participation of barrio residents in the consejos comunales was significantly lower (18 percent) than the rate of participation in AVs in the urbanizaciones. However, the comparison is rendered somewhat inexact by the differences in the purpose and composition of these two organizations. Unlike the AVs, which are made up of residents, consejos are constituted by delegates (*voceros*) of social organizations. Future surveys should examine as well participation in barrio assemblies.

By far the most common form of involvement up to August 2006 in barrios was with the Barrio Adentro health committees. Only the educational missions (Robinson I and II and Missión Rivas, which provide adult secondary education) incorporated more people into government programs.[7] Only thirty-two respondents reported that they were paid for their community work; of sixty-four leaders, only twelve (18.8 percent) identified themselves as leaders. We did not survey residents about MERCAL, probably the program with the most negative reputation for corruption, and one where patronage might be most effectively dispensed for political gain (see chapter 7, "The Misiones of the Chávez Government," by Hawkins, Rosas, and Johnson).

Final Considerations

We find that well-organized barrios showed higher levels of involvement in organizational life than found in the more affluent urbanizaciones—somewhat at odds with theories positing strong civil society is correlated with a strong middle class. I would venture that the rates of participation in misiones, communal councils, and other grassroots organizations are fairly high by any standard. However, we are in uncharted territory regarding the level of participation necessary to make participatory democracy a success. Is a participatory rate of 25 to 30 percent high enough to make twenty-first-century socialism, predicated upon new participatory networks of governance and the local level, viable?

The Venezuelans in our survey did not on the whole seem ready to embrace workplace democracy in conventional industries. Judging by the relatively low levels of support for auto-gestión, even in these more activist communities, residents were not supportive of overthrowing the capitalist order. Their moderate views are consistent with attitudes expressed a generation ago (Martz and Baloyra 1979). Venezuelans in these communities do seem open overall to greater worker democracy—but they do not seem ready to embrace worker self-management. It is important to bear in mind that the cogestión scheme being implemented in Venezuela has a goal more radical than the co-management corporation laws prevailing in Germany. The Venezuelan system is intended to allow a transition to full ownership and management control of workers.

Although our respondents showed little enthusiasm for political parties, and although barrio residents are somewhat more likely than their counterparts in the urbanizaciones to value substantive equality and inclusion as basic to democracy, neither group seems prepared to dispense with liberal norms of democracy. Both sides showed a surprisingly high degree of tolerance for the other's right to participate in local affairs. Even though parties are in disrepute in Venezuela, a majority of barrio residents surveyed refused to eliminate party competition as desirable. Venezuelans living in more organized communities continued to value some important characteristics of liberal democracy. It suggests to us that in Venezuela embracing participatory democracy does not mean repudiating all values associated with representative or liberal democracy.

We did find that barrio respondents were more likely than those in urbanizaciones to value characteristics of democracy associated with inclusion and social equality—substantive measures, not merely procedural. We would hasten to add, however, that these differences are not stark. Many respondents in the more affluent communities valued equality; and levels of tolerance and respect for democratic procedure were notable in the poorer communities. This suggests some basis for consensual politics. Also, since tolerance of opposing views is necessary to work in a representative democracy, would that not be all the more true for a participatory democracy?

Notes

The data for this study were generated through a survey completed August 1–7, 2006, financed by the Faculty Research Grant Program of Webster University.

1. See López Maya (2005, 360–64) for a balanced evaluation of the successes and failures of participatory democracy in Venezuela.

2. Victory speech given December 15, 2006, at the Teresa Carreño Theatre in Caracas.

3. In 2008 Chávez did move to nationalize several other industries that had been privatized in the 1990s. Perhaps more significant, the government refused to nationalize several factories, the most outstanding being Sanatarios Maracay SA, where worker *tomas* (takeover) had occurred.

4. Latinobarómetro is an annual survey conducted throughout the hemisphere. Reports may be found at http://www.latinobarometro.org.

5. Of barrio respondents, 57 percent expressed sympathy for the MVR.

6. Keep in mind that while respondents of urbanizaciones were far more likely to eliminate party competition, they are highly overrepresented in terms of the general population, 50 to 80 percent of which live in poor neighborhoods.

7. Unfortunately, our question asking in which missions people had participated did not discriminate between being a beneficiary of the program and participating as an educator or provider.

CHAPTER TWO

Participatory Democracy in Venezuela

Origins, Ideas, and Implementation

Margarita López Maya and Luis E. Lander

Since 1999 the Bolivarian government has been promoting "participatory and protagonistic" democracy in response to a broad and deeply felt aspiration in Venezuelan society that dates back to the 1980s. Unlike the case in the countries of the Southern Cone, in Venezuela democracy was never interrupted by military dictatorship in the 1960s and 1970s. For this reason, in the 1990s Venezuelans did not experience a transition from authoritarianism to a restricted democracy, as occurred, for example, in Chile or Argentina. On the contrary, diverse and ever-expanding social and protest movements, as well as some political parties, demanded a reform of the state in order to achieve a more "profound," more "integral" democracy. This demand was, in one way or another, frustrated by several governments, including those of Jaime Lusinchi (1984–89), with his failed "Reform of the State," Carlos Andrés Pérez (in his second presidency, 1989–93) with his neoliberal reforms, and Rafael Caldera (in his second presidency, 1994–99) with his postponed constitutional reform. Only the Bolivarians had the political will to accomplish the task; upon assuming power in 1999 they almost immediately initiated the process of writing a new constitution. They elected and installed a constituent assembly to produce a constitution that made a reality of demands postponed for years. The "Exposition of Motives" in the 1999 Constitution of the Bolivarian Republic of Venezuela says that the Republic has been "re-founded" to establish "a more democratic society. Not only is it the state that should now be more democratic, but also society." Democracy, by this logic, ought not to be restricted exclusively to the political sphere; it should impregnate all the spaces of social life.

This newly born democracy incorporated in its discourse novel proposals to address grave problems of exclusion and social injustice afflicting the majority of the country. For this reason it ran counter to the globally hegemonic way of thinking and has been viewed with suspicion and frank aversion by some socio-political actors and political players in Venezuelan society, as well as by hegemonic actors in the global capitalist system. It also initially awoke suspicion among groups and political actors of the left, among other reasons because it originated mainly from sectors—including the military—quite alien from the traditional left, and because its philosophical bases are rooted in sources distinct from traditional Marxist thought.

Foundations

"Participatory and protagonistic" democracy, as outlined in the Constitution of 1999, proceeds fundamentally from the progressive liberal thought of Jean-Jacques Rousseau and John Stuart Mill, and also from more recent ideas about democratic socialism by Nicos Poulantzas. Works by these authors, among others, were widely disseminated and debated in Latin America in the 1970s and 1980s, but their ideas were discarded in the Southern Cone after the fall of the military dictatorships, in favor of a more procedural or restricted type of democracy. The terrible experience of authoritarianism and abuses of power in this period dictated a more cautious approach to a democratic transition. By contrast, broader ideas about democracy fell on fertile soil in Venezuela. Already in the time of President Lusinchi social organizations and political parties of opposition sought to incorporate modalities of direct democracy into proposals to reform the state. But it was with the hegemonic shift toward the Bolivarian forces that these ideas prospered, germinating in Chapter IV of the new constitution, which in the Exposition of Motives consecrated citizens' rights to direct, semi-direct and indirect participation, not only through the vote in electoral processes but also by way of the "formulation, execution, and control of public administration" (Constitución de la República Bolivariana de Venezuela [CRBV] 1999). In this respect the change of emphasis from the Constitution of 1961 is notable. While representative democratic institutions are maintained, now participation in all spheres of the state is regarded as a key educational practice for transforming fundamentally unequal social relations. For its part, the *Líneas generales del plan de desarrollo económico y social de la nación 2001* (hereafter *Guidelines*) provided the orientation for public policy for the constitutional period that ended in January 2007, the conclusion of Chávez's first term, The *Guidelines* held that participation would stimulate self-betterment, inculcate co-responsibility, and give impetus to the "protagonism" of the citizens. According to the Bolivarian project, these are the sources from which a society characterized by equality, solidarity, and democracy will emerge.

The Political Sphere

One of the central ideas of the Constitution of 1999 is well expressed in the first part of Article 62: "All citizens [*ciudadanos y ciudadanas*] have the right to freely participate in political affairs, *directly or via their elected representatives*" (emphasis added).[1] This part of the text also delineates the separation of Public Power into three levels—the national, the state, and the municipal, with National Public Power organized into five powers, formally independent of one another. In addition to the three powers traditionally found in a representative democracy—legislative, executive, and judicial—the CRBV incorporates civic and electoral powers that formally increase autonomy and independence. These institutions of Public Power are responsible for controlling other powers and for administrating electoral processes. By incorporating elements of more direct or participatory democracy into the representative model, the constitutional text strives to prove false the presumed antagonism between representative and participatory democracy.

In practice the equilibrium between participation and representation has been quite precarious. The Bolivarian project tends to privilege characteristics of direct democracy—participation and protagonism (the right of the people to play an active role in policymaking)—in the implementation of policies (see chapter 3, "Urban Land Committees," by García-Guadilla). Nevertheless, even taking into account advances in the development of modes of popular organization and their capacity to influence complicated political decisions, it remains clear that crucial aspects of national and international policy stand beyond reach. In some key respects representation has been weakened by concentration of power, by poorly constructed collective leadership, and by personalism in the figure of the president. Sectors of the opposition focus on these issues, complaining about weaknesses in representative aspects of democracy, such as the separation of public powers and their lack of independence.

The new model has been put to the test on several occasions. From the approval of the constitutional text until the narrow defeat of the constitutional reform project in December 2007, there occurred two presidential, two parliamentary, two regional, and two municipal elections, plus a presidential-recall election. In all but the December 2007 referendum, the forces supporting the Bolivarian project were victorious; but the electoral process has been burdened by strong polarization, tensions, and contradictions. The legal framework governing elections is the Organic Law of Suffrage and Political Participation, promulgated in May of 1998. When this law was under discussion there were sectors, today mainly grouped in the opposition, which advocated a purely personal system—that is, a uninominal system in which voters opt for candidates, not for parties via a list. In the end a system more adapted to the country's electoral tradition was established. Although broad space for personalized voting was included, it was combined with a system of proportional representation in order to guarantee that deliberative bodies would better reflect the diverse positions existing in society.

However, in the parliamentary elections of 2000 there occurred an incident in a small state in the interior that, though it had little impact at the time, in other, later elections acquired national importance. The state of Yaracuy, until the gubernatorial elections of 2004, had been governed by a member of the opposition party, Convergencia. In the parliamentary elections of 2000, the governor, Eduardo Lapi, came up with a scheme that proved exceptionally fruitful for his personal political organization. He created a group called La Alianza por Yaracuy—LAPY—phonetically similar to his name, though ending in *y*. Under this name he formally listed candidates postulated by name (that is, presented by LAPY), separating them from those on the party list presented by Convergencia. This technique meant that for the National Assembly, with little more than 40 percent of the vote, the governor won four of the five deputies allotted to the state on the proportional ballot; for the state Legislative Council, with little more than 53 percent of the votes he obtained six of the seven deputy positions being contested via "first past the post."[2] At the time, a complaint was filed with CNE and in the courts, but the maneuver was not invalidated.

The results clearly stood as a distortion of the principle of proportional representation established in Article 63 of the Constitution of 1999 as well as the mechanism outlined in the Organic Law of Suffrage and Political Participation. The latter, in articles 12, 14, 15, and 17, establishes the manner by which equilibrium between the personalized vote and proportional representation is guaranteed. Subsequently, in the municipal elections of 2004 government supporters adopted this strategy, and they repeated it for the parliamentary elections of December 2005. Again complaints were filed against the maneuver, which came to be called popularly *morochas* (for its use by two parties that essentially are "identical twins"), but based on the precedents established in 2000, both the National Electoral Council and courts set aside demands for its invalidation. This was one of the reasons, though not the only one, that a majority of the opposition organizations gave to justify their decision to abstain from the parliamentary elections of December 2005. As a result of this abstention, the National Assembly came to be constituted totally by pro-government deputies, making it a body that inadequately represented the entire society and weakening its role in the political system.

On the other hand, we can also highlight several improvements in the democratic condition. From 1998 to 2006, the number of Venezuelans with the formal capacity to exercise their political rights increased faster than the growth of the population. While the total population of the country from 1998 to 2006 increased by a little more than 3.2 million people, the Permanent Electoral Register (Registro Electoral Permanente—REP) increased by more than 4.95 million. Through the so-called identity mission, efforts have been intensified to issue and distribute updated identity documents to the adult population that lacks them, and to register those that have the right to vote but are not on the REP. These initiatives have been aimed, with success, at converting noncitizens—without identity or political rights—into full citizens.

Polarization, although attenuated after the presidential recall referendum of August 2004, remained an uncured illness in Venezuelan society. In all of the electoral processes after 1998 it has been evident in the geographic distribution of results. In predominantly lower-class areas, the results have almost always favored the Bolivarian process; in areas that are mostly of the middle and upper classes, the results have almost always opposed it (L. Lander and López Maya 2005; López Maya and Lander 2006). The social policies discussed below are directed at the low-income majority of the population. For that reason these sectors positively evaluate the actions of the government—although they are often critical about inefficiencies and weaknesses in implementation. By contrast, sectors of the population with middle or high levels of income— the minority—often fail to appreciate the government's efforts in social policy. The pattern was somewhat altered in the December 2007 constitutional reform referendum, when high rates of abstention and even defeat for the president's reform proposals characterized results in many populous urban barrios. The Chavistas prevailed in a second referendum repealing term limits on certain elected officials, including the president, but the results of the mayoral and gubernatorial elections of February 2009 were mixed. The pattern of polarization was evident again as the Chavistas overall did well in poor rural areas and barrios nationally, but with important exceptions in some key cities and urban states. The outcome of National Assembly elections scheduled for 2010 produced similar results. Chávez remained popular through early 2010, but there were signs of popular fatigue with continued problems of governance.

The Focus on Social Justice and Equality

Supporters of the Bolivarian political project understand democracy not only as the enjoyment of civil liberties and the exercise of political rights but also, in a very emphatic way, as social justice and social equality. The concept of democracy had a similar connotation during the period of two-party hegemony: political democracy was considered the route to social justice. This understanding of democracy is deeply engrained in Venezuelan political culture, evolving at the end of the twentieth century into an unfulfilled promise of representative democracy (see chapter 1, "Defying the Iron Law of Oligarchy I," by Hellinger). For that reason, when Venezuela undertook in 1999 a substantive and profound transformation of representative democracy, it sought to address a pending issue from the era of Punto Fijo.[3] The search for social equality as an explicit objective distinguishes Venezuela's democratic proposal from others in the region, and this is one sense in which we can properly use the term *revolution*. Thus the Constitution of 1999 establishes in its second article (on the fundamental principles of the Republic), "Venezuela is constituted as a Democratic and Social State of Law and Justice which in its legal order and actions holds as highest values life, liberty, justice, *equality, solidarity*, democracy, *social responsibility* and in general, the preeminence of human rights, ethics, and political pluralism" (emphasis added).

When referring to the problem of social inequality and the strategy for overcoming it, *Guidelines* explicitly rejects a stress on compensatory mechanisms. Such an approach assumes that the material deficiencies of the majority are accidental, provisional, or individual, as signified by the concept of poverty in the neoliberal social-policy orientations used by previous governments. The point of departure for this new perspective is an understanding of social inequality as social exclusion. This is closer to the meaning articulated by the United Nations Development Program in the 1990s and 2000s: poverty as exclusion from access to social rights, even exclusion from the human condition as a member of a society (United Nations 2010, especially chapter 4). The objective of the state's social policy, then, is building inclusion, reestablishing the human condition, fulfilling social rights, and treating persons as social subjects capable of determining and being co-responsible for their life conditions. The orientation of the *Guidelines* is holistic; that is, social exclusion is diagnosed as a structural problem of society, not of individuals. It can only be corrected by applying public practices that relate issues of social equality to the nation's economic, territorial, cultural, and international policies, and that try to progress on all of these fronts simultaneously. This is what the document calls in chapter 1 the equilibria that ought to be constructed, one of which—social equilibrium (the others being economic, political, territorial, and international)—would focus the actions of the state on resolution of the problem of exclusion.

As a strategy to reach social equilibrium, the *Guidelines* considers the work of two fundamental actors to be decisive: first, the state in all of its administrative levels and branches, as the creator of conditions that make possible the empowerment of citizens; second, citizens, who through their participation in families, communities, and organized groups are transforming themselves into political subjects with values such as solidarity, respect for democratic procedures, and co-responsibility.

The identification of *two* key actors, with distinct obligations and duties for the achievement of a common goal, differs from the framework for public planning used by previous governments, when the main actor was the interventionist state, creator of conditions that would make possible modernization and the acquisition of citizenship. The state's activities, in the hands of both parties, were oriented toward social transformation. The *Guidelines*, in contrast, speaks of the state as "accompanying" citizens, families, and organized communities; the state should not be predominant in the creation of the conditions of citizenship. In this scheme the state is a facilitator of empowerment for those who ought to make decisions and control public administration. The state ought to guarantee human rights, but citizens, families, and community organizations, through their participation in public administration, are the only ones who will make possible participatory and protagonistic democracy, by assuming an active and directive role in the solution of problems. The Constitution says in article 62, "All citizens have the right to participate freely in public affairs, directly or through their elected representatives. The participation of the people in the formation, execution and control of public administration is the necessary medium to achieve the protagonistic role that guarantees their complete development, individual as well as collective. It is the obligation of the State and duty of the society to facilitate the creation of conditions more favorable for its practice."

Within this logic, in order to reach a social equilibrium, the *Guidelines* presents three foci around which politics should revolve, each one pertaining to a distinct and crucial dimension of the structural condition of exclusion, and all promoting popular organization and mobilization.

1. The correction of the unjust distribution of income and wealth.
2. Overcoming discrimination in access to fundamental human rights such as nutrition, health, housing, and education.

3. Development of full citizenship, which is characterized by members of society possessing attributes such as solidarity, responsibility, and participatory and democratic attitudes.

This manner of addressing exclusion is coherent and attractive, with the potential to be effective in the pursuit of the articulated objectives. Through a variety of policy instruments these three foci have been implemented in Venezuela over the last eight years (1999–2007). And it is apparent that the popular sectors have been experiencing surprising levels of social mobilization, providing them with increasing levels of organization and a growing sense of efficacy.

Social Policies and Results

Now we turn to consideration of some of the many instruments of social policy deployed by the Chávez government since 1999, which seem to have contributed toward the dynamic organization and lively mobilization of diverse popular sectors, a phenomenon that has been noted repeatedly by researchers, observers, and international journalists, and is reflected in the statistics presented below.

Rectification of Income and Wealth Inequality

The Law of Land and Agricultural Development (approved via the Enabling Law in November of 2001) and Decree 1.666 of February 4, 2002 (which relates to the regularization of tenancy of urban land occupied by informal settlements of popular communities), stand out in the government's efforts to redistribute wealth. Both legal instruments seek to democratize property in Venezuela. For citizens to exercise their right of property, they must first hold assemblies to constitute organizations called Urban Land Committees (CTU) in cities and Rural Land Committees (CTR) in the countryside. In addition, the community must define the boundaries of its territory and write its history, among other requirements. This opportunity to obtain property rights has fomented intense popular mobilization, organization, and self-governance.

The mobilization stimulated by the Land Law almost immediately generated intense conflict in the Venezuelan countryside, the antagonists being landowners on one side, and the state and peasants on the other. This conflict contributed to the confrontation between the Chávez government and entrepreneurial sectors, which resulted in the attempted coup of April 11, 2002.

Since then, conflict over land in the countryside has, with some variation, continued. In 2004, several human rights organizations and the attorney general denounced the assassination of at least seventy-three peasant leaders, some by hired assassins, for defending the Land Law and seeking adjudication of rural property through formation of CTRs. The 2004–5 report from PROVEA (Venezuelan Program for Rights Education and Action, a leading human rights organization in the country) indicates that if the disappeared included in the reports of some peasant organizations were to be counted, by the second semester of 2005 the number would have reached one hundred killings (PROVEA 2005, 220). In its report for 2005–6, PROVEA denounced the assassination of five more peasants (2006, 213).

With regard to urban land tenancy among popular sectors, the new Venezuelan policies were unprecedented. Andrés Antillano (2005), an activist with the Urban Land Committees, maintains that the committees, created by Decree 1.666 in February 2002, have maintained an important autonomy of action versus the bureaucracy of the state. According to the National Technical Office for Regularization of Land (OTNRT)—charged with coordinating aspects of this process—by the middle of 2005 there were almost six thousand CTUs already constituted and organized into a network. They were present in the majority of the barrios of the largest cities in the country, covering a population of close to one million families. Based on a conservative estimate of four persons per family this would amount to a fourth of the poor urban population of the country. Some one hundred thousand adjudications of property titles for urban land have taken place. Antillano describes some characteristics of these CTUs that explain their success:

1. Organized popular struggle for regularization of urban land tenancy precedes Chavismo. It formed part of the Assembly of Barrios that came to play an important role after the Caracazo of 1989. Although the Assembly disappeared around 1994, organizations that formed part of it emerged again in 2001 as a consequence of the approval of forty-nine laws via the Enabling Law in November of that year. Popular urban communities complained that their aspirations had not been incorporated into any of these laws that were to give birth to the "refounding of the Republic," leaving them excluded once again. With the publication of Decree 1.666 in response to this complaint, the process began to take shape; however, rather than the government taking the lead, it unfolded in autonomous form, in part to the political crisis that ravaged the government and obliged it to direct its attention elsewhere. Only after two years was the OTNRT cre-

ated. The diversion of the govenrment's attention elsewhere fortified the independence of the CTUs.

2. The CTUs, as stipulated by the decree creating them, have a territory that the community conceives and delimits. These social territories both strengthen in CTU members feelings of belonging and ownership and promote solidarity and self-government.

3. The CTUs are constituted via an assembly and through participation of the majority. They must fulfill certain requirements, such as laying out a map of the community (the territory) and reconstructing its history, in order to be able to register with the OTNRT. This process provides recognition of leaders with deeper roots in the community, as well as links among members.

4. The CTUs are famous for their flexibility and organizational versatility. Efforts were made to simplify the procedures to constitute a CTU, to facilitate processes of organization of sectors traditionally alienated from participation in formal organizations. This freed them to some degree from the need to rely on parties, non-governmental organizations or government bureaucrats. On the other hand, no scheme of organization is proscribed, which allows each CTU to adapt itself to the idiosyncrasies of its community. (Antillano 2005, 211)

Some activists claim that a tension exists between the CTUs' autonomy and their dependence on government institutions. This tension permanently threatens their dynamism; conflicts are frequent and their resolution remains uncertain. Toward the middle of 2006, the director of the National Office for Regularization of Land, an institution within the office of the Vice Presidency of the Republic, reported the approval of a total of 210 million land titles authorized to CTUs, benefiting more than two million Venezuelans.[4]

In a similar manner to the CTUs, the Technical Water Workshops (Mesas Técnicas de Agua—MTA), defined by Santiago Arconada Rodríguez as "an organized community response to problems or concerns arising in relation to potable water service or sanitation" (2005, 189), were formed by popular organizations active before the Chávez government.[5] They have their origins in the parish governments promoted in Libertador municipality by Mayor Aristóbulo Istúriz—at that time of the Causa Radical party—during the period 1993–95. MTAs were converted into a national policy instrument on the initiative of activists who participated in that experience and after 1999 supported the Chávez government. Since that time they have expanded—and like the CTUs maintain with difficulty their autonomy and vitality—having managed to extend themselves across the better part of the urban and rural geography of the country. They have been an important factor in many communities' successful resolution of problems related to potable water and sanitation, and they have created more complex organizations, such as Community Water Councils, which function as intermediary institutions linking the MTAs with local governments, public water enterprises, and other MTAs.

Another key feature of the attempt to rectify income and wealth inequality that has received significant government support since the defeated oil strike-sabotage of 2002–3 is the effort to promote the social economy, understood as an alternative, more democratic, more cooperative, and more collaborative form of production and service. The Exposition of Motives of the Bolivarian constitution (CRBV 1999) calls for greater equilibrium between economic efficiency and social justice, "allowing freedom of private initiative and preserving collective interest." Article 308 obliges the state to promote and protect diverse forms of community organization for employment, including cooperatives, peasant enterprises, microenterprises, and small and medium industry. Article 70 recognizes cooperatives as forms of popular initiative and participation in social and economic affairs, and calls for laws to be passed to establish conditions for their successful functioning. In addition, Article 118 establishes that the law ought to recognize the specific nature of these organizations as generators of collective benefits. Article 184 requires that laws create flexible mechanisms for participation by community organizations in the administration of decentralized services or services transferred from states or municipalities. This article mentions services in the areas of health, education, housing, culture, sport, environment, maintenance of industrial areas, neighborhood security, and the like. On August 30, 2001, the Special Cooperative Associations Law was passed, fulfilling the constitutional mandate.

The growth of these community organizations over the years has been spectacular. According to the National Superintendency for Cooperatives (SUNACOOP), the number registered by December 2005 was 102,568, which indicates a great leap in relation to the 24,433 registered by August of 2004 or the 10,032 counted in June 2003.[6]

The social economy is supported by a system of microfinancing—by Banco del Pueblo Soberano, Banco de la Mujer, Banco de Desarrollo Social (Bandes), among others—in order to give financial and technical support to those involved in grassroots social and economic organizing. Programs that teach commercialization of production and training for co-entrepreneurs and workers also undergird it. The social economy is rooted in the popular demand for democratization of the market (Vila Planes 2003). In fact since 2003, when the national government gained control of PDVSA, there has been rising support for so-called business circles, some specifically for cooperatives and small and medium entrepreneurs, where they open up bidding for contracts for the goods and services purchased by the public sectors.

Combating Exclusion

The government has developed several significant means to combat exclusion. Here we point out a few that in their formulation, or because of the availability of trustworthy information, can provide a preliminary description of the direction of such programs in meeting the constitutional charge to promote participatory democracy.

National Identity Plan (Plan Nacional de Identidad—PNI)
The lack of state-recognized identity is a radical manifestation of exclusion. In recent decades, due to the retreat and weakening of the state, the problem of lack of official identity documents increased in Venezuela, with the consequent violation of human rights that this implies. To not exist legally is to be unable to access basic services, the education system, the social security system, or to establish family status. In 2000, with the technical assistance of UNICEF, the national government began an operation under the title "Soy venezolano, soy venezolana" ("I Am Venezuelan"), creating Hospital Units for Civil Registration of Births (UHRCN) in order to guarantee that all those born in public hospitals obtain at that time their citizenship and officially register a name. Approximately 94 percent of Venezuelans are born in public institutions. The first UHRCN was created in 2000 in the state of Zulia; later, the Concepción Palacios Maternity Clinic in Caracas put one into operation, registering on average sixty births daily. In 2003, the goal was to add a UHRCN to four more establishments in the Metropolitan Area of Caracas and spread the PNI to eight more states. The plan also called for the gradual modernization of the Civil Birth Registry. Under this program there has been a massive effort to increase registration via mobile operations and more widely dispersed registry centers. At these centers citizens can either update or obtain for the first time their identity document rapidly and efficiently. According to information on the official web page of the Ministry of Planning and Development, 8,212,659 identity cards had been issued by October of 2004 to Venezuelans who needed new documents or simply had never registered; and 653,306 children and adolescents had acquired their identity documents.[7]

Bolivarian Schools and Little Simóns (Simoncitos)

Inclusion through access to a quality education from the earliest years—a right also stripped from the popular sectors by the reduction of the state and social spending in decades past—has been advanced by Chávez government since 1999. It has successfully boosted school enrollment, which had been decreasing consistently since the 1990s—independent data have demonstrated this year after year (see PROVEA 1999, and subsequent years). According to official data, by the beginning of 2005 there were around 3,807 Bolivarian schools functioning. The 2005 annual report of the Ministry of Education and Sports said that in the entire country the number of Bolivarian schools reached 4,732, with 887,769 attending through the ninth grade (PROVEA 2006, 114). The Venezuelan state has managed to reverse the drop-out rate and has struggled to eliminate hidden enrollment fees that some public schools required from parents, in violation of the constitutional right to free education. It has also provided free uniforms and textbooks as an incentive to return to school. But perhaps most important, the state has provided children with a full day of school instead of the half day instituted in previous decades—although this is still not a reality in all Bolivarian schools. A full school day permits parents to work, especially the mother, who is often the head of the family, and also provides children that attend these schools two meals and two snacks daily. PROVEA, based on official indicators, recorded that real public expenditure *per capita* in education for 2005 increased 4.1 percent, while the previous year it had increased 31.1 percent. As a percentage of gross national income, public spending on education in 2005 was around 4.2 percent (PROVEA 2006, 100). The simoncitos, for their part, are a new version of pre-school education that seeks to correct exclusion and social inequality, both affective and cultural, that begins before basic education. The government has argued for the necessity of making this level obligatory, which it has never done before, and declared in its annual report of 2005 that the program had reached an enrollment of 880,639 children.

The Missions

The missions are social programs that aim to ease access to various social rights and are thought of as temporary or emergency policies to deal with urgent necessities of the popular sectors. The missions have perhaps obtained the most international recognition, though this does not mean that their functions and characteristics are understood in a systematic way. The first of these missions was undertaken a little after the government brought the oil strike of 2002–3 under control and was called Misión Robinson, after the pseudonym "Samuel Robinson," used by Simón Rodríguez, Bolívar's teacher.

Misión Robinson I had as its goal eradication of illiteracy in Venezuela. The methodology of this mission, known as "Yes, I can," was developed by the Cuban pedagogue, Lenola Relys, and adapted to the Venezuelan context by local teachers. It has been praised by UNESCO, among others. In sixty-five sessions of two hours each the participant—called a "patriot"—is schooled in the rudiments of reading and writing. Misión Robinson I relies upon a facilitator, called the "volunteer," in many cases a youth from the same community, and also a teacher or a retired teacher, who is given training. A textbook and supporting material are provided. According to the national census of 2001, there were 1,154,120 million illiterate Venezuelans. Utilizing official figures collected by the volunteers, the number actually reached 1,252,226. A few months later came Misión Robinson II, through which the newly literate patriots were helped to obtain a sixth-grade diploma after two years of study. If we keep in mind that 52 percent of the registered illiterates were younger than thirty, we can appreciate the significance of this program for awakening future expectations for more than a half million Venezuelans. In October 2005, the country was declared by UNESCO to be free from illiteracy, after having carried out numerous initiatives to bring this program to the far corners of the nation, where there are communities of indigenous people and peasants who have not been able to exercise their rights to education. Other missions centered on the right to education are Misión Ribas and Misión Sucre, also created after the oil strike to address the exclusion of large popular sectors and certain middle-class sectors from access to secondary and higher education.

Since 2004 the government has been increasing the number of missions—stimulated by increasing fiscal income stemming from the advancement of oil reform, which has permitted greater control over the activities of the industry, combined with the hike in oil prices on the international market. Among the many missions currently functioning we would highlight Misión Barrio Adentro, which has established a system of primary and preventive medicine in popular communities; Misión Mercal, a food commercialization and distribution network aimed at the popular sectors; Misión Vuelvan Caras ("about face"), whose job is to train participants—called "lancers"—for work in and promotion of so-called endogenous development centers; Misión Guaicaipuro, which promotes access to rights for indigenous communities; Misión Miranda, which seeks to improve conditions for the military sector; Misión Piar, which serves miners; and Misión Negra Hipólita, for the indigent population.

All these missions are significant for achieving in theory the elimination of exclusion, but we do not have sufficient independent information to evaluate them with a high degree of confidence. Nonetheless, in what follows we review some data about Barrio Adentro and Mercal, two of the policies that are most supported in the popular sector and most recognized with political impact nationally and internationally.

Plan Barrio Adentro, converted in 2004 into Misión Barrio Adentro, emerged as a presidential initiative to promote development in health, education, culture, and sport in the most deprived communities of the country—communities that demonstrated active and sustained support for the Chávez government during the political crisis of 2001–4. This mission is basically focused on offering barrio residents onsite health services including free medical attention, including free prescriptions and supplies of medicine, home health services, and twenty-four-hour-a-day medical care.[8] Through an agreement between Cuba and Venezuela, Cuban medical professionals began in April of 2003 to offer medical assistance alongside Venezuelan doctors in the Caracas metropolitan area, and the program was expanded in 2004 to cover all of the states and cities in the country. The number of Venezuelan health workers participating was initially minimal, since conditions in the urban barrios where they have to work are not attractive, and the Federation of Venezuelan Doctors launched ferocious opposition. Nonetheless, in 2004 Venezuelan doctors and nurses were incorporated, and the resistance of the medical association softened, given the clear benefits of the mission and its positive political impact. For 2005, official data indicate that almost twenty-one thousand Cuban doctors and five hundred nurses were working in poor communities; there were six thousand Venezuelan doctors and twenty-six hundred nurses (PROVEA 2007, 171). Barrio Adentro II was also launched in 2005; its objective is to set up centers for holistic diagnosis and free clinics in popular urban barrios, with the capacity to render health services at a level higher than those available in the Barrio Adentro centers.

The provision of preventive and primary care medical services, by bringing medical personnel to popular communities, involves the organization of Health Committees that, as with the CTUs and MTAs, make decisions in assemblies. They are charged not only with receiving and helping the doctor in his or her activities, but also with improving the integral health of the community to which they belong. Unlike the case with the CTUs and the MTAs, there was not any significant previous organizational experience with respect to health care in the Caracas barrios, nor in most of the other cities in the country. This policy was clearly initiated by the state, which has had a greater influence on its development than in the case of the CTUs or the MTAs. Available information does allow us to conclude, however, that the processes of organization and administration have been fundamentally rooted in the concerns and aspirations of the communities (see Alayón Monserat 2005).

For its part, Misión Mercal—also created after the difficult experiences of the oil strike—has been establishing a network for distribution and commercialization of food and other basic necessities. This mechanism's price controls and subsidies distinguish it from what was earlier provided through the private sector. Its goal is to assure the nutritional security of the population, especially those sectors with scarce economic resources. Mercal has been constructing a network with both fixed and mobile outlets and incorporating individual, collective, and family merchants who voluntarily enter into the system. It has been coordinated mainly by members of the Venezuelan Armed Forces. Since 2003, according to official information, it has established at the national level 34 supermarkets—large capacity establishments usually the property of cooperatives or of the state—201 Type I mercales and 1,105 Type II mercales, which are general stores smaller than supermarkets, which also can be either publicly or privately owned; 393 mobile *mercalitos* whose vehicles cover diverse routes in places difficult to access or in situations of emergency; and 13,973 mercalitos, or *bodegas populares*, which are private and permit the incorporation of families from the popular sectors in the network. The discounts are around 40 percent relative to the private production networks of commercial food, and for 2006 it was estimated that this mission reached about half the population.[9]

The missions have attracted a great deal of attention in Latin America. Carlos Eduardo Febres (2005), an expert on social policy, suggests that if they are indeed conceptually similar to the compensatory policies and orientations of neoliberalism, they differ in that their extent and coverage give a "degree of universalism" that the other programs lack. Also, in popular imagination they differ from these earlier programs because they are seen as achieving social inclusion. Febres emphasizes the symbolic side of these missions, that is to say, the strength they derive from the discourse and images accompanying them. Misión Identidad, for example, has been promoted with the slogan, "Soy venezolano, soy venezolana," directly stimulating the development of a sense of belonging to the nation via access to citizenship; Misión Robinson's "Yo si puedo" reinforces feelings of self-esteem; Misión Sucre denotes its student as "winners." More recently, and through their own initiative, indigent people have begun to organize themselves into a mission, Misión Negra Hipólita, to gain access to the right to employment, and call themselves "nomads"; members of Misión Vuelvan Caras, with its goal of overcoming the high rate of unemployment, call themselves "lancers." Changes of name are also changes of image. This, of course, is reinforced by the discourse of the president, which is constantly filled with symbols and historical antecedents to give impact to every official act associated with the missions.

Participation for Empowerment

The third focus of social policy has as its goal the creation of solidaristic, participative, co-responsible, and democratic citizens, which will enable a new relation between state and society. Toward this end, much like the multiple organizational forms promoted by policies described above, as well as the constitutional provisions that open various levels of public administration to political activity, these participatory policies seek to transform Venezuelans into politicized citizens sharing responsibility for solving their problems. Among the constitutional provisions we would highlight referendums in their various modalities (consultative, approbatory, revocatory, and abrogative); assemblies of citizens; legislative initiatives; local public planning councils; and parish councils, among others. Toward the beginning of 2006 a great impetus was given to the creation of the communal councils (*consejos comunales*), organizations in which all the aforementioned organizations are locally articulated. In April 2006, the National Assembly produced the Communal Councils Law, and approximately $1 billion was expended to finance projects presented by these councils in that year. Along with this initiative was announced the creations of "people's banks" as financial instruments to manage these resources.

During the presidential recall referendum of 2004 the suitability of these various forms of participation was put to the test. Sectors and organizations opposed to Chávez mobilized to collect the required signatures and, having complied and fulfilled their requirement, organized the vote to revoke the presidential mandate. For their part Chavista forces encouraged popular mobilization with the goal of supporting the president. This type of popular organization, emerging in the din of the polarized confrontations of recent years, is by nature defensive and given cohesion by the charisma of President Chávez. Organizations, such as the Bolivarian Circles in the first years of the government, the electoral battle units (Unidades de Batalla Electoral—UBE) later, or the squadrons and battalions of the Miranda Campaign in the presidential elections of 2006, incline toward a cult of personality. If they have indeed rendered important political results, not only did they not favor, they also became obstacles to the autonomous organization of the popular sectors and their capacity to make decisions in an independent manner.

A Preliminary Evaluation

The focus on social policy in the Bolivarian project aims to address conditions of exclusion. This is not just a matter of increasing income or providing better services. Exclusion is recognized as a historical problem, and these social policies seek to establish, or in some cases re-establish, conditions of citizenship. Unlike previous policies, the fundamental orientation of change is the development of an organized citizenry capable of making decisions and taking responsibility for solving their problems.

Nonetheless, thinking about the popular sectors and movements in Venezuela in recent decades, it is obvious that the relation between the two subjects of social transformation, that is, the state and the organized citizenry, is unequal. The Venezuelan state can count on financial, institutional, and organizational resources that give it political and economic advantages with respect to the popular sectors. And the initiatives and pressures of the state endanger the autonomy of civic and community organizations.

The popular movement, at the beginning of this new political project, was drained by almost two decades of neoliberal policies. The movement existed before Chávez, but it lacked an organic base, tradition, and networks which might have given it the strength and autonomy to take action vis-à-vis the state. Disorganized, dispersed, and fragmented, this earlier popular movement began to co-exist after 1999 with multiple popular organizations that have been stimulated by the government through the various policies and social programs described above.

Sociologists such as Edgardo Lander (2004) maintain that while it is natural for the state to mobilize and organize its bases of support, such initial relationships of inequality lead to at least two routes toward which the transformation of society may be directed. The easiest is a return to a pattern of clientelism and paternalism, as has happened countless times with Latin American populism, and in particular with Venezuelan populism in the twentieth century — primarily as exemplified by the history of Acción Democrática (AD) political party. The state in this scenario controls and colonizes society and the popular movement. This can result in mobilization and social advance as well as organization. But autonomy is absent and people's capacity for social control and feelings of efficacy is weakened. The top strata of the state, in the person of officials in key posts in public administration, distribute resources and decide upon practices and orientations. Self-governance and independence are not promoted; instead the passive acceptance of bureaucratic transmission of public resources is encouraged. There exists no real social control, no transparency, and corruption is facilitated. This is in essence an authoritarian path, one historically known and tirelessly repeated in Venezuela in the twentieth century.

The second path or paradigm, according to Lander, would be participatory and democratic. It would imply sustained stimulus on the part of the state and a greater plurality of social and productive organizations, along with respect for their development and advances toward greater levels of autonomous participation in public administration and acquisition of control over it. An indispensable requisite for this route would be the creation of dense organizations and the constitution of new, intermediate levels of articulation among popular organizations. These latter would also be autonomous, able both to mediate between society and the state and to fortify the popular movement as interlocutors in various types of public administration.

Another crucial condition for this desirable scenario is the increased institutionalization of types of public administration that allow for continuity, universalistic criteria for access to rights and resources, and real capacity for public control.

A look at the development of the multiple instruments of social policy that have emerged during the Chávez government currently reveals dynamic mobilization and popular organization with few precedents in the history of the country. CTUs, Health Committees, cooperatives, self-governing community housing organizations, CTRs, mercalitos, and the like have increased in number and coverage throughout the length and breadth of the country. The enthusiastic participation of previously excluded social sectors has been increasing and extending throughout all of the country. This is especially true since 2003, when the state managed to gain control over the petroleum industry and reform the oil regime, with a consequent increase in fiscal income to finance these many social policies. This dynamism has produced some efforts at coordination among popular organizations, as well as the search for intermediate spaces, such as the Social Connection for Popular Power (2004) or the Communal Councils for Water. Nonetheless, participatory and organizational enthusiasm has not always implied greater autonomy in popular mobilization and organization.

In April 2006 the National Assembly approved the Law of Communal Councils, intended, according to article 2, to be "instances of participation, articulation and integration among diverse community organizations, social groups and citizens that permit the organized citizenry to directly exercise control over public policies and projects aimed at answering the needs and aspirations of communities in the construction of equality and social justice." According to this proclamation, the communal councils are offered as forms of empowerment and autonomous participation by the popular sectors organized into them. But the law also contemplates the creation of various types of higher entities—National, Regional, and Local Presidential Commissions of Popular Power and the National Fund for Communal Councils—whose members are all designated directly by the President of the Republic. These bureaus approve or reject projects presented by the communities and assign the necessary financing. Clearly, this is a structure that potentially can restrict the autonomy of community and grassroots organizations and facilitate the construction of patron-client networks. Furthermore, the proposal for communal councils was not sufficiently informed by the previous successful experiences of participatory organization, such as the MTAs, the Self-Governing Community Organizations (Organizaciones Comunitarias Autogestionarias—OCAs), or the CTUs, and it is not at all clear what the articulation and integration among them will be. Will the old organizational forms be supplanted by communal councils, or are we dealing with the construction of a relationship of harmonious coexistence among diverse organizational forms?

Equally problematic is the low priority assigned to establishing a process of institutionalization of these new forms of social policy. Such is the case with the missions, which have been created as a way of getting around the inoperability or frank opposition of traditional institutions of social policy. But to this date they have not been regularized by law. Nor are there clear accounting and auditing procedures. For example, in the case of Misión Mercal—created to take charge of commercialization and distribution of foodstuffs for the popular sectors, with the prominent participation of the military in its administration— denunciations of corruption are increasing without leading to investigations that clear suspects or sanction the guilty. Other frequent complaints indicate political discrimination (in the form of denying access to micro-credits) against organizations that have carried out actions or manifested opinions contrary to the government, or that simply do not show support (see chapter 7, "The Misiones of the Chávez Government," by Hawkins, Rosas, and Johnson, on clientelism in these programs).

Another crucial issue is the financial viability of these policies. There is no doubt that extraordinary revenues have allowed the government to finance this multi-dimensional strategy to attack the problem of social exclusion. Nonetheless, are these programs economically sustainable in the future?

There are also tendencies in the composition of revenue that are difficult to interpret. The massive indirect value-added tax has been slowly diminishing, which alleviates pressure on prices for the population with fewer resources. The reduction in use of indirect taxes also is due to the reliance on extraordinary resources of internal origin—especially the availability of resources previously deposited in the Macroeconomic Fund for Investment and Stabilization (associated with increased oil income from previous periods) and to funds stemming from devaluation of currency by the Central Bank. To this can be added changes to the Central Bank Law that permit the Executive to withdraw so-called "excessive international reserves" (Magallanes 2005). The state has improved the system of tax collection, registering record statistics in combating fiscal evasion. The predominance of this scheme of public finance has reduced fiscal pressure on society in general, although without improving the progressivity of financing public expenditure. The reliance on oil income in fiscal spending also puts social policies in a position of financial instability.

In sum, the future remains open to contradictory tendencies, and it will be Venezuelans, organized and energized by the process of social and political change, who have the last word about the direction that they end up taking. Participatory democracy and more recently twenty-first-century socialism are utopian horizons full of reefs to navigate and challenges to overcome. We Venezuelans have experienced the abundance of the petro-state as well as the setbacks that occur when prices fall. Overcoming the dilemmas experienced within Venezuelan society for decades would distinguish a real and profound democratic transition toward social inclusion, from yet another populist, demagogic government in our history.

Notes

1. Though a "definitive" and final version of the constitution was published in March 2000, I quote here from the December 1999 publication. All translations are my own.

2. More information on this election may be found at the website for Venezuela's National Electoral Council, http://www.cne.gov.ve.

3. The Punto Fijo era refers to the democratic regime initiated in Venezuela after the fall of the dictatorship of Marcos Pérez Jiménez on January 23, 1958.

4. Congresso Bolivariano de los Pueblos (CBP), "Más de 2 milliones de venezolanos beneficiados por comités de tiereras," September 26, 2006, www.congresobolivariano .org.

5. Arconada's experience as an activist began in the Southwestern Caracas parish of Antímano during the administration of Mayor Aristóbulo Istúriz in Libertador municipality from 1993–95. (Libertador municipality is the most populous of the five that make up the metropolitan area of Caracas.) He was a Community Administration official for the state company, Hidroven, and is now an official for the Community Participation Administration of the Ministry of the Environment, which has responsibility for MTAs.

6. See the 2004 and 2005 reports by PROVEA, as well as the web page for SUNACOOP, http://www.sunacoop.gov.ve.

7. See the website of the Ministry of Planning and Development at http://www.mpd.ve/venezuela-nva.

8. For more information on Misión Barrio Adentro, see their website at http://www.barrioadentro.gov.ve.

9. See the Misión Mercal web page, at http://www.mercal.gove.ve. Additional information may be found at the page for *Aló Presidente*, President Chávez's weekly talk show, at http://www.alopresidente.gob.ve.

CHAPTER THREE

Urban Land Committees

Co-optation, Autonomy, and Protagonism

María Pilar García-Guadilla

The Urban Land Committees (Comités de Tierra Urbana—CTUs) are among the most important popular social organizations that emerged from participatory democracy sanctioned in the Bolivarian Constitution of 1999. They have had a broad impact on the right of citizens to dignified and adequate housing and to city space. According to information from the National Technical Office for Regularization of Urban Land Tenancy (Oficina Técnica National para la Regularización de la Tenencia de la Tierra Urbana—OTNRT), by 2005, there were almost six thousand CTUs nationally, with a presence in the majority of Venezuela's poor *barrios* (shantytowns). They cover close to one million families, that is to say, four to five million persons.[1]

In the Gramscian approach to civil society, the term *social movement* is understood as the space in which social subjectivities are constructed. These social subjectivities are characteristic of new collective actors that promote alternative modes of citizenship and social action. Working within this perspective, one of the goals of this chapter is to determine if the CTUs can be considered a social movement. That is, do they share a collective identity that transcends specific demands regarding regularization of land tenancy and improvement in living conditions, and can they create a collective identity around the struggle for inclusion, equity, cultural diversity, and democratization of decision making? Have they the capability to enrich social and cultural identities and in this way contribute to the pluralism of urban life? Can they generate an alternative project for society, independent and diverging from the state, one that transcends more immediate material demands and permits the construction of hegemony for social transformation?

In order for civil organizations to construct an alternative social project they need autonomy, understood as the capacity to make decisions independently from the government, political parties, unions, and other organizations. For Katsiaficas (2007) this autonomy implies the exercise of direct democracy. We begin with the premise that neither the CTUs' ideological affinity with the government's political project, nor the fact that they were spawned from this project, precludes their autonomy. The government could relate to these organizations in multiple ways: (1) promoting and safeguarding these new identities; (2) co-opting these identities in favor of political objectives that differ from the essential principles and values of these organizations; or (3) sometimes promoting their identities, other times co-opting them. These civil organizations can also respond in different ways to each of the government's possible approaches.

Given that the identities and subjectivities we are studying here form part of a process that is still under construction, this analysis of the CTUs as a social movement and the description of their level of autonomy will rest on an evaluation of their praxis and will be confined to a few key moments in this process, that is, when they have had to politically position themselves in defense of President Chávez's leadership as members of the Bolivarian project. We will analyze whether or not the CTUs conserved the values and principles of their collective identity in these situations, and whether they were able to steer clear of the acute political polarization that has marked the relationship between the state and organized civil society since 2001.

Segregation and Exclusion: Housing Policies, 1958–1999

One characteristic of Venezuelan urbanization patterns has been the construction of highly segregated social spaces, a consequence of an economy based on oil revenues (*renta petrolera*), which has generated strong social and territorial disequilibrium. More than 50 percent of the urban population lives in what have been designated as "informal settlements, shantytowns," or barrios without access to legal property rights over the land they occupy and without being fully articulated into the formal or planned city recognized and attended to by the state and the market.

Not only are these barrios segregated from the formal city, they are spaces of exclusion in as much as residents suffer from deficits of adequate and dignified housing, basic services such as water, and infrastructure such as schools and health centers. Residents have low rates of schooling and high rates of unemployment, general mortality, infant mortality, and homicides. In sum, the barrios are spaces that violate the fundamental human rights written into the Bolivarian Constitution of 1999.

For some authors, the term *exclusion* does not adequately capture the mode by which the barrios and their inhabitants relate to the larger city; they prefer to use the term *segregation*, which expresses the subaltern relation between the formal city and its inhabitants. The establishment of the barrios in the 1950s and 1960s was the result of an economic policy of import substitution, the beginnings of representative democracy and modernization policies for the cities, including the construction of great works of infrastructure and new urban residential areas for the middle and upper classes where the popular sectors of the population were excluded. As Antillano puts it, the popular sectors were taken into account in so far as they served as builders of the city, as a cheap source of labor and a mass of voters, and given that they needed a place to live, they built the barrios. Thus, the barrios, as inexpensive settlements resulting from the unequal distribution of petroleum income, provided a sort of surplus value for the city: urban, economic, and political surplus (2005, 206).

In general, Venezuelan state housing policies have been characterized by serious disarticulation, resulting in an underserved market for housing that has, in turn, led to unplanned and informal mechanisms for building in the cities. From the initiation of democracy in 1958, and even before, the Venezuelan state took on responsibility for solving the problems of or improving poor barrios—as can be seen in huge housing developments, such as the 23 de Enero, constructed during the dictatorship of General Marcos Pérez Jiménez (1948–58), and Caricuao, constructed during the presidency of Raúl Leoni (1964–68). Many of the barrio-improvement policies emphasized massive production of homes or the financing of isolated residential developments, abetted by a booming oil economy. In this way the Venezuelan state adopted a paternalistic role, acting as producer, manager, and financier not only of urban land and development projects, but also of low-income housing (Baldó 2002, 349).

From 1958 to 1979 the government tended to minimize the contribution of the private sector, of non-governmental organizations, and of other community actors in solving the housing problems that affected an ever-greater proportion of the population. Additionally, the absence of a legal framework governing the participation of the citizens in barrio-improvement programs contributed to scarce community involvement in these efforts. During this time various institutions were created with the goal of solving problems of the barrios. These included FUNDACOMUN (the Foundation for Municipal and Community Development), founded in 1962 to finance housing developments and service

infrastructure and to provide technical assistance to municipal councils; and
FONDUR (the National Fund for Urban Development), founded in 1975 mainly
to carry out a program of land acquisition. Housing cooperatives were created;
mass construction of homes, popular residential areas, and improvements in
barrios were undertaken; and housing subsidies were instituted. Nevertheless,
due to the lack of continuity and the isolated character of these efforts, the deficit of housing worsened, as did the quality of life in the barrios.

The decade of the 1990s was marked by a profound economic, political,
and social crisis due to the incapacity of the centralized state to offer solutions
to the problems of the barrios, which by then affected more than half of the
population residing in the cities (M. Rivas 2004, 219). According to the National Population Census of 2001, close to 90 percent of the Venezuelan population was living in cities, and more than half the urban population lacked access to the formal market of housing and had therefore to resort to their own
solutions.

During the 1990s a policy of decentralization was implemented, based on
legislation passed in 1989 and 1990. As part of this process, responsibilities
and power were transferred from the central government to local and regional
governments, and regulations were provided for local-level community participation. However, this change amounted to more of a transfer of functions and
responsibilities than a transfer of the economic resources needed to carry them
out. In addition, community participation was limited to information and consultation. One could say, then, that the decentralizing process was aimed more
at perfecting a model of representative democracy—making changes "so that
everything would continue the same"—than at constructing legal instruments
to encourage a deepening of the democratic process (García-Guadilla 2002).

Despite this shortcoming, there were some improvements in the barrios as
a result of the creation of the National Housing Council (Consejo Nacional
de la Vivienda—CONAVI) and the passing of a Housing Policy Law, modified
in 1993. A system of national technical assistance, which became an "intermediary between the State as facilitating agent and the communitarian sector,"
was institutionalized; and the formation of Community Housing Organizations
(Organizaciones Comunitarias de Vivienda) was encouraged (M. Rivas 2004,
221). Some of the most important positive efforts in this period were provided
through the creation of the National Program for Providing Infrastructure and
Services to the barrios (Programa Nacional de Equipamientos de Barrios) and
"Project CAMEBA," both of which focused on improving the quality of life of
barrio residents, establishing as a priority the incorporation of communities in
the process of rehabilitating their barrios.[2]

Citizenship, Participatory Democracy, and the Right to Housing: 1999–2005

Citizenship in this context refers to the status of the person living in the city, whereby "individual rights of expression and construction of collective identities, participative democracy, and basic equality among residents" are fully recognized (Borja 2003, 22). Given the dialectical relationship between city and citizenship, the values linked to the city only emerge when the citizens' rights are recognized in real life, not only as a formality. Thus the construction of citizenship should be understood as a transforming process that allows the citizen to become a subject (in the sense of a protagonist) with rights and responsibilities, someone who can have impact on the government of the polis. The formal recognition of the status of citizen, that is to say, the recognition of an individual's rights, including the right to decent housing and the right to participate in policymaking, was consecrated in the Constitution of the Bolivarian Republic of Venezuela (1999). Their concrete realization in the policies of government has occurred in several distinct phases.

When Chávez assumed the presidency in 1999, public policies were reoriented toward the poor sectors. Under the banner of "inclusion of the excluded," structural changes were proposed regarding the conception of barrios and how to address the problems affecting poor people, including housing. To achieve this objective, President Chávez proposed deepening the model of participatory democracy and increasing the attention to those Venezuelans excluded economically, socially, and spatially.[3] The residents of barrios are doubly excluded (materially and symbolically) from the right to the city and to citizenship, or from those rights that, according to Borja (2003), the city should offer. As Andrés Antillano puts it:

> Material denial is accompanied by symbolic denial: the barrios are not represented in urban images; they are outside of cartography. They do not appear on maps, are not registered in land cadastres and censuses; their stories are not told; they are not considered at times of taking inventory of patrimony. Barrios do not exist in the rhetoric of the city, save as danger or abnormality. . . . The barrio is defined more by what it lacks than what it is, by its negation more than its affirmation. (2005, 206).

One of Chávez's first proposals for the new constitution was the creation of new participatory ideas and widening of mechanisms of participation for incorporating the population into the solution of their problems. As provided by Article 70, "Participation, involvement and protagonism of the people are the means for the exercise of sovereignty . . . in social and economic affairs, it can be manifested by: citizen service centers, self-management, co-management, cooperatives in all forms, including those of a financial character, savings funds, community enterprises and other forms of association guided by the values of mutual cooperation and solidarity. The law shall establish conditions for the effective functioning of means of participation foreseen in this article" (CRBV 1999, Article 70).

The right to housing is also embedded in Article 82 of the constitution. Studies undertaken by CONAVI estimate that there exists an accumulated deficit of 1,620,000 housing units—which includes one million existing units requiring improvement or remodeling—generating a net need for 620,000 new units (F. Villanueva 2008). Given the accumulated deficit of housing, CONAVI proposed a new national housing policy oriented toward reducing the social debt—that is, the state's obligation to persons with low income who, despite having constructed a great part of Venezuelan cities on their own, live without basic services and the most elemental infrastructure.[4]

This policy was developed with an urban component as well as a social component. The first is oriented toward the attentions of families through public works that will contribute to the transformation of the habitat and improve the standard of living; the second has the goal of promoting new channels of active community participation in the collective management of the city. This means that organized communities are to have an important role to play in the planning, development, and governance of the barrios, as mandated by the new constitution.

Struggles for Citizenship and Inclusion:
The Right to Housing and to a Better Habitat

The constitutional right to housing and to residential landownership was not new and did not take place in an organizational vacuum. Previous governments had attempted to address these issues from different perspectives because citizens affected by the housing problem mobilized in the past, using various organizational forms to demand their rights, including the right to regularization of land tenancy. An intensification of popular urban struggles took place during the crisis of the 1980s and 1990s in response to neoliberal policies that were not holistic and included privatization of basic services (Arconada Rodríguez 2005; López Maya 1999; Cariola and Lacabana 2005).

From an organizational point of view, one of the most important precedents was the Assembly of Barrios (Asamblea de Barrios) of Caracas, which was founded in 1991 as an outgrowth of an earlier initiative, the Working Round-table of Residents of the First International Meeting for Rehabilitation of Barrios. The Assembly of Barrios lasted through 1993 and brought together more than two hundred leaders of the barrios of Caracas. They made a significant contribution to the definition of a program of struggle for these communities. According to Andrés Antillano, one of the founders of the Assembly, "The proposal for regularization of tenancy over land occupied by residents of popular communities, the discussions about physical rehabilitation of barrios, the proposals for co-management of water service, [and] the demand for local self-governance all contributed, among other things, to enunciating and forging a plan of struggle of Caracas barrios" (2005, 208). The Assembly of Barrios represented a space in which existing demands were recognized and given political articulation. Before that time such demands had been dismissed as reformist by activists, as occurred with some actions taken in the case of the dense multi-family housing Superbloques del 23 de Enero (discussed by Velasco in chapter 6).

The participatory dynamic and the focus on rights inscribed in the Bolivarian Constitution of 1999 inspired new models of community organization. Presently, popular social organizations are being sponsored by the government under a political model that encourages participation by responding to the demands of the popular sectors. The government has directed technical help and considerable financial resources (provided by high oil revenue) to most of these popular organizations with the hope of obtaining their political support. These factors explain the explosion of organizational forms promoted by the government, among them the Bolivarian Circles, the CTUs and the communal councils (*consejos comunales*).

Nevertheless, unlike the bottom-up organizational processes represented by the Assembly of Barrios, which permitted them to maintain autonomy versus the government and political parties, the new organizational forms inspired by the conception of participatory and protagonistic democracy in the new constitution were promoted from above, that is, by the president of the republic. Such is the case with the CTUs that stemmed from a presidential decree.

During his electoral campaign of 1998, Chávez declared himself in favor of popular organization, and early on his administration promoted community participation through the formation of the Bolivarian Circles. These circles were created by a presidential decree in accordance with Article 52 of the constitution, were assigned to the Ministry of the Secretariat of the Republic and have the objective of "popular organization to seek the welfare of the community . . . health and housing."[5] The circles were closely linked at birth to Bolivarian ideology and to the Chavista political party of that time, the Fifth Republic Movement (MVR). This political association, as well as the partisanship of its members, considerably reduced the diversity of participating sectors, distancing the circles from their original objectives and facilitating their political co-optation (García-Guadilla 2003; see also "The Misiones of the Chávez Government," by Hawkins, Rosas, and Johnson, chapter 7 in this volume).

Urban Land Committees in Law and in Practice

The constitutional text and legal regulations operative in 1999 sought to channel demands for greater civic participation that surged as a result of criticism of representative democracy (García-Guadilla 2005).[6] The Constitution of 1999 recognizes not only the obligation of the Venezuelan state to guarantee the right of every person to adequate housing, but also the right of all citizens to participate via various methods in public affairs and in the formation, execution, and control of public administration (Articles 6, 62, and 70). To this end Presidential Decree 1.666, which started the process of regularization of land tenancy in popular urban settlements, was promulgated on February 4, 2002.

The process is initiated by the formation of a CTU and the gathering of information by the OTNRT, the supervisory agency. Among requisites for official recognition are a census of the barrio, a cadastral survey, and a Barrio Charter (Carta del Barrio), culminating with adjudication of title to land. The land occupied by a community can belong to the state or be private. In the case of public property, it can belong to the municipality or to the central government. Municipal governments can either facilitate or make more difficult the process of regularization of tenancy of land, depending on whether they favor or oppose this policy.

Despite their commonalities, such as their identification with organized communities and the shared goal of regularizing tenancy of residential land, the CTUs have developed great heterogeneity in practice. CTUs differ from one another regarding the existing legal status of land in the communities where they are found; the economic, social, and political actors with whom they interact; their established alliances and articulations with other groups; the tradition of struggle of their members; the stage of the process of regularization at which they find themselves; and even the strategies they have used to achieve their objectives.

Given this variability, the evaluation of whether the CTUs have a transformative potential as a social movement and, for that reason, capacity to construct new subjectivities and autonomous social projects, or whether, on the contrary, they can be co-opted and reoriented toward electoral political objectives or neo-clientelist practices, requires that we understand and compare two facets—their legal or institutional dimension and their praxis.[7]

Article 82 of the constitution recognizes adequate housing as one of the rights provided under Chapter V, "On Social Rights and those of Families," and it adopts the definition of the different aspects of housing outlined by the United Nations Committee of Economic, Social, and Cultural Rights (CESCR) in 1991, that is, legal security, availability of services, affordability, habitability, accessibility, location, and cultural adequacy. To this end, President Chávez issued Decree 1.666 in 2002. This decree sought to begin the process of regularization of land tenancy in barrios and low-income neighborhoods of the country's cities and towns and to submit for public consultation proposed legislation that would govern this matter.[8] Article 1 provides that the decree "has the goal of initiating the protagonistic participation of organized communities in order to achieve the regularization of urban land tenancy in popular neighborhoods through proper inter-institutional coordination." The first provision of Article 3 contemplates the "formation of Urban Land Committees to initiate the process of regularization of land tenancy," thus establishing CTUs as the organizational form that will accomplish the decree's objectives.

The decree assigned the OTNRT, an entity within the vice-presidency, the functions of stimulating citizen participation through the formation of CTUs; of carrying out enrollment in and registration of information about CTUs; of advancing procedures for social and inter-institutional coordination necessary for regularization of land tenancy; and of collating and studying information about the situation of property and land tenancy in barrios and popular neighborhoods. The OTNRT was also assigned the task of facilitating the process of public consultation regarding the proposed "Law for the Regularization of Land Tenancy in Popular Settlements."[9]

The process of regularization of urban land tenancy is embedded in legislation that regulates the tenancy of public as well as privately owned land. If indeed Decree 1.666 raised the possibility of regularizing tenancy in popular settlements on state-owned land, negotiations about private land remained governed by the Civil Code. To include private land in the larger process of regularization would require promulgation of a special law. These legal limitations complicate the process of regularization because to resolve the difficulties that entangle the legal status of land requires the involvement of multiple actors and, therefore, alliances and interrelations among them. Additionally, the legal situation of land can vary from one municipality to another according to their relevant ordinances. For example, in the case of Baruta, an opposition-controlled municipality in the metropolitan Caracas area, some of the ordinances that regulate the transfer of land are inconsistent with provisions in the presidential decree.

In August 2004, Chávez announced the creation of the Housing Mission (Misión Vivienda). In November, the CTUs presented their proposal for the function of this new social mission. This proposal was the product of a debate on the national level, which also served to reinforce spaces for articulation of CTUs on the parochial, municipal, regional, and national levels. The fundamental element of the proposal is the conception of regularization of land tenancy as an integral process implying legal urban and physical regularization. Legal regularization implies property rights. Urban regularization refers to the establishment by consensus of norms of co-habitation that respects the particularities and idiosyncrasies of each barrio; it calls for a constituent process and for community self-governance. The instrument for this process is the Carta del Barrio (the Barrio Charter).[10]

In sum, the existing legal framework is oriented toward dismantling the dynamics of spatial segregation that more than half of Venezuela's urban population suffers in order to build to achieve a more democratic and equitable society and to satisfy peoples' demands for inclusion, democratization, and equity. Given this legal and institutional foundation, one would predict that the CTUs would be democratic in their structure and functioning as well. By the statutes, the CTUs are privileged spaces for participatory democracy where important decisions, including their very constitution, ought to be made in assemblies of citizens. The Municipal Technical Offices for CTUs in the Caroní and Libertador Municipalities (Oficina Técnica Municipal Caroní 2004; Oficina Técnica Municipal Caracas 2005) define them as "models of horizontal and autonomous organization that have as their goal the realization of all activities undertaken by a community to achieve acquisition of urban land and to seek a solution to urban problems" (Oficina Técnica Municipal Caroní 2004, n.p.).[11]

Each CTU works with the double purpose of achieving regularization of land tenancy and of developing processes to make decisions about holistic improvement of the barrio or popular neighborhood. According to the directives of these Municipal Technical Offices for CTUs, their sphere of action ought not to be greater than two hundred families; their structure ought to be democratic; and their members ought to be chosen through elections in assemblies of citizens held in popular sectors. The CTUs can structure themselves into commissions, such as census, cadastre, barrio charter, communications, resources, community action, institutional relations, and others they deem necessary and suitable to carry out their work effectively. They should be structured to function in a horizontal and flexible manner and should render an account of their activities to the higher levels of the National Technical Office, attached to the Vice-Presidency of the Republic. On the other hand, the process of making decisions and the timeline for activities are not to be decided by the CTUs but must be discussed and approved in the assembly of citizens. Assemblies are supposed to be held periodically, and their convocation must be announced six days in advance via media at the disposal of the community (Guiffrida and Salcedo 2005, 62–63). Generally, members of the CTUs have had experience participating in other forms of organization linked to the theme of housing such as the Barrios Assembly and other civic associations.

According to the presidential decree, the functions of the CTUs, besides organizing discussion and formulation of observations and proposals for legislation, are to collate information or inventory homes in the barrios; to generate provisional maps identifying geographical boundaries of the community; to identify the spontaneous and historical organization of their barrio, its zones, and uses; to elaborate lists of members of the community in order to develop a document recognizing the existence of the barrio; and to participate in the design, execution, and follow-up of public policies for holistic rehabilitation of their community.

To constitute itself, a CTU must first delimit a geographic space—known as a *polygonal*—defined in terms of the uses, customs, history, and traditions of the community, and not in terms of technical criteria. The CTUs can cooperate or coordinate efforts with other CTUs, sectors, and barrios or popular housing projects. The knowledge that members of a CTU have about their polygonal is fundamental to gathering the information required to complete the process of regularization of land tenancy. This reference to a concrete territorial space permits the orderly participation of citizens in the process of regularization and in activities associated with each polygonal. The information developed by the CTU can be checked and validated through oversight by the communities themselves. The *legitimacy* of the CTUs is bestowed as a result of their confirmation in an Assembly of Citizens with the participation of 50 percent of the families that form the polygonal.

The Barrio Charter (Carta del Barrio) required of each CTU expresses its *identity*, as it embraces the history of the community and the barrio from their founding, their idiosyncrasies and traditions, as well as the norms of neighborhood life decided collectively by the community. The political value of the charter is rooted not only in bestowing this common identity but with regard to establishing the minimum norms of group life, committing all of its members to a collective project.

Consider, for example, the barrio León Droz Blanco, in Caracas, located in the vicinity of the Central University of Venezuela on land deeded to the Metro de Caracas. Confronted with threats of eviction several times, this community decided to opt for collective title over the land. The collective ownership of the land and the rules for sale of goods built on it, as well as the history of their struggle against eviction, are established within the Barrio Charter of this community, as reported by Antillano:

> Without having laws that regulate these matters, nor with legal precedents, the neighbors constructed a formula in which, if indeed each family can dispose of the possessions and land that they occupy, this [land] is property of an association constituted by the totality of families of the barrio, which among other things is charged with regulating the use of space (common and family), authorizing sales and rentals, establishing and overseeing norms of living together, deciding about litigation and about actions of the incumbent collectivity, etc. (2005, 214)

This example shows how the CTUs organize democratically according to their needs and make decisions on the basis of communal solidarity.

The Political Dimension and Praxis of the CTUs:
Class Identity and the Right to the City

Currently, the demands for regularization of land tenancy and for adequate and dignified housing are expressed in the demand of the popular sectors to live in the city. Therefore the struggle for land is a demand not just for resources but for a right; it is a political demand. In turn, this political contention stands in relation to the fact that the popular sectors are considered and consider themselves the excluded of the city, and as such they construct their identity based on the rights of citizenship. We are not saying by this that the inhabitants of the barrios have been excluded as a policy of the state, but that they are inserted into the city in a subaltern manner (Antillano 2005). Two cities are produced: the formal city and the informal or self-constructed one.

The conception of housing as a basic right was neglected by democratically formed governments and by the platforms of the political parties that preceded President Chávez. The right to citizenship is embodied in the constitution; thus the demands of the popular sectors focus on making this constitutional precept a reality. Their demands go beyond inclusion in the city since they include the right to cultural diversity and to construct the city collectively within a pluralist vision where everybody fits. That is to say, they demand the right to "habitat" and "to inhabit" under *new* forms and models of the city, which require a collective and plural construction (Antillano 2005).

Having been excluded from the formal city, they have had to construct their own habitat. The struggle for land not only is a demand of a material character but also is a demand for the right to live in the city, thereby encompassing a political agenda. The struggles of the CTUs also express an element of class identity, since their self-definition depends on the idea of being an excluded class. From the 1950s to the beginnings of this century, the term *marginal* has been used by theorists who try to explain poverty and by government programs designed to confront this condition. To refer to these sectors in this way, despite the fact that they constitute more than half the population, implies an integrationist, not a pluralist framework of analysis.

For this reason, any sociopolitical analysis of the CTUs ought to approach the study of the actors and the popular sectors in terms of how conflict over land expresses the struggle against social, political, and economic exclusion, that is, the struggle to cease being invisible and to participate in the political decision-making process. We need to keep in mind the connections between, on the one hand, demands that are apparently socio-economic and, on the other hand, the political conflicts in which they are embedded. These latter struggles express a "subjective objectivity" and actions that position the CTUs as agents of the popular classes (Múnera 1998, 81). In this way the demand for the right to dignified housing (including the right to ownership of land) and participation in policy decisions concerning the city become political and a claim for their urban identity and visibility (Salazar 2003). As Antillano puts it,

> Struggles that earlier seemed reducible simply to the socio-economic sphere (traditionally seen with disdain by political activists) now adopt political modes of expression and content. The struggle for water has been converted into a struggle over how to distribute services and what is the role of the state in their provision; fights over wages become mobilizations for work and against the economic model, etc. . . . In the case of the Urban Land Committees, their objectives are inscribed within what in their own debates has been called the "holistic regularization" of barrios, which could define a program for democratization of the city and against urban segregation. (2005, 212)

It is worth highlighting that this type of participation claims to rescue the way of life of the popular sectors. The Assembly of CTUs for Metropolitan Caracas has argued that barrios "express a basic and primary scheme of space and urban order with a character of their own, that ought to be respected and taken seriously, even ought to be the point of departure for all urban intervention" (Asamblea Metropolitana de Comités de Tierra Urbana de Caracas 2004, 8). This holistic approach, called "integral regularization," questions the more traditional model of barrios based on consolidation, under which interventions are partial, do not reflect holistic diagnoses, and make the participation of communities dependent upon institutions. Integral regularization also questions the policy of physical rehabilitation of barrios articulated in the Law of the Subsystem of Housing and Habitation Policy of 2000, which "places emphasis on financial aspects and privileges the aspect of construction over other dimensions closer to the life and needs of barrios; does not recognize the struggle and identity of popular urban settlements, imposing a technocratic vision alien to the barrio; [and] favors administrative, political, and technical intermediation, requiring communities to resign themselves to acceptance of the decisions of others" (Asamblea Metropolitana de Comités de Tierra Urbana de Caracas 2004, 7).[12] Through the cultural vindication of the way of life of the barrio, the CTUs together with other popular sectors fight for a democracy of difference or of complex equality, that is to say, for the "equality of opportunities to affirm difference and protect themselves against mechanisms of social exclusion and cultural discrimination" (Hopenhayn 2000, 116), independently from the causes of exclusion.

Constructing of Citizenship and Autonomy: Potentials and Limitations

The CTUs seek to influence legislation and public policies dealing with housing and habitat—in other words, to carve out and construct spaces of decision making and power. Their demands have an antagonistic character since their struggle expresses resistance to the dominant discourse regarding land and adequate housing, as well as to the subordination that inhabitants of the barrios suffer in relation to the rest of the city.

But the CTUs not only participate in this antagonistic manner; they also interact with institutions of the state within the framework of government policies that stimulate civic participation by the popular sectors. While this stimulation of participation from above could lead to a new form of political clientelism threatening organizational autonomy (García-Guadilla 2002, 2008), the treatment of the historical needs of popular sectors as rights should lead scholars to explore popular participation as an exercise in the construction of citizenship.

It is necessary to point out that the human rights perspective does not dis-

allow the existence of any link whatsoever between the state and the participation of citizens (Guillén and García-Guadilla 2006). Such a relationship does
not contradict the role of the state as guarantor of rights but instead recognizes the state's and society's co-responsibility in carrying out human rights
policies in general, and the right to housing in particular.[13] For civil organizations, autonomy is defined in terms of the relation they establish with the state
and with the administration of government, as in the case of social and human
rights organizations. Conceptualizing participation and relationship to the state
in this way, the CTUs demand the right not only to adequate housing but to
co-responsibility with the state in the administration of this policy. Thus, the
CTUs do not simply define themselves as autonomous by virtue of being nongovernmental. Unlike many organizations of civil society, the CTUs consider autonomy to reside in the nature of their demands and alternative vision of society.
Their demand for titles to land and rights of tenancy is associated with protection of individuals and communities against eviction, not just with the economic
value of the land. They also demand the right to maintain their culture and mode
of living and to the democratization of the land, which they consider "a fundamental requirement not only to make viable housing policy with a massive impact; this is also an essential instrument to achieve territorial equity" (Asamblea
Metropolitana de Comités de Tierra Urbana de Caracas 2004, 7).

Critical Junctures and Networks as a Potential Source of Co-optation

As already mentioned, Urban Land Committees define themselves as autonomous in terms of their impact on the definition of policies of the state and
the possibility of inserting their project for an alternative society in such policies. Nonetheless, studies carried out in the Baruta and Sucre municipalities of
Metropolitan Caracas and in the Caroní municipality in Ciudad Guayana suggest they do not always achieve this autonomy. In some cases, the informal organizational structure that prevails in their praxis shows that the CTUs depend
upon the hierarchical structure of the Bolivarian Circles, other government
programs such as the Missions, and even the Electoral Battle Units (Unidades
de Batalla Electoral) and that they are activated politically to win elections, as
will be discussed below. This has meant that in certain critical junctures, political pressure from MVR and most recently the PSUV (the Unified Socialist Party
of Venezuela), and even from President Chávez, bears down on them to mobilize in support of government candidates.

Given that social movements are defined by their daily praxis with respect to the strategic demands tied to their identity, the temporary abandonment of their roles and identities to mobilize in favor of political parties and other political organizations does not necessarily imply that they have renounced their autonomy. It means that the CTU has been *temporarily* deactivated as a result of the conflicting loyalties of its members.

Among the organizations that have emerged from within President Chávez's political project there are competing views regarding the best strategy to follow during periods when the sociopolitical project they share is threatened. Should they remain at the margins of the political struggle or become part of it? The CTUs use different strategies at different times. When the continuity of the sociopolitical project that spawned them is threatened, the CTUs tend to mobilize as part of the political parties or machine that support President Chávez. Nevertheless, once the threat is over, they return to their original social spaces and to the defense of the identities that they collectively constructed.

As indicated above, the relations between the CTUs and the other social organizations existing in the barrio should be horizontal and complementary. That is, each organization is autonomous and seeks to define its own attributes and develop its work in a parallel manner, in order to achieve the primary objective of improving the quality of life of the barrio's population.

Nevertheless, this autonomy is not always possible when the CTUs find it necessary to work with political organizations or with the government. This is because at the beginning of the Chavista era there were not strong grass-roots social organizations on which the MVR or President Chávez could rely; thus, when the government needed support, it turned to organizations such as the Bolivarian Circles or the CTUs in search of a political clientele that could be mobilized electorally.[14] At least until the creation of the PSUV in late 2006, President Chávez based his support more on a direct appeal to the people than through a party. He repeatedly refers to and addresses them as *el Pueblo* (the People), *el Soberano* (the Sovereign) and *el Poder Popular* (the Popular Power). He stimulated the political mobilization of popular organizations such as the CTUs and most recently the Communal Councils, which are supposed to be embedded in popular power. In the case of the Communal Councils, the most important social organizations created in 2006 by President Chávez, it is too soon to know whether they will remain autonomous or they will be penetrated by the PSUV.

An example of this political support was the mobilization of the CTUs through the Electoral Battle Units in favor of the MVR and the no vote in the 2004 presidential recall.[15] Similarly, the CTUs, as well as other pro-Chávez popular organizations were politically mobilized in the October 2004 election of governors, mayors, and legislative councils.[16] Nonetheless, neither the CTUs nor many of the barrios were as active as before in mobilizing for the constitutional reform packages proposed by President Chávez and defeated in December 2007. This could mean that the temporary abandonment of autonomy may be contingent on other political factors. Another significant aspect that could threaten autonomy is the creation of the communal councils by the president and the role he gave them of building popular power. In this organizational scheme, the CTUs were supposed to form part of the communal councils as one of its multiple committees. This could contribute to disarticulate and demobilize the CTUs from their original identities (García-Guadilla 2008).

The attempts by the MVR and its political allies, such as the Comando Maisanta, to penetrate popular social organizations, including the CTUs, contributed to their temporary demobilization in terms of their primary identity. For example, during the frustrated coup of April 2002 and throughout the oil strike from December 2002 to February 2003, the political-network strategies developed by the vertically structured MVR managed to penetrate the organizational fabric of the CTUs, bringing as a consequence the eclipse, although only temporarily, of their original objectives and identity as CTUs.[17]

In this way the CTUs have tended to integrate themselves into a submerged and invisible political network favoring Chávez, which blooms and becomes visible in moments of crisis or in electoral cycles when political power is in play. When the CTUs are mobilized as part of this network they cannot define themselves as social movements, as they become extensions of the Electoral Battle Units, the Bolivarian Circles or the government party. Nonetheless, once the electoral process is concluded or the political crisis subsides, the CTUs return to their more permanent organizational space and primary social identity—that is, the defense of their constitutional right to inhabit the city as citizens.

To understand how the CTUs are networked it is necessary to analyze the context (national, regional, or local) where relations are forged, as well as the type of relation (with state's institutions, with other social and political organizations, or among themselves). Analyses of CTUs in Caracas and Ciudad Guayana indicate that in addition to their formal affiliation and relationship with the Vice Presidency of the Republic, and more recently with the Ministry of Habitat and Housing, some of them have been linked informally with government-promoted missions, with the MVR party, and with the Bolivarian Circles (Contreras 2005, 2006; Guiffrida and Salcedo 2005).

Due to the great multiplicity of organizational types that exists in the popular sector, it is common for the coordinators and members of the CTUs to belong to several organizations, meaning they usually have a rich history of organizational participation. Indeed, simultaneous membership in other social organizations per se does not necessarily imply a threat to autonomy; these various identities may be complementary. However, when political and social identities enter into conflict, simultaneous membership in political organizations, such as the Bolivarian Circles, the old MVR, or the new PSUV, could encourage neoclientelist practices and undermine autonomy (García-Guadilla 2002, 2005). In general, multiple memberships have tended to find expression in parallel and complementary forms without affecting the core identity of the CTUs. But in situations of acute political crisis and in the presence of high levels of polarization (as existed between 2002 and 2004), the identities associated with these memberships have become mixed and politicized—temporarily leaving a vacuum in the core identity and space occupied by the CTUs.

In some communities a relational space has been constructed between the CTUs and parish assemblies, and this represents another social articulation. The goal of this relationship is for communities to exchange experiences regarding the process of regularization of land tenancy, clarify doubts that arise because of the absence of a clear legal framework, coordinate mutual support, and coordinate with other institutions and actors involved in the process. One of these spaces is the Assembly of CTUs for Metropolitan Caracas, created to implement Article 52 of the 1999 constitution requiring public functionaries to render accounts of their actions to the communities. Officials of the Office of Cadastre of the Municipality Libertador in Caracas and of the National Technical Office frequently attend this assembly to explain to the community advances and difficulties in the process of regularization of land tenancy.

The Assembly of CTUs for Metropolitan Caracas has met informally since the beginning of 2002 and constitutes an arena for debate and articulation. Its origins were in meetings of urban planners, architects, human rights activists, and residents who debated aspects of the working document that would later be approved as Presidential Decree 1.666. This initial space for weekly meetings began to attract an increasing number of residents; in order to maintain its dynamic development, over time it transformed itself into a formal assembly. Particularly notable is that participation in the Metropolitan Assembly varied according to the theme under debate and according to particular needs and the type of work unfolding in the CTUs' communities. Not all of the CTUs participating in the Metropolitan Assembly are also part of parish assemblies; nor do all CTUs attend the metropolitan one.

Another space for articulation of CTUs consists of national conferences that evaluate the politics of the state regarding regularization of land tenancy and make proposals for the design, implementation, and evaluation of policies. For example, a national conference of CTUs was held in November 2004 at the Bolivarian University of Venezuela, where CTUs discussed the advancements and difficulties in the process of regularization of land and designated a commission of the Metropolitan Assembly to systematize their concerns and elaborate a working paper of proposals to the Housing Mission (Misión Vivienda).

Just as they are demanding a role in influencing public policy, the CTUs are also demanding participation in the equitable distribution of resources—most importantly, land. The CTUs do not receive monetary resources from the state to pursue this objective; the communities themselves provide voluntary contributions for the functioning of the committees, including making their homes available for meetings. Nonetheless, the scarcity of resources for the gathering and distribution of information, and the limitations of space for assemblies and meetings, can tempt the CTUs to become part of the extensive populist and clientelist webs and networks that have created the government.

The fact that the CTUs do not have the legal existence necessary to receive resources has created a situation where, as of this writing, they have not fallen into neoclientelist practices. This has favored their autonomy relative to their interlocutor, the state. In addition, the focus on rights has permitted the CTUs to maintain a critical outlook, to ask for a rendering of accounts regarding the state's use of resources designated to address their needs. As a result of the speech by President Chávez in August 2005 in the Poliedro of Caracas, when he authorized direct financing of social sectors, some CTUs created parallel civil associations to receive funding, which could potentially create conflict between members and change the character of CTUs.

Although it had not apparently become a practice as late as 2006, a potential factor leading to clientelism is the possibility of paying wages for organizational labor. In the government and also in the communities there exist two views on this idea. One current view insists this type of community work should be voluntary. The other, represented for example in some of the CTUs in the Municipality of Caroní (in Bolívar state), suggests the need for salaries for people who participate actively in the CTUs—above all for the coordinator, so that he or she can devote full time to the work. Should this latter position win, it would open the doors to co-optation and clientelism, with the consequent loss of autonomy.

Tensions, Challenges, and Questions

The Bolivarian process is threatened by the contradictions that are implied by a project of social transformation occurring in a profoundly polarized society.

This is reflected in the praxis of the CTUs, where one observes a tension between two tendencies: one that promotes autonomy by focusing on the self-governing, protagonistic role that is at the core of their identity; another that pushes them toward neoclientelist co-optation by the government and the political parties that support it.

The focus on rights favors pursuit of a project for alternative and inclusive citizenship associated with the praxis of social movements. If indeed the CTUs' demand for citizenship, as well as their demand for the right to construct their own model of habitat, are intrinsically political and based upon the defense of a citizenship of difference, the fact that such rights are rooted in the constitution and law prevents easy co-optation by the state and political parties. Another element favoring autonomy for the CTUs is the constitutional and legal framework that defines them as democratic and self-governing organizations that must be structured horizontally to foster democratic decision-making processes. In addition, the long organizational trajectory of the popular sectors that today form the CTUs is an important factor in favor of continuing autonomy.

Among the factors that might pose obstacles to the exercise of autonomy, are their creation via presidential decree and their institutional adscription to the Vice Presidency of the Republic. Both are potential mechanisms of political co-optation to the extent the CTUs' objectives are conditioned upon political loyalty—especially given the relationship of the popular sectors with such a highly charismatic leader as Chávez. Another challenge, stemming from the foregoing ones, is the possible institutionalization and bureaucratization of the CTUs by the state in its quest to satisfy demands, which could cause competition for resources among institutions and the CTUs. The state needs to ensure that the Proposal for Integral Transformation (Propuesta de Transformación Integral) is expressed as a coherent policy, and that it transcends the housing policies of past governments, adopts the priorities of the CTUs, reflects local characteristics, and exercises real co-responsibility in policy creation. Another challenge for the autonomy of the CTUs lies in the need to strengthen their identities and organizational spaces and to focus on their own objectives.

The diversity of new types of participation that surged with the Bolivarian Constitution of 1999 and was in many cases promoted by President Chávez challenges the CTUs to deal with the complexity of self-management and collective work. The fact that in the popular sectors, organizations with a broad trajectory, such as the Health Care Committees, come together with more formal organizations imposed from above, such as the health misiones, that respond to a different organizational logic and a different type of participation (see chapter 2, "Participatory Democracy in Venezuela," by López Maya and Lander), tends to create confusion about the definition of *participation*. Are we meaning participating in the definition of the "issues" and of local, regional, and national policies as the CTUs or the Health Care Committees pretend, or are we talking of participating in carrying out policies that have already been defined from above, that is to say, from the presidency of the Republic, as is the case with the misiones?

In the context of promoting new types of organization, another challenge for the CTUs is how to articulate themselves with the new organizations, also created by President Chávez, that overlap and share the same geographical space and demands but have different logics and potentials for autonomy. The profusion of organizational types and forms began with the Bolivarian Circles, which ended up responding more to a political logic than to their original objectives of organizing the communities to confront deficiencies in housing, services, and urban infrastructure. Later on, the CTUs were created by decree and they were allotted the same territorial spaces which led to overlap with the Circles in certain functions. Nevertheless, for reasons explained in this work, the CTUs seem more immune to political co-optation and responded more to the logic of a social movement. In a majority of cases their position vis-à-vis political power is "to change the world without taking power" (Holloway 2002). Finally, in response to President Chávez's call to "deepen and radicalize the revolution" after his re-election in 2006, communal councils were declared the enactment of the Popular or Communal Power, the "Sixth Power" included in the constitutional reform proposal defeated in December 2007. Once again, their geographic spaces and allotted functions tend to superimpose themselves in some cases, and complement in others, over those of the CTUs. On the other hand, the overlapping of territory, structure, functions, and roles of communal councils and the implicit political logic to which they respond as the enactment of the Sovereign bring with it the danger that the CTUs will either be absorbed and lose their autonomy or will be displaced and disappear (GAUS-USB 2006, 2009). This indicates that the CTUs may have to choose either to adhere to the political logic of "transforming the world *with* power" by entering into the political machinery and lose their autonomous space and identities, or to maintain their autonomous organizational spaces at the cost of losing their character as strategic sociopolitical actors.

Another factor to keep in mind regarding autonomy is the possibility that temporary demobilizations in favor of political objectives could become permanent, leading to the abandonment of the organizational space proper to the CTUs. Their penetration by political parties or political organizations—

whether they are called electoral "commands," "Bolivarian Circles," or "Electoral Battle Units"—or their displacement by communal councils could lead to a redefinition of identity as political rather than social.

The possibility of coordinating members being paid could bring as a consequence the creation of leadership answering not to democratic but to individualistic criteria. It is also worth noting the possibility, mentioned in presidential speeches, of shifting economic resources directly to the CTUs or to other entities with similar functions. This might create competition between different organizational entities or even put political loyalties ahead of the identity of the CTU.

Finally, the tension between autonomy and co-optation also arises from the dilemma confronting social organizations that have identified with the Bolivarian project put forth by President Chávez, in which two visions, or two positions, relative to *political power* present themselves. One position is to remain as a social movement "transforming the world without taking power"; the other is to shift away from social organization and "linking to power to change the world." Hellinger notes a similar contrast in his chapter "Defying the Iron Law of Oligarchy II," in this volume. According to their legal definition and to their self-defined identity, the CTUs have tended to locate themselves in the first camp, even though today there exists, given their affinity with the hegemonic project of President Chávez, strong pressure on the part of government and political parties to shift toward the second position.

Is it possible to resolve the problem of inclusion and generate new forms of inclusive citizenship without taking power? Is power necessary to transform the condition of exclusion for those who inhabit the popular sectors? Can struggles for inclusion be rooted in social identity? How can new constitutional provisions and rights be made to permeate society? What role does political culture play? These are some open questions for new Bolivarian social organizations, whose *praxis* needs to be deepened further, since it is in praxis that social movements manifest, and, it is in praxis where their capacity for transformation resides.

Notes

1. The information and theoretical development for this chapter come from different sources. The theoretical framework is based on discussions about social movements, popular subjectivity, identity, autonomy, and citizenship over the last years with various research assistants of the ten-year project "The Constitutionalization of New Citizenships and Rationalities: Social Actors and Management of Sociopolitical Conflicts in

Venezuela," which I coordinated, and was financed by the Fondo Nacional de Ciencia y Tecnología (FONACIT) of the Ministry of Science and Technology. I want to highlight in particular Carolina Salazar, who was working on this topic for a master's thesis in political science under my supervision and whose ideas have greatly contributed to this chapter. In addition to documentary information, the analysis of the CTUs is based on empirical information about three CTUs of the popular sector (or *barrio*) Toro Muerto in Ciudad Guayana, Bolívar state, which was developed by Verónica Contreras during her internship in the mayor's office of the Municipality of Caroní for the Universidad Simón Bolívar. This internship was completed in the summer of 2005. Also, this chapter is based on data that were collected expressly for this work by urban planning students under my direction, about an additional seven Land Committees from different popular barrios of Caracas. To all, I extend my thanks and recognition.

2. Both housing and barrios improvement programs were written into the Law for the Subsystem of Housing Policy (October 1998), which was focused on two sectors of the barrios La Vega (UPF-10) and Petare Norte (UPF-04). (The initials UPF refer to Physical Planning Unit.) For information on Decreto 140 (April 20, 1994), sponsored by FUNDACOMUN, see their website at http://www.fundacomun.gov.ve.

3. Here I refer to "President Chávez" instead of the "government" because most such decisions have been the sole responsibility of the president; in many cases decisions are made through presidential decrees.

4. See "Creación y Reseña Histórica del CONAVI," http://www.conavi.gov.ve/portalvivienda/queesconavi.htm.

5. See "Círculos Bolivarianos," Gobierno en Línea, http://www.gobiernoenlinea.ve/cartelera/CirculosBolivarianos.html.

6. Some of the criticism of representative democracy has focused on the incapacity of resolving problems of poverty and social inequality, and on the failure of political parties to mediate between the state and citizens (García-Guadilla 2003, 2005; López Maya 2005; Ellner and Hellinger 2003).

7. I use the term *neoclientelist* to differentiate the search for sinecures or privileges on the part of social organizations in their relation with the State, from those more traditional and individual *clientelist* behaviors. The latter have long existed in Latin America in the relationship between individuals and political parties, including the party of government (García-Guadilla 2002) in the sense of reproducing old relations with instances of power in order to receive privileges and immediate responses to their demands.

8. Three legislative proposals were drafted: the first, from the Primero Justicia party (opposition), titled "Law of Regularization of Urban Land Property and Urbanization of Popular Barrios," submitted to the National Assembly on April 30 of 2002; the second proposal, by four pro-government deputies, titled "Law of Regularization of Land Tenancy in Popular Settlements," submitted on May 21, 2002; and the third, representing the official proposal of the government and its supporters in the National Assembly, and also the proposal of the CTUs themselves, submitted in November 2005.

9. Article 3, Decree 1.666.

10. See "La Asamblea Nacional de la República Bolivariana de Venezuela Decreta," http://www.acnur.org/biblioteca/pdf/6650.pdf.

11. See ibid.

12. There are three proposals defined in this Propuesta de los CTU a la Misión Vivienda: democratization of land, holistic transformation of barrios and neighborhoods, and the creation of new popular settlements within a progressive and holistic housing approach (Asamblea Metropolitana de Comités de Tierra Urbana de Caracas 2004).

13. Guillén (2002) proposes five levels of participation in government policies in the case of human rights organizations that help to understand the different possibilities social organizations have of interrelating with the government. *Organizations for Denunciations and Information*: This level of participation refers to the use of institutionalized mechanisms for channeling denunciations, such as judicial power or citizen power. It involves also writing reports denouncing or informing about specific issues addressed to the authorities and the public opinion. *Organizations for Elaboration of Proposals*: It means designing and presenting to the appropriate authorities public policies proposals to solve social and political problems. *Organizations for Negotiation in Making Decisions*: In this level of participation, in addition to elaborating proposals the organizations pressure the state for the right to participate in decision making. *Organizations for Policy Implementation*: This level refers to carrying out public programs for the benefit of society. *Organizations for Evaluation and Follow-Up*: These are organizations that are charged with defining benchmarks and monitoring and evaluating the development of public policy.

14. The organizational structure of the pro-Chávez MVR tended to penetrate the CTUs in search of people who could be politically mobilized in the same way that past political parties, such as AD, COPEI, MAS, or Causa R, were using the symbolic appeal of community participation.

15. It should be noted that the same occurred with social organizations of the opposition, which not only linked themselves with political parties and the opposite mass media throughout the campaign for a yes vote in the presidential recall referendum but were themselves its promoters.

16. In the case of social organizations opposed to President Chávez, there was more heterogeneity among opposition political parties. For this reason, there was no clear line of action coming from the political parties, leaving each individual the option of supporting a political party or abstaining. In any case, they also follow the political lines of the parties of the opposition.

17. To some extent, other organizations, such as the Water Technical Roundtables (Mesas Técnicas del Agua), Health Committees, and some organizations of women at the popular level were also penetrated and their original objectives were temporarily put on hold.

CHAPTER FOUR

Catia Sees You

Community Television, Clientelism, and the State in the Chávez Era

Naomi Schiller

In the sociologist Javier Auyero's critique of the paradigm of clientelism, he argues that "'political clientelism' has been one of the strongest and most recurrent images in the study of political practices of the poor—urban and rural alike—in Latin America, almost to the point of becoming a sort of 'metonymic prison' for this part of the Americas" (1999, 297). As Auyero notes, scholars typically define political clientelism as the hierarchical relationships through which impoverished "clients" exchange their political loyalty for political, economic, or cultural resources from elite "patrons" who are usually politicians. My aim in this chapter is a prison-break of sorts. I examine how leaders from Catia TVe, Caracas's most prominent community media outlet, responded to an attack on one of their producers in order to reflect critically on the usefulness of the analytic category of clientelism.

The privately owned commercial media, scholars, and commentators often portray state-funded media organizations, like Catia TVe and other nascent barrio-based media outlets, as clients of President Chávez who produce positive representations of the government in exchange for resources. I highlight instead what the theoretical model of clientelism makes impossible to identify and assess: the political practice of state making that takes place among grassroots media activists every day. Conventional theories of clientelism are contingent on a reified state-society boundary, which limits our ability to assess changing and competing notions of the state in Venezuela and the shifting relationships between barrio activists and the government. Moreover, such theoretical approaches to clientelism, which assert distinct boundaries between state and society, prohibit an analysis of how activists use assumptions about the state and society for their own benefit. The state is granted meaning on an

everyday basis through debates over issues of autonomy and exchanges between grassroots media makers and government actors. Activists at times strategically position themselves outside the state, even while in their everyday
practice they traverse and challenge this boundary.

Attention to the shifting notions of what *the state* means in daily life is crucial to understand how barrio-based political activists negotiate contradictions, engage government actors, and make gains for their political projects.
Since 2000, community media outlets in Caracas have expanded from informal
groups of activists documenting everyday life in their impoverished neighborhoods to licensed broadcasters who use state funds to train and equip their
neighbors to be radio and television producers. (Sujatha Fernandes also explores this theme in chapter 5, "Radio Bemba in an Age of Electronic Media.")
In the 1990s, Catia TVe's founders considered their media productions the
"voice of the voiceless" against the elite-controlled commercial media and the
ruling parties of the government. More recently, Catia TVe and other community media producers have found themselves in a different position. As of 2007,
Catia TVe received the bulk of its funding from the government by broadcasting segments several times daily about the supposed advancements of Chávez's
self-proclaimed Revolution.

The debate over how to respond to the attack by a commercial journalist
on one of their producers revealed Catia TVe's efforts (1) to negotiate the distinct demands and agendas of their diverse interlocutors (other community
media makers, their imagined viewing audience, and various government institutions) and (2) to broker power in a way that advanced the station's agenda.
Catia TVe's response provides insight into how community producers understand the impacts of their own media organization and their use of social networks and competing notions of the appropriate relationship between their
organization and the government.

This chapter draws on thirteen months of ethnographic field research among
community media producers in Caracas over a period of four years, between
2003 and 2007. As an observant participant, I accompanied staff and volunteers
into the field where they filmed meetings, marches, press conferences, and folk
performances. Additionally, I attended workshops, conferences, and meetings
in poor neighborhoods and state institutions alongside Catia TVe producers.[1]

Perspectives on Clientelism

The central question animating the vast scholarship on clientelism concerns
how power is leveraged through relationships of exchange between two groups

or individuals that have unequal access to resources (Gellner 1977). Much contemporary scholarship in political science and sociology focuses on the role of
clientelist practices in creating or perpetuating fragile democracies, authoritarian governments, and weak states outside of the United States and Western Europe. Recent assessments of the consequences of political clientelism
on citizenship practices in Latin America argue that democratic pluralism and
broad-based participation in civil society are eroded when social actors think
of their relationship with the state as one between client and patron rather
than focusing on their rights and duties as citizens (Fox 1997; García-Gaudilla
2002; Gay 2006).

Critics contend that clientelism has strong roots in Venezuela, where petro-
dollars have created a "culture of rent-seeking" (Karl 1997). Hugo Chávez's
electoral successes are explained within this framework. Thus, some scholars
conclude that the large number of national electoral contests that Chávez has
won over the past decade (over a dozen), is the result of the patronage channels that distribute funds for health, housing, nutrition, and education programs (Corrales and Penfold 2007). Poor people, numerous scholars purport,
are the most susceptible group to enter clientelist exchanges due to their financial vulnerability (Penfold-Bencerra 2007). In addition to reducing the political allegiance of the poor to basic economic rationalism, scholars maintain that
what is developing in Venezuela is a form of what Jonathan Fox (1997, 394) has
called "authoritarian clientelism" where the denial of political support for a
politician can result in a threat to livelihood.

The political clientelism paradigm is contingent upon the classic liberal
conception of democracy where a strong, autonomous, and universally accessible civil society separate from the state regulates and influences the government to act in the interest of the majority. This theoretical perspective positions the state as a coherent entity situated above and distinct from the rest of
society. Scholars who embrace clientelism as a useful explanatory framework
(Gay 2006; Fox 1997) assume a coherent and unitary state that works in a top-
down manner rewarding and recruiting actors with selective incentives in ways
that strengthen particularistic identities, power hierarchies, and processes of
exclusion.

Alternative Anthropological Approaches to Clientelism and the State

After the zenith of ethnographic studies of patronage in the 1960s and 1970s,
anthropologists have largely abandoned the theoretical rubric of clientelism

(Zinn 2005). Refusing to accept the covert assumption that relations between patron and client were always based on exploitation, anthropologists have argued that relations of interdependence between groups of unequal power need to be approached as an object of empirical analysis (Scott 1977, 37). Shifts in anthropological methodology to "study up" (Nader 1972) and the epistemological turn away from the notion of static bounded "cultures" have encouraged a revised approach to discourses of corruption such as clientelism (Zinn 2005).

Rejecting assertions that endemic corruption is a social pathology unique to underdeveloped nations and criticizing the ways in which the clientelist paradigm excludes assessments of "cronyism among equals or elite nepotism" (Zinn 2005, 230), this recent work also reflects critically on the political context of neoliberal policies that produces the frame for the concepts of corruption and clientelism (Haller and Shore 2005). The so-called culture of clientelism that many assert pervades Latin American societies is critiqued as an essentialist explanation for Latin America's poverty and allegedly weak democratic institutions, which deflects attention from the historical and contemporary conditions that have shaped and undermined Latin American political trajectories and democracies.

Challenges by anthropologists and some sociologists to the clientelism paradigm have come from two directions. Some scholars have argued for an alternative reading of clientelism; others have chosen to rethink the nature of the state and of the divide between it and society as described by classical political theory. Those arguing for an alternative reading of clientelism challenge the notion that informal exchanges through personal networks are dysfunctional aspects of state institutions and find that these practices are often central to governmental functions, even in nations widely considered democratic (Lomnitz 1988; Lomnitz-Adler 1992). These scholars assert that the distribution of resources through personalized channels can but does not always generate forms of top-down control. According to this critique, those who receive such resources cannot be understood as unsophisticated, passive, and uncritical (Auyero 1999, 2000; Gay 1998; Lazar 2004). Without examining social fields from the client's point(s) of view (Auyero 1999; Burgwal 1995; Silverman 1977) we miss how marginalized groups negotiate dense political networks and exercise complex logics of problem solving.

In the past fifteen years, new approaches to the study of corruption have emerged in combination with researchers' effort to re-examine what *the state* means in everyday life and to challenge received understandings and approaches to the state's force and formation. Scholars influenced by Foucault's theorization of power have extended his critique of the notion that state power emanates from a centralized authoritative headquarters (Foucault 1978, 1984). Timothy Mitchell has highlighted the specific tactics of power made possible through the use of the culturally constructed idea that the state is an abstract and autonomous structure separate from society (Mitchell 1991). He makes the crucial insight that rather than being simply descriptive, the ersatz distinction between state and society contributes to the creation of the relationships of force that the dichotomy pretends only to describe (Mitchell 1991, 1999; Steinmetz 1999).

Akhil Gupta's groundbreaking work (1995) on narratives of corruption in rural India vividly reveals how talk of corruption enables citizens and bureaucrats to imagine and create the state on an everyday local basis. *Ideas* about and *representations* of the state are not merely reflections of the material world, these scholars contend, but actively shape and produce that world. A body of scholarship has emerged that examines how and why the state is imagined, practiced, and represented as a *thing* that appears coherent, supreme, natural, and agentive (Coronil 1997; Ferguson and Gupta 2002; Hansen and Stepputat 2001; Joseph and Nugent 1994; Nuijten 2003; Scott 1998; Taussig 1993; Trouillot 2001).

Rethinking the State in Venezuela

The Venezuelan case is a significant and challenging context to pursue a different approach to the state than the traditional clientelism paradigm permits, because the Chávez government itself has engaged in the central theoretical issues being debated here. The anthropologist James Ferguson recommends that in order to advance new perspectives on emerging ideologies rather than simply reproducing normative theory in situations where "the analytical tools closest to hand are themselves part of the social and cultural reality we seek to grasp" requires "a heightened level of reflexive scrutiny of our categories of analysis" (2004, 383). In this vein, I very briefly assess the practical and theoretical implications of the official government and community media discourse as well as the scholarly assessments of the nature of the relationship between citizens and the state.

One of the declared aims of the Chávez government is "to create a new relation between the State and society" with "the objective of transforming the Venezuelan into a politicized citizen that has joint responsibility for the solutions of their own problems" (López Maya 2005, 359 [my translation]; see also "Participatory Democracy in Venezuela" by López Maya and Lander, and

"Urban Land Committees" by García-Guadilla, in this volume). A prominent slogan of Chávez's government is "El estado somos todos" (We are all the state). The legitimacy of Chávez and the Bolivarian Revolution relies on the claim that there is a new geometry of power in Venezuela and that the Revolution is a social movement catalyzed from below by the people. Most scholars of Venezuela from across the political spectrum have been critical of the Chávez government's claims to remake the relationship between state and society. The sociologist Edgardo Lander noted, for example:

> As long as the state exists, democracy requires and necessitates the recognition of the inevitable (and necessary) tension between the state and the multiplicity of organizational forms and autonomous associations that exist in society. To look for a way to resolve this tension via the incorporation of these multiple modalities of organizations and associations inside the state, or in the search for an identity pueblo-state, would threaten the existence of autonomous environments not submitted to the logic of the state. (2007; my translation)

While Lander's fears about the balance of power between official government projects and nongovernment initiatives might be warranted, this chapter takes a different approach. My analytic point of departure is *not* an "inevitable tension" between state and society or the assumption that autonomy from the state is necessary or possible for nongovernmental organizations in any state context.

Instead, I take seriously how barrio-based media makers who depend on government resources imagine, discuss, and engage the logic of the state, the tension between state and grassroots groups, and notions of their own autonomy. I consider everyday debates, reflections, and negotiations of relations of exchange to be forms of state formation (as do Joseph and Nugent 1994; Hellinger, this volume, chapter 8). Attention to changing and sometimes incompatible ways that people imagine, speak of, and approach state institutions allows for an analysis of how members of poor communities in Caracas understand and create political force. Do Catia TVe producers see themselves as part of the official government project or logic? Is the state understood as the locus of power? Do community producers worry about risks of government co-option? How do they view the relationships between community and government projects? Is there, as Monique Nuijten asserts, an "unbridgeable gap between people and the state" (2003, 10)?

While scholars have assumed that within an electoral democratic system the only power marginalized subjects have is their vote, my study of Catia TVe re-

veals a changing dynamic wherein political subjects have different sources of
leverage due not only to their long-term political and personal alliances with
individuals now in key government positions, but also as a result of the way
in which the polarized political battle in contemporary Venezuela has been
fought largely in the terrain of media and through televisual spectacle (see
also the chapters by Fernandes and Acosta-Alzuru in this volume). It is no surprise that Chávez would demonstrate a keen interest in the production of popular media that exhibit the government's success and support among the poor.
Grassroots media producers skillfully negotiate the recent increase in the symbolic value of their productions in the changing cultural and political economy
of the Venezuelan media world. Catia TVe is therefore a particularly rich social
site to explore the failure of the clientelism paradigm to capture shifts in political subjectivities and everyday debates over the meaning of the state.

Few scholars have addressed grassroots video's complexities as a tool for social transformation. Patricia Aufderheide, however, points out that early optimistic celebrations of grassroots video production in Latin America assumed
that technology itself could break down social inequalities, media messages on
their own could be libratory, and media production was intrinsically empower-
ing (2000, 224–25). Anthropologists have examined the critical questions concerning the pitfalls and possibilities of cooperation between the state and
grassroots media initiatives (Ginsburg 1991; Wortham 2004). Ethnographic research follows everyday relationships, processes of decision making, and how
the actors involved perceive these processes. This research traces the cultural,
financial, and political relationships involved in the flow and exercise of power
that shape media representations. I build on scholarship on state-funded cultural production that asserts that even when television is government-funded,
it cannot be reduced to a hegemonic state apparatus; within state-run culture industries, producers negotiate and struggle to express their views (Abu-
Lughod 2005; Mankekar 1999).

Catia TVe's Origins: Don't Watch Television, Make It!

Media and politics have become increasingly inseparable in Venezuela. Since
the collapse of traditional political parties in the 1990s, media outlets have
not simply provided a terrain for political debate; rather, media spokespeople
are now key political actors who shape politics in ways intended to resonate
with local and global audiences.[2] Representation on television is understood by
many as equivalent to social and political existence in Venezuela (Duno Gott-

berg 2004, 130). As one media producer at Catia TVe told me, "If you see your-self on television, you say, yes, I exist. And part of that [process] is understand-ing that you are part of this reality and that you have to solve its problems." Becoming media producers and creating images of poor people and poor neigh-borhoods, in other words, is important for groups to become political actors.

Catia TVe had its origins shortly after the 1989 Caracazo (the massive urban uprising against the implementation of structural adjustment policies) when residents of a small neighborhood in west Caracas began organizing a local Casa de Cultura (Cultural Center). A middle class student, Blanca Eekhout, was living in the barrio at the time doing political organizing and working on her undergraduate thesis on the *cine club* (film club) movement.[3] A few young men from the neighborhood together with Eekhout appealed to the Federation of Centers of Cinemagraphic Culture, a state initiative, to secure funds for the Casa de Cultura to purchase a 16-mm film projector in order to start a local film club. The film club aimed to strengthen community collaboration by bringing the neighborhood together to watch and discuss movies collectively. The seeds for Catia TVe, which takes its name from the poor western region of Caracas referred to colloquially as "Catia," were planted in the early 1990s when the Casa de Cultura presented a proposal to the mayor's Cultural Commission and received funding to buy a video camera. Catia TVe is a pun that means "Catia sees you." The film club's screenings expanded to include the documentaries made by members of the community, and for the first time residents of the bar-rio saw their own images projected on screen.

Ricardo Márquez, one of the founding members of the film club and Catia TVe's current director, grew up in the neighborhood where Catia TVe was founded. In an interview with me, Márquez explained that the impetus for Catia TVe sprang from the private media's biased portrayal of Caracas's poor neighborhoods.

> When they [commercial media] come to a poor neighborhood they de-nounce the murders, the criminals, the rapes. But they've never come to document the community organizing itself, the community fighting for its children, the community doing cultural activities. Nothing. They come to make news that bleeds. . . . So community media has established itself to fill this gap that for so many years the commercial media has left open.

Márquez stressed the importance of media content about barrios that high-lights their political agency and community organizing. The founders of the film club understood the media produced by and for their community not only as a way to valorize and re-present Caracas's barrios but also as part of an effort to organize for better living conditions. Moreover, they recognized that filming and screening productions of their barrio was an excellent tool to encourage their neighbors to participate in community meetings.

In 1998, organizers from the film club met a group based in the state of Táchira, Venezuela that was experimenting with media technology in order to try to implement a local television project. With their help the founders of Catia TVe planned to mount their own signal to broadcast their video productions. Blanca Eekhout became the first director of Catia TVe. The station's official slogan became "Don't Watch Television, Make It!" ("¡No vea televisión, hágala!"). In 1999, Eekhout and other young producers from the neighborhood caught Chávez's attention when he was inaugurating a nearby hospital in west Caracas. As the station's lore goes, Chávez was surrounded by the usual mob of reporters, when Eekhout called out: "President Chávez, what do you have to say to the people of Catia?" Chávez, it is said, took several more steps before stopping still in his tracks, curious to know what station was reporting for Catia, the impoverished, densely populated area of west Caracas. According to Catia TVe staff, this meeting initiated a series of talks between community media producers and government officials that helped propel the media reform legislation the following year that allowed community media stations to become licensed legal entities. This personal history with Chávez no doubt has been pivotal for the station's ability to secure funding and has solidified their sense of personal commitment to the president.

Márquez, Eekhout, and Catia TVe's other founders expanded their project to include community organizers living in other nearby barrios. Ana García, one of the current assistant directors at Catia, and her sister Margarita were involved in the local Health and Urban Land Committees in their neighborhood in 2000 when Blanca Eekhout and Ricardo Márquez invited the two sisters to join a discussion about the media. Ana García noted to me:

> Blanca's proposal was to have discussions about communication and what kind of communication we were seeing. And of course, beyond what kind of communication we were seeing, how we were doing so many things and no one was seeing it. Commercial television spread information about our community when someone killed someone, and of course pornography, sexuality, violence. But it never spread information that our community was organizing itself, that it was transforming itself to change things. No one was seeing that. So we started analyzing and thinking. All the things we had accomplished and no one knew about them.

For long-time activists like the Garcías, making community television was an extension of their community activism, and the process of media production was a powerful tool to involve their neighbors in community projects. For the first time, the García sisters began to think seriously about the role of the commercial media not only in spreading negative messages about barrio communities but also in eclipsing the work they were doing to solve problems in their neighborhoods. As Faye Ginsburg (1991, 1994) and Terrence Turner (1991) have noted, the social process of media production is not only a *means* of representing culture but is also an *ends* of activism and social reproduction.

With a small grant from Venezuela's Ministry of Communication, Catia TVe could begin broadcasting two hours daily from a small office in a local hospital, and Chávez inaugurated the station in 2001. With their miniature digital video cameras and experience with filmmaking, Catia TVe members documented the activity in the streets during the April 2002 coup attempt against Chávez. Several Catia TVe founders participated in re-launching Venezolana de Televisión (VTV), the only state-run television station that existed at the time, on the air after it was shut down by supporters of the coup. Over five years later, members of Catia TVe staff regularly spoke of those days and expressed their belief that they played an important role in restoring Chávez to power. These memories, invoked and narrated again and again, serve as a message to themselves and whoever might be listening that poor people have the power to shape national political trajectories. The experience of the coup and its dramatic reversal made vividly apparent for many at Catia TVe how the state is a human construction.

In 2003 Alfredo Peña, the mayor of Caracas at the time, evicted Catia TVe from its original headquarters in an unused room of the local hospital in the neighborhood where the station's founders lived. Peña, a former journalist and one-time Chávez ally, claimed that the broadcast waves of the station's transmitter were a hazard to the hospital's patients. However, just a few months earlier the Ministry of the Interior had granted Catia TVe a rent-free fifty-year lease to an abandoned state-owned building in a poor neighborhood of Caracas. The move had been slow because Catia TVe's founders had to raise the money to restore the dilapidated building. The media publicity generated by Catia TVe's eviction from their original headquarters proved to be a boon in gaining recognition nationally and internationally. As a victim of the opposition to Chávez, Catia TVe gained notoriety and support among Chávez supporters and the government. With loans from PDVSA, the state-run oil company, the founders of Catia TVe were able to build their dream headquarters, bought video equipment and computers, and hired more staff. In order to repay the

PDVSA loans, Catia TVe broadcast lengthy infomercials promoting PDVSA several times daily. After the loans were paid off, in order to finance the station Catia TVe continued to broadcast PDVSA infomercials as well as other infomercials that championed the government's projects.

As of 2007, Catia TVe had a paid staff of thirty, the majority of whom came from the poor neighborhoods of Catia. Volunteers at the station are organized into small production teams called ECPAIs (Equipos Comunitarios de Produccion Audiovisual Independientes or Independent Community Teams of Audiovisual Producers). These volunteer teams attend a free video-production workshop that includes training on how to operate miniature digital video cameras and use editing software; discussion and practice of collective decision making and leadership; and lessons in media history and literacy. Then they must by law create 70 percent of the station's programming; the paid staff at the station can contribute only 15 percent. The law regulating community media also stipulates that the directors of community media cannot be party officials, members of the military, or employees of private mass media. Like all community, state, and commercial media outlets, Catia TVe must by law interrupt their programming for *cadenas*, the nationwide simultaneous radio and television government broadcasts that preempt all regular programming.

From the beginning, Catia TVe's programming included short educational and public service documentaries, which covered neighborhood events, local history, and some short fictional films treating various issues such as health care, refuse management, and domestic violence. Although the staff claims that Catia TVe's signal reaches the homes of half of Caracas's almost five million people, in fact, the signals' reach is unpredictable due to Caracas's uneven landscape; moreover, the repetitive and unscheduled programming and the low production quality of sound and lighting limit audience numbers. In addition, because their television signal is broadcast terrestrially and requires a conventional aerial to receive the signal, the population with digital cable television in Caracas cannot easily tune in to Catia TVe. It is quite common to see satellite dishes for Direct TV, the most popular digital cable provider in Venezuela, perched atop houses even in poor neighborhoods. Most often, people tune into Catia TVe to watch themselves, their own video productions, or people they know.

The station's producers recognize that the viewing audience is small but express ambivalent attitudes about the importance of a large audience. Most Catia TVe producers do not approach viewers as an "object to be conquered" by the one-way flow of information (Ang 1991, 23). Instead, they understand participation in the process of media *production* as the central site for cultural and political struggle. Catia TVe's slogan "¡No vea televisión, hágala!" is more than just a catchy phrase; it asserts Catia TVe's aim to generate producers rather than audiences. The station, in practice, functions predominantly as an audio-visual training center that encourages local participation in projects to ameliorate neighborhood problems and educates community groups about the importance of media democratization. Nevertheless, Catia TVe leadership has sought exposure of the station's programming on nationally and internationally broadcast state-run television stations. Between 2002 and 2006, Catia TVe had a weekly one-hour timeslot on VTV, the main state channel, whose signal reaches across the country. Beginning in 2006, Catia TVe began contributing material to a daily program of community media on Vive TV, another state-run television channel, whose broadcast signal reaches most of the national territory.

Given their relatively small viewing audience, Catia TVe's prominence and political clout cannot be attributed only to the impact of their programming but also to a combination of (1) people's expectations about the immediate ability of television to reach and influence the station's imagined audiences and (2) the daily practices of Catia TVe's producers and leaders. Government officials imagine that Catia TVe's audience is people from poor neighborhoods, while people from poor neighborhoods who seek out the station to register complaints or cover community events often imagine that the viewing audience of Catia TVe is the government, if not Chávez himself. The consistent presence of Catia TVe's leaders, moreover, as spokespeople for the community media movement on state television and in face-to-face settings at community organizing meetings, press conferences, and marches establishes the station as the leader of the community media field. Catia TVe gains much of its clout among community activists as well as government supporters as a symbol of the progress of the poor and the democratization of communication in Venezuela.

Placing the Story

At an anti-Chávez student march in July 2005, Noe Pernia, a well-known reporter from RCTV, a major commercial television network in Venezuela, angrily approached José Lara, a young staff member from Catia TVe. Pernia reached for Lara's video camera and in a raised voice stated: "Stop filming me, you spy, and tell your papa Chávez to buy you a new camera." The two men struggled over the camera, then Lara broke free and fled with it. Although the small viewing screen had been torn off during the scuffle, the camera continued to record throughout the entire episode.

The Pernia-Lara scuffle was a fortuitous opportunity for Catia TVe to bolster its prominence in the media world of Caracas. The effort to redress the conflict, moreover, became an occasion where community media makers articulated competing understandings and preoccupations concerning the station's relationship with the state.

The political significance of the RCTV journalist's attack in 2005 must be understood within the highly polarized media world of Venezuela. Both Catia TVe and Pernia, the commercial reporter, depicted the incident as representative of the larger struggle between the commercial media and the Chávez-aligned media. Catia TVe recognized the attack as an opportunity to reveal what they saw as the hypocrisy of commercial media's claims that they are the victimized and silenced party in the conflict. Catia TVe staff and volunteers asserted that attacks against commercial journalists and assertions that Chávez had placed limits on freedom of speech had received much attention internationally while acts of aggression against community media outlets had gone largely unrecognized by the national and international commercial media.[4]

When Lara returned to Catia TVe after the confrontation with the RCTV reporter, rather than immediately broadcasting the footage of what had taken place, one of the station's assistant directors, Ana García, insisted that Lara go with her directly to the main state channel, VTV, to report the incident. Meanwhile, other staff members worked on publicizing the story on a pro-Chávez website and making copies of the footage to send to both state television channels (VTV and Vive TV). Their communication strategy to disseminate news of the attack made clear that the station's staff did not see their own television station as an effective vehicle for the instant dissemination of news. Instead, the Internet and state television were the preferred channels of communication. Producers recognized that these outlets are more effective than their own station to reach a large audience immediately.

Upon hearing the news of Lara's scuffle with Pernia, Catia TVe's director, Ricardo Márquez, began making feverish phone calls from his cell phone to lawyers, community media colleagues, and Blanca Eekhout, the former director of Catia TVe and at that time president of both VTV and Vive TV. Another staff member called a longtime friend who had just begun working for Telesur, the international news channel modeled after CNN, which Chávez inaugurated in 2005. These long-term ties between barrio-based activists and newly established government officials require ongoing renewal and delicate management; Catia TVe staff must decide when and how to call on their support network in the official domains of power.

A few hours later, a Catia TVe staff member found a letter that Pernia, the RCTV journalist, had posted on an Internet site about his confrontation with

Lara. Pernia wrote that he was easily able to identify the "government spy" at the demonstration because "journalists and reporters know one another, it's like an instinct that unites us, and permits us to watch each other's back."[5] Pernia admitted to breaking the camera and maintained that it was not until after the incident that he learned that Lara worked for Catia TVe, which he labeled "the trash boot-licking network of the regime" (*bodrio comunicacional lamebotas del régimen*). Pernia clearly did not recognize Lara, a community media producer, as an authentic journalist. For Pernia, Catia TVe's barrio-based origins and state funding were enough evidence to prove that the station served as an apparatus of the government.

Catia TVe members understood this letter as all-out declaration of war against community media. The staff was outraged by Pernia's comments but found most of his insults comical. Jokingly, they called one another *espía* and *sapografo*, a derogatory name Pernia had labeled them (roughly translated as journalist-spy). Significantly, they did not jokingly call one another *lamebota del régimen*. While it seemed laughable that anyone would accuse them of being spies, the accusation that they were inappropriately linked and subservient to the government was decidedly *not* funny. The silence around this insult revealed the anxiety concerning how the station's funding from and close alignment with the government make them vulnerable to claims that Catia TVe lacks independence.

Catia TVe's overlapping agenda and involvement with government projects leaves them vulnerable to the charge that they are not sufficiently autonomous to exercise the kind of editorial objectivity traditionally understood to bolster democracy. International visitors repeatedly ask Catia TVe staff how they can maintain their autonomy given their financial dependence on state funds. The staff asserts that they will openly criticize Chávez and the government if they believe it is necessary. In practice, during the period of my research, Chávez was never openly criticized on Catia TVe's airwaves. However, Catia TVe programming is often sharply critical of the bureaucratic inefficiency and other shortcomings of state institutions and their failures to meet needs. The station regularly covers their neighbors' *denuncias* (complaints) about corruption or their inability to gain access to government assistance. Catia TVe staff members make it clear that they do not pretend to be impartial and, in fact, some dismiss objectivity outright as an impossible position that neither state-funded community media nor commercial media outlets can maintain. They often highlight how commercial producers are dependent on transnational capital through advertising contracts.

Nevertheless, the station's ongoing reliance on the broadcasting of infomer-

cials that celebrate the advancements of the government was a topic of constant debate inside the station. Some producers worried that their ability to
criticize the government was compromised by their financial relationship with
state institutions, such as PDVSA. Other Catia TVe producers argued that the
oil resources belong to the people and that the days were long over when grassroots organizations had to struggle "tooth and nail" to maintain their operations. The official PDVSA infomercials continue to play on Catia TVe, which
serves to legitimize the state oil company's message that, for example, "*Now,*
the oil belongs to all Venezuelans." But these government-produced propaganda segments are framed in a sequence of Catia TVe programming created
by Catia TVe's barrio-based producers to highlight the problems that continue
to plague poor neighborhoods. This framing creates space to contradict the
government-produced messages that they broadcast.

The internal conflict over the station's dependence on state resources is
illustrated by two assertions made by one of Catia TVe's assistant directors,
Hector Alvarez. Alvarez noted at a gathering of community media producers,
where representatives from the state Ministry of Information and Communication were also present,

> State publicity can also harm us in the sense that if we have a denuncia
> [complaint] and we take a political position against some functionary,
> they could block us saying, "Cut their publicity." And we could say, well,
> we'll continue functioning *or* we can continue with the denuncia. How
> can we make a participatory budget [where viewers fund the station]
> that guarantees our independence, independence as a media, indepen-
> dence from the bourgeois state, from the old state?

Here Alvarez articulates the concern that Catia TVe cannot achieve or maintain
editorial independence when their budget is controlled by people who work in
state institutions. However, when I later interviewed Alvarez and asked him
about the conundrum of autonomy, he dismissed the notion that Catia TVe
should attempt independence from the state. I asked Alvarez how he understood Catia TVe's relationship with the state and he explained:

> One understands that in other countries, or even here before the revolu-
> tionary process, to be dependent on the state was bad, to be connected to
> the state was bad. Now we are talking about *taking* the state. More than
> that, we are in a process of taking the power and destroying the state to
> construct a popular one. . . . To be independent of a state that is a revo-
> lutionary state, that's a position of the right wing, it's a reactionary posi-
> tion, no?

The shift between describing autonomy from the state as necessary to asserting that it is impossible when "popular" movements are "taking the state" probably in part reflects the difference in his primary audience (other community media producers and government representatives versus me, a North American researcher). Nevertheless, the distinct perspectives Alvarez articulates—on the one hand advocating for financial independence in order to secure editorial control, and on the other hand advocating for the creation of a new revolutionary state—reflect the practical and ideological struggle taking place within many grassroots media organizations.

Advancing these conflicting ideas of the state is part of a process of everyday state making. Alvarez struggles to articulate definitively the appropriate relation between the state and community media. In his daily work Alvarez collaborates with and at times contests projects that fall under the rubric of "state." Some state projects are motivated and organized by groups that are more closely aligned with his goal of creating a revolutionary state than others. He attempts to assert independence from the government while at the same time attempting to remake the state. Shaping how the state is conceived of and imagined can have real, practical effects on political action; this dynamic cannot be accurately understood through a lens of normative theory which assumes that the opposition between state and society is natural and, indeed, necessary for any form of democracy.

In the days following the Pernia attack, I observed Catia TVe leaders and staff maneuver through various networks, often using assumptions about the division of state and society to their benefit. I accompanied Lara and two other staff members from Catia TVe to different media outlets where they tried to publicize news of the attack. At the office of the newspaper *Ultimas Noticias,* Venezuela's highest circulation paper and often editorially sympathetic to Chávez, Catia TVe staff members were unsuccessful.[6] The woman at the front desk of the newspaper's headquarters curtly informed the Catia TVe staff that the paper only takes denuncias in the morning. Without personal connections, Catia TVe members were not able to pursue unofficial channels at the paper. In any event, Catia TVe producers did not see newspaper coverage as a priority; they never returned to *Ultimas Noticias* to report the attack against Lara. In contrast, at Vive TV, the state television station created in 2003 with Blanca Eekhout as president, Catia TVe staff members quickly passed through the front security desk, entered the station, and were greeted warmly with handshakes and hugs from people they knew. After a short conversation with a friend about how best to light a studio space for television, Catia TVe staff arranged an interview to discuss the Pernia attack on a Vive TV program later that day. The media coverage culminated later that week when Andres Izarra, the Minister of Information and Communication at the time, called an official press conference to highlight the issue.

Catia TVe used the media airtime obtained through their social and professional networks not only to promote the sensationalist news of the Pernia attack but also to advance their approach to communication. For example, during *En Confianza,* an early-morning talk show on VTV, the Catia TVe director Ricardo Márquez and two volunteer producers were invited to discuss the attack. Márquez was repeatedly asked by the show's male host to explain the impact that Catia TVe's message has on their communities. There was an awkward pause in the over air-conditioned television studio when Márquez did not deliver the kind of answer the host seemed to be expecting. Márquez attempted to explain that Catia TVe is not interested in the impact of their programming on a passive audience but rather in producing active community participants and social communicators. In this moment, Márquez distinguished Catia TVe's project from that of the official state media and pressured the state media to think about audiences not as passive vessels to be filled with messages. Márquez seized the opportunity on the nationally broadcast talk show to advocate for a different approach to communication than VTV practices. He encouraged viewers to participate in community media production as a way to engage in local political struggles and advance neighborhood projects.

Catia TVe's denunciation of Pernia on the airwaves of state media advanced both the government's and Catia TVe's agendas. Catia TVe granted state media cultural and political legitimacy by demonstrating that they, in fact, do represent the people (*el pueblo*) by not only showing their solidarity with community media but also allowing space on state media for the grievances of el pueblo (see Gupta 1995, 388). Grassroots media with non-professional production values carry much symbolic weight for politicians whose legitimacy depends on displaying their commitment to popular publics.[7]

The station's long-term relationship with Blanca Eekhout, the original director, who could exert considerable influence on state media as president of Vive TV, was crucial to their ability to gain access to the major state channels and officials. Eekhout's rise to prominence in state media was a result of her grassroots media credentials. For close to a decade, Eekhout lived in the poor neighborhood where Catia TVe was created. In a 2003 interview, Eekhout, characterized this period to me as "a foundational experience" that taught her the extent of stigmatization that barrio dwellers experience and the lack of basic services that plagues everyday life. When Vive TV hastily went on the air for the first time in 2003, Catia TVe producers provided vital technological knowledge to assist in its launch. The station's programming often replicates the immediacy of community media productions with documentaries about the lives of Venezuela's rural and urban poor. Vive TV's vice president, Thierry Deronne, also co-founded a community television station in the city of Maracay, called Teletambures. In 2007, several of Vive TV's newest employees were producers from poor neighborhoods who had received their training at Catia TVe.

The shared personal histories and intertwined intellectual and political development of Vive TV and Catia TVe's leadership shape how community media activists understand what *the state* means, as reflected in my conversations with former Catia TVe volunteers who went to work for Vive TV. A young man from a poor neighborhood who had worked at Vive TV for just a few months expressed disillusionment at not having the freedom that he had at Catia TVe to include *all* aspects of peoples' experiences. He was instructed to exclude criticisms of the shortcomings of government programs in the segment he was producing for Vive TV. When I asked him in 2007 if he felt like he was part of the state, he noted, "I don't feel part of the state as such, as an institution. I don't feel like an institution. I feel like a person that, well, is being helped economically but I continue with my same ideals, with my same desire to continue going out into the street to say, well, this crap isn't working, and we are going to tell people." Such perspectives further enrich our understanding of the complexity of everyday state formation taking place in the networks between and within community and state television stations. This producer expressed fond memories of the editorial control he exercised over audiovisual material at Catia TVe, in distinct contrast to his experience at Vive TV. This difference highlights how community media outlets do in fact provide unique spaces for expression.

The circulation of material resources and knowledge between Catia TV and Vive TV represents more than political loyalty. This dense network of relationships enhances barrio-based producers' access to government decision-making processes and provides these producers with insights into the limitations of working directly for a government-run institution. These relationships and experiences, which are of course embedded in social hierarchies, are nevertheless part of the construction of changing practices of representation, interpretation, and interpellation that shape how people understand the state.

After their experience on the state television channels, and ten hours after the incident, Catia TVe went on their own airwaves to discuss and play the footage of Pernia's attack. There was an air of excitement in the television studio as Márquez, together with two other male staff members, prepared to discuss the incident live during their weekly one-hour talk show. Two male and one female staff members operated the massive professional studio cameras, purchased by the station with funds from PDVSA. Márquez immediately framed Pernia's attack as an act of aggression against el pueblo by Chávez's opposition. Under the bright studio lights, Márquez looked directly into the camera and stated:

> Freedom of speech belongs to every inhabitant of the planet. It doesn't belong to the oligarchy with their spokesperson and their microphone and their private channel in any part of the world. It belongs to the people, and we are fighting here at Catia TVe so that it will be that way. They are going have to get used to seeing more ECPAIs from Catia TVe. . . . Every day, more and more, the government authorities and the opposition are going to have to agree to be interviewed and answer to the ECPAIs.

Márquez positioned Catia TVe and its volunteer media producers as a force that both the opposition *and* the government had to recognize as legitimate, and he stressed that Catia TVe was outside formal government apparatuses.

The program was interrupted twice. First, an official *encadena*, a government segment that legally preempted all regular programming, boasted about the recent progress of government programs. Márquez and his colleagues sat patiently, exhibiting neither frustration nor concern at being interrupted. Later, there was a scheduled break for the government-produced publicity that Catia TVe regularly broadcasts to fund the station. These segments also celebrated improvements in the government's delivery of services. When the program continued, these interruptions of the people's voice by the government went unacknowledged. Márquez and his co-hosts did not understand government publicity as a breech of their space of expression. Rather, they identified with the political project being celebrated in these interruptions.

Márquez invited viewers to call the station and voice their support and opinions about what should be done in response to the Pernia attack. His teenage niece was standing by to answer calls. Over the course of the hour, seventeen people called the station. Most callers were from barrios on the poor side of town, although one viewer called from a middle-class neighborhood. Several of the callers were affiliated with Catia TVe or lived in Márquez's neighborhood. The majority suggested that Catia TVe organize a march to RCTV, the commercial television station, to protest the attack. At the end of the program, Márquez invited community media producers and activists to attend a meeting at Catia TVe the next day to discuss what action should be taken.

Debating Redress

Sixty people involved in community television, radio, newspapers, and Internet sites gathered in Catia TVe's basement screening room the day after Pernia's attack to discuss the crisis and to strategize about the appropriate response. The group, two-thirds men and one-third women, sat in rows facing the front stage. Present were the directors of the most prominent community radio stations, a founder of a prominent pro-Chávez website, a lawyer who had agreed to represent Catia TVe, and many teams of volunteer producers from Catia TVe. Márquez positioned himself at the front of the room and welcomed everyone. He asked Lara once again to recount the incident. By that point, Lara had described the attack multiple times to radio and television reporters and his delivery was effective in promoting palpable anger among his audience. Márquez then opened the discussion with the proposal that they organize a demonstration outside the office of the Public Prosecutor two days later to demand that the government take legal action against the RCTV commercial reporter. He asserted that the majority of people who called and e-mailed the station about the incident advocated that Catia TVe organize a large demonstration in front of RCTV, the commercial television station. Nevertheless, Márquez was forceful in his belief that to hold a demonstration in front of RCTV would simply be falling into a trap of provocation. "It is better," he asserted, "to pursue this matter through official channels." Márquez ceded the floor for debate. Another Catia TVe staff member acted as the meeting facilitator, keeping a cue of names of people who wanted to speak.

"We need to organize a massive boycott against the commercial media stations," a community radiographer argued. A woman representing another barrio-based radio station asserted, "This is our fault because we sometimes think the revolution is complete. We need to organize the community media movement and integrate ourselves. Chávez has his bodyguards, but we have no protection. We have to protect ourselves." Another member of a volunteer production team from Catia TVe waved the 1999 Venezuelan Constitution above his head and pleaded to the group: "We can't let them provoke us; that's exactly what the opposition wants. We should follow the channels established by our Constitution." The next speaker, a man from a radio station, disagreed: "We can't just depend on our little Constitution. We have to defend what we've built. The state isn't in charge of the people. . . . Our mistake is to believe that the revolution is over. We can't just sit here and talk. This is a struggle against imperialism. We need to fight."

One of the codirectors of Catia TVe noted, "We have to organize and agitate people to take to the streets and to move on from the 'light' revolution. Since the referendum, nothing has been done.[8] We have to seize the media and build socialism." Someone else suggested that they organize a march to RCTV.[9] Several people spoke at once sparking a ten minute dispute over whose turn it was to speak. A man from yet another radio station eventually asserted his place in the speaking cue and commented, "We can only resolve this in the streets." A final commenter, a volunteer from Catia TVe, urged the group not to be provoked into rash action and that they had enough proof to win their case in court.

The smattering of applause died down as Márquez stood up in front of the group: "This attack against Catia TVe is an attack against all community media, against the *campesinos* [the peasants]. I agree with what our friend has said about taking the struggle to the streets, but we need to start with official channels. Catia TVe will be the center of this battle against the commercial media." Márquez urged the group to come to a consensus to hold a demonstration in front of the Public Prosecutor, as he originally proposed. He effectively wove a language of resistance through his proposal, incorporating aspects of what many of the speakers had said during the meeting, and located Catia TVe as the nucleus of the community media movement. Still, his proposal to demonstrate outside the office of the Public Prosecutor did not reflect what the majority in the room advocated as the appropriate course of action. Many people seemed frustrated that the government was not doing enough and wanted to use Pernia's attack to spark mobilization in the streets. Despite the hour-long discussion that reflected multiple perspectives, the group agreed with little debate, some more hesitantly than others, to adopt Márquez's plan, and promised to publicize the demonstration over their radio stations, in community meetings, and on the Internet. The proposal Márquez outlined before the discussion began was the course of action that was agreed upon at the end.

In this meeting, Catia TVe, which bills itself the "voice and image of the people," found itself in the delicate position of quelling grassroots voices of resistance. Catia TVe staff and volunteers voiced the more moderate perspectives about how they should respond. Márquez's direction of redress toward the state seems to have kept in check the more radical possibilities of the Bolivarian movement. Although several media makers did not feel that official legal channels was the best avenue of redress, it seems that they agreed to go along with Márquez's plan not only because of his effective leadership style but also because they recognized that he possessed the necessary social capital to negotiate through official channels and gain access to resources. It is clear that there is a complex web of relations through which Catia TVe negotiates their connections with the government and other community media producers, while at the same time less established community media outlets often depend on Catia TVe as brokers between themselves and government actors.

Hierarchical social networks, which link Márquez and Catia TVe to state actors and resources, probably influenced Márquez's decision to take the matter to the courts. He tempered the reactions of other community media producers to make the political scenario easier for the government. However, Márquez's actions can also be examined as an effort at everyday state making. The acts of waving the Constitution above their heads and asserting that state agencies are the appropriate place to lodge their complaints and demand justice instantiated the state as a legitimate institution within their reach and open to their influence. Yet, Márquez's call for a demonstration outside the public prosecutor's office suggested that state institutions had to be pressured to provide justice quickly through media attention and by a demonstration of the people's support for Catia TVe. In an interview with me two years later about Catia TVe's relationship with state institutions, Márquez said,

> I understand that there are many groups and social organizations that try to demarcate themselves from the state or from the government. But I believe that really in this moment, that's not the correct thing to do. I believe that what should be more important is, how do we contribute to the construction of the new state of the future? . . . Of course there are many revolutionaries that dreamed of armed struggle, of a guerrilla fight with the execution of traitors. But in Venezuela we are creating a historic process via an electoral path, with a military guy at the head, with a process where the people have come out to defend the institutions and it was the people that maintained those institutions in power. This, all of this, one has to know how to interpret and know how to manage things.

Márquez asserted not only that social organizations should take part in building a new state, but also that they had in the recent past assumed responsibility for defending state institutions (i.e., during the 2002 coup attempt and the 2003 oil strike). His statement was perhaps also an effort to deflect criticisms of Catia TVe for its close relationship with government. Nevertheless, Márquez's notion that the state needs to be co-constructed by nongovernment actors was a notable departure from seeing the state as impenetrable and beyond the influence of barrio-based organizations.

This meeting of community media activists also highlighted how the messiness of collective organizing is never far from the surface. Beneath the appearance of consensus at the end of the meeting, there was a level of political maneuvering and vying for power within the community media movement, contestation that could undermine its coherence and organized articulation. Community media groups compete with one another for government resources and many have asserted that they would prefer to be self-sustaining (see Fernandes's chapter). James Ferguson and Akhil Gutpa recommend that we question not only the "commonsense assumptions about the verticality of states" but also the "many received ideas of 'community,' 'grassroots,' and the 'local,' laden as they are with nostalgia and the aura of authenticity" (2002, 990). Antagonisms, conflict, and jostling for power take place not only between government actors and grassroots activists but within community organizations. Catia TVe, like most organized groups, is made up of individuals with different views and aspirations who compete for leadership. At times, the ability of community media producers to accomplish goals is obstructed by leaders who speak in their name. Catia TVe's cooperation with other community media organizations is sometimes impeded by their direct relationship with government officials. Participation in state making does not necessarily entail challenges to hierarchical social organization among barrio activists.

The demonstration held in front of the office of the public prosecutor two days after the attack attracted a crowd of about two hundred people, far fewer than some Catia TVe staff people were expecting. At one point, it seemed that there were more media producers covering the event than demonstrators. There were several journalists and camera crews from VTV, the main state network; Telesur, the new hemispheric cable news channel; RCTV, the private channel where Pernia worked; several reporters from community radio stations; and a reporter from a prominent pro-Chávez website. Catia TVe assigned one of its most physically imposing volunteers to act as a bodyguard for the RCTV reporter to protect him from potential aggression from the ranks of the community station's own supporters. The crowd shouted at the RCTV crew, "¡Golpistas, que se vayan!" ("Coup plotters, get out!").

The demonstration served two purposes: it was an opportunity for the community media groups in Caracas to show their support for both Catia TVe and one another, and it was a chance to generate more publicity for community media on a national and international scale. The demonstration also helped to legitimize and naturalize the state as the arbiter of justice. The choice to pursue the matter through official state channels worked to place the state in peoples' minds as the appropriate locus of political activity. Yet the demonstration, staged outside a state building, also contributed to a portrayal of the community media in Catia as independent of state institutions, a distinction that grants both the government and Catia TVe political capital. As Timothy

Mitchell notes, "producing and maintaining the distinction between state and society is itself a mechanism that generates resources of power" (1999, 83). In the end, the most important outcome of the response to the confrontation was the circulation of the event in the news (print, radio, and television). The effort to force the state to serve justice quickly was unsuccessful. The commercial journalist left the country shortly after the incident, and the legal case still had not been resolved by 2008.

Conclusion

While scholars have shown that in Venezuela both state and grassroots actors produce spectacular, magical displays that serve to promote and fetishize state power (Coronil 1997; Karl 1997; Taussig 1997), by examining grassroots actors' networks and everyday relations with state actors, we also find that people recognize the state as a collection of multiple agencies, organizations, levels, and agendas that are in their reach and can possibly be transformed. This insight allows them to undertake social action that cannot be dismissed as merely illusionary. Their actions have the potential to transform how they see their role in local problem solving and how they approach state institutions. Acknowledging community media producers' crucial role in everyday forms of state formation does not mean, however, that Catia TVe or other barrio-based organizations have been successful in "taking the state." Catia TVe, in fact, has not been compensated for Pernia's attack. Moreover, grassroots producers who enter state-run television stations struggle with censorship, and Catia TVe staff and volunteers worry about their editorial autonomy given the station's financial dependence on state institutions.

Nevertheless, the ongoing debate about the state taking place within Catia TVe challenges the "topographic metaphor" (Ferguson and Gupta 2002, 983) of the state as an abstract coherent entity above society that is implicit in much of the discourse of clientelism. Personal relationships with Eekhout and others who assumed key leadership positions in state institutions play an important role in how people's understanding of the state is shaped by their "particular locations and intimate and embodied encounters with state processes and officials" (Sharma and Gupta 2006, 11). They use social networks to participate in government processes.

Assumptions that the relationship between grassroots groups and government institutions is always vertical, automatically induces corruption, and creates weak democracies inhibit an analysis of the multiple impulses at work.

Social networks, while embedded in hierarchies, can contribute to encouraging participation and involvement in decision making. In the changing political landscapes in Latin America "openings from above and pressures from below have produced *a series of hybrid political relations* that question if not defy standard categories of classification and analysis" (Gay 2006, 197; emphasis added). In Venezuela, grassroots movements and the state are intimately intertwined. It is necessary not only to move beyond the assumption that the state is the repressive headquarters of power, but also to refocus our vision to see grassroots efforts, as Ferguson suggests, not necessarily as "local, communal, and authentic, but worldly, well-connected, and opportunistic" (Ferguson 2004, 394).

The issue of state funding at Catia TVe is a subject of constant debate and reflection. Expressions that "we are all state," "we are separate from the bourgeois state," "the state money is ours," and "we need financial independence from the government" compete and overlap. Rather than seeing Catia TVe's decision to look to the state to resolve the conflict with Pernia as an indicator of a lack of autonomy, as the co-option of social movements, or as the assertion of domination through clientelist exchanges, we might instead view this tactic as grassroots actors attempting to use the leverage they have to create state institutions that they can trust to serve barrio interests.

I have examined how ideas about the state are produced and circulated among community media producers who depend on the state to support their grassroots projects and who seek to redefine the state's role in the everyday life of Venezuela's poor majority but nevertheless remain wary of co-option. Haunted by the dichotomy between barbarism and modernism that lies behind many critiques of Chavismo, essentialist notions about the entrenchment of a so-called culture of clientelism in Venezuela hinder analysis of how social networks can be crucial elements of everyday participation in democratic state formation (Ellner and Hellinger 2003). Rather than defining a state as undemocratic, networks that contain relationships of unequal power are part of the way the state is constantly reproduced and experienced. In the long run, scholars need to approach this constellation of political practices as something that is not unique to Latin America. This case study of a community television station in Caracas should be taken as an illustration of a more global process.

My argument is not simply that clientelist practices are as legitimate as other forms of politics heralded by liberal conceptions of democracy. Rather, I have argued that traditional theories of clientelism that rely on a constitutive opposition between state and society cannot capture the complexity of these emerging state-barrio relationships, the everyday work of state making, and the negotiations of power taking place. Viewing traditional clientelist bonds as the simple exchange of political loyalty for resources or favors precludes an examination of not only the work and skill it takes to negotiate social networks but also the ways in which barrio-based actors might re-imagine and recreate the state through these very networks. This case provides insight into how the boundary between state and society can be strategically used to generate resources of power.

Intellectually normative boundaries (such as the divide between state and society), on which the theories of clientelism are based and which influence analyses of contemporary Venezuela, must be checked against developments of thought and practice among the organized poor. Beneath the surface of what seems for many critics of Chávez to be an unquestioning support for government on the side of Chavistas is a serious vying for power and a jostling of interests and forces seeking to determine the path that the Bolivarian Revolution will take. Community media actors are playing a key role in this struggle in an effort to secure access and participation for poor communities. The process of community media production in contemporary Venezuela is not only a means to create programming with a message, but also a social practice that produces ideas, relationships, and access to the state. The station bolsters the legitimacy of Chávez's government and also challenges the government to follow a redistributive project.

If one rejects both the frequently advanced notion that petro-dollars inevitably create rent-seeking, unproductive citizens and the modernist development discourse that makes clientelism a scapegoat for the failure of certain nations to modernize, it is necessary nevertheless to evaluate how personal networks operate in the context of severe political polarization. In the case of Venezuela, one set of actors has the cultural or social capital to appeal successfully to the government, while an opposing set of actors has the economic and political capital to appeal to international agencies and the United States government and wields considerable social and financial capital of its own. It remains to be seen, of course, whether Catia TVe members can create long-lasting state institutions that accomplish greater redistribution of resources and are founded through participatory democratic means. My fieldwork suggests that Catia TVe's visibility and status as the most prominent center for community media production creates the possibility that even when the government agenda and the community television agenda do not coincide, Catia TVe can intervene in political discourse, go against the grain of the official state message, and defend what they see as the interests of their community.

Notes

1. The conclusions I develop in this chapter build on this data, as well as on over fifty interviews with Catia TVe's staff and volunteers, Vive TV staff, and government officials.

2. The "spectacularization of politics" on television has been most visible during significant moments in Venezuela's recent history, such as the 1989 urban uprising known as the Caracazo, Chávez's televised apology for his 1992 coup attempt, and, most recently, the 2002 coup against Chávez (J. Hernández, 2004).

3. In order to protect privacy and confidentiality, I have changed names, except those of public figures such as government officials, the most prominent leadership of Catia TVe, and commercial journalists.

4. Two years later in 2007, debate over whether Chávez was democratizing or clamping down on freedom of communication increased when President Chávez decided not to renew RCTV's broadcast license after fifty-three years in operation, forcing the station to become a subscription satellite and cable network in order to remain in business. While I do not explore in this chapter the implications of this decision, my case study provides insight into the community media producers' overwhelming support of Chávez's decision to license the bandwidth formerly occupied by RCTV's broadcast signal to a new state-run television station instead.

5. The quotation appeared on a page of the Internet site noticierodigital.com, no longer in existence. It was reposted later on page 21 of http://www.redescualidos.net/forum. My translation.

6. *Ultimas Noticias* is known among Catia TVe staff to be somewhat more "balanced" between Chavista and opposition perspectives than the other major daily newspaper, which they assert leans decidedly toward the opposition.

7. Moreover, within the tense debate over whether the Chávez government has expanded or collapsed spaces for free expression during the 2007 nonrenewal of RCTV's license to broadcast, the government relied on displays of community media outlets as proof of the democratization of media access.

8. Chávez had won the August 2004 presidential recall referendum with 59 percent of the vote.

9. This suggestion must be understood within the context of Venezuela's recent history. Many private media outlets were fully complicit in the 2002 coup that briefly ousted Chávez. On April 13, 2002, two days into the coup, a violent demonstration was held by Chávez supporters outside the offices of RCTV, as well as the other private television stations and newspapers to demand that the media end the news blackout and report the popular resistance against the coup that had emerged to demand Chávez's return to power. The demonstrators also demanded that the news outlets call for Chávez's return and threatened journalists with violence if they did not comply. This difficult and violent past formed the backdrop for the Pernia-Lara drama.

CHAPTER FIVE

Radio Bemba in an Age of Electronic Media

The Dynamics of Popular Communication in Chávez's Venezuela

Sujatha Fernandes

HOST: Our great friend Nicolás Díaz is calling from the sector Santa Cruz. They have a *cofradía* [brotherhood] for the organization of San Juan Bautista of Macarao, and they're inviting all of the community in general to participate in the Encuentro de Tamboreros [Meeting of the Drummers] that will happen tonight in the street Río de Santa Cruz, on Saturday July 2—today—at two in the afternoon. And they're telling us that the girls are making a *sancocho* [traditional soup] there. And we'd like to give space on the air to Nicolás. Good day, Nicolás!

NICOLÁS DÍAZ: How are you, my friends, from Radio Macarao, from the parish Macarao. . . .

HOST: We're well and we want to say hi to all the people out there. We want to let you know that you're on air right now.

DÍAZ: Of course, and the neighbors from the parish, all our colleagues, the community radio, and all within this alternative movement, in search of a process of change and transformation. Look, we're here. The proposal is for the people to come by, to the shopping centre, between the basketball court and the plaza. Right now there's an important team making the sancocho . . . Joana, Materano, el Yoyo, Carmen Medina, Otilia. Here is the precious Guaya Márquez, Cecilia Salazar, Josefina Márquez, *la niña* Judith Vázquez, and Tiago. And of course, what we want is simply to give a kick start to this activity, something that, within our community activities in the parish, is necessary. (*Radio Macarao*, July 2, 2005; my translation)

The residents of the Caracas parish of Macarao have been celebrating the popular fiesta of San Juan since 2002, and the local radio station has been an important tool in helping them to organize this event. On a Saturday afternoon as residents take care of household chores, drop by to visit the neighbors, or prepare the evening meal, they listen to the local community radio station. They might stop by the plaza to see the drumming, or join in the dancing and partake in the traditional sancocho, or soup. Nicolás Díaz is calling in to the radio program on his cell phone, drawing on innovations of cell-phone technology and radio transmission to publicize his event. The mention of people's names, streets, and locations indicates the highly localized nature of community-based media.

Radio bemba, a figure of speech in the Caribbean meaning gossip or word-of-mouth communication, has found a new mode of expression in electronic technology. Community radio, assemblies, and newspapers form a layered set of publics that have expanded dramatically since Chávez was elected president. What is the relationship of community media to the state, and how do the connections of media producers to the state impact its functioning? How have community media contributed to new forms of participatory democracy?

Scholars have had different interpretations about the contributions of community media to a democratically functioning society. Some argue that locally produced media can foster plural spaces of communication and discourse, even taking up a decidedly oppositional stance in the case of minority groups (Urla 1997). Some suggest that in a moment of greater media consolidation and concentrated ownership, community media can democratize access to the means of cultural production. This makes possible meaningful self-expression and the right to be informed, which lie at the base of participatory citizenship (Remedi 1997). Others express concerns that the politicization of community media could make it vulnerable to partisanship and monitoring by the state (Tanner Hawkins 2006). While my study of barrio-based community media in Caracas bears out these diverse views, it also shows the field of community media to be a heterogeneous one, with media producers establishing different relations to the state. I propose that we look at the local orientation and social base of the media, the degree to which they facilitate deliberation and democratic decision making, their relationship to state funding, and access to technical knowledge as key factors.

There are multiple media collectives affiliated with groups in the barrios that have organic leadership. There are those who are linked to tightly knit, cadre-based organizations, where a smaller leadership usually makes decisions. There are some who have acted as brokers between the government and barrio groups (see Schiller's chapter, "Catia Sees You"). There are others with less formal structures, which operate through assemblies and collective decision making, at times leading to the emergence of informal cliques. Certain groups have sought to make strategic connections with state institutions in exchange for resources; others tend to rely more on self-financing. All of these groups have found common ground in the various electoral campaigns and initiatives in support of Chávez, restoring Chávez to office after the 2002 opposition-led coup and working to defeat the recall referendum of August 2004. But I argue that while some groups find it easier to maneuver among various levels of government, others have less access to state funding, privileging instead work in local spaces and a connection to the life of the barrio. An exploration of community media illuminates the new forms of associational life that have emerged in an age of electronic media. This study reveals the complex dynamics of power and negotiation in Chávez's Venezuela, as newspapers and radio and television stations balance their desire for autonomy and locality with an orientation to funding bodies and state institutions, albeit in varying ways. This balancing act is part of ongoing efforts to create spaces of participatory democracy and agency in the Bolivarian Revolution.

Communications Technology and Associational Life

Several scholars have addressed the reasons for the centrality of communications technology to new forms of associational life. The availability of communications technologies such as cable television and electronic audience feedback has led to political messages being constructed more through the mass media than through parties and interest associations (Bennett and Entman 2001, 16). Transnationalization is located primarily in the field of communications such as satellites and computer networks, which has meant that issues of nationality are also increasingly addressed in this field (Martín Barbero 1993, 208). The massive growth of communications technology has also facilitated the entry of citizens into the public sphere, especially where political parties and unions have failed to address their needs (García Canclini 2001, 23). But as many of these scholars acknowledge, the spaces available within the mass media are limited; although media culture is now much more a part of everyday political life, functions of deliberation, organization, and representation play a minor role.

Given the limited spaces available within the mass media for creative political action and deliberation, community activists and barrio residents have begun to utilize technological advances to produce their own alternative forms of communication. In the popular parish 23 de Enero (discussed in Velasco's chapter, "We Are Still Rebels"), there are about one hundred cybercafés serving some eighty thousand inhabitants. In a small sector of this neighborhood, Barrio Sucre, with a population of five thousand people, there are seven cybercafés. Most of these cybercafés have about ten computers, and they are always occupied. There are also Centros de Comunicación (communication centers), which emerged due to the availability of flat rates for cell phones. Since it is expensive to call cell phones from home or another cell, and because many people in the barrios do not have home telephone lines, street vendors set up booths where you can make calls. These centers are a vibrant part of the informal economy and communication technology. Text messages on cell phones are another utilized technology that has become an important part of local communications, as are *motorizados*, or motorbike workers, who work as messengers and run errands through the congested streets of the barrios (see Duno Gottberg 2006 and "The Color of Mobs" in this volume). All of this technology has come to be utilized by social movements in Venezuela, and in particular by community radio.

Radio has been one of the most important media of popular communication because of its privileged relation to popular culture. As Jesús Martín Barbero (1993, 181) argues, radio counterbalanced the unifying tendencies of television. Radio has a way of capturing the popular world through music, sports, and colloquial expression; it is able to attract more varied publics; and it is able to facilitate new social identities not related to traditional party and union politics. The radio is a part of life for most households in the barrios of Caracas. It is generally on all day in the home, whether as the sole source of information and entertainment, or as background noise. People will switch between government or private channels and local community stations. The hills and high locales of the barrios of Caracas (and the shantytowns and favelas of other Latin American cities) create an advantage for community radio stations, which are able to reach larger territories due to the natural height of their antennas. For example, Radio Negro Primero in Barrio Sarría has only a 14-watt transmitter, but it is located close to the Avila, a twenty-six hundred–meter-high mountain from which its transmitter operates.

Radio technology is basic and accessible as compared with television and print media. The community radio station Un Nuevo Día, located in a poor barrio in the hills above the old highway out of Caracas, began in the bedroom of one of the women residents. The residents put a borrowed mixer, a compact disc player, and a microphone on the woman's dresser, and they broadcast their signal on a small transmitter. Invited guests would sit on the woman's bed, and people would send in text messages via cell phones. This story is similar to many experiences of radio collectives globally (Remedi 1997).

By contrast, community television has been more dependent on state financing, and community newspapers have had a much harder time sustaining themselves due to a lack of resources and of people to write reports. Gustavo Borges, one of the founders of *Sucre en Comunidad*, a local newspaper in 23 de Enero, says that as community print media experienced an upsurge in 2004 to 2005, printing presses realized that they could make money from printing the newspapers and began raising their charges. For many community newspapers these prices became unaffordable and put them out of business. But radio and print media are also integrated in various ways. Interviews on radio are sometimes transcribed and reprinted in newspapers, or newspapers have spaces on radio programs. *Sucre en Comunidad* has a slot on Monday and Friday mornings on Radio Comunitaria San Bernardino; *El Tiempo de Caricuao* carries transcriptions of radio discussions about local history. Murals are also a popular alternative to newspapers, and have been referred to as a form of "street journalism." Mural brigades in the barrios, such as La Piedrita in 23 de Enero, paint over old murals and replace them with new ones regularly.

The Emergence of Community Media in Venezuela

There occurred a surge in community media in Venezuela after 2002, not only broadcast but in print as community newspapers began to appear in the barrios. In addition to legally recognized and funded broadcast stations, hundreds of other unsanctioned stations emerged, created and operated by a range of local groups throughout Venezuela. Not only have alternative radio, television, and newspaper outlets appeared in urban areas but they have flourished in the Amazonian south, the coastal north (with its rich Afro-descendant culture), and the Andes.

There are several reasons for this explosion of community media. One was the passage of new laws by the Chávez government in 2000 and 2002, which facilitated the legal recognition of clandestine radio and television stations. The Ley Orgánica de Telecomunicaciones (Organic Law of Telecommunications), passed in June 2000, promoted the right of community radio stations to exist. In January 2002, another law, entitled Reglamento de Radiodifusión Sonora y Televisión Abierta comunitarias de Servicio Público, sin fines de lucro (Regulation of Open Community Public Service Radio and Television,

Non Profit), established the conditions under which authorization would be granted to community radio and television stations. Following these laws, the government made substantial sums of money available for authorized community media. In late 2004, five billion bolívares (US$2.3 million) was given to community radio and television stations in grants for purchasing equipment, and at the end of 2005, sixty-five of these stations had received new equipment (Tanner Hawkins 2006). The funding available to community stations created an incentive for people to create their own stations and to seek authorization.

Another reason for the dramatic increase of community radio stations in this period was the desire of popular sectors to have control over the means of communication following the media blackout engineered by the opposition during the coup against Chávez in 2002. Chávez was removed from office on April 11, 2002, and at that time, the opposition journalist Napoleón Bravo came on the air and falsely broadcast that Chávez had resigned. While the opposition was taking over the presidential palace, the private media replaced its regular news broadcast with cooking shows, soap operas, and cartoons. The public was deprived of access to information, as the orchestrators of the coup took the government-owned television station, Channel 8, and several community radio and television stations off the air. During this time, it was mainly the alternative print media that was able to get the message out to the people about what was happening. According to Roberto, a worker at the Caracas Municipal Press, activists came to the press and labored to produce one hundred thousand copies of a bulletin, informing people about what was happening. Radio Fe y Alegría managed to continue transmitting during these days and began to make announcements about the coup. Through the bulletins, alternative radio, radio bemba, and the exchange of text messages through cell phones, people were able to pass on the news of the coup and come out onto the streets in massive demonstrations that would help put Chávez back into power two days later.

Several people noted that the events of the coup were the incentive that led to the formation of their own radio station. Rafael Hernández was one of the founders of the movement Macarao y su Gente, which emerged during the late 1980s in the popular parish of Macarao. Although the movement had dissolved in the mid-1990s, after the coup Hernández and some of the others formed a radio collective and began working to put their radio on the air. Hernández explained: "After Chávez regained power, on April 13, we decided, look, we have to accelerate the process of installing our radio because this [destabilization by the opposition] will go on and somehow we have to keep the people informed and we have to counter the negative campaign of the commercial media."[1] The media collective in Macarao had been given some equipment from the

Foundation for Culture and the Arts of the Mayor of Libertador Municipality (FUNDARTE) in 2001, including a low-power transmitter, an antenna, microphones, and recording equipment, but they were unable to go on the air because they lacked an office space for the station. When they heard the news of the coup on April 13, the media collective took the equipment to Miraflores, intending to begin broadcasting from there along with other radio stations. But the popular mobilization was swift, and Chávez was returned to power before they could set up their equipment. A week later, a resident of Macarao made available a small office space to the collective and on April 22 the first signal of the radio went out.

The combination of the new legislation, increased government funding available for the community radio and television stations, and the determination of the popular sectors to have access to their own media following the coup contributed to the growth in community and alternative media. Certain radio stations with a longer history and trajectory, such as Radio Negro Primero and Radio Perola, served as a nucleus for the multiplication of radio stations. In an interview, a worker at Radio Negro Primero described how once they received their authorization, they duplicated their application for other groups: "The detailed project that we presented to the government to obtain authorization was copied by twenty different groups; they copied the same project and put their signature, they just changed the name of the barrio." Legal assistance, technology, and technical skill were passed from one radio collective to the next, allowing for the rapid creation of functioning radio stations. Media activists went from urban to rural areas, bringing equipment and demonstrating technical basics of radio transmission. The idea caught on and before long low power radios mushroomed in cities and rural areas across Venezuela. Yet in the overall media landscape, community media still holds a relatively small percentage of the airwaves. Only 5 percent of the radio spectrum belongs to community radio stations, while 85 percent of the airwaves are still in the hands of private capital, and 10 percent are in the hands of the state.

Community media are distinguished from government and commercial media in several ways. For Gustavo Borges, community media need to reflect the essence, struggle, and spirit of the barrio, with reports produced by people living in the barrio. Commercial media tend to be focused on the negative elements of barrio life—complaints about the lack of services, violence, crime, and ranchos that collapse—without recognizing the positive aspects. Reporters from government-controlled media such as *Vea* are generally sent to the barrio when there is an official event, such as the inauguration of a new popular health clinic. According to Borges,

When they come, it's because there's going to be a big assembly, or an extraordinary event. But in the barrios there are extraordinary events every day. In a barrio where there's a high degree of delinquency, a high rate of drug addiction, of vagrancy, or where the kids have nothing to do, when a young girl decides to form a volleyball team on her own initiative and her own resources, this is an important act.

From the perspective of community media, the construction of news—as either the sensational reporting of tragic events or the media spectacle created around official inaugurations—needs to be reconfigured to privilege the everyday events that take place in the lives of ordinary residents of the barrio. By inviting the residents themselves to do the reporting—the organizer of the volleyball team, the housewife who teaches a literacy class, or the sisters who started a health clinic in their spare room—community activists, says Borges, emphasize the participatory nature of community media.

Community media are also distinct in that people reject the label of professional journalists and prefer to see themselves as popular communicators. The authority or knowledge that comes from textbooks and communication degrees is less valuable than immersion in the community and knowledge of the barrio. Carlos Carles is one of the founders of Radio Perola in the parish of Caricuao. With his signature baseball cap, baggy clothing, and goofy grin, he looks like just another one of the *chamos*, or kids, at Radio Perola. "We try to demystify certain concepts people have about knowledge," said Carles. "An old guy from the community who works with kids or organizes a soup kitchen has much more value to us than a cookie-cutter radio announcer with a melodious voice who doesn't tell us anything about what's happening in our community."

Practical experience is also valued more than formal training. An interaction between an established journalist from the opposition and a popular communicator from a local community radio station illustrated this difference. The established journalist, who was criticizing the community radio activist, said, "I have done a course of five years to train as a journalist. What have you done?" The popular communicator replied, "We did a course of three days, 11, 12, and 13 of April." The days of the coup were a baptism by fire for community media activists; the activist establishes his credentials not in any school or course, but in the growing collective awareness that took place during those days.

Locality, Place-Based Consciousness, and Identity

Community media activists draw on place, locality, and cultural identity in creating alternative languages of resistance and oppositional discourses to the private media. Arif Dirlik sees place and locality as signifiers for processes, rather than locations conceived in narrow geographical terms. While some theorists have tended to use terms such as *local* and *place-based* interchangeably, in opposition to terms such as *global*, Arif Dirlik (2001) argues that the global and local are always producing each other, and that the reassertion of place may provide a means of critiquing the power asymmetries implicit in globalization. This is precisely what is taking place in the case of community media in Venezuela, where the geographical specificity of community media has emerged in response to the homogenization of private media under processes of neoliberal reform. As in the United States, the consolidation of ownership in Venezuela has resulted in syndicated programming and market-researched playlists, which has in turn led to less diversity, fewer viewpoints, and a devaluing of the regional and local (Huntemann 2003, 78). By contrast, community media proponents have sought to ground their operations in the place of the barrio. Community media networks are based in local neighborhoods—examples include Radio Perola in the community of Caricuao, Radio Macarao in the parish Macarao, Radio Al Son del 23 in the parish 23 de Enero, Catia TVe in the parish of Catedral, and Radio Negro Primero in Pinto Salinas. These stations are part of the social and cultural life of the barrio and are often sustained by the barrio. But as I explore in this section, retaining their local vision versus developing broader audiences is a key tension faced by community media.

The themes that the community media address are generally local; they deal with everyday life in the barrio or the cultural life of the community. On radio and television there are talk shows, educational programs, cultural shows, sports segments, local history programs, children's shows, cooking shows, and a variety of music programs, including salsa, bolero, hip-hop, rock, and *llanero*, or country music. Community newspapers have editorial pieces and discussion sections, articles about sports teams and cultural events in the barrio, and pieces on local history, health, and politics.

The programming on community media is linked to cultural activities in the barrio, such as the religious festivals of San Juan and Cruz de Mayo. At the start of this chapter, I described the role of radio in promoting the San Juan fiesta in Macarao. Similarly, the radio program *Tambor y Costa* on Radio Comunitaria de la Vega helps to organize the Encuentro de los Santos Negros (Meeting of the Black Saints) as well as other fiestas in the parish. Francisco Pérez and Gilberto

Sandoja from the station frequently travel to the coastal zones during the fiesta time to record festivities for later play-back on the show. In July 2003, *Sucre en Comunidad* had a report about the celebration of Cruz de Mayo in the sector La Piedrita in 23 de Enero, with information about the history of the fiesta and the organizing committee. Catia TVe regularly makes short documentaries about fiestas in different parishes.

Popular communicators are concerned to integrate local media with the life and culture of the residents. Media activists promote and organize activities such as children's vacation plans, sports events, and musical activities, such as karaoke festivals. During the summer of 2005, the Radio Perola activists Carlos Carles and his wife Eli Flores were busy organizing a community children's vacation camp in the Andean state of Mérida. Carles announced on *Tomando Perola* (Taking Perola) that there was space for three hundred children and one hundred adolescents between twelve and fourteen years of age. Carles and Flores were working with Radio Eco in Mérida, as well as Radio Horizonte and Radio La Zulita to provide this opportunity for the children of the neighborhood. At the same time, Radio Macarao was organizing a karaoke festival in the street, by the Metro station. The residents entered the competition, and prizes were given by small businesses in the barrio. The radio station Al Son del 23 helped to facilitate dance classes, doll-making workshops, and boxing lessons for members of the community, and they organized a vacation plan for local children.

The radio is used as a means of reflecting on the meaning of the geographical and everyday place of the barrio. In 2005, four young women from the parish of Caricuao, aged seventeen to twenty-one, had an hour-long program on Radio Perola on Saturday mornings, titled *Poder Popular* (Public power). The young women, Maria Cristina, Gladys, Clara, and Lilibet, divided *Poder Popular* into distinct segments. These included an invited guest to speak about a specific topic relevant to the community, a news segment, a roundtable discussion about a particular current event, and then a segment called "Community Realities." During this final segment, the young women debated with each other, as well as with listeners, who called in or sent text messages via their cell phones. When I visited, the young women were addressing the theme "Living in the Barrio."

Maria Cristina introduced the segment.

Ok, it's 10:44 in the morning; we're entering the section, "Community Reality." Today, we're commenting on the theme of community in the barrio, because we speak about the barrio and we live in a barrio, but we don't know what the word barrio means. It's like that. So, look, when we try to find the meaning of the word barrio, for all that we can find in the library, in dictionaries, sometimes we still don't understand because the meaning can only be found in being with the people, in the verbal, in the physical, with the people. And at times it's important to know how the barrios began.

Maria Cristina contrasts the knowledge produced by written texts with the local and situated knowledge that is learned through daily life: it comes from "being with the people, in the verbal, in the physical." Clara chimed in on the discussion,

Exactly, supposedly we all live in a community, we should help each other out, like we commented in the first program. I agree that a barrio is not only the place where you live, it is to share our daily existence with each other, because they are the people who are closest to you, those who really know the problems that exist in the community. A barrio is not simply a hillside of stairs, a barrio is the community, it's your house, you are close to it, you live there. So, why should you be ashamed that you live there? I live in a barrio, Santa Cruz de las Adjuntas. And the reality is not what they have told you earlier—that if you live in a barrio you don't have a future, that if you live in a barrio you are a nobody. It's not like that.

As the children of parents who have migrated from rural areas, these young women have grown up their entire lives in the urban centers. They feel the stigma of being from the barrio, and at the same time this is where they seek meaning and identity. Gladys, one of the young women, says that "the barrio is a place and a way of life at the same time." Gladys's observation illustrates the notion of place as both location and process. The barrio is a physical space of narrow lanes and steep staircases, bodegas and open plazas, but it also encompasses a set of relations of power, kinship, and territory. Through their involvement in the radio, the young women are creating a place-based consciousness, connecting place to social identity. They are transforming stigmas of place and culture into positive signifiers of collectivity and community.

The interconnections between place, culture, and identity are apparent in the names of radio stations. The station Radio Negro Primero takes its name from both the barrio Negro Primero located in the parish and a mythical hero. According to media activist Madera, part of the project of community radio is claiming these local heroes who have been eclipsed by official history: "Everyone knows Bolívar, Francisco de Miranda, all the great leaders, but Negro Primero was a sergeant, a middle-level cadre. . . . We are revindicating those from below, those eighty percent who are segregated by official history, from *el negro* Sambo Andresote to Alí de España." Other stations also draw on the narratives of mythic chiefs and anti-heroes as they describe their own projects. Angel from Radio Tiuna noted that the station takes the name of a mythical indigenous chief: "Tiuna is one of the chiefs from here, from Venezuela. When the Spanish arrived they fought with Tiuna, with Guaicaipuro, all of these chiefs who were here, who are native to this country." Carles from Radio Perola incorporates the anti-heroes of Venezuelan history into the popular figure of Bolívar. On the show *Tomando Perola*, Carles describes Bolívar: "Simón Bolívar was not Bolívar. Simón Bolívar was also Páez, he was also Zamora, he was also Boves, he was also Piar." Carles refers to this mix of celebrated *caudillos* (leaders), radical populists, and anti-heroes, some of whom were suppressed within official historical narratives, only to be appropriated and recirculated in popular oral traditions.

Community media producers make claims to indigenous and black identity as a way of positioning themselves in broader relations of class and marginality. Carles identifies *el pueblo* (the people) as descendants of the indigenous chiefs: "We are the children of Guaicaipuro, those who screamed in the last moments of their lives, 'Come, Spaniards, and see how the last free man of this land dies.'" For Carles, el pueblo is an embodiment of their ongoing struggle against the colonizer: "We are children of indigenous resistance, Caribbean indigenous resistance. They almost wiped out our population, but we will not accept that the invader, the colonizer, can wipe out our dignity and our territory." Carles invokes the specter of indigenous resistance, not as a past historical relic but as a means to recreate a sense of collective action. More broadly what is taking place is a reframing of el pueblo from the virtuous foundations of the mixed-race nation to el pueblo as a marginalized, excluded majority who are seeking recognition and their rightful share in the country's wealth.

Popular communicators also elaborate and construct notions of blackness. Madera, a brown-skinned man in his late forties with a shaved head and a beard flecked with white, is a broadcaster on Radio Negro Primero. Neatly attired in a shirt with a collar and a pen in one pocket, he speaks slowly, carefully considering his words,

> Ok, continuing here from 101.1, Radio Libre Negro Primero. Only for black women and men. If you're not black, please change the dial, that's how we say it. Because blackness is not a problem of the color of your

skin, blackness is a problem of feeling, of commitment to others. . . . That's why we do this program, only for black men and women, to make visible what here they want to make invisible—that here there is no racial problem, that here there is no ethnic problem, more than racial, ethnic. So, we make it visible from Radio Negro Primero.

Madera's style is tongue-in-cheek; in making his program "only for black men and women," he is being provocative. Madera uses the radio as a tool to counter the invisibility of black people in society and his polemical style invites people to engage in debates about race. At the same time, he does not define blackness only on the basis of skin color or ancestry; he defines it as a "problem of feeling, of commitment to others." Madera gives the example of Ricardo Guerrero, a white drummer from the popular parish of La Pastora, who for Madera embodies this more spiritual notion of blackness. Identifications of blackness and indigeneity are often used to refer to a shared condition of marginality, or in this case solidarity with others, rather than physical characteristics or lineage.

There is little space for the discussion of cultural difference within either the state-run media or the private media. Madera says that the question of race has been invisible, or taboo, within Venezuela society: "Nobody here talks about the Afro problem. . . . I'll give you the example of our Constitution, that talks of the plural and the multiethnic. It names the indigenous, and then the whites, but the black is just assumed." The airwaves may provide new spaces for rethinking blackness and black subjectivity. As Kathy Newman argues in her piece on black radio in the 1940s and 1950s in the United States, while blacks were left out from mainstream visual representations, black *sound* found a niche in music and radio (2003, 122). Similarly, in Venezuela where racialized notions of good presence have led to the exclusion of blacks even in government television, there may be more opportunities in radio to assert a black presence through sound.

Local history programs on radio are one means of connecting expressions of cultural identity with narratives about place and of linking these to political projects over the reorganization of space. Popular historian and history professor Freddy Hurtado from the parish of Caricuao, has a local history radio show called *Programa Etnografía* (Ethnography Program), which he does on Radio Perola, Radio Macarao, and Radio Antímano, and he also writes articles in *El Tiempo de Caricuao*. Hurtado says that while official history is constructed through printed archives, popular history draws on the living archives: historical memory and oral histories of the residents. He is mostly concerned to excavate the history of the parishes and to tell the stories of the indigenous

Toromayma people who inhabited these parishes before they were invaded and displaced by colonizers. On his program on Radio Perola in January 2006, Hurtado said that knowing local history is the basis of regional and then national history and that "local power is the first expression of popular power." In contrast to the official versions of indigenous resistance and defeat, Hurtado speaks of the conquest and sacking of the country, and the massacre of the indigenous population, which he says need to remain present in the memory of barrio residents and young people. During his two-hour programs, he interviews popular historians; he recounts stories of colonial conquest; he tells stories about locales such as the metro station and what happened in those locales in the past; he talks about the roots of popular music; and he mentions popular drinks, such as the *solesombra*, which, he says, used to cost one bolívar.

The construction of this place-based historical memory is part of the project to create a sense of community and a shared past and moreover to reclaim public spaces that have been privatized or abandoned in recent decades. As Hurtado has mentioned in his show on Radio Perola, the parish of Caricuao has no Casa de la Cultura, and the local sports center was privatized. Spaces that were previously centers of community life were gradually sold to the private sector by local politicians or occupied by gangs, taking them out of the hands of the community. As a result, public space has become more militarized, with an increasingly repressive police presence in the barrios. The project of reclaiming these spaces is about not only confronting drug dealers or working with young people to give them employment and direction, but also demilitarizing the barrios. As Carles said on *Tomando Perola*: "We don't have to militarize our barrios or our communities; rather, we have to fill them with happiness, with color, with collective experiences, and important experiences." Community media activists have promoted community-based models of violence-prevention, in contrast to a law-enforcement model (Hayden 2004, 270). This is a crucial step toward opening spaces for increased participation and renewed cultural life.

Barrio-based media producers make appeals to the local—they address local themes, they seek to integrate their programming into the life of the barrio, and they address local history. This space of the local is vital in defining new forms of collectivity. Yet it is important to be aware of the ways in which local forms are themselves integrated with and produced by broader global forces. Most community radio stations and newspapers have websites, where they maintain blogs, livestream their shows, and connect with audiences and publics outside their immediate vicinity. Like other locally based social movements that, as Arturo Escobar (2001 205) says, "borrow metropolitan discourses of identity," community media activists draw on transnational articulations and narratives.

Also, media activists receive international support and participate in global exchanges and forums. But at the same time, the defense of place serves as an ongoing reminder of the power relations that shape the configurations of what Dirlik (2001) has called "glocality." It is through a reassertion of place-based memory and consciousness that corporate and private claims can be contested.

Holding on to place-based politics often comes into conflict with other tendencies, such as the desire of some stations to have a broader reach. The radio station Al Son del 23, operated under the auspices of the militant organization Coordinadora Simón Bolívar (CSB) is a case in point. The station was inaugurated in January 2006, and it functions in the headquarters of the CSB in La Cañada, a community of popular housing projects where the CSB was born. Ronald, a young man who works at the station as an operator, mentioned, "Now we would like to buy a satellite of 17 watts to cover 100 percent of Caracas and part of Miranda. We are now covering almost all of Caracas, but we want to cover more, there's a part where the signal fails." The television station Catia TVe also aims for this kind of broad reach. It began with a transmitter of 30 watts that covered the parishes Sucre, Los Junquitos, 23 de Enero, and La Pastora. It has since moved on to a high-potency transmitter that attempts to cover the entire metropolitan region of Caracas, although in reality the coverage is much more uneven. Other stations, such as Radio Macarao, are critical of this move and are committed to retaining the local nature of their programming. According to Hernández, community radio relies on highly localized codes and language—names of places, people, and events that may have no relevance to someone in another sector or barrio. "If there is a party in Kennedy, why do the people in Negro Primero need to know about it?" he posed. For stations such as Radio Macarao, a radical agenda is inseparable from a politics of place, which is more important than expanding their audience base and outreach.

Spaces of Deliberation and Collective Decision Making

Critical debate and deliberation play an important role in the functioning of community media, which have become a central means by which barrio activists engage in dialogue about the issues facing their community and formulate collective strategies. Bolivian activist Oscar Olivera (2004, 130) says that in the contemporary era, the site of working-class political deliberation has shifted from unions and party caucuses to the informal sector: "Deliberation—which for us encompasses expressing opinion, debating, deciding, and putting into practice—now occurs in the new world of labor that the *modelo*, or neoliberalism, has created." The local radio station is used by a range of groups to discuss ideas and promote their activities, including land and health committees, and soup kitchens. The producers of radio shows are often members of these different committees, and they report back on their progress and achievements. Although the missions and committees have often been designed and receive support from the Chávez government, the degree of democratic functioning depends on the integration of these programs into organizing structures, such as community assemblies and radio.

Assemblies have been integral to the formation of several community newspapers, as well as radio and television stations. *Sucre en Comunidad* had its origins in a broadsheet known as *La Esquina Caliente* (The hot corner), which was created by participants of street assemblies who regularly convened in the Plaza Bolívar. Radio Rebelde (Rebel radio) in Catia emerged from an assembly called by community leaders. Assemblies continue to be important in the daily functioning of many community radio stations. The rooms that house radio stations can also be converted into assembly and meeting halls. Radio Negro Primero has a large room from which it can broadcast and facilitate debates and discussions among members of the barrio during the regular programming.

Community media networks vary in terms of their internal democracy, decision-making structures, and participation. The radio station Al Son del 23 adheres to a more centralized style of decision making. Juan Contreras, the president of the CSB, is the general director of the radio station and has the final decision about programming and content. One of the station operators described the process: "If someone approaches us and has a well-organized project, we will study it and then Juan Contreras as the general director makes the decision about whether or not to accept it." This style of decision making fits with the general style of the CSB as a cadre-based organization with a strongly directive leadership. Although there is space for discussion and debate in meetings and on the air, the parameters are often defined clearly by the directive.

Other stations, such as Radio Negro Primero, Radio Perola, and Radio Macarao, function through a constant process of assemblies, meetings, and consultation. At Radio Negro Primero, the process of decision making is fairly diffuse and fluid. There is a committee that consists of all those who are active in the functioning of the radio, and they meet twice a week, either early in the morning before people disperse to do their work for the day or in the evening when people are back in the station. There are special meetings of the committee to discuss the budget, reporting back on the previous year and projecting the budget for the year to come. If a serious dispute arises, say between the radio station and the community, or regarding something that was said on the air, then the committee reconvenes to discuss the issue and decide what to do. Rather than a fixed structure, there is what Fernando Barret refers to as "a custom, a habit, a culture of convening assemblies to discuss things." He continued, "Our decisions are collective, talked about, and discussed methodically." The flexible structure helps them to respond quickly to events. For instance, when I was visiting the station one day, the activists were trying to decide whether to respond to the *buhoneros* (street vendors) who were demonstrating in Sabana Grande for relocation after their businesses were shut down by the Chavista mayor. The activists convened an assembly in the morning and decided that the issue was an important one not being covered in the government press, and so they sent the director of the station to cover the events for the radio.

Radio Perola also has a fluid and flexible structure. Decision making is done through popular assembly, which is convened regularly by the coordinating team (*equipo de coordinación*). There are small assemblies consisting of fifteen to twenty people and larger assemblies of fifty to seventy people. Carles describes the process of decision making as a "permanent assembly": "We reach agreements. We often say very critical things at times, but it is necessary in order to organize ourselves." They will discuss their work plans, the division of tasks, the programming, and the everyday functioning of the station. Like Barret, Carles sees this process of decision making in assembly as a habit that is inculcated over time: "It is a practice, that nobody instructs anyone else, nobody learns alone, human beings learn in collective, and this process of collective learning is a process of liberation as well." The assemblies are not seen purely as decision-making forums, but as spheres of dialogue that help them collectively build a political analysis and strategy.

The efforts by some community radio stations to establish fluid mechanisms of deliberation, flexible processes that can respond quickly to events, and a culture or habit of decision making through assembly has strengthened the internal democracy of those stations. However, at times the lack of a formalized structure can itself lead to the emergence of an informal de facto leadership. The absence of explicit and formally structured work teams may encourage the emergence of cliques and concentrate power in a few leaders. The general directors of the radio stations are male leaders or couples who have power to give orientation and direction to the radio.[2] Many of these leaders have a daily or weekly show—like Juan Contreras's daily morning show, Carlos Carles's daily *Tomando Perola*, or Rafael Hernández's weekly *La Revista de la Mañana*—that sets the agenda for the station. It is assumed that these male leaders provide an ultimate guidance to the collective, an assumption that is part of the broader political culture of centralized leadership.

Radio Macarao has implemented a more organized structure than the other radios. The communicators meet together in teams in order to distribute the tasks of running the radio more evenly. There is a production team that works on programming and seeks to fill empty spaces and ensure there is a balance between music, news programming, and community programs. At one point, this team decided that there were too many music programs, so they organized a weekend workshop to orient producers toward community programs, teaching them skills of doing interviews and reporting. There is a technical team, to monitor the technical needs of the station; an administrative team that oversees the functioning of the station; a publicity team, to look for local advertising and sponsorship; an education team, which organizes workshops; and a cultural team, to arrange cultural events in the community and forums. For example, the cultural team organized a public forum to discuss the evolution of Macarao as a parish, its recent history, and what the people of the neighborhood want for the future of their parish. Every team has four or five people who are in charge of their area and who report back to the broader assembly on their activities and decisions. The assembly consists of between eighty and ninety people who are actively involved in the functioning of the radio. It is the assembly that decides on the editorial lines of the radio, to the extent that such lines exist.

By participating in assemblies and work teams, residents learn skills of deliberation and collective decision making. This involves listening to others, respecting the opinion of others even when it is different to one's own, and learning to lose when one is outvoted by other members of the assembly, practices that reflect attitudes uncovered by Hellinger in his survey research (see "Defying the Iron Law of Oligarchy I" in this volume). In principle, most radio stations adhere to the notion that communication should be free, which means giving access to a plurality of voices on the air. Radio Macarao allows all residents of the barrio, regardless of their political affiliation, to participate in the station. As Hernández recounted, there are people involved in the daily running of the station who signed against Chávez in the referendum, or do not identify with Chavismo. And there are people, such as Hernández himself, who support the current of change associated with Chávez but do not see themselves as Chavistas. This plurality is not the norm, and Radio Macarao members have come under criticism for it, and have even been accused by some Chavistas of being *escualidos*.[3] For Hernández, this is part of a struggle against unilateral modes of thinking: "There cannot be only one way of thinking, because this goes against the principles that I conform to as a communicator. . . . Dialogue is confrontation, discussion, collective growth. If we're all in agreement, hey, it hardly makes sense, does it?" Listening, contentious argument, and re-spect are crucial aspects of collective decision making and community media production.

Self-financing, State Funding, and Technical Knowledge

Community media networks vary according to the localism of their work and the degree to which they facilitate deliberation and debate about the function-ing of the station and issues affecting the community. Another factor differen-tiating community media is their access to state funding and their degree of integration in the informal economy of the neighborhood. Some community media draw on their political connections to gain authorization and resources, some have tried to sustain themselves through local community support, and others rely on a combination of state and local funding. Stations with larger transmitters and broader coverage are more likely to attract bigger advertising grants from state bodies, and in turn these greater funds increase the techni-cal capacity of those stations. Meanwhile, stations focused on their local areas with basic technology and low power transmitters have less need for large endowments from the state. The access to technical knowledge has also been an important factor in ensuring democratic control and local management of radio resources.

Infrastructure, financing, and sale of airtime are crucial factors that influ-ence the nature of community media. A handful of Caracas-based stations and newspapers receive all of their funding from state institutions and do not need to raise money from the community or through local businesses. The news-paper *El Tiempo de Caricuao* has been strongly affiliated with the Chávez gov-ernment. Leonardo Heredia, one of the media activists with the newspaper, said that it started when they met with Chávez and he suggested they begin a community newspaper. Their first article was titled "Doing Politics in the Bar-rio," and it was written by Chávez himself. The newspaper is affiliated with the Bolivarian Bloc of Alternative and Community Media (Bloque Bolivariano de Medios Alternativos y Comunitarios), a grouping of government-affiliated community-media organizations.

In contrast to these state-affiliated community media, most barrio-based media seek some level of autonomy from the state. Critics of the opposition tend to see all community media as instruments of the Chávez government. An article published in the private daily *El Universal* on June 26, 2005, refers to the community radio stations as "radio-electronic media of the state," which are "employed for propaganda and political proselytism." The writer laments what he sees as the lack of quality and cultural homogeneity of the community stations and their bias in favor of the Chávez government. But this kind of analysis misses the negotiations and often quite heated disagreements between government bodies and community activists, as well as the subtle interplay between struggles for autonomy and forms of negotiation.

Media activists from Catia TVe and Al Son del 23 have successfully integrated themselves within official networks, using their political connections—often with former comrades and barrio activists now in official positions—to bargain for resources and visibility. The founders of Catia TVe and Al Son del 23 tell of how they approached Chávez personally with their projects and received support. While Chávez was visiting Catia, Blanca Eekhout was able to have a moment with Chávez to explain the idea of the community television station. Chávez intervened to speed up the authorization process, and Catia TVe was legalized in May 2002 (Tanner Hawkins 2006). The members of the CSB also sought a direct audience with Chávez as a way to promote their radio station. In 2002, Chávez came to record his weekly program *Aló Presidente* in a small hall near the Cristo Rey theatre. One of the leaders of the CSB, Cristel Linares, approached the president at this event and gave him their proposal. Nearly three years later, for lack of a locale and available frequencies, the radio was still not functioning. Guadalupe Rodriguez from the CSB went to see Chávez when he was presiding over the granting of land titles in Petare. She introduced herself as a leader of the CSB and said that in 23 de Enero they still had no community radio station. Eventually, the CSB took over the headquarters of the Metropolitan Police (PM) in their sector, a deteriorated building where activists and delinquent youth of the barrio were often hauled to be interrogated, detained, and sometimes tortured. With the tacit support of the Chavista mayor Juan Barreto, they took over the building and reclaimed it as their new headquarters, setting up the radio station there. According to Rodriguez, they received support from Chávez for the purchase of new computers and technical equipment for the radio.

The CSB and Catia TVe have strategically chosen to make themselves legible to the state in order to access resources. James Scott (1998) defines *legibility* as the ease of assimilation into an administrative grid, the ability of a given set of local practices to be aligned with the categories of the state. These groups have incorporated state slogans into their programming and have demonstrated their acumen in negotiating among various levels of government. The CSB fostered their links with Barreto's office, and used their strength as an organized group to obtain funds for refurbishing their premises, to pay for buses to take them to events, and to sponsor conventions and forums. The mayor's office paid for a computer center on the premises of the organization's headquarters, providing seventy-four brand new computers. At this center, the CSB holds classes in "computer literacy" for residents of the parish and other parishes in Caracas. Catia TVe also has a large building for its premises and receives most of its financing from the National Council for Culture (CONAC) and Petroleum of Venezuela (PDVSA), which helps with the large expenses of maintaining a television station. State funding provides a steady source of income, which may give the stations more political clout. For example, in "Catia Sees You" (chapter 4, this volume), Naomi Schiller recounts that when a reporter from the commercial channel RCTV confronted a young Catia TVe reporter and broke his camera in July 2005, the incident received wide coverage on state television broadcasts on VTV and Vive TV. The minister of information and communication then, Andres Izarra, called an official press conference on the issue. Although the young reporter was never compensated for the attack, Catia TVe used its contacts and access to media time in order to publicize its encounter with the opposition reporter.

Communicators from Radio Negro Primero also strategically made themselves legible to various state institutions, obtaining large amounts of state funding. After gaining authorization from the state, Radio Negro Primero moved to spacious new premises outfitted with a media cabin, Internet stations, and several new computers. The activists from the station submitted projects to various state institutions such as the Intergubernatorial Fund for Decentralization (FIDES) and the National Commission of Telecommunications (CONATEL). They were successful in obtaining numerous grants which helped cover their bills and facilitated the purchase of further equipment like recorders and financing of media courses. The core budget of the station is around 4.5 million bolívares (US$2,143) per month, which includes bills for rent, electricity, water, and a nominal salary for full-time staff. They use the grants and some small state advertising to cover this budget.

The workers at Radio Negro Primero have tried to use forms of democratic assembly to manage their relationship with the government. At one point, the government decided to install Infocentres, or small Internet booths with web links to government sites, on the premises of Negro Primero. There was disagreement about this among workers in the station, so they had an assembly to discuss it. After arguments for both sides were presented, they finally agreed to allow it. Making the decision on their own gave the workers a sense of agency over the installation of Infocentres. Radio Negro Primero also earns money through cooperatives; the workers have an audiovisual cooperative where vol-

unteers edit videos and DVDs, and an editorial cooperative that produces publications. These services and products are sold to government agencies to raise
money for the radio operation.

Other radio stations combine smaller amounts of government funding with
their own funds and local community contributions. Radio Perola has an agreement with the Ministry of Popular Power for Communication and Information
(MINCI) and CONATEL, whereby they received a computer, a mixer, and a new
transmitter. But according to Carlos Carles, the majority of the equipment used
in Radio Perola was bought or secured by members of the station and the community. Some community radio stations stretch the funds they receive from
the government. Radio Comunitaria de Petare received twenty-four million
bolívares (US$11,429) toward station functions for a period of six months from
the cooperative fund created by Chávez, which they stretched to last thirteen
months. Radio Activa la Vega received nine million (US$4,286) from CONAC to
buy new equipment, but they used the money to buy second-hand equipment,
and with the extra money they bought four antennas, which they donated to
other stations.

These radio stations rely heavily on voluntary labor and donations of equipment and resources. As Francisco Pérez from Radio la Vega said, "Sometimes
I do work here and there, and if I earn good money I put it toward the station
funds. Likewise, the other day, Gilberto had some work painting a house and
put in twenty thousand *bolos* (US$9.50)." Unlike the larger and better financed
community radio stations like Negro Primero, Radio la Vega is a small operation squeezed into a tiny room with the console piled on top of the computer
tower, and stacks of boxes and books taking up most of the space. Radio la Vega
is not able to put together the programming of the larger stations, but there is a
strong sense of ownership by the members of the media collective, due to their
personal financial contributions.

Likewise, Radio Macarao has received state support in setting up the station, but they prefer to maintain the everyday running of the station through
the contributions of local businesses. Radio Macarao received authorization at
the end of 2005, and in March 2006 the media collective began to build new
and larger premises for the station. The station was given twenty-seven million bolívares (US$12,857) by CONATEL for basic infrastructure, and another
grant from MINCI for electricity, air-conditioning, and equipment, such as a
new, higher-potency transmitter, a larger antenna, a computer system, recording equipment, and a high-quality microphone. The technicians from MINCI
installed the equipment and trained the members of the collective to use it.
These grants from institutions helped the radio to begin functioning in its new

premises, but they do not cover everyday expenses such as rent, services such as electricity and water, and payment of the operators and technicians.

To pay the monthly bills, Radio Macarao raises money through advertisements from the government, fund-raising events in the neighborhood, and contributions and advertisements from local businesses. Radio stations are permitted to sell five minutes of airtime per hour to local commercial enterprises. As a community radio station, the law prevents them from selling airtime to large corporations. The amount the station charges for the publicity depends on the kind of business. In Radio Macarao, larger businesses pay a monthly fee of six hundred thousand bolívares (US$186); established middle-size businesses such as a bakery, a shoe shop or an auto repair shop, pay a monthly fee of two hundred thousand or three hundred thousand bolívares (US$95 or $143); and small businesses pay around one hundred thousand bolívares (US$48). Radio Macarao has been successful in building a broad base of local financing. About 60 percent of their monthly income comes from fifty local businesses, and another 40 percent comes from state advertising from the Ministry of Finance, MINCI, and the national water company Hidrocapital. Through these transactions, radio stations tap into the vibrant informal economy that exists at the margins of the formal economy.

At times there can be conflict between the desires to build a base of financing through local businesses, and the potency of the transmitter. Radio Comunitaria Un Nuevo Día has a transmitter of 10 watts, which reaches most of the homes in the barrio. But there are no businesses in this barrio, and the transmitter does not reach to the central area of Catia, where local businesses are situated. Luis Peña, a member of the station, says, "If we go around soliciting publicity, what am I going to say to the owner of the bakery if he asks me whether the radio will be heard in his sector? I have to say, 'no.'" To reach the center of Catia the radio would need a transmitter of at least 100 watts. This would give it broader reach and possibilities of publicity, but it would reduce the highly local nature of the station, which has had a strong base in the barrio from the start.

Foreign funding is another source of income that is becoming increasingly important for financing community media. The newspaper *Sucre en Comunidad* has several digital cameras and a computer, and some of this equipment was donated by foreigners who sign up for Gustavo Borges's barrio tours through the paper's website. A Brazilian organization donated a transmitter to Radio Alí Primera, which they purchased in Rio Grande do Sul and sent to the southern state of Amazonas. The volunteers of Alí Primera made the fourteen-hour journey south to the Amazonas to pick up the transmitter. Although these alternative means are not easy, activists pursue them as a means of expanding and diversifying their resource base.

While some community media are more closely connected to the Chávez government through funding structures, others seek alternative means to reduce their dependency on the state and become self-financing. "The idea is not that we should be community media sustained by the state, but rather we have the capacity to be self-sustaining," said Carles. "Because if they give you money and they give you your daily bread, they begin to ask, why are you doing this, why are you doing that? We prefer autonomy in what we do." This insistence on autonomy is often at odds with the actual practices of stations such as Radio Perola, which does accept state funding. But media producers are also aware of the compromises that they may have to make to continue receiving state funding. Borges noted that there are major contradictions in receiving funding from officials such as the city mayor, because that may prevent the media from criticizing the mayor when basic services are not functioning. Or if the community newspaper is criticizing the oil company PDVSA about not maintaining its gas installations in the barrio, PDVSA may retract its funds. For these reasons, Borges has worked hard to secure a diverse base of advertising from local businesses and service providers in 23 de Enero for *Sucre en Comunidad*, including plumbers, radiator cleaners, grocery stores, bakeries, printers, internet cafés and clothes stores.

Community radio stations prefer to train their members in the technical aspects of managing the station, rather than rely on officials from CONATEL. The Christian radio station Fe y Alegría has carried out workshops for community radio stations on technical aspects of radio. At Radio Al Son del 23, three teenagers from the barrio were trained by Fe y Alegría, and they are responsible for sound levels, engineering, and production during broadcasts. These teenagers are also teaching other workers at the station how to manage the technical aspects. Beyond the radio, these youth are also working on the web page for the radio, and they have been creating and editing short videos. At Radio Negro Primero, the workers hold workshops in technical aspects of radio for other community radio stations, and those trained in technology often help out at other radio stations. Most stations recognize the importance of training their workers in technical aspects in order to defend the autonomy of the station. In a few cases, lack of technical knowledge has compromised the ability of the community workers to manage the station. After receiving authorization from CONATEL, Radio Rebelde in Catia found that the regulatory agency began to restrict access to persons who they deemed do not have the correct technical expertise. As activist Jesús Arteaga noted, "It was highly undemocratic, a radio managed without community input. . . . It didn't stimulate organization of any kind and the community was not represented in the board of directors." In June 2004, the station was without a signal for several weeks due to a technical problem, and because of the monopoly over technical expertise by a small group of people assigned by CONATEL, the activists were unable to resolve the problem. Technical knowledge can be used as a form of maintaining control by a small elite and excluding broader participation in the running of the station.

Conclusion: Emerging Blocs of Political Agency

Within the movement of community media, there have emerged distinct blocs, each with their own ethos, visions, and agendas. There are those organizations and media groups, such as CSB and Catia TVe, who are connected with the state and seek to expand their programming beyond their immediate territory. Although Schiller ("Catia Sees You") reports a highly democratic culture at Catia TVe, there is a danger that such funding may cause them to rely more on centralized methods of decision making, a cost of their success in obtaining large grants from state institutions and government-owned companies.

There has also emerged a heterogeneous group of media collectives, popular organizations, and cultural groups such as Radio Perola, Radio Macarao, Radio Negro Primero, and *Sucre en Comunidad* who retain a strong orientation to the local. Many of these groups operate through fluid and non-hierarchical forms of decision making, which at times produces its own de facto leaderships. But they are committed to experimental methods of critical engagement, building autonomous sources of financing and sustainability, and creating spaces for deliberation about issues in the community.

During negotiations with the state over media regulations and in clashes with major television networks, Catia TVe producers tended to align themselves with state agencies such as CONATEL. On November 14, 2004, CONATEL invited community media organizations to a meeting to discuss the formation of a cooperative to administrate a grant of five billion bolívares given by Chávez for community media groups. Radio Perola, Radio Negro Primero, Catia TVe, and other authorized stations were present at the meeting, but no unauthorized stations had been invited. Eli Flores from Radio Perola pointed out the exclusions from the proceedings by CONATEL, and she requested that some money be set aside to help unauthorized stations to complete the arduous process of authorization and that the meeting be postponed so that the unauthorized groups could also be a part of the discussion. The groups present voted on this motion, and the representative from Catia TVe among others voted in favor of continuing that evening without the unauthorized stations. Radio Perola, Negro Primero, and Radio Macarao left following the vote, refusing to participate in the discussion, while Catia TVe producers remained.

Producers from Catia TVe have acted as mediators, channeling discontent and urging moderation. In this volume, Schiller describes a meeting of community media groups in response to the incident where a reporter from a major television network RCTV confronted a young staff member from Catia TVe in July 2005. While members of Radio Negro Primero, Radio Libre, and Radio Perola among others spoke about the need to take to the streets to pressure the government to take action, the volunteers from Catia TVe urged a moderate approach and encouraged the group to work through official channels. By contrast, the former set of community media groups used the assembly and the radio station as a means to deliberate collectively and then act on their interests, often in tension with official directives and institutions.

Clearly then, in order to understand the relationship between community media and the state in Chávez's Venezuela, we cannot treat barrio-produced media as a homogenous grouping. This study has shown the differences among various media collectives as crucial to the ways that they negotiate with the state. We can conclude that the greatest potential for developing forms of participatory democracy may not be with those that are identified with or against the government, but those who retain a level of organizational independence, while making strategic alliances with the state.

Notes

1. I conducted interviews and made observations during nine months of field research in Caracas between January 2004 and January 2007.

2. Notably, this is a phenomenon mostly in Caracas, as outside of Caracas there are radio stations that are led by women.

3. "Squalid ones," Chávez's term for opposition supporters.

CHAPTER SIX

"We Are Still Rebels"

The Challenge of Popular History in Bolivarian Venezuela

Alejandro Velasco

On April 2, 2005, voters in the 23 de Enero neighborhood in downtown Caracas took to the polls to participate in a historic election. Over two dozen candidates representing a wide variety of local groups, but linked nevertheless in shared support of President Hugo Chávez, sought to consolidate a single slate of pro-government forces ahead of nationwide neighborhood elections scheduled for August. At first glance these local level primaries, unprecedented in Venezuela, highlighted the gains of grassroots activism under Chávez.[1] Indeed since first taking office in 1999, Chávez's calls to consolidate *poder popular*— popular power—by promoting grassroots participation in the democratic process had remained a common discursive thread. But beyond a dynamic electoral agenda including six nationwide referenda in six years, concrete signs of how "participatory democracy" might in fact be consolidated on the ground remained scarce. In this context, promoting organic community leadership through local-level primary elections lent credibility to what had largely remained an unfulfilled promise.

Yet a closer look reveals more about the limits than the possibilities of popular power under Chávez. Indeed primaries in the 23 de Enero reflected long-simmering tensions between national Chavista parties and "Electoral Battle Units" (UBES), which emerged in June 2004 after anti-Chavistas mounted a successful signature drive demanding a recall referendum against the president (Izarra 2004). That the referendum took place at all reflected the failure of Chavista parties to convince enough voters to refrain from signing petitions calling for the vote. Ironically Chávez himself secured their defeat, long railing against bureaucracy and elitism in political parties of old, but in the process undermining the credibility of political parties at large, including his own.

By contrast, the UBEs functioned as five- to ten-person committees designed to mobilize voters at the most local level by bypassing party bureaucracy.[2] By August, UBEs and their grassroots get-out-the-vote campaign helped score a referendum victory for Chávez. In October, they would secure another victory, helping Chávez-backed candidates sweep regional elections.

These various successes pitted locally based UBEs against national Chavista parties as competitors for the role of legitimate interlocutors of popular power. Unsurprisingly, that contest came to a head in the run-up to local elections in 2005. Along the way UBE members alleged they were barred from state media, denied electoral resources, and prohibited from running as official Chavista candidates. In response, UBEs and other neighborhood groups in 23 de Enero formed "electoral committees" to conduct independent primaries (CSB 2004). Once held, the winning candidates created United Popular Front 23 de Enero (Frente Unitario Popular 23 de enero—FUP23) as an electoral vehicle to run in the August elections, eventually finishing third in the neighborhood behind the officially sanctioned Chavista party and the Communist Party, both with national reach. Days later, FUP23 candidates staged a protest at the doors of the National Electoral Council (CNE) to denounce the pressures to which they had been subject throughout the campaign process.

This chapter examines the genesis of political dissent among urban popular sectors otherwise identified with Chavismo. Indeed, as a grassroots challenge to a political project that claims grassroots participation, the primaries were certainly remarkable; that they took place in the 23 de Enero was even more striking. An amalgam of 1950s-era superblocks and densely packed squatter settlements, *el 23*—as the neighborhood is widely known—has long been considered one of the staunchest bases of urban popular support for Chávez, the kind of place that journalists use words like *bastion, stronghold,* and *hard core* to describe (Parenti 2005; Relea 2005; Rohter 2000). It is here that Chávez comes to cast his own ballot, amid enthusiastic crowds. Several of the programs that would become highly popular *misiones* were piloted in el 23.[3] And election returns from nationwide contests consistently locate el 23 as one of the three major areas of electoral support in Caracas for Chávez and pro-government candidates.[4] But as the primaries reflect, alongside these expressions of support also arise direct challenges to the hegemony of Chavismo. In October 2004, when the newly elected Chavista mayor of Caracas announced his choice for *jefe civil* (the highest, parish-level civilian authority), local groups staged an insurrection and installed their own appointee. Earlier, armed groups disenchanted with what they regarded as the government's inability to confront the opposition government of Caracas, coordinated an assault against city police, forcing Chávez to distance his government from what he referred to as "anarchic groups" in el 23 (Rojas 2002; Viloria 2002).

What accounts for these conflicting currents of loyalty and disloyalty in the heart of Chavismo? How do we make sense of these wide-ranging expressions of local autonomy, from primary elections to armed conflict? What influences shape popular understandings of the limits and possibilities of revolutionary change in Venezuela? And what are the contours of what Sujatha Fernandes (2006) has called "critical social movements," neither independent from nor beholden to Chávez? To be sure, internal tensions are common among movements struggling to consolidate transitions from one regime type to the next (Mayer 2000). In Latin America, two decades of research have exposed the fraught nature of revolutionary dynamics, more often marked by the push and pull of local and national sectors than by the design of central leaders and parties; more often characterized by everyday claims to rights and citizenship than by disputes over material interests and resources (James 1988; Joseph and Nugent 1994; Rubin 1997; Winn 1986).

Yet as David Smilde notes in his introduction to this volume, the relationship between urban popular sectors and the Bolivarian Revolution continues to be seen primarily in terms of Chávez's enduring leadership, based in turn on emotional links and the distribution of goods and services (see "The Misiones of the Chávez Government," by Hawkins, Rosas, and Johnson, in this volume; see also Hawkins 2003; Roberts 2003). Those taking a longer view point to Venezuela's economic downturns of the 1980s, and the ensuing disenchantment with a once-famed pact system, to suggest that popular sectors are what drive Chavismo's most radical tendencies (Corrales 2006; Ellner 2005).[5] In either case, assessments of popular sectors' political culture seem again and again to derive from top-down structural analyses that leave local trajectories of organizing and mobilization unexamined, thereby marginalizing the complex and contradictory ways in which popular sectors engage with the Bolivarian Revolution. As Daniel Levine has noted, "The protest cycle of the last decade or so draws on a long, and as yet, for the most part, unwritten history of organization, communication, and the articulation of positions. New groups and informal networks were created, whose continuing social presence shaped new issues, and served as points of attraction that elicited citizen interest, gave experience in common action, and nurtured activism on a small scale" (2002, 260).

This chapter traces patterns of local activism in el 23 before both the onset of economic crisis in the 1980s and the rise of Hugo Chávez in the 1990s. It mines this period for clues about how urban popular sectors came to understand their relationship with the state. These popular histories pose a challenge to a political project aimed at consolidating a "complete break with the past," in the process marginalizing local traditions of struggle and giving rise to tensions well expressed in the caption of a local placard: with or without revolution, "Seguimos siendo rebeldes" (We are still rebels).

Founding Paradoxes in the 23 de Enero

In December 1955 General Marcos Pérez Jiménez, who had cemented dictatorial rule three years earlier, inaugurated Venezuela's largest public housing project in downtown Caracas (Pérez Jiménez 1955). In its first phase it consisted of thirty-five rectangular monoliths, eleven of them as high as fifteen stories, built to accommodate fifteen thousand residents (López Villa 1986; see figures 1 and 2). But the neighborhood was meant to house more than people. It also symbolized the promise of Pérez Jiménez's "New National Ideal," his vision of a modern, urban nation built on the foundations of massive public works projects (López Villa 1986, 1994). Indeed, rural migration patterns going back to the mid-1920s, coupled with grandly conceived but poorly implemented urbanization policies in the 1930s and 1940s (Almandoz 1999; Frechilla 1994), contrived by 1950 to generate over twenty-eight thousand "miserable *ranchos*" in and around Caracas hillsides, "generally [consisting of] one cardboard-walled room, wooden planks and a zinc roof" (C. Villanueva and Cepero 1953, 115). The figure represented 25 percent of Caracas households. It also marked a twofold increase in just nine years.[6] But more importantly for the dictatorship (and in contrast to some revisionist ideas about the ranchos and barrios discussed by García-Guadilla in her chapter, "Urban Land Committees"), according to its principal urbanist, Carlos Raúl Villanueva, the proliferation of ranchos "in the face of Caracas's steady growth, seemed like an implacable indictment." Indeed, "housing construction in these sectors [had] been completely anarchic and in many cases clandestine," amounting to an imminent "threat" against "society," "the individual," and the "aesthetic" integrity of all public works projects planned for Caracas within the soon-to-emerge New National Ideal (Banco Obrero 1954). In order to score "another conquest in the state's program of social action in favor of the least favored classes," according to Villanueva, ranchos "had to disappear" (1953, 115).

And disappear they did, in a "battle against the rancho" officially announced in 1951 (Banco Obrero 1951). In the area that would become the 23 de Enero, Pérez Jiménez condemned ten barrios for demolition, making use of a 1947 law enabling expropriation "in areas considered essential for the security or

Figure 1 Aerial view of 23 de Enero housing blocks. Photo in both the Banco Obrero and the Ministerio de Obras Públicas archives, reproduced in "La vivienda popular en Venezuela," *Integral*, no. 7. Caracas: Facultad de Arquitecturay Urbanismo, Universidad Central de Venezuela (1957).

defense of the Nation."[7] In the construction frenzy that the historian Ocarina Castillo D'Imperio (1990) has aptly named "the bulldozer years," homogenizing the problem made possible homogenous solutions that could be implemented quickly and prominently to effect a decisive victory. The superblocks well fit these needs. Introduced in 1951, in concept the blocks consisted of free-standing *unidades vecinales* (neighborhood units) equipped with terraced duplex apartments, roof-top walkways and greeneries, and collective services at both roof level and on the first floor (López Villa 1994; C. Villanueva and Cepero 1953). By 1957 the finished project would grow to encompass seventy-eight buildings, including thirty-eight fifteen-story "superblocks." All told the new neighborhood was capable of housing nearly seventy thousand people (Carlson 1961). In naming the neighborhood 2 de Diciembre, the 1952 birth date of his dictatorship, Pérez Jiménez confirmed what its unparalleled dimensions suggested: the superblocks were the "material expression" of *perezjimenismo*, the president's broader ideological vision for a modern Venezuela (López Villa 1986); their working-class inhabitants were symbols of the regime's popular

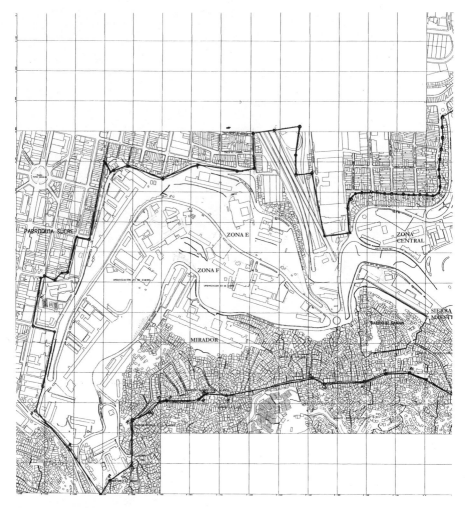

Figure 2 Map of the 23 de Enero parish and its subdivisions. Source: Provided by Alcaldía de Caracas (Caracas mayoralty), obtained in 2002.

foundations. Located within sight of the presidential palace, defense ministry, and Congress, the blocks formed a symbolic axis reflecting Pérez Jiménez's control over society's principal elements.

But the dictatorship's swift and uncompromising attacks on ranchos had established a matrix of confrontation that closed off dialogue with the state, thus channeling even mild discord toward an only option of resistance. For instance in clearing the terrain for 2 de Diciembre, demolition teams had made no distinction between ranchos and "well-constituted and traditional" barrios.[8]

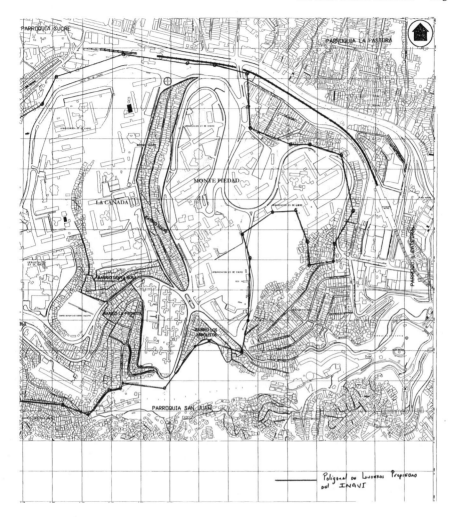

In turn, residents forced to move to the 2 de Diciembre faced their relocation in various ways. For some, especially recent arrivals to Caracas, the move represented, as Pérez Jiménez had intended, a marked improvement in their standards of living. For others, primarily among those who witnessed their longtime communities razed to make way for densely packed superblocks, forcible relocation generated predictable discontent. In both cases, the common thread lay in experiences of community life forged around both material demands and clandestine political activity in their barrios. This camaraderie and its attendant organizing networks persisted and at times grew stronger in 2 de Diciembre, as entire neighborhoods were moved en masse, often to the same building, sometimes to the same floor.

Consider the following example. On April 30, 1949, neighbors in the Tiro al Blanco sector in northern Caracas published the inaugural issue of *Laberinto*, an independent biweekly broadside. On the front page, in what would become a standard feature, was a description of the community's basic needs, water constituting an early lack. Other sections included a murder-mystery serial novel, a literary segment featuring poetry, birthday announcements, and a "muchachas del barrio" feature showcasing an interview with a local female youth. *Laberinto* illustrates the associative networks that underlay community activism in urban popular sectors later forced to relocate to the superblocks. Indeed in 1955, Tiro al Blanco became the first neighborhood razed to relocate its residents to the just completed 2 de Diciembre.

Expropriations and adjudications persisted as a major source of disaffection toward the state. During its construction between 1954 and 1957, work on the 2 de Diciembre took place in six-month cycles. From December to May construction slowed almost to a standstill before commencing again at breakneck speed around June. On the one hand this peculiar practice made possible, indeed necessary, record-setting rates of construction.[9] On the other hand, it meant that all work—from evictions, to temporary relocation, to leveling, to construction, to adjudication of new housing—took place simultaneously. The resulting bottlenecks in expropriations and adjudications were a tinder box of bitterness, as many forced from their homes in June were further forced to wait months beyond December to return to what the regime had billed as "paradise lost" (López Villa 1986) even as new apartments sat vacant.[10] In the fourth trimester of 1957, so as to accommodate the third, final, and largest phase of 2 de Diciembre, expropriations spiked 500 percent, marking an unprecedented rise that translated into unparalleled social frustration.

This simmering frustration in late 1957 coincided with mounting pressures from both military and civilian sectors for Pérez Jiménez to resign. Yet by the time authorities understood the unintended consequences of their hasty urbanization agenda there was little room for a selective response, leading instead to broad militarization of the neighborhood beginning in December 1957. Far from neutralizing clandestine political work, the government's response helped to expand networks of solidarity among residents, fueling the kind of key urban support for the struggle for Venezuelan democracy that would prove vital in lending popular legitimacy to the military coup on January 23, 1958. Within days, the 2 de Diciembre "went from being a symbol of the dictatorship to a symbol of the democratic victory against it" (Orellana de García-Maldonado 1989, 172). An unsigned article in *El Universal* stated, "The fury unleashed upon residents of that populous neighborhood," alongside the final demise of Pérez Jiménez, "gave rise to a proposal asking the Board of Governors [*Junta de Gobierno*] to change the name of the superblocks from 2 de Diciembre to 23 de Enero."[11] Renamed 23 de Enero, it would again honor both popular strength and the promise of a republican ideal, only this time at the service of a new liberal democratic order. And just as it had during the dictatorship, a tense interplay between conflict and support marked the state's relationship with its namesake community.

"La Pelea Era Brava" (The Fight Was Fierce): The Ambiguous Politics of Radicalism, 1960s

In the wake of Pérez Jiménez's ouster, political elites sought to consolidate democratic order by opening spaces for dissent under carefully crafted rules of consensus building. Moving away from the zero-sum politics that had doomed earlier efforts at democratization, political, military, clerical, and labor leaders agreed to what Fernando Coronil has referred to as an "agreement to make pacts," steering economic and political incentives to opposition seen as legitimate through a well-oiled institutional apparatus (1997, 229). Meanwhile opposition considered "illegitimate" faced marginalization and punishment. The result was a system highly efficient at managing conflict from within but highly inefficient at handling conflict from without, leading to party splits and guerrilla conflict that would shape Venezuela's political landscape for much of the 1960s.

In el 23, the tension between conflict and consensus that underlay Venezuela's political system during the years of democratic transition would find expression through a seeming paradox: while electoral support increased for the nascent democratic regime, violent opposition also found a strong and lasting base. The roots of this tension lay in what residents recall as the National Guard's "occupation" during the second presidency of Rómulo Betancourt (1958–63), which gave shape to an undercurrent of radical political action in the neighborhood. The occupation responded to urban guerrilla activity during the transition to democracy, creating a climate of intense conflict in el 23. Period headlines give a sense of the violence: "23 de Enero . . . Gunned Down," "1500 National Guardsmen and Political Police Agents Assault 23 de Enero," "Unrest All Day in 23 de Enero: Six Dead, Forty Wounded," "Disorder

in 23 de Enero."[12] Because it was set against the backdrop of the consolidation of democracy, the militarization of a neighborhood ironically named after
democracy's founding date seemed all the more striking. Indeed, these contradictions and the violence that characterized them were not lost on residents,
even among those who professed loyalty to the parties then in power, AD and
COPEI, respectively. Ramón López, a lifelong AD militant whom I interviewed
in 2005, heavily criticized Betancourt and the difficulties his administration's
record in el 23 created in the campaign for his eventual successor, Raúl Leoni.
Still, voter rolls in el 23 grew during the elections of 1963, 1968, and 1973, even
if not apace with national levels, as did preferences for the bipartisan system
(Consejo Supremo Electoral 1983). What accounts for this apparent contradiction, and how deep did popular support for representative democracy and its
leading parties run in practice?

Testimonies offer partial answers. By the mid-1960s, the insurgency settled
into stalemate after any real chance of victory crumbled; popular support faded
for radical leftism while it increased for the bipartisan system. Electoral statistics, insurgent leaders' memoirs, and institutional analyses of Venezuela's party
system sustain this long-held view in the literature.[13] But local testimonies offer
new insight into the troubled context in which this process took place, suggesting that just correlating the unfeasibility of guerrillas' military objectives
with waning urban popular support offers an incomplete view. For example,
AD militants in el 23 point to a kind of pathological aversion to communism
in barrios. Ramón López, an AD militant since the 1940s and among the first
residents of the 2 de Diciembre neighborhood, noted in an interview with the
author: "AD always had more support than the communists. No one liked the
communists. Do you know why no one liked them, why the people never liked
the communists? . . . because they have that vision, of communism, what they
do is kill people to take over their stuff, that's a vision that's been created, from
Russia to Venezuela."[14]

Yet this political-culture analysis underestimates the lasting influence of the
Communist Party of Venezuela (PCV) in organizing against the dictatorship
among popular sectors like those resettled in el 23 (Ray 1969). Despite its exclusion from the Pact of Punto Fijo that shaped representative democracy after
1958, the PCV was well represented in the Caracas congressional delegation
elected that year, including one envoy—Eloy Torres—from el 23, who in 1962
would go on to participate in a failed coup against the government of Rómulo
Betancourt. Through its weekly organ, *Tribuna Popular*, the PCV also targeted
el 23 as a source of support, publishing a weekly column under the title "En el
23 de enero" about social and political goings-on in el 23 throughout 1958 and
1959. In 1960 it expanded its column to include all barrios of Caracas. Between

1962 and 1969 *Tribuna Popular* was banned as part of the counter-insurgency campaign waged during the administration of Raul Leóni (AD). When it was again legalized, *Tribuna Popular* continued its column on el 23, this time under the title "Tribuna del 23."[15] Meanwhile Eloy Torres and his wife Carmen would continue to participate prominently in the social and political life of Venezuela in general and their neighborhood in particular. While Eloy would go on to help found the Movimiento al Socialismo (MAS) party in 1971, Carmen dedicated herself to bringing material benefits to el 23 in the form of health centers and forming women's action committees to solicit gas and telephone service.[16]

Torres's partisan affiliation signals another problem with applying a strict political-culture analysis to el 23. Classifying all 1960s guerrilla movements as communist overlooks the insurgency's ideological fault lines, which were soon exposed by the state's increasingly effective military campaigns. What complicated the picture was the high representation of disenchanted AD militants in the ranks of the insurgency. In fact, it was generational and ideological fissures within AD that fueled three well-documented splits in the party between 1958 and 1968. Each break led to the creation of new, more militant factions that promoted guerrilla warfare against a system by which they felt betrayed as socialists. In this context, while all insurgents believed that the social democracy Betancourt promoted after 1958 was neither socialist nor democratic, their struggle was marked more by doctrinal debates regarding the contours of real democratic socialism than by plotting the task of wresting political power in the soviet or Cuban style. The result was a series of internal fractures in which the PCV constituted only one tendency among many, more often lending a voice of criticism than of support to guerrilla warfare (Alexander 1969; Velásquez 1979). In this context, residents of el 23 were more likely to view insurgent actions in their community as strands of student protest movements than as communist take-over campaigns.

Seen as students rather than hardened political partisans, insurgents in el 23 benefited at times from a parental kind of support, as when women lent their homes as impromptu safe houses or makeshift infirmaries. Consider the following testimony from Lourdes Quintero (LQ), at the time a mother of two toddlers in block 37 of Zone F. Recalling armed clashes in the early days of the insurgency, Señora Quintero related the following to me (AV) in a 2005 interview:

LQ: One time the police were chasing some kids, students, coming up [the stairs] with crates full of bombs. We opened the door [and said], "Leave those bombs here and keep on running."

AV: They came in?

LQ: Yes, we opened the door. . . . They were running, yelling, "Help us! Help us! Help us!" And we opened the door, and they left a crate here and then we threw it down the chute, all bombs. There were many, the fight was fierce [*la pelea era brava*].

To be sure, it is difficult to glean the extent to which these forms of seemingly spontaneous support reflected broader ideological affinities. In the case of Quintero's testimony, however, what emerges is a pattern of material aid for the insurgency that seemed to reflect a spirit of pragmatic solidarity. Recalling another instance, Quintero noted,

AV: But did you sympathize with the students? That is, did you understand them?
LQ: Well, it's not that we understood them, but we helped them.
AV: How did you help them?
LQ: For instance one time a kid burned his back with a bomb, because when he threw it, it fell on his back. Two kids brought him here, we kept him, treated him, well, we helped them, we gave them water, and food, and whatever we could. They were going around hurling . . . and this was full of students, but I don't remember for what purpose, why, how it all started. I know it was during the government of Betancourt, very tough.
AV: Were the students communist?
LQ: Apparently. They came here for that. They came from below for that. Downstairs it was full of tanks.
AV: And were there many soldiers or police?
LQ: Many military, not police, military.
AV: And did you have to help a lot of people?
LQ: Yes of course, everyone around here helped the students.
AV: So the people in the building helped?
LQ: Of course, they were young kids, students.
AV: And were there people who did not want them here?
LQ: No, everyone lent a hand, some didn't because they were afraid, but others did, we helped them a lot, because they were young students.[17]

What this interview suggests is that behind the waning urban popular support for 1960s insurgent movements, or behind rising acceptance of representative democracy, lay more quotidian concerns regarding violence and the attendant difficulties it posed for everyday life. In el 23 these concerns gave rise to at least three political choices: (1) participation in national elections as a form of punishment vote (*voto castigo*) against radical leftism; (2) participation in national elections to reject leftist political parties born in the wake of pacification—an early 1970s policy of granting amnesty to demobilized guerrillas in order to incorporate them into the political system—considered tautologically as sell-outs (*vendidos*) for acceding to the plan or "the same radicals" (in either case untrustworthy); and, (3) participation in national elections as an admission of defeat by rank-and-file militants and sympathizers of the guerrilla movement, and as an attendant recognition that social democracy as represented by AD had indeed won and should therefore be afforded a vote of confidence.

Consider the testimony of Ravin Granier Asuase Sánchez, who as a teen in the 1960s participated in the urban guerrilla campaigns in el 23. He recalled an AD rally in the early 1970s: "When I saw an Acción Democrática rally come down this road, openly identified as *adecos* [AD partisans], I felt that, well, that we were screwed. When I saw that march come by here with people carry Acción Democrática flags, for me that was the final proof that we were screwed. . . . We, in that era, were defeated by the *adecos*."[18] Admissions of defeat among demobilized guerrillas occasionally translated into very active—and paradoxical—cooperation with the state, as was the case with those from el 23 who went on to fill the ranks of the military, the urban or political police services, or the intelligence agencies, in short the same repressive apparatus against which they had squared off as insurgents.[19]

The common thread during the 1960s was the way in which the political struggle between the Punto Fijo establishment and leftist guerrillas was overwhelmingly focused in el 23, even if statistically the levels of ideological adherence to either front were limited. On the part of insurgents, their emphasis on doctrine rather than popular support exposed their indifference toward social goals. On the part of the state, its inattention to the social demands of el 23 was manifest in the performance of its Worker's Bank (Banco Obrero—BO) charged with running el 23. During the dictatorship the BO had pursued a housing policy almost exclusively focused on urban centers and Caracas in particular, as the superblocks well illustrated. On coming to power in 1958 under Betancourt, AD reversed this policy, focusing on rural areas and urban construction outside Caracas.[20] But the BO proved institutionally ill-equipped to handle the dramatic turnabout without sacrificing efficient management of its superblocks in Caracas.

This was especially true in el 23 where nearly half of the apartments were seized by squatters in the days immediately following the fall of the dictatorship, which generated an immense challenge when rents were normalized, resulting in staggering financial losses for the BO in the ensuing years.[21] At the same time, squatter settlements arose in areas of el 23 that had been designated as parks and footpaths, presenting new challenges and requiring more investment in infrastructure and maintenance at precisely the time when the fledgling democratic regime moved the foci of its development policy outside Caracas.[22] In this context el 23 became a state burden not just politically but also administratively, and the latter lost out. What was sidelined, then, by both militant activists and the state, was attention to residents' social demands: efficient water, sewage, and waste management services; roads and elevator maintenance; and more public spaces. Against this backdrop, pacification under President Rafael Caldera (1969–73) created an aperture for community work to take the forefront in organizing in el 23, rather than political militancy. Against this backdrop, an alternative current of activism gained force, one emphasizing community needs over political aims and resorting to unarmed, if not always passive, forms of collective action to achieve results.

Community Activism and Student Protest, the 1970s

In March 1969, Rafael Caldera was sworn in as president in what would be seen as the defining moment of Venezuela's democratic consolidation, marking as it did the third consecutive handover of power from one president to the next, and the "first time power had ever been handed over to an opposition party—with a plurality of barely 30,000 votes out of almost 4 million ballots cast" (Daniel Levine 1973, 3). Two months later, residents of the La Libertad sector of 23 de Enero shut down streets in protest against water shortages.[23] Some among the protesters considered the shortage part of a government reprisal for the "repeated complaints we have made against the various institutions that service our sector, and which have culminated in our refusal to pay some of their fees."[24] Two weeks later, residents in another popular sector of Caracas staged a copycat action in protest over water service shortages in their community. The rash of street actions over public services would prompt stern reactions from state officials who, in a pattern repeated throughout the decade, struggled to admit deficiencies while also reproaching neighbors on their tactics (Medina 1969b).[25]

Much as Caldera's election marked a turning point for Venezuelan democracy's institutional stability, the May 1969 protest also signaled a shift in residents' approach to organizing and mobilization. In particular, it inaugurated an era of collective action spearheaded by neighbors at large rather than by partisan extremists, with aims that centered on local concerns and community demands rather than seizing state power. Groups such as the Social, Cultural, and Artistic Movement (Movimiento Social, Cultural, y Artístico—MOSCA) in the Sierra Maestra sector and Like Desert Raindrops (Como Gotas de Lluvia Sobre el Desierto) in Zone E, as well as a wide range of dance groups from across el 23, organized musical and theatrical events, held art and crafts workshops, and promoted health and drug awareness campaigns. In the Central Zone, the Christ the King (Cristo Rey) cultural complex experienced something of a renaissance after a decade of neglect. Its movie house, its theater, its meeting rooms, and its "Liberty Park" and hatch shell all began to draw more and more use.[26]

Community-oriented activism also provided a space for clientelist co-optation. The case of Block Number 31 in Zone E is instructive. Years of silence in this sector geographically separated from the main body of el 23 gave the building a reputation as a "white elephant."[27] According to some the moniker derived precisely from its self-sought isolation from the more direct forms of confrontation with the state that characterized other sectors. For others it referenced a perception that residents stood staunchly behind the long dominant AD political party, represented in elections with the color white. The man who organized the block, as residents recall, was a member of the same Metropolitan Police widely derided in most other sectors as the repressive arm of the state in el 23. He was also a ranking AD militant who skillfully exercised that clout to forge patronage ties with residents and over the years cemented authoritarian control of the local comité social—the organic predecessor to what became formally constituted condominium associations in the mid-1980s.[28]

The tension between co-optation and protest spawned debates that were at times ideologically driven and violent; occasionally organizers arrived home to see their doors blackened and burned, and they speedily scoured the classifieds for home sales far from el 23. Francisco Suarez, from his apartment on the fifteenth floor of a Monte Piedad superblock, could see threats against his life painted on the walls of the building facing his.[29] His participation with the AD-controlled junta de vecinos—neighborhood association—prompted this attack. Eventually, the president of that junta was forced to move to Guarenas, thirty minutes east of Caracas, after a pipe bomb was detonated on her doorstep.[30] Still, internal debates more often reflected quotidian concerns about conditions of life in a nation of growing contradictions, and about how these contradictions played out in a state-owned and administered neighborhood that was Venezuela's largest urban housing project. For nearly two decades comités sociales in each building provided a space for this kind of rich discussion demanding concrete deeds. Generations of activists first found their organizing zeal here; Juan Contreras, today a founding member of the socialist inspired Coordinadora Simón Bolívar in the La Cañada sector of el 23, recalls cutting his political teeth as the youngest president of his building's comité social, at first sparring with and later securing the respect of older AD and COPEI militants for his work in organizing youth events, cleaning brigades, and other events.[31]

But while on the one hand pacification—and recognizing defeat in the 1960s armed struggle—prompted activists in el 23 to develop a social vocation over and above partisan political commitment, on the other hand pacification brought renewed confrontation with the state, primarily involving youth. Long-haired youth, at the time pejoratively referred to as *melenudos*, reportedly had their heads shaved on their way to and from school.[32] Andrés Vasquez, then a teenager, recalled other forms of harassment, as well as the consequences of resistance:

> They used to make you sweep that whole thing—that was good—you ventured outside and then you had to sweep half the block before going to work or going to school. To talk back (*ponerse rebelde*), there were many rebellious youth who resisted, well they beat them, they shot at them, in fact there was, Cheo is still around, Cheo had his leg blown off, he's still around. And that's how they killed many people, they killed so many people here.[33]

Periodical sources support Mr. Vásquez's testimony. Between 1972 and 1979, local high-school and middle-school students in el 23 staged on average five major protests a year resulting in clashes with police and garnering national press coverage.[34] Reasons varied widely, from reinstating dismissed teachers, to improving school resources, to opposing the military draft (López Maya 2006). For some, protesting reflected mere curiosity, an opportunity to engage in youthful adventure and rebelliousness. At times, even the threat of protest yielded positive results. In June 1974 authorities at the Banco Obrero ceded a local youth center, used to promote cultural and drug prevention activities, to police. In response students at the nearby Manuel Palacios Fajardo high school, mounted a public challenge, contacting media and promising to take to the streets should the measure go ahead.[35] Two weeks later, in an appearance in el 23, the Caracas mayor personally overturned the measure, while also promising new resources to revitalize the center.[36]

Over time, however, the tenor of student protests grew increasingly contentious, even lethal, while aims and outcomes grew less clear and effective. Earlier in the decade staging barricades, hurling rocks, and firing Molotov cocktails against police had marked the range of the students' collective action. Yet by decade's end the violence routinely extended to setting ablaze local stores and public transportation vehicles and exchanging gunfire with police and national guardsmen, leaving in its wake scores of injured police and several dead students. Between 1977 and 1979, seven youth died of gunshot wounds received while protesting in el 23 (López Maya 2006). The result was a cyclical pattern of mobilization and repression, where ill-defined protests led to violent clashes resulting in student deaths, in turn generating more protests and violence. A team conducting research in el 23 in the 1980s concluded, "The youth's effervescence was so brutally repressed [in the 1970s], by different means, that to be young actually constituted a crime" (Pacheco, Elba, and Mirian 1987, 124).

While students were at the forefront of protest events in the 1970s, mobilization during the decade extended to sectors whose immediate needs had grown sharper during the previous decade's era of democratic consolidation. Indeed, pacification opened new spaces of collective action at a time when urbanization in Caracas reached new levels of haste. Between 1961 and 1973, as planning policy shifted away from Caracas, the capital's population jumped over 60 percent, from 1.6 to 2.6 million, bringing new housing, sanitation, and transportation demands to an increasingly saturated city whose poverty rates now hovered around 50 percent (Briceño 1973). In el 23, protests over access to housing and sewage by those who had squatted during the 1960s, and over improvements to basic infrastructure by superblock residents, marked the tenor of mobilization throughout the 1970s (López Maya 2006).

But much as the 1969 protest had heralded, water would prove a major mobilizing factor. Aging pipes and equipment at the city water service, when coupled with recurrent droughts and rapidly increasing demand, created cyclical water shortages in Caracas generally but popular sectors in particular (Leyton 1976). Not unlike student protests, civic protests grew increasingly contentious over the course of the decade. In September 1976, lightning damaged Caracas's main water supply station. After three weeks without water, neighbors in the same La Libertad sector that had set the stage for the 1969 protest took to the streets, shutting down main access roads. When police arrived, gunfire erupted, leading to one dead and one wounded (Urbina 1976). A year later, similar protests over water shortages resulted in the deaths of two minors (Brando 1977). And in October 1978, two more died when another demonstration demanding water service turned violent, including a ten-year-old shot while he played at home by a stray bullet from the events below (F. Gómez 1978; Urbina 1978). Commenting on the violence Interior Minister Manuel Mantilla labeled the protestors "maniacs of disorder," "who try to find problems where none exist" (C. Alvarez 1978a, 12). Meanwhile, then-President Carlos Andrés Pérez went further, noting that "events like those of 23 de Enero make existing public service deficiencies more acute" (C. Alvarez 1978b, 16).

Pérez's comment laid bare the paradox of collective action in el 23 during the 1970s: though characterized by an explosion of mobilization, it was a
time nevertheless marked by little in the way of organization. Yet by decade's
end signs of an emerging unity between militants skilled at tactical organization and residents simmering with mounting frustrations had begun to surface.
Police reports of the October 1978 violence, for instance, noted that "hooded
protesters (*encapuchados*) with high caliber rifles" took part in the events, reflecting a modality of violence seldom seen since the days of urban guerrilla
war in the early 1960s (J. Pérez 1978, 52). In this context, political activism
did not disappear entirely; though its reach had grown much more limited,
its constituency had passed to new generations of activists who had cut their
teeth in local struggles over community demands. Continuing state violence
throughout the 1970s provided a space for older groups of militants to continue their work with a rising generation of activists in el 23. Other militants
from the 1960s continued to be politically active in el 23 but through subliminal
rather than clandestine means, shifting their energies to what one veteran of
the urban guerrilla referred to as "cultural work," like organizing street theater
troupes, musical ensembles, and athletic events.[37] In this context, where in general terms a pendulum between political and social activism swung during the
1960s and 1970s respectively, the 1980s would witness a synthesis of the two
overarching trends.

Toward a Synthesis of Politics and Protest, 1980s

By the late 1970s the tenor of popular consciousness in el 23 reflected outrage
at the combined impact of crime, repression, and structural decay into which
the neighborhood had devolved over the previous decade. The result was a
confluence of the contentious, though locally oriented, collective action of the
1970s, and the systemic critiques of representative democracy of the 1960s.
Consider the case of the Grupo de Trabajo La Piedrita (GTLP). The GTLP operates in one of the oldest squatter settlements in el 23. It sits strategically at the
crossroads of four sectors, which rendered it a favored spot for criminal, and
especially narcotics, activity during the early 1980s. By the mid-1980s neighbors formed a working group to seek collective solutions to a scourge threatening to unravel their once close-knit community, a phenomenon playing out
throughout el 23. Their response was twofold: on the one hand, they renewed
a sense of pride and solidarity in their community through the organization
of festivals for local youth, the formation of a "muralist brigade" to propagate

messages of solidarity, and the construction of a commons where strict rules of conduct were observed and imparted to all members; on the other hand, they exercised police action against criminal elements, whether or not they came from outside the neighborhood.

On the face of it, then, the GTLP arose as a primarily social response to crime and its consequences for community life. In fact, politics underlay nearly every facet of the GTLP's trajectory, from its inception to its strategies to its goals. For founders of the GTLP, crime and drugs in el 23 were but another effect of state repression. In this they concurred with a widely held perception in the parish that government policy to neutralize dissidence in el 23 explained the explosive rise of violent delinquency starting in the mid-1970s. In their cultural work the GTLP likewise incorporated music and images reflecting demands for social justice, rebukes of representative democracy, rejection of state violence, and the memorialization of activists gunned down either by thugs or police. But especially in their police actions the GTLP drew directly from a tactical repertoire that picked up from the associations that some members forged in the 1970s with veterans of the so-called Tactical Combat Units (Unidades Tácticas de Combate) of the 1960s, who were living in or near their community.[38]

The case of the GTLP is relevant because it helps illustrate what by the 1980s became the driving debate among the more militant wing of activists in el 23: how—if at all—to combine social and political organizing in their community. The debate reflected a synthesis in the dialectic between political and community work that had marked the previous decades of activism. Eventually, this synthesis would be manifested in the seizure of a dozen state vehicles over Christmas 1981. The *secuestros* (hijackings) followed from an unprecedented state effort to privatize the long beleaguered Caracas waste management service, the first venture of its kind in post-1958 Venezuela. The move promised a new era of efficiency in the handling of the city's trash. However, a kickback scandal and poor coordination botched the transfer of services to four independent firms, leaving mounds of refuse in the streets and in the headlines. Facing a potential public health crisis in time for Christmas, hundreds of firebrand youth, stay-at-home women, and card-carrying party militants in the Monte Piedad and Sierra Maestra sectors of el 23 began seizing whatever garbage truck drove by. Protesters placed signs reading "hijacked" on the vehicles and resolved to return them undamaged only after they had seen "the last ounce of trash removed from the area."[39]

Over the next four weeks, as state officials offered one stopgap measure after another, neighbors seized more and more state- and privately-owned public service vehicles, expanding their demands from a general clean-up of the area to a comprehensive renovation of the community's aging infrastructure. To sustain the protest over time, neighbors relied on an intricate system of task sharing drawn from el 23's multiple organizing traditions. Erstwhile guerrillas and militant youth formed the core of those who staged the roadblocks, seized the vehicles, and kept guard overnight, drawing from their tactical experience forged in the fray of anti-establishment conflict. Housewives (*amas de casa*) gave the protest its public face, speaking to reporters about the nature of their specific grievances and following up to ensure the coverage was *fidedigno*, or fair. During daily assemblies at the various buildings in Monte Piedad where vehicles were being detained, the community at large discussed their options as days turned to weeks, also setting up guard shifts to ensure the vehicles' safe-keeping. When it seemed like attention to the protest was waning, and the state was ready to wait them out, neighbors organized mass rallies to which other sectors of el 23 contributed representatives to assist with logistics and stand in solidarity.

In the process, national media picked up the story and sympathetically reported on its progress.[40] President Luis Herrera Campins personally inter-vened, "furiously" chastising heads of public institutions and ordering an im-mediate cleanup of the neighborhood.[41] The city council moved to penalize waste management authorities. Elsewhere in Caracas, other communities threatened copycat demonstrations in a bid to draw attention to problems be-setting their own neighborhoods. By January 19, 1982, a month after it began, the protest reached its climax. Firebrand youth, grandmothers, party activ-ists, former guerrillas—together reflecting the protest's remarkable breadth—packed a local school and bore witness as heads of public service institutions signed legal documents committing their agencies to revamping the commu-nity (M. Hernández 1982). Within days, work crews began the monumental task of removing tons of waste, refitting long-stalled elevators, installing phone service, rewiring power lines, and repaving local roads, among other tasks. It was the most extensive overhaul of the area in over a decade. And, as residents had vowed all along, once repairs were under way they began to release the vehicles that made it all possible.

The secuestros presented Venezuela's political order with an enduring prob-lem, one that would not be resolved by purchasing elevators, paving roads, or installing phone service, and one which residents tactically deployed to mobi-lize city councilmen, national media, military generals, state intelligence agen-cies, heads of public institutions, and even presidents around their demands. Indeed, on the first day of the protest neighbors hinted at why a local affair could manage so much traction: responding to reporters, "[they] said that their action is an opportune contribution to help the contractors fulfill their promise to 'clean Caracas in December.'"[42] In the discourse of the hijackings, the radical character of the neighbors' methods insisted on rather than challenged the overall legitimacy of government institutions. From the viewpoint of the state this modality marked a significant enough departure from prior narratives of violent protest to limit severely its standard response options. From the neighbors' perspective, however, the hijackings more accurately reflected a long gestating convergence of once-competing traditions of mobilization: support for the liberal-democratic regime through clientelist networks, anti-establishment guerrilla strife, and community-oriented activism. Each strand found expression in collective leadership as residents hijacked the property of the state while adopting its logic of accountability.

As the conflict dragged on into 1982, the Caracas city council debated the merits of the residents' tactics. Its president denounced the measure as "beyond all established order, it is lamentable that this should take place for the simple reason that it has negative consequences . . . especially when there are perfectly acceptable mechanisms to reach an understanding."[43] A Christian-Democrat councilman concurred, criticizing residents for presumably acting against their own interests by letting themselves be manipulated: "By no means do I think violence is the solution. . . . If the community allows itself to be taken by activists who don't want solutions to problems because they live off of that cauldron, they will never be able to live decently." A councilman for the MAS party offered lackluster empathy while supporting dialogue: "I understand that what took place in 23 de Enero is a reflection of dramatic neglect that affects the people of that area, forced to use extreme measures, even though I think that the correct approach would be to attack the root of the matter and the most convenient initiative to that end is dialogue." But Gladys Gavazut, an independent, broke ranks and issued a blanket condemnation of the council while lending full support to residents' measures:

> The Council has ceased to be a popular instrument to become a museum instead, and the participation offered by [the government] was nothing more than a ploy that was discarded when they realized that it might be useful for the people to hold accountable, at a given time, those who direct the fortunes of the nation. . . . I justify [the secuestros] and even more in the case of a neighborhood that has been so beaten. The time comes when a community tires and takes actions that are the externalization of a *pueblo* that cannot find solutions to the problems it faces.

In the press, beyond near daily coverage, columnists reflected on the underlying implications of the secuestros. The artist Mateo Manaure, who years earlier had collaborated in the design of 23 de Enero, offered a scathing rebuke of public officials who would fail to see the larger problems of representation exposed by residents' protest, opting instead to focus on the legal aspects of the secuestros:

> To claim their rights turns them into enemies of the government, into dangerous people, when reality is different: they are the symbols of a *pueblo* . . . that continues to hang on to the hope that Venezuela will go down the path of authentic legality. . . . The very fact that there exists a popular sector like 23 de Enero, which keeps alit the torch of just claims, is living proof that the light of hope has not died out. It is also testimony that there is a Venezuela that is beaten, but not defeated. (1982, A4)

For Manaure the implication was a clear portent of things to come: "*Pueblos* always have an intuition that permits them constant reflection. Ours is an intelligent *pueblo* that has kept a stoic vigil which, at a given moment, will upend all deceit . . ." (1982, A4).

Manaure's exhortation to view the secuestros as a larger commentary on the broken pacts between the state and its citizens and to view the illegality of the secuestros ironically as a plea for "authentic legality," laid bare a deeper reality about el 23: that residents could mobilize political sectors on behalf of a democratic claim even while engaging in extra-legal tactics reflected their paradoxically privileged position vis-à-vis a state by which they felt ignored. In this space, between the civic attributes of their claims and the uncivil character of their means, neighbors experimented with how to respond to the effects of a coming economic crisis and its attendant expressions in distribution lapses and incipient privatization efforts. Indeed, by hijacking the property of the state while adopting its logic of accountability, residents of el 23 were marking not just a new modality of protest but also the emergence of a new consciousness of participatory politics in Venezuela.

The success of the secuestros transformed more than the physical face of el 23. It also redefined the boundaries of legitimate protest in Venezuela, as neighbors wove tactics forged in the fray of urban guerrilla struggle and loyalty to the Punto Fijo system born through years of electoral participation, to challenge representative rule where it proved most vulnerable: in its own logic of accountability. Much as it had in the past, el 23's symbolic weight and strategic location amplified the scope of the secuestros, turning a local action over public service deficits into a larger reflection of popular unrest with the

failings of an entire system of governance and with its initial attempts at reform. In the wake of the secuestros a new era of popular mobilization ensued,
one where community struggles were imbued with political content as usually
mainstream sectors embraced a leadership and tactical repertoire fashioned
around radical ideological goals. But these sectors also placed limits upon insurgent leaders and tactics, forcing once anti-establishment groups into negotiating with Venezuela's state. As community activists gained a radical political
edge, one-time insurgents came to recognize the legitimacy of the representative system. The result was a hybrid political consciousness that held direct
action tactics and loyalty to the founding premises—and promises—of liberal
democracy as complementary rather than antithetical.

These moments in the early 1980s gave rise to an alternative practice of
democratic pluralism among urban popular sectors. This practice drew simultaneously from institutional and extra-institutional, legal and extra-legal traditions of popular mobilization forged against the backdrop of nearly twenty-five
years of representative democracy. As a result, it contained radical elements
of direct action that nevertheless did not preclude loyalty to liberal government, in its forms of accountability, institutionalism, and representation. It
was through this fraught but effective convergence that urban popular sectors
sought to stake a claim in reforming the state.

Revolution and the Challenge of Popular History

The trajectory of organizing and mobilization in el 23 sets in relief a key challenge of revolutionary movements. Namely, how do political projects founded
on the premise of marking "brutal ruptures with the past" address the challenge of history (Mayer 2000, 27)? Indeed as Hannah Arendt reminds us, "The
modern concept of revolution [is] inextricably bound up with the notion that
the course of history suddenly begins anew, that an entirely new story, a story
never known or told before, is about to unfold" (1963, 28). Yet as Frederick
Corney notes for the case of 1917 Russia, revolutionary beginnings are contingent on the rise of "a new historical genealogy," capable of subsuming competing experiences of the pre-revolutionary past within a unified and unifying
meta-narrative of the revolutionary present and future. Over time, "told and
retold, [new genealogies] become constituent parts of the social fabric, erasing
or pushing aside alternative histories" (Corney 2004, 48).

It is this pursuit of subsuming not just competing ideologies but entire
"alternative histories" of struggle under a grand narrative arc of sudden and

inevitable rupture with the past that challenges us to conceptualize revolution not only in terms of what is ushered in but also, and perhaps primarily, in terms of what is ushered out in the fray of regime consolidation. It also suggests that revolutions confront their greatest challenge not in the construction of the future, but rather in the reconstruction of the past in ways commensurate with grand projects of radical change, all the while contending with conflicting memorializations of pre-revolutionary history.

The trajectory of organizing and mobilization in el 23 highlights one such alternative history and challenges the Bolivarian Revolution's designs to refound the nation (López Maya 2000). Indeed, as the Bolivarian project seeks to consolidate what Chávez has long characterized as a "new historical phase in Venezuela" (Muñoz 1998, 410–11), it has come increasingly to rely upon a historical genealogy that rests on the rise of Hugo Chávez as the redeemer of long-suffering popular sectors, whose political awakening can be traced, at best, to the mid and late 1980s.

Yet the case of el 23 suggests otherwise. What it shows is that popular sectors, informed by long struggles to consolidate the promises of effective government, unleashed early on a contest over competing visions of democracy and revolution. Indeed, el 23's symbolism and location fueled intense co-optation efforts; over time partisan networks emerged throughout the neighborhood on the basis of access to and allocation of state resources. Similar organizing trends informed by partisan political motivations also developed elsewhere in el 23. Yet when these networks failed to reap community benefits, residents deployed the same symbolic and spatial qualities to mobilize media attention around forms of collective action that moved in and out of the terrain of legal and extra-legal protest. These tactics gave rise to alternative local networks of resistance that arose in parallel to clientelist webs in el 23. In other words, in the 1960s anti-establishment groups waged urban guerrilla struggle, while in the 1970s community groups emphasizing local needs took to the streets to protest public service deficiencies. Their convergence in the early 1980s would signal the rise of a distinctly popular political culture able to navigate both liberal and radical tendencies.

Against this backdrop, el 23's history of organizing and mobilization sets in relief the need to cast urban sectors as a fraught constituency imbued with its own ideological contradictions, which changed over time as residents' disenchantment with national politics ebbed and flowed, incorporated patterns of representative democracy while also crafting more radical strategies and interpretations of democratic change out of their experiences with the failures of the Punto Fijo regime. The shifting loyalties, contradictory tactics, and internal divisions that underlay these seemingly at-odds traditions ensured that visions of a democratic society would vary as widely as the strategies used to wage protest against the state's shortcomings. For some, it would involve expressing political dissent through local primaries. For others, it would involve more radical means, like taking up arms to defend against reformist currents in government.

Yet the common thread remained as it does today, a sense of community built around the pursuit of a contingent autonomy, neither fully independent from nor fully beholden to the state. As such, it is a relationship marked by negotiation and conflict, drawn in turn from an experience of activism dating to well before the rise of either Hugo Chávez or economic crisis in Venezuela.[44] As one long-time activist in el 23 comments, "Chávez did not produce the movements, we created him. He has helped us tremendously, but what is going on here cannot be ascribed solely to Chávez" (Parenti 2005). Revisiting the Punto Fijo period with an eye toward local politics provides the basis for understanding how, when, and why internecine struggles emerge from the initial stages of radical change.

Notes

1. Political parties in Venezuela had held primary elections sporadically in the past, but only at the level of presidential elections. Notably, Acción Democrática held different types of primary elections to select its presidential candidates in 1973 (indirect primaries), 1988 (electoral college), and 1993 (direct primaries), while COPEI held primaries in 1988 (Alcántara Sáez 2002).

2. Hugo Chávez, *Aló Presidente* episode 193, June 13, 2004.

3. In April 2003, 53 Cuban physicians arrived in ten parishes in Caracas, including 23 de Enero. These doctors were the first in a program that would become Barrio Adentro, aimed at providing popular classes with direct access to primary health care (D'Elia 2006). In May 2003, Chávez granted the first urban land titles to Urban Land Committees (CTUs) from four Caracas communities, including 23 de Enero. CTUs were organized to help normalize tenancy for squatter communities in Caracas, a program that generated an enormous amount of organizational and electoral support to Chávez (Coleman 2003). In August 2005, Chávez again provided CTUs in 23 de Enero with the first funds based on a "communal project" proposal, a project that would set the stage for eventual "communal councils" entrusted with management of community resources ("Contruyendo el Poder Popular," June 13).

4. In the 2004 presidential recall referendum 69 percent of voters in 23 de Enero voted against the proposal to recall, behind Antimano (77 percent) and Macarao (74 percent). In parliamentary elections in October 2004, Chávez's party, the MVR, ob-

tained 90 percent of the vote, behind El Junquito (92 percent), Catedral (92 percent), and Macarao (91 percent). In the 2006 presidential elections, el 23 returned 76 percent for Chávez, the largest percentage of support behind Antimano (81) and Macarao (79). Data available from the website for the National Electoral Council, http://www.cne.gob.ve.

5. Steve Ellner, examining competing currents within Chavismo's leadership, captures the debate between on one hand "the call for an immediate creation of parallel organizations and institutions to replace the old ones and achieve a complete break with the past" (what he refers to as "revolutionary opportunity"), and on the other hand, "ushering far reaching change short of revolution or socialism . . . [including] the creation of mass based parties and democratic institutions," or "non-revolutionary transformation" (Ellner 2005, 161–62). Javier Corrales, examining similar tensions pitting radical approaches toward effecting change against reformist currents of long-term institution building within the confines of liberal democracy, argues that the two currents emerge from the alliance of military and leftist civilians that long formed the core of the clandestine movement to overthrow Venezuela's bipartisan system (Corrales 2006). Yet both leave unexplored the ways in which these undercurrents of ideological complexity also permeate popular sectors, imbuing Chavismo with conflicting pressures of their own but from below. In Ellner's case, popular sectors emerge as the civil-society complement to radical currents within Chavista policy making, again and again constituting the most "hard-line" among Chávez's constituency (Ellner 2005). For Corrales, problematizing the image of Chavismo takes the form of a "supply-side theory" capable of accounting for why and how seemingly contradictory social sectors—mid-level military officers and leftist intellectuals—found common cause in the 1990s. This strategic alliance, notes Corrales, was eventually successful at channeling an already radical popular mass constituted in the wake of market reforms in the late 1980s and early 1990s: "Blaming neoliberalism . . . helps to provide a partial answer to the question of the origins of chavismo: it explains the demand side but not the supply side. It can explain the rise of the poor, and the overwhelming demand for a radical change in politics, but it does not explain the actual change provided" (Corrales 2006, 9).

6. "La vivienda popular en Venezuela," *Integral* 7 (1957).

7. The expropriated barrios were, successively, Cerro Belén, Monte Piedad, Colombia, Las Canarias, Cañada de la Iglesia, Cerro San Luis, Los Flores, 18 de Octubre, Barrio Nuevo, and Puerto Rico (de Blay 1959; López Villa 1986). Marcos Pérez Jiménez's decree can be found in Pérez Jiménez 1954.

8. López Villa 1986, 169. López Villa has found that of the ten barrios that 2 de Diciembre replaced, three were founded in the late nineteenth century, one in the 1920s (its landowner directed the urbanization process therein), one in the early 1930s (again through an urbanization process directed by its landowner), and three later that decade.

9. One fifteen-story superblock was built in thirty-eight days. "La vivienda popular en Venezuela."

10. Crests and troughs in the rate of expropriations help explain the model's cyclical

nature, although the pattern in terms of grievances took place on alternating cycles. See, for instance, *Actas del Banco Obrero*, vols. 44 and 47 (Banco Obrero 1956, 1957).

11. "161 muertos y 477 heridos es el balance trágico de la lucha por la libertad." *El Universal*, January 24, 1958.

12. "Ametrallados el 23 de enero, Barrio Union y Simon Rodriguez," *Tribuna Popular*, October 27, 1960; "1500 guardias nacionales y esbirros de la Soto Pol asaltaron el 23 de enero," *Tribuna Popular*, October 28, 1960; "Disturbios durante todo el dia en la urbanización 23 de enero" *El Nacional*, October 27, 1960; "Desordenes en el 23 de enero, Lidice, Sarria, y otros sectores," *Ultimas Noticias*, May 5, 1962.

13. Explanations for the demise of armed struggle in Venezuela have come primarily from the leadership cadre of the 1960s guerrilla movement. The earliest attempt came from Teodoro Petkoff, who identified Bhreznev's invasion of Czechoslovakia in 1968 as the critical juncture in global socialist thought, marking a break between Dubcek's humanist socialism and neo-Stalinism. In this context, socialism in Venezuela—though it remained a goal—would not be achieved by imposition but through electoral means, although whether or not the Prague Spring and its end proved to be a fitting pretext or an intellectual fine-tuning leading to surrender of armed struggle by Venezuelan cadres remains an open question (Petkoff 1970). In 1973 the electoral defeat of the Movimiento al Socialismo (Movement toward socialism, MAS) political party—founded by and comprised largely of demobilized guerrillas—prompted Petkoff again to defend the decision to surrender armed struggle (Petkoff 1976; Ellner 1988). Toward the end of the 1970s, previous guerrilla leaders were openly calling for an end to intellectual justifications for demobilization and instead, in a confessional tone, for acknowledgment of the mistake represented by their decision to pursue armed struggle in the first place (see "Un ex-guerrillero que abandonó la clandestinidad para hacer política," *Ultimas Noticias*, August 15, 1977). By the early 1980s, consensus among previous guerrilla leaders was reached on the tactical error represented by armed struggle. In this context, a wave of oral histories emerged to narrate the tactical details of Venezuela's guerrilla conflict, rather than its intellectual merits or faults (García Ponce 1977; Rangel and Blanco Muñoz 1981; Rangel 1990).

14. Ramón López, interview with the author, Caracas, 15 February 2005.

15. Ibid.

16. "En el 23 de enero: Inaugurado consultorio médico gratuito *Jesus Yerena*," *Tribuna Popular*, September 3, 1970; "Gas directo y telefonos para el 23 de enero exige comité por unidad de mujeres," *Tribuna Popular*, May 7, 1970; see also L. Pérez 1976.

17. Lourdes Quintero, interview with the author, Caracas, February 16, 2005.

18. Ravin Granier Asuase Sánchez, interview with the author, Caracas, January 25, 2005.

19. "Jefes guerrilleros fueron detenidos al inscribirse en servicio militar," *Ultimas Noticias*, January 12, 1968.

20. For Rómulo Betancourt the 23 de Enero superblocks were but a "costly and anti-human" solution to Venezuela's urban housing shortage, concentrating Caracas's primacy and therefore leaving the countryside, AD's traditional base of support, unat-

tended (Betancourt 1959, 10). In this context, the Banco Obrero moved away from high altitude, high-density structures to promote housing alternatives away from Caracas (Sarli 1996). The most celebrated case of planned urbanization in the 1960s was that of Ciudad Guayana, 250 miles southwest of Caracas (Peattie 1968).

21. "Habitantes de los cerros ocuparon los bloques todavia no inaugurados," *El Universal*, January 26, 1958; "Los desalojados de los cerros ocuparon los bloques de Monte Piedad," *El Nacional*, January 30, 1958. By 1982 the BO's balance of payment deficit had reached US$560 million (C. Alvarez 1982).

22. As early as January 31, 1958, just over a week after the January 23 coup, newspapers reported the rise of squatter settlements in the green areas between the superblocks; see "Se construyen ranchos en varias zonas verdes," *El Nacional*, January 31, 1958. A year later, press reports continued to record the ongoing phenomenon; see "Ranchos se estan construyendo en las faldas de las urbanizaciones obreras," *Ultimas Noticias*, January 19, 1959. Meanwhile state officials responded by constructing additional water and sewage lines, as well as additional schools, literacy programs, and cultural centers to meet the demands posed by these new residents. See "Estudiaran los problemas de los pobladores de la 23 *de enero*," *El Nacional*, February 26, 1958; "Ampliaran canales de desague en la 23 *de enero*," *El Nacional*, June 4, 1958; "Creadas tres escuelas para la 23 de enero," *El Nacional*, June 14, 1958; and "Programa de alfabetización y extensión cultural financiara el Banco Obrero," *El Nacional*, August 13, 1958.

23. "Enardecidos por la falta de agua habitantes del 23 de enero bloquearon las avenidas con barricadas," *El Nacional*, May 5, 1969; see also Medina 1969a.

24. "Considerán represalia contra el sector falta de agua en el 23 de enero," *Ultimas Noticias*, May 7, 1969.

25. "No se debe llegar a la violencia para pedir regularidad de un servicio," *El Universal*, May 6, 1969; "Por orden del Presidente sigue al servicio de la comunidad el Centro Cristo Rey del 23 de enero," *El Nacional*, June 19, 1974.

26. "Por orden del Presidente," 1974.

27. Hipólito Rondón and Sánchez Nada, interview with the author, Caracas, February 26, 2005.

28. Josefina Hernández de Machado, Pedro Gerardo Cadiz, Diego Carvallo, and Nuria Márquez, interview with the author, Caracas, March 12, 2005.

29. Francisco Suarez, interview with author, Caracas, July 20, 2005.

30. Hipólito Rondón and Sánchez Nada, interview with the author, Caracas, February 26, 2005; Francisco Suarez, interview with author, Caracas, July 20, 2005.

31. Juan Contreras, interview with the author, Caracas, February 23, 2005.

32. "Melenudos acusan a policias de perseguirles injustamente," *Ultimas Noticias*, March 17, 1969.

33. Andrés Vásquez, interview with the author, Caracas, January 29, 2005.

34. "5 Heridos en la balacera: Mataron a liceista en el 23 de enero," *Ultimas Noticias*, March 15, 1978.

35. "Desalojados jóvenes del 23 de enero del único local donde realizaban actividades culturales," *El Nacional*, June 1, 1974.

36. "Por orden del Presidente," 1974.

37. Gustavo Rodríguez, interview with the author, Caracas, August 23, 2005.

38. Nelson Santana, interview with the author, Caracas, January 23, 2005; Valentín Santana, Henry Aguero, Carlos Ramirez Guacaran, Ramón Molines, José Angel Pabon, Javier Ramon, Wilmer Carreño, and Carlos Julio, interview with the author, Caracas, January 25, 2005; Valentín Santana, interview with the author, Caracas, June 4, 2005.

39. "'Secuestraron' a cuatro camiones del I.M.A.U.," *Diario de Caracas*, December 21, 1981. The IMAU is the Instituto municipal de aseo urbano (Municipal waste management institute).

40. Amaral 1982; "En el 23 de enero siguen secuestrando vehiculos oficiales," *El Nacional*, January 8, 1982, 15; Moreno 1982.

41. Argotte 1981, 8; "L.H.C. 'furioso' dio 48 horas a los servicios publicos," *Diario de Caracas*, December 23, 1981.

42. "Los vecinos dijeron que su acción se convierte en una contribución oportuna al cumplimiento de la promesa de los concesionarios de la recolección de basura de 'limpiar a Caracas en Diciembre'"; "'Secuestraron' a cuatro camiones del I.M.A.U.," *Diario de Caracas*, December 21, 1981.

43. All city council quotes are taken from Lombardi 1982.

44. As Sujatha Fernandes argues, "To see Chávez as an independent figure pontificating from above, or popular movements as originating in autonomous spaces from below would be to deny the interdependencies that have made possible Chávez's emergence and sustained access to power" (2006, 18).

CHAPTER SEVEN

The Misiones of the Chávez Government

Kirk A. Hawkins, Guillermo Rosas, and Michael E. Johnson

The goal of several contributors to this volume is to determine whether Chavismo and the Bolivarian Revolution are capable of creating the kind of participatory democracy the movement advocates or if instead there is some re-
version to traditional forms of clientelism and top-down control. Each of these
contributors affirms that the answer to this question is not an exclusive choice
but is instead a matter of degree and variability. For example, they show that
in many regards the movement's programs and organizations (community
media, Urban Land Committees, neighborhood associations, and so on) demonstrate autonomy, but that in other areas these programs and organizations
have the potential for and sometimes show signs of submitting to party bosses
and Chávez himself. They also show that the strength of local identities differs
across and within organizations and across time, and that financial incentives
are increasingly present but vary considerably in their size and effect.

In this chapter we also consider this question by engaging in an analysis
of the *misiones,* or social programs of the Chávez government. However, we
hope to further problematize the analysis by showing that understanding Chavismo—or more particularly, the movement since the approval of the 1999
Constitution and the abortive coup of 2002—is not a matter of a single dimension, however continuous the scale. Rather, we must take into account the possibility of an additional mode of citizen-politician linkage, one with a problematic relationship to the principles of participatory democracy. Specifically, we
refer to *charismatic linkages* with a *populist discourse.*

As we will see in the case of the misiones, the Bolivarian Revolution often
cannot be characterized as either programmatic (a concept we define below) or
clientelistic but must instead be treated as charismatic. As with a clientelistic
mode of linkage, the movement manifests a strong top-down quality in the re-

lationship between citizens and politicians; but in this instance the relationship arises from a powerful belief in the ability of the leader to provide transcendence and moral-political renewal, and not merely from perceived material benefits. The movement is also populist in the sense that it relies on a Manichaean discourse of a collective, popular will pitted against a conspiratorial elite (and not because of any claims that economic policies are unsustainable or that the political leadership is insincere, as we will clarify below). This discourse gives rise to other phenomena that are widely commented on nowadays in Venezuela, such as extreme polarization and the use of partisan criteria in the distribution of government goods and services. In this regard too there is a resemblance to clientelism, but with an important qualitative difference— the criteria to receive goods and services are rarely explicit, let alone understood by beneficiaries. Along this charismatic-populist dimension too there are varying degrees, not stark categories, and we reaffirm what we insist are the impressive accomplishments of the misiones, as well as the stated vision that motivates them. But we insist that Chavismo cannot be understood without introducing this third mode of citizen-politician linkages.

In what follows, we present some of the findings from our study of the misiones, carried out primarily during June and July 2005 and consisting of interviews with ministerial officials, an on-site survey of approximately 140 aid recipients and workers, and a statistical analysis of program allocations in three of the misiones. The situation in Venezuela is constantly evolving, and some of the data provided here are now out of date. However, we feel that our analysis provides an important snapshot of the Bolivarian Revolution at a moment of great popularity and strength.

Basic Concepts

As originally developed by anthropologists and subsequently by political scientists, clientelism was seen as a relationship of dyadic, unequal exchange, usually accompanied by some kind of patrimonial values system (for a recent restatement of this conceptualization by a political scientist, see Mainwaring 1999, chapter 9). According to this view, clientelism naturally resulted in a top-down relationship or a lack of capacity for autonomous action, the latter being the hallmark of civil society, or our associational life outside of the family and the state. For both classical liberal and radical participatory theorists of democracy, an autonomous civil society is ultimately necessary for full and effective democracy (for the classical liberal view that informs much of our own work, see Diamond, Schedler, and Plattner 1999; Linz and Stepan 1996). We share this concern for autonomous association and will address the concept in the case of the misiones.

More recently, however, political scientists have shifted the study of clientelism to emphasize the complementary notion of conditionality (Kitschelt and Wilkinson 2006). Clientelistic relationships are conditional in the sense that goods and services provided by the government are not dispensed using universalistic or means-tested criteria such as need or merit. Instead, electoral criteria are used: no vote, no goods or services. For theorists of democracy, conditionality has negative moral implications (see O'Donnell 1999). If democracy is premised on the idea of the fundamental legal equality of each human being, enshrined in the principle of "one person, one vote" and the principle of citizenship, according to which each legally defined person enjoys the same bundle of rights and duties with respect to the community, then the conditionality inherent in clientelism is undemocratic. In clientelism, there is no fundamental equality before the law because rights derive from partisanship rather than citizenship. Scholars who emphasize this aspect of conditionality do not set aside the unequal distribution of resources and status that constitute the focus of older studies of clientelism; they simply see them as complementary. Inequality is both an important condition facilitating the emergence and persistence of conditionality and a likely outcome. Therefore, in our study of the misiones, we will consider both their top-down qualities *and* the presence of conditionality in the way they distribute goods and perform services for Venezuelans.

The relationship, or linkage, between citizens and politicians can assume various forms (Lawson 1980; Kitschelt 2000; Roberts 2001). Clientelism is one mode of linkage; another, which is often seen as the mirror-image of clientelism, is programmatic linkage, so-called because parties and politicians tend to compete around universalistic visions of what they will do for the entire community if elected to office. Whereas clientelism emphasizes top-down relationships and conditionality, programmatic politics assumes full rights of citizenship and conceives of politicians as true representatives of citizens, who are sovereign.

In contrast to clientelistic or programmatic linkages, the charismatic mode of linkage is an extraordinary one in which citizens support a single, quasi-divine leader who provides transcendence, a sense of moral renewal and connection to things "outside of" or more permanent than the individual himself (Weber 1946; Marcus 1961). Charismatic movements (and they are almost always organized as movements) offer radical programs that sweep aside old institutions. In this regard they differ from clientelistic forms of politics, which are usually more mundane relationships emphasizing material benefits and reciprocity; and from programmatic politics, which are usually institutional-ized. Of course, charismatic leaders resemble programmatic parties and poli-ticians in that they offer some kind of vision or program for change, perhaps even a well-defined ideology, but participants primarily find meaning by link-ing themselves directly to the leader and not so much by following an estab-lished set of principles. In a charismatic political movement, one cannot find meaning in politics-as-normal (voting and showing up for neighborhood meet-ings) but must become a whole-hearted, constantly and personally active sup-porter of the leader. Charismatic modes of linkage also manifest a kind of con-ditionality, in that non-adherents to the movement may be rejected as morally inferior, but this outcome depends on the particular discourse of the move-ment. Some charismatic movements are tolerant and pluralistic, such as the nonviolent independence movement of Ghandi or the civil rights movement in the United States.

This brings us to the final concept we explore here: populist discourse. Charismatic modes of linkage can draw from many different democratic dis-courses. The Bolivarian movement, we suggest, draws from a populist one. By this, we do not mean a set of misguided economic policies that sacrifice long-term growth for short-term benefits, or "economic populism" (Dornbusch and Edwards 1991). Nor do we mean a particular stage in the development of late-industrializing, former colonies that promotes import-substituting industrial-ization based on a coalition of blue-collar workers, the middle sectors, and small-scale industrialists (Di Tella 1965; Germani 1978; Cardoso and Falletto 1978; Ianni 1975). Instead, we mean a kind of weak ideology that posits a Mani-chaean conflict between a unified will of the people (seen as the embodiment of the side of Good) and a conspiring elite that has subverted this will (Laclau 1977, 1985; de la Torre 2000; Mudde 2004; Panizza 2005). A populist discourse is the opposite of both elitism, which sees the side of Good as the will of an en-lightened elite, and pluralism, which is not Manichaean and instead argues for the inevitability of different popular wills and the need for political institutions to forge compromises among these views (Mudde 2004; Hawkins 2009).

A populist discourse has significant observable implications. It polarizes the population into those who see themselves as the true people and those they have rejected for equivocating support or for opposing the movement. Dis-senters are quickly demonized, and undecided voters are pressured to take a stand. As with clientelism, populism produces a kind of conditionality in terms of who receives the benefits of the movement if it comes to power, but the conditionality will be infused with strong moral elements and may result from an implicit, rather than explicit, collusion among adherents to the movement. Thus, adherents will claim that they are open and tolerant, but they will only be tolerant of (minor) differences among adherents. Outsiders are not considered citizens or part of the people; they are an "other" that can be legitimately ignored or suppressed.

Origin and Development of the Misiones

Since early 2003 the government of Hugo Chávez has implemented a series of special programs for carrying out the socioeconomic goals of the Bolivarian Revolution. These misiones, listed in table 1 along with their emphases and rough dates of inauguration as of 2007, cover an incredible variety of social objectives designed not only to bring the benefits of the welfare state to the poor, especially those in the informal sector, but to alter the governance of the economy from one emphasizing atomistic participation in the market to one relying on cooperatives, state coordination, and local know-how—in a word, what the government celebrates as "endogenous development." The misiones incorporate Venezuelans into a growing, parallel, state-sponsored economy that competes with the traditional private sector and ultimately seeks to supplant it. These objectives are not just empty rhetoric. The misiones are financed through direct transfers of several billion dollars in revenues from the state-owned oil company (transfers that are free from regular congressional budgetary oversight), making them the best-financed of any of the programs of the Bolivarian Revolution studied in this volume and one of the largest social funds implemented in Latin America over the past two decades. Thus, they represent a crucial component of the government's goal to create "socialism of the twenty-first century" and its program of participatory and protagonistic democracy. The misiones constitute a variety of reforms that draw on oil revenues to avoid the politically explosive problems of massive redistribution. Without them we cannot explain the government's ability to combine the Bolivarian Revolution with democracy.

We focus here on five of the most well-known and successful misiones: the three that deal with remedial education (Robinson [both phases], Ribas, and Sucre), the one that works with health care (Barrio Adentro), and the one that offers subsidized food (Mercal). Our access to data on these programs varies considerably and is summarized in table 2. Basic information about policy output and aggregate performance for all of these misiones is available from vari-

Table 1. Misiones by origin and area of emphasis

Misión	Date of founding (date of presidential decree)	Area of emphasis
Barrio Adentro	April 16, 2003 (December 14, 2003)	Health care
Robinson	May 30, 2003 (July 2003)	Remedial education (literacy)
Robinson II	October 28, 2003	Remedial education (primary)
Sucre	July 10, 2003	Decentralized university education
Ribas	November 17, 2003	Remedial education (secondary)
Guaicaipuro	October 12, 2003	Communal land titles, human rights for indigenous groups
Miranda	October 19, 2002	Creation of a military reserve based on citizen militias
Piar	October 1, 2003	Assistance to small-scale miners while promoting environmental sustainability
Mercal	April 22, 2003	Subsidized food
Identidad	February 3, 2004	New national identity cards; record keeping on aid recipients at Misiones
Vuelvan Caras	March 12, 2004	Endogenous, sustainable economic development (vocational training, co-ops)
Habitat	August 28, 2004	Housing
Zamora	January 2005	Land redistribution/reform; elimination of latifundismo
Cultura	July 14, 2005	Sponsorship and dissemination of popular culture in the arts
Negra Hipólita	January 14, 2006	Assistance to other marginalized groups (handicapped, addicts, homeless)
Ciencia	February 19, 2006	Local scientific research through collaborative efforts
Madres del Barrio	March 6, 2006	Social assistance for indigent mothers and female heads of households
Arbol	May 28, 2006	Reforestation, environmental education

Note: Misiones studied in this book are highlighted.

Sources: Ministerio de Poder Popular para la Energía y Petróleo (formerly http://www.mem.gob.ve/misiones/index.php [when accessed in 2006]; now http://www.mem.gob.ve/); United Nations Population Fund (http://www.unfpa.org).

Table 2. Data sources on the misiones: Number of sites visited (number of total interviews)

Data source	Robinson	Ribas	Sucre	Mercal	Barrio Adentro
On-site interviews	3 (14)*	—	—	—	7 (27)
Nonrandom interviews	—	—	8 (50)	12 (46)	—
Ministerial interviews	Yes	Yes	Yes	—	—

Note: All interviews conducted between June 27 and July 16, 2006.

*Because we visited only three non-randomly selected Robinson sites, we generally do not include information about those responses.

ous government websites, especially the site for the *Aló Presidente* television program.[1] For two of the misiones (Robinson and Ribas) we were able to speak directly with officials in the government ministries; for another two (Barrio Adentro and Mercal) we instead obtained information through on-site interviews with workers and aid recipients, primarily in the Libertador municipality of Caracas (between twenty-seven and forty-six interviews at seven or more different sites for each misión); and for the remaining misión (Sucre) we obtained information through both ministry-level and on-site interviews (fifty interviews at eight sites in Libertador). Only the on-site interviews for Sucre and Mercal used random sampling, which limits the generalizability of some of the findings we report below. On-site interviews of both workers and aid recipients were conducted so as to ensure confidentiality.[2]

Educational Misiones

In our research we examined all three of the educational misiones, although we studied Misión Sucre the most thoroughly. These misiones seek to provide education to Venezuelans who have traditionally been excluded from public or private schools; most are remedial and, with the exception of Sucre, not intended to supplant regular public education. Ideally, an adult student could achieve literacy in Robinson, Phase I, and acquire a grade-school equivalency degree in Robinson II; obtain a high-school equivalency in Ribas; and receive a university degree in Sucre. All three misiones use standardized, national curricula that incorporate distance-learning techniques (usually videocassettes with a classroom facilitator) and are usually taught as night or weekend classes. All of the program curricula include traditional subject areas such as science, math, language, and history, but parts of the curricula have a strong ideological flavor emphasizing the Bolivarian Revolution, and all of them encourage community activism and service. The curricula for Robinson and Ribas are both based on Cuban programs and were initially designed and taught with the aid of Cuban educational advisors.[3] Registration and materials are free for students, and one-fourth to one-fifth of all students receive a monthly need-based scholarship of what was then about 160,000 bolivares (about US$80).

Classes are offered at a variety of locations, often with more than one classroom at each site. While some are dedicated buildings, most are facilities ordinarily used for other purposes, such as regular public schools, military bases, universities, and rented homes. Each misión is housed under a different government ministry, only one of which (Misión Sucre) is under the direct supervision of a regular educational ministry.

Misión Robinson

According to government statistics,[4] nearly all of the country's estimated 1.5 million illiterate citizens have learned to read and write since the implementation of Misión Robinson in July 2003, with nearly 130,000 facilitators at about an equal number of sites working in this first phase of the program. The second, newer phase was equally extensive, with nearly 1.5 million students in four cohorts and about 100,000 facilitators in about as many sites as of late 2005.

Of the three misiones, Robinson has perhaps the longest pedigree and the strongest grassroots orientation. The literacy program was among the first begun by the government (inaugurated in July 2003) and uses a well-known Cuban program, "Yo, si puedo" (Misión Robinson n.d.). When the program started, classes were initiated by volunteers who canvassed their neighborhoods for students and acted as the first facilitators, often running classes out of their homes. Training of facilitators was sporadic, and in many cases was postponed in order to carry out classroom political discussions in conjunction with the campaign for the 2004 presidential recall.[5] As of 2005 there were still no educational or experiential requirements to work as a facilitator or supervisor of Robinson I, and while all Robinson II teachers were required to be high school graduates, only 10 percent had previous teaching experience.[6]

With time, however, Misión Robinson has become more standardized and regulated. Decisions about new sites and the management of old ones are now controlled by the office of the national coordinator, and most individuals begin their studies in Robinson by attending courses at an already established site. Prospective students are required to show their government identification card or a copy of it, state their objectives for studying at the misión, and commit to finishing the program. As of late 2005, about one hundred thousand students in the two Robinson programs had received the standard monthly scholarship.[7] The distribution of scholarships was poorly regulated during the first year of the program, and problems with patronage and cronyism (*amiguismo*) surfaced; the office of the national coordinator subsequently required an applicant to demonstrate need, although approval for each scholarship was still granted by the multisite coordinator. In other areas of the country at the time we conducted our interviews, scholarship awards had been suspended while these problems were ironed out.[8] Every ten classroom sites (each with their own facilitator) was governed by a supervisor selected by the municipal or parish coordinators, and these coordinators in turn reported to state coordinators who reported to the office of the national coordinator. Unlike the other two remedial education *misiones*, classes in Misión Robinson were frequently offered throughout the day (morning, afternoon, and evening), usually Monday through Thursday, for three-hour blocks (none of the Robinson sites that we visited held weekend classes).

Misión Ribas

Also started at the end of 2003, Misión Ribas is a high-school equivalency program and is currently run by the Ministry of Energy and Oil and the national oil company, Petróleos de Venezuela, S.A. (or PDVSA), rather than any of the educational ministries. At the end of 2005 it had more than six hundred thousand active students and about thirty thousand graduates with over thirty thousand classrooms in over nine thousand locations and thus typically reached well below the parish level (i.e., the administrative level below the municipality).[9] About 25 percent of students (over 173,000) received the monthly need-based scholarship. The only requirements to matriculate in Ribas are that applicants be at least eighteen years of age and have completed their primary education, either through regular schooling or through Misión Robinson. The Ribas curriculum consists of two levels that essentially correspond to Venezuelan middle school (grades seven to nine) and high school (grades ten to twelve). Classes proceed in three-month blocks, and new cohorts of students are admitted at the beginning of each block. Classroom facilitators are required to have a baccalaureate degree; at sites with more than one facilitator (or sometimes covering several sites) there is also a coordinator.[10] As with Robinson, most courses are taught using some form of distance learning with occasional live instruction. Class size ranges from ten to thirty students. The curriculum is broad and integrates standard areas of instruction (math, science, language, geography, history) with additional components of civic education, service-learning projects, and jobs skills (Misión Ribas n.d.c). Most courses are taught in the evening on a Monday through Friday schedule (two hours each night, forty-five minutes per class period) or in the afternoons on a Saturday through Sunday schedule (four hours each day).

Misión Sucre

Misión Sucre is an alternative university program run by the Ministry of Higher Education and was formally started with a presidential decree issued in September 2003. At the time we conducted our research, the program had about 250,000 students enrolled[11] and about twelve thousand instructors. According to government data (Ministerio de Comunicación e Información 2005), over eighty thousand students were receiving the monthly need-based scholarship. The program currently includes a small number of universities with actual campuses (most notably the Universidad Bolivariana de Venezuela) and a much larger number of students in local satellite campuses spread throughout urban areas of Venezuela, typically with one campus per municipality or, in highly populated municipalities, one per parish. This helps to achieve the program's goal of municipalizing university education.[12] Each satellite campus houses only a few major programs, with these programs distributed among neighboring satellite campuses in order to provide as complete a slate of majors as possible while offering majors that fit with economic opportunities in the region (e.g., tourism, petroleum, or agriculture). Courses are normally taught by part-time instructors with baccalaureate degrees and experience in the field rather than full-time faculty with post-graduate degrees and research obligations, although some regular university professors participate in the program as volunteers. Instructors who are not already government employees receive a stipend for their service. Students who wish to participate in Sucre are required to have a high school diploma (or equivalent from Misión Ribas) and were formerly required to successfully complete a six- to eight-month preparatory course, the Programa de Iniciación Universitaria (or PIU); this last requirement was done away with in January 2006.[13]

Noneducational Misiones

The two noneducational misiones we consider here—Mercal and Barrio Adentro—are organizationally very similar to each other but different from the educational misiones. Both of these focus more on resolving basic, short-term material needs rather than on long-term problems of human capital formation. Consequently, their services do not require an extended commitment after an application procedure, but can consist of a single visit to a dedicated locale that essentially has an open-door policy. Both programs use full-time employees that receive a more significant salary (over US$700 per month for the Cuban doctors) but still operate outside of the regular civil service regulations. Predictably, workers in these programs are more dependent on the incomes they receive through the misión, and, particularly in the case of Mercal, they seemed to manifest less of the idealism and autonomy that we felt in the educational misiones.[14]

Mercal (short for Mercados de Alimentos, C.A.) is a chain of small, government-owned supermarkets offering basic foodstuffs at subsidized or wholesale prices, often 40 percent below the regular market price. The program has been in existence since the beginning of 2004. The chain is run as a semi-autonomous, government-owned enterprise under the Ministry of Nutrition. At the time of our study, over 209 government-owned stores operated nationwide (including thirty-two "Supermercal" stores), as well as 870 cooperative-owned locales and more than 12,000 street markets, or Mercalitos.[15] Supermarket locations are generally open during daylight hours. According to our on-site interviews and observations, customers are able to buy as much of any product as they like, but there is frequently rationing for high-demand products (such as meat and milk) or products that might be re-sold on the black market. When high-demand products are available at stores, there is usually a long line of customers; in these instances, admittance is first-come, first-serve, except for the elderly and young mothers with infants, who are allowed to move to the front of the line. No identification is required. Most Mercal stores that we visited were staffed by four or five individuals, including a manager and a guard at the door, who were nearly always full-time, non-civil-service employees. Employee training seldom occurs and only takes place on-site.

Barrio Adentro is, together with Misión Robinson, probably one of the best-known of the misiones. Begun in early 2003 as a program under the Libertador Municipality, the Misión today provides free medical care across the country, relying initially on Cuban medical doctors (nearly twenty-two thousand at the end of 2005) who came for eighteen-month stints through an arrangement with the Cuban government, as well as a number of Venezuelan nurses or assistants (about sixty-five hundred at the end of 2005), who were usually medical students at Misión Sucre.[16] The Misión originally focused its efforts on primary care, provided at cheaply built clinics (visible throughout Venezuela because of their hexagonal, bare-brick design) staffed by one or two doctors who usually live on the premises. Some additional clinics provide basic dental care or optometry. However, much as with Mercal, Barrio Adentro has expanded beyond the original primary-care clinics to include additional tiers with successively more sophisticated diagnostic and treatment centers; these are fewer and, at the time of our study, were in the process of being created. The eventual aim is to consolidate much of the traditional public health care system within Barrio Adentro while maintaining its emphasis on free health care and expanded local access. As of the end of 2005, government statistics proudly indicated that over 160 million visits had been made since the program's inception, 3.7 million of these in optometry and 14.5 million in dental care.[17]

The process for receiving services at Barrio Adentro primary care clinics is similar to that for Mercal. Patients wait in line and are received on a first-come, first-served basis, although at some of the sites we visited, long lines prevented some patients from being seen before the clinic closed. Unlike at Mercal, service recipients at Barrio Adentro are generally required to provide basic identifying information before receiving services (including name, age, *cédula* number, symptoms, and medical history), but our visits showed us that this was largely a formality for data collection or for help in making a diagnosis. Once admitted, patients received individual attention from a doctor, although occasionally patients met with nurses and physician assistants while the doctor was seeing other patients. Both nurses and doctors frequently made the rounds of the neighborhoods where they served, either visiting shut-ins or carrying out neighborhood health campaigns.

Initial Analysis: Top-Down or Bottom-Up?

The first question we address is whether or not the misiones are governed "top-down" or "bottom-up." That is, we ask if they foster the autonomy of activists and participants and more generally contribute to Venezuelan civil society. Our answer to this is that the misiones are in fact very top-down. While they make some noteworthy, largely indirect contributions to Venezuelan civil society, they are heavily dependent on funding and decisions made by national leaders. In most senses they are simply part of the state. Yet this does not mean that they are clientelistic, nor is this finding by itself a sufficient cause for concern for proponents of participatory democracy. Let us explain this in more detail.

In a variety of ways the misiones do embody the bottom-up quality of the Bolivarian government's efforts to create a "participatory and protagonistic democracy." The misiones are founded on a very programmatic, idealistic notion of appropriate public policy. All of them ostensibly use means-tested criteria that direct the efforts of each misión to a particular sector and, more particularly, to the poorest or least-advantaged people in that sector. This idealism surrounds and informs the ethic of workers, who were frequently referred to as "volunteers" by cabinet-level officials and by the people we met during our on-site visits. Many of the workers and managers that we met showed considerable enthusiasm for their work and for the overall project of the Bolivarian government. This sense of idealism and autonomy was highest in the educational misiones, which made heavy use of part-time workers, many of whom were full-time government employees elsewhere (e.g., public school teachers), who were not allowed to receive any remuneration for their additional service. The misiones not only improve the material quality of life of participants (and aid workers who receive stipends), but they bring together and energize potential activists and provide resources for political mobilization (education, a larger disposable income, free time, etc.). Some misiones, particularly the educational ones, also contribute directly to Venezuelan (and especially Chavista) civil society through the requirement that participants create and participate in community projects and work to give members of their own communities a political voice.

That said, the misiones themselves are almost entirely government financed and controlled, with a trend toward greater centralization. Few aid workers are entirely unpaid, and even those that are truly volunteers (such as many of the teachers in the educational misiones) are not working in organizations of their own design or control. Although the potential for micro-management by National Coordination offices is often limited by practical concerns (leadership and management of sites is often controlled by management at intermediate administrative levels, not the National Coordination), there is usually only a thin veneer of self-governance at the community level. For example, scholarships in the Ribas program are distributed at each class site according to a vote or consultation between the facilitator and the students, but the overall number of scholarships per site is determined by administrators at the state and national level. Likewise, Barrio Adentro clinics are typically supported by a neighborhood Health Committee (Comité de Salud) that provides volunteer support for the doctors in the clinic, but these committees have only come into existence since the creation of the clinics and have narrow functions that depend on the existence of the clinic.

To get a better handle on the question of connections between the misiones and civil society in Venezuela, we included a question in our ministerial-level interviews about whether there were any meaningful ties between personnel in their misión and different sectors of civil society, and we asked a similar question in our on-site surveys of misión workers. In particular, our on-site surveys asked aid workers if they or their co-workers participated in "popular organizations in their community, such as the Círculos Bolivarianos, the Urban Land Committees, the Water Committees, Neighbor Associations, Neighborhood Meetings, or some NGO."[18]

At the ministerial level, officials could rarely think of any consistent contacts between their personnel and Venezuelan (Chavista) civil society. The only instance mentioned was in an interview with officials at Misión Vuelvan Caras (a misión we did not emphasize in our survey because the program was on hold during the summer of 2005), who said that some of the national leaders of the misión were originally members of a certain Chavista nongovernmental organization.[19] Leaders at many of the misiones instead emphasized the strong presence of people who had been or still were regular employees of related or preceding government agencies. For example, leaders of the educational misiones mentioned the presence of regular teachers from the public schools and universities, and contacts at Vuelvan Caras mentioned former employees of the National Institute for Cooperative Education (or INCE).[20] In many instances this was simply a shift in employment duties, albeit one that these employees gladly accepted. The clear exception here was Barrio Adentro. The Venezuelan Colegio de Médicos generally opposed Chávez and was not willing to participate in the misión.[21]

In our on-site interviews, we found some limited mention of participation in (Chavista) civil society. Twenty-nine of sixty-six workers we surveyed (not a random sample) mentioned a specific Chavista organization to which they belonged. These numbers are lower if we consider only Sucre and Mercal workers, who were randomly sampled—only about ten out of thirty-one workers that we surveyed in these two programs mentioned a specific Chavista organization.[22] Thus, probably fewer than half of the workers in the misiones were members of other Chavista organizations that could be considered part of civil society. Although these would be high levels of activity for average Venezuelans, they are not very high for activists and community organizers. In fact, they are much lower than that of the members of Círculos Bolivarianos that we surveyed in 2004 (Hawkins and Hansen 2006), where we found that about 71 percent of the respondents were members of some kind of voluntary association that could be considered Chavista. Although these two surveys (Círculos Bolivarianos and misiones) used different instruments that should make us cautious about offering precise comparisons, the results suggest that overall participation in civil society by misión workers is only moderate and probably lower than that of other Chavista activists. We cannot be certain if the misiones are detracting from civil society by absorbing individuals who were previously participating in other organizations, or whether they complement the Chavista movement by incorporating Venezuelans who would otherwise not have been active in anything. But follow-up interviews with a few former members of the Círculos that we conducted in 2005 indicated that at least some of those individuals had given up their activities in the Círculos precisely in order to work in the misiones (Hawkins and Hansen 2006).

While the misiones' direct contribution to other areas of civil society was only moderate, they did have considerable interaction among themselves. These associations were usually officially sponsored. For example, most of the Venezuelan nurses or assistants at the Barrio Adentro clinics at the time we did our interviews were medical students from Misión Sucre, which had been given the task of training a cadre of Venezuelan doctors that could eventually replace the Cuban ones at Barrio Adentro clinics; Misión Robinson included instruction on basic health care that was prepared and sometimes administered by Barrio Adentro workers; and Mercal stores often included pharmacies that were staffed and administered by Barrio Adentro workers and located near a Barrio Adentro clinic. Many of the misiones were associated with cooperatives that have been organized under the aegis of the Ministry for People's Economy and the Misión Vuelvan Caras. All of this cross-fertilization was an efficient, indeed, crucial way of creating the parallel economy and society that the government envisions; however, it tended to contribute less to autonomous organization.

Thus, we feel confident in saying that the misiones are more top-down and less autonomous than the other instances of the Bolivarian Revolution that are considered in this volume, with some important variation across misiones (educational misiones versus Mercal and Barrio Adentro). Again, though, this may not mean very much. Social programs in many other countries are also carefully managed by national government officials, especially when such high levels of funding are at stake. And the misiones are largely an original creation of the state with very little independent trajectory. From this perspective, the fact that they encourage any kind of grassroots activism at all should be considered a remarkable achievement. But if we are hoping to test whether the Bolivarian Revolution is really achieving its goals of a participatory, protagonist democracy by analyzing the top-down quality of the organization, the misiones may not be our best case.

In addition, as we have already pointed out, the mere absence of autonomy and bottom-up organization is not itself an indicator of clientelism, but could instead reveal the presence of charismatic linkages. To determine which of these modes of linkage is present, we would need to know more about the quality of the top-down relationship. Is there a coercive element to the relationship, or is it the product of a strong affective tie? Are the misiones seen as part of an ordinary, quid-pro-quo, paternalistic relationship between participants and the state, or are they associated with a radical reform of institutions and the moral renewal of the state? And if it is the latter, what particular democratic discourse motivates participation—a populist one or a pluralist one? We turn to these questions in the next section.

Analysis: Charismatic Linkage and Populist Discourse

We argue that the data from our study of the misiones indicate a strong charismatic linkage with a populist discourse, rather than either a strictly clientelistic or a programmatic one. To make this case, we will present first some of our key findings beyond the basic descriptions we have already provided and then an analysis of how they fit together.

Finding 1. Strong Electoral Bias in Allocation
and Weak Association with Means-Tested Criteria.

Probably our key finding is that the municipal- and parish-level allocations of the misiones are not strongly associated with their ostensible means-tested criteria. Program allocations have only a weak or non-existent correlation with poverty and education at the aggregate level, even after we control for other important factors. Instead, we find strong evidence that allocations are based on partisan or electoral criteria, although these criteria vary according to the type of program.

In order to determine what criteria were used in allocating misión programs across localities—programmatic, clientelistic, or charismatic/populist—we statistically analyzed key policy outputs for three of the misiones for which we were able to find data: the number of students by municipality for Misión Ribas, the number of scholarship recipients by municipality at Misión Sucre, and the number of Mercal stores (Type I) by parish. We analyzed these program outputs rather than actual budget figures because the latter have not been made available by the government, at least when we conducted our analysis. Data for the first indicator were provided to us directly by government officials, while data for the latter two indicators were found on government websites (www.misionsucre.gob.ve and www.mercal.gob.ve) and downloaded in July 2005.

A more detailed description of this analysis is found in the Appendix. Here we will simply present a broad sketch of the analysis and results. Our key causal and control variables were:

— the *total population* of each locality, measured using data from the 2001 Census;

— the *level of poverty*, measured using the percent of houses in the locality with access to some kind of regular sewer access, so that higher numbers correspond to richer communities (again using the 2001 Census);

— the level of *education*, measured as the percent of the population with at least some college education (again, using the 2001 Census);

— the degree of *political support for Chávez* in the circumscription, which we measured as the percent of the vote for Chávez in the 2000 presidential race, using data from the National Electoral Council.[23] We chose not to use the election results for the more contemporaneous presidential recall election in August 2004 because most of the initial misión allocations were made before that date.

In order to test for the possibility that several of these effects were non-linear — that is, that allocations were actually highest at middle ranges of poverty or electoral support — we included squared versions of these indicators in our statistical models. This was especially important in the case of electoral support, where we had strong reason to suspect either a direct, linear relationship (more support for Chávez, more allocations — a typical sign of conditionality) or one in which swing or undecided districts were the ones being targeted (indicating a more cynical attempt to buy new votes).

In the case of the two educational misiones for which we have data, Ribas slots and Sucre scholarships, we found strong evidence that programs were targeted using electoral criteria (see table 3). In particular, we found that the municipal level of electoral support for Chávez in 2000 was an excellent predictor of the number of scholarships distributed in the municipality through these programs. Scholarships were more numerous in swing or undecided municipalities, that is, in those that provided Chávez with shares of the presidential vote hovering around 58–60 percent, even after controlling for population size. In contrast, poverty and education indicators had no statistically discernible association with Sucre scholarships, suggesting that these were not allocated to districts according to their levels of poverty or even the number of Sucre students in the municipality.[24] Ribas looked somewhat different, in that

Table 3. Results—Deviation from the expected distributions

	Sucre scholarships	Ribas students	Mercal stores	
			(1)	(2)
Constant	−4.574	−6.504	−9.115	−8.828
	(0.638)***	(0.695)***	(1.344)***	(0.664)***
Chávez support	0.073	0.100	0.046	0.015
	(0.018)***	(0.019)***	(0.035)***	(0.005)***
Chávez support^2	−6.06E-04	−9.28E-04	−2.56E-04	
	(1.52E-04)***	(1.66E-04)***	(2.79E-04)	
Sewer	1.044	4.123	−0.948	0.760
	(1.026)	(1.116)***	(1.906)	(0.392)***
Sewer^2	−0.902	−3.606	1.304	
	(0.770)	(0.838)***	(1.507)	
Population (log)	0.704	0.899	0.618	0.630
	(0.030)***	(0.033)***	(0.066)***	(0.065)***
Percent college	0.006	0.001	−0.001	
	(0.007)	(0.008)	(0.033)	
Adjusted R^2 (pseudo R^2)	.0692	0.735	[0.308]	[0.307]
F (p-value)	125.2	153.8		
	(0.000)	(0.000)		
LR χ^2 (p-value)			235.29	234.98
			(0.000)	(0.000)
Level (N)	Municipality	Municipality	Parish	Parish
	(335)	(333)	(1,066)	(1,066)

* is when $p < .10$; ** is when $p < .05$; *** is when $p < .01$

levels of poverty were a good predictor of the allocation of students (as poverty increases in a municipality, the number of Ribas students first goes up, then down), but our measures of support for Chávez were again very strong predictors and suggested an electoral logic in the distribution of scholarships.

In the case of Mercal (for which our data are at the lower jurisdictional level of the parish), we also found evidence that electoral concerns, rather than parish-level poverty, drive the allocation of food stores across the country. Here our best fit to the data is a model that includes only linear effects (Model 2 in the appendix). In other words, parishes that delivered more support for Chávez in 2000 were much more likely to receive a store through the Mercal program. We interpret these results as suggesting that stores were not

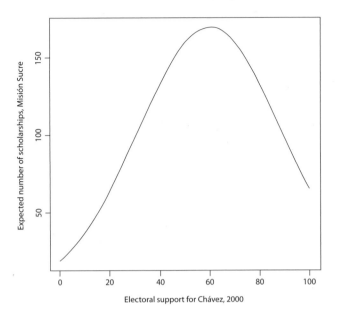

Figure 1 Relationship between electoral support for Chávez in 2000 and number of Sucre scholarships awarded.

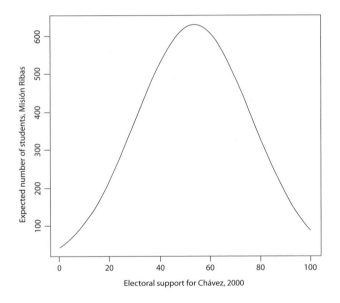

Figure 2 Relationship between electoral support for Chávez in 2000 and number of students, Misión Ribas.

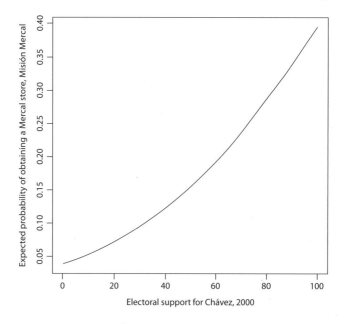

Figure 3 Relationship between electoral support for Chávez in 2000 and location of Mercal stores.

targeted to swing or undecided constituencies, but to core ones. These results hold after controlling for population (which again has a strong association) and poverty. Interestingly, poverty does have a statistically discernible association with the allocation of Mercal Type I (see chapter 2, "Participatory Democracy in Venezuela," by López Maya and Lander, for a description of types of Mercal stores), but the association is in the wrong direction. Our results indicate that richer parishes actually stand a *higher* chance of receiving a Mercal. This may be a result of the fact that our dataset does not include other components of the program that may be designated for poorer urban areas.

We depict these findings in figures 1, 2, and 3, which indicate the expected distribution of Sucre scholarships, Ribas students, and Mercal stores (measured on the vertical axis) conditional on the percent of the 2000 vote for Chávez in a particular circumscription (measured on the horizontal axis). As can be seen, the relationship between partisan support and the first two measures of Misión output is an inverted *U*, with expected allocations peaking at around 50 to 60 percent of the vote for Chávez. Thus, we can say more specifically that these particular educational programs were targeted to districts that delivered a bare majority of votes for Chávez in 2000, with expected allocations falling off as the municipal electoral share in 2000 becomes higher or lower.[25] In contrast, the probability of locating a Mercal store peaks in parishes with 100 percent support for Chávez.

Finding 2. Strong Attachment to the Leader
among Workers and Aid Recipients.

In addition to analyzing decisions about the misiones from the top levels of government, we also studied the attitudes and experiences of aid workers and recipients on the ground. Specifically, as already mentioned, we surveyed 139 workers and recipients in the Libertador Municipality of Caracas, including random samples of about 10 workers and 40 aid recipients at Misión Sucre, and 15 workers and 30 recipients at Misión Mercal. In both cases we found unusually high levels of support for and affective attachment to Chávez.

Consider aid workers first. As we found in our previous study of the Círculos Bolivarianos (Hawkins and Hansen 2006), there seems to be a high level of affect for Chávez that drives much of the workers' participation in the misiones. Nearly 88 percent of all the workers we surveyed (N = 41) and 91 percent of workers in the randomly selected sites (N = 32) indicated that they would vote for Chávez if elections were held the next day, even though the actual vote for Chávez in the 2004 recall election in these same areas of the Libertador municipality was only about 57 percent (63 percent in randomly selected localities). When asked an open-ended question about what word or phrase would characterize their feelings toward Chávez, most of these workers used phrases indicating a strong charismatic tie, such as "amor," "ídolo," or "lo adoro."

Perhaps more tellingly, these results were repeated and amplified in the case of aid recipients. A slightly smaller 82 percent of all recipients (N = 66) and 83 percent of recipients at the randomly selected sites (N = 35) also indicated they would vote for Chávez, and nearly as many of them expressed feelings for Chávez that indicated a strong charismatic tie. Not only was this level of support much higher than that found in the population as a whole, but it went in exactly the opposite direction of what we would have expected based on the partisan profiles of these programs that we uncovered in our earlier statistical analysis. That is, the percent of support for Chávez among the program recipients was actually higher in Misión Sucre (86 percent; N = 21), which is located disproportionately in swing districts, than it was in Misión Mercal (79 percent; N = 14), which is located more in core districts. The small number of respondents means that we cannot place too much stock in these last results (a t-test indicates that this difference is significant at only the $p < 0.30$ level), but they confirm that the profile of aid recipients at the misiones is much more Chavista

than the average population, even in parts of Caracas that are known as Chavista strongholds.[26]

Finding 3. No Apparent Coercion and Low Awareness of Conditionality.

The third finding we mention is the virtual absence of any kind of overt coercive apparatus in distributing the benefits of the misiones to recipients. In our
survey, we included a module of open-ended questions about whether any partisan criteria were used to determine who received services.[27] Only one of the
137 respondents who answered these questions indicated that there was any
overt conditionality in receiving services, which is consistent with Hellinger's
finding (see chapter 1, "Defying the Iron Law of Oligarchy I," this volume) of
high levels of tolerance in relatively organized barrios. Most respondents em-
phatically denied that this took place and affirmed that services were available
to all, whether opposition or pro-government. Obviously, respondents could
have been trying to give the "right" answer to our interviewers, but we took
great pains to ensure the confidentiality of respondents, and our experience
suggested that most respondents were giving us honest answers and would
have admitted—even defended—conditionality if it existed openly. We base
this claim on two observations. First, although interviewees initially received
us with different levels of trust across sites—in some, we were first perceived
as foreign spies, while in others we were seen as possible government inspec-
tors—we always got the same answer regarding partisan conditionality. Second, a number of respondents actually thought that conditionality would be a
good thing, and they seemed disappointed that it was not being used.

At the same time, in an interview during the recall campaign a year earlier,
at least one program director had admitted screening participants based on
partisan qualifications. Likewise, in our follow-up questions regarding conditionality, a few respondents to the current round of surveys said that they felt
compelled to attend pro-Chávez rallies. And it was clear that during earlier
periods such as the recall election, facilitators in the educational misiones had
engaged in pro-Chávez propagandizing and used class time for political activism.[28] This is consistent with observations made by López Maya and Lander in
"Participatory Democracy in Venezuela" and García-Guadilla in "Urban Land
Committees" (chapters 2 and 3, this volume). Nevertheless, few respondents
seemed to think of these activities as a kind of conditionality. After all, most of
them strongly supported Chávez, and they suggested that others who had received the benefits of these extraordinary programs should feel the moral obligation to do so as well.

We conclude that screening sometimes occurred and more than likely there was some kind of self-selection of aid recipients and workers, particularly in the educational misiones, but that the misiones were not using any kind of overt conditionality at the time we studied them. The strong ideological element in the curriculum of the educational misiones and the general, politicized environment of all the misiones was a sufficiently strong deterrent to potential recipients who opposed the Bolivarian Revolution. This may explain the unusually high levels of support for Chávez among Sucre participants that we noted above (as opposed to Mercal) and the fact that participants and workers generally expressed an obligation to support Chávez and actively did so, especially in the classrooms. But the people we surveyed had no sense of program benefits being directly based on their participation or that they would be expelled or excluded for wavering in their support. Furthermore, none of the recipients or workers was aware of the kinds of political targeting that our district-level data later revealed, nor were we aware of this ourselves until after we had run the statistical analysis. If conditionality is used by site directors or higher officials, it cannot be very effective because it is not clearly communicated.

Discussion of Results

How do we make sense of these key findings? Our first conclusion is that the misiones clearly do not represent a purely programmatic linkage. Whatever the universalistic outlook at the ground level, the weak association between program allocations and means-tested criteria at the district level—and the strong association with the electoral profiles of municipalities and parishes—suggests that the principle of citizenship is not fully honored by the top administrators of the misiones. This in itself is a significant, negative finding that should call for much closer scrutiny of the misiones: these particular programs are apparently not being allocated where they are most needed, at least not according to criteria of poverty and educational access. If the misiones, one of the centerpieces of the government's efforts to achieve endogenous development, are only weakly associated with universalistic criteria, we cannot conclude that the Bolivarian Revolution represents a new, programmatic form of linkage in Venezuela, at least at the top levels of the government. This threatens to undermine the democratic goals of the movement.

At the same time, it is clear that the misiones are not simply a return to the clientelism of the Punto Fijo era. Certainly, there are some hints of the old paternalism evident in the gradual tendency toward bureaucratization and control of the misiones by national administrators, as we can see most clearly in the changes taking place even in the educational misiones, such as Misión Robinson. New forms of corruption and clientelism are emerging in other areas of public administration, especially the state oil company. Yet it is striking that the misiones we studied did not seem to be using any kind of overt conditionality. Aid workers and recipients were unaware of the partisan criteria that are apparently being used to allocate sites across localities. If conditionality is part of what we define as clientelism, and if this conditionality needs to be overt or at least expected by program participants, then the misiones do not support the idea that the Bolivarian Revolution is clientelistic. The top-down controls that we saw were not largely the result of coerced exchange.

This leaves open a third possibility: that the misiones embody a charismatic mode of linkage, and in particular one with a populist discourse. We argue that this interpretation allows us to make the most sense of our findings. The charismatic underpinnings of the misiones can be seen most easily in the peculiarities of their top-down organization. It seems clear that the top-down quality of the misiones is based not only on simple bureaucratic constraints (which is not a particularly interesting finding) but a strong affective bond. Overt conditionality is not present, and yet both the workers and participants in the misiones have an unusually powerful inclination to vote for Chávez, to accord him affection or even reverence, and to sacrifice many of their programmatic objectives for the greater good of the movement. All of these are indicators of charismatic linkage.

While the fact that our respondents' "employer" is Chávez might make them more willing to vote for him out of fear or duty, this relationship cannot as easily compel affection. This might help explain why participants in the misiones (as well as those in other organizations studied in this volume) were so willing to provide partisan support to Chávez and his movement at key electoral moments such as the presidential recall, and much less support at midterm elections. Not only did their participation help protect their programmatic objectives (if Chávez lost, the programs might have been cut off), but it reaffirmed their commitment to a revolutionary movement for change and moral renewal. As Hellinger reminds us in this volume, Chávez's greatest and most effective source of electoral activism is the UBEs, the remnants of the Círculos, and other instances of the revolution that are more truly part of civil society; it is not the political parties. The fact that this activism is stronger in the educational misiones than in the more "professionalized" ones such as Mercal seems to confirm this pattern.

The misiones also seem to embody a strong populist discourse. One reason to suspect this is the ambivalence of misión managers and administrators toward screening and partisan considerations in district-level allocations. It is easy, but probably incorrect, to interpret these as mere vote-maximizing behavior. As we have already suggested, program directors at the local level seem to have engaged in screening, not true vote-buying. The evidence we have of this kind of behavior at the site level indicates an attempt to keep out the unfaithful rather than openly bid for votes and political support. This is a very different kind of conditionality.

The electoral allocation of misión programs across districts is another anomaly that the populist discourse helps explain. Why would program directors use these criteria without telling anyone? Surely the allocations would have a more potent electoral effect if they were known or at least widely suspected, as under the old Punto Fijo system. The answer is that such conditionality looks especially cynical for a populist movement. Even politicians under programmatic forms of politics will avoid revealing this kind of targeting if they can help it; electoral targeting clearly violates the universalistic principles they campaigned on and undermines their credibility. For a populist movement that proclaims its unique ability to represent the will of the people, however, the implications are worse: not only has the movement come dangerously close to rewarding the unfaithful in a bid to win their affection, but the movement's leaders are as much as admitting that they would not have broad popular support otherwise.

We see added evidence for this populist discourse in the lack of concern and even awareness of the fact that participants and workers were overwhelmingly Chavista. While emphasizing the openness of the misión, a national director of Sucre acknowledged during an interview with the authors in 2005 that opponents of the Bolivarian Revolution tended to exclude themselves from consideration as instructors: "People who aren't with the program [proceso] don't participate."[29] With a little less self-awareness, an official of Misión Ribas stubbornly insisted in a 2005 interview that there was "at least one" anti-Chavista he knew of at the ministry-level organization. And while the vast majority of our local interviewees insisted on the fact that the misiones were open to all, the profile of our average respondents indicated that almost no one in the opposition was willing to take them up on that offer. Critics of the misiones might be inclined to see some of these expressions of ecumenism as an effort at deception, but we feel that the reality is much less cynical. If activists see the Bolivarian Revolution as representing the true will of the people, they may have a hard time conceiving of how any program such as the misiones could be exclusionary or, if it were, why this would be problematic. If anti-Chavistas or fence-sitters refuse to come, it is their own fault—how could they oppose something so good?

Thus, the populist discourse leads to a curious set of contradictions. At the aggregate level, programs are placed where they will make the most electoral difference, but no one goes so far as to use open conditionality. Site directors screen recipients but do not tell recipients that they are doing it. And program directors, workers, and participants in the educational misiones insist on an open-door policy of the program, but without creating a curriculum that is sufficiently neutral to ensure cross-partisan participation.

Conclusion

Like the other contributors to this volume, we find a strong top-down quality in the misiones of the Chávez government; the lack of autonomy and the contribution to civil society may be the least among any of the programs studied here. However, we take this less as a sign of the reemergence of traditional forms of clientelism (although this is always a potential) and more as an indicator of bureaucratic necessity and the charismatic underpinnings of the Bolivarian Revolution. Rather than characterize Chavismo as either programmatic or clientelistic, we place it in a third category of charismatic-populist. Participants and workers in the misiones show an unusually high level of support and affection for Chávez (demonstrated in our surveys and in key electoral moments over the past few years), they give this support without any sense of individualized, overt conditionality in the receipt of government goods and services, and they seem unaware of or unconcerned by the fact that few non-supporters of Chávez are using these same programs, despite the open-door policy at program sites. Educational programs in particular are suffused with an ideological, partisan atmosphere that seems bound to make anti-Chavistas and even many undecided voters feel uncomfortable. These are not intentional efforts at exclusion, but a natural outcome of a movement that relies heavily on the figure of Chávez and sees him and the movement as the embodiment of the popular will.

Matters look worse when we move above the grassroots level. We find only a moderate association between the ostensible universalistic criteria of the misiones and the district-level allocation of program services, such as student slots, scholarships, and stores. On its own, these results might simply indicate carelessness or some lack of bureaucratic rationality, but we find that program allocations *are* correlated with the distribution of Chávez support in the 2000 election: swing or undecided districts are much more likely to receive Sucre scholarships and additional student slots for the Ribas program; core districts are much more likely to receive Mercal (Type I) stores. These results undermine any claims that the national government pursues purely universalistic, programmatic objectives. However, the lack of any accompanying awareness of this distribution among aid recipients and site workers indicates that there is some ambivalence about how these allocations are made and that this is not simply a return to the clientelism of the past. National leaders still take seriously the proclaimed objectives of the movement and the preferences of grassroots activists, and to a large extent they share these objectives.

Our analysis has at least two implications for the other studies in this volume as well as a more general appreciation of the accomplishments of the Bolivarian Revolution. First, many of the kinds of top-down organization that seem to be emerging in other instances of the movement analyzed in this volume may also represent a charismatic linkage rather than a clientelistic one. We hope to have convinced readers that this interpretation is an alternative worth considering. Second, it is essential to study the revolution not just at the ground level, in the communities where state programs interact with ordinary citizens and their associations, but at the systemic level where the control of national leaders predominates. This is not to play down the extraordinary ethnographic research that is currently being conducted on the revolution, which is nicely reflected in this volume; we applaud this effort to understand the movement from the vantage of its actual, everyday participants and have tried to do the same. However, the misiones show that we miss important parts of the picture unless we take into account the broader institutional context of the Bolivarian Revolution in which these particular instances of popular activism occur.

Appendix

In order to test our alternative notions about the underlying logic of the misiones, we statistically analyzed key policy outputs for three of the misiones for which we were able to find data: the number of students by municipality for Misión Ribas (which we sometimes refer to as the number of slots); the number of scholarship recipients by municipality at Misión Sucre; and the number of Mercal stores (Type I) by parish, using information from the misión website (http://www.mercal.gov.ve/).

To circumvent concerns about reverse causality—that is, the possibility that anticipation of support in future elections would determine misiones expenditures in the present—we measured all independent variables almost five years prior to the period in which we collected the misiones indicators. Our key independent variable, *Chávez support*, is the degree of political support for Chávez in any given circumscription (municipality or parish, depending on the program we analyze). We use the percent of the vote for Chávez in 2000 and also include its squared value to capture nuances in Chávez's spending behavior in contested districts. Our key control variable to gauge the level of poverty, *sewer*, is the percent of dwellings that had access to a regular sewer connection (sewer line or septic tank), and is calculated as the ratio of houses in this category to total number of houses in the municipality/parish. This control variable is an important one, because there is a fairly high correlation ($r = 0.25$, $p < 0.000$) between poverty levels and the vote for Chávez in any municipality. The two other control variables we include are *population* and *pct college*. The former is simply the total population in the territorial unit (municipality or parish) according to the 2001 Census. Most of these data are from the Nomenclador program available from the National Institute of Statistics (INE), which provides the final government estimates from the census. Unfortunately, these data were only available at the municipal level, and so in some cases we resort to preliminary parish-level estimates provided directly by Census officials at the INE.[30] *Pct college* is a measure of education level that reports the percent of the population with at least some college education; these data are also taken from the tables provided to us by the INE. We include this variable with our analyses of the educational misiones as an alternative way of gauging the degree to which they use universalistic criteria. Thus, we would expect expenditure in remedial education to be higher in municipalities with lower levels of education. Since distribution of *Sucre scholarships* is positively skewed, we consider a log transformation to normalize its distribution.[31] Moreover, though scholarships and the number of Ribas students come in integers, their sheer numbers are such that we can consider *Sucre scholarships* and *Ribas students* to be continuous variables for practical purposes. We thus resort to OLS analysis of these variables. In contrast, *Mercal stores* is a proper "count" variable at the municipal level; at the parish level, however, the dichotomous character of this variable makes us prefer a logit/probit specification.[32]

Table 3 presents estimates from three different models, one for each of our dependent variables. The estimates in table 3 largely confirm the importance of electoral criteria in the allocation of goods and services under the misiones, rather than the universalistic criteria that our respondents suggested. Consider first the models for *Sucre scholarships* and *Ribas students*, whose estimates are reported in columns 1 and 2. The first thing to note is that our control variables—*population, pct college,* and *sewer*—have very mixed effects that are generally not in accord with claims of universality. While the size of the population is clearly our strongest predictor of the allocation of Sucre scholarships and Ribas students (more densely populated municipalities receive more scholarships and have more students), the level of education in the community has almost no relationship to the number of scholarships or students.

Most significant, the effect of poverty is practically nil in the case of scholarships, where we would expect poverty to be an additional criteria of the national coordinators, and is large only in the case of Ribas enrollment. In these specifications, we have included *sewer* and its squared term to capture a potential nonlinear effect of poverty on scholarships and student slots. The logic is that these programs should initially benefit middle-class households, as rich households are presumably wealthy enough that they can purchase university and high school education in the private arena, whereas poor households are only just beginning to acquire the educational credentials they need to qualify for the university or high school programs. Consequently, more scholarships per capita should be going to municipalities that are toward the middle of the distribution in terms of poverty. Be this as it may, neither the main nor the squared term of *sewer* displays an effect parameter centered away from zero in the case of Sucre scholarships. In the case of Ribas enrollments, there is a fairly large, statistically significant effect of poverty (we can expect three hundred to four hundred more students in municipalities with moderate levels of wealth as opposed to poor or wealthy municipalities), but this is where we would least expect it, as student enrollment should probably be correlated more strongly with education than with wealth.[33]

In contrast, we find that both of our indicators for *Chávez support* have large, statistically significant signs in both models, suggesting strong associations with the allocation of Sucre scholarships and Ribas slots in the municipality. The combined effect of these indicators in table 3 is such that we expect the distribution of scholarships and students to be at a maximum in swing municipalities. Specifically, given the coefficient estimates, the number of scholarships and students is expected to be highest in municipalities where Chávez won about 60 and 54 percent of the vote, respectively. Municipalities with a middle level of support for Chávez are expected to receive about one hundred more scholarships and have five hundred to six hundred more students than municipalities that were strongly in favor of or against Chávez. These are large effects, given that the mean numbers of scholarships per municipality is about three hundred and the mean number of Ribas students is about eighteen hundred.

The model for Mercal offers a similar set of results that again confirm the importance of electoral indicators. It should first be noted that our inferences in this case are much more precise, largely reflecting the fact that we observe *Mercal stores* at the parish rather than the municipal level; thus, our number of observations increases from 335 to 1,134. Two different columns in table 3 offer alternative parameter estimates from a probit model of Mercal store location. As these indicate, the location of Mercal stores is first and foremost a function of population size. Once we control for the effect of this variable and poverty, however, we find the combined effect of our two indicators of Chávez support to be large and positive (linear). Specifically, a parish that is uniformly in favor of Chavez is 35 percent more likely to have a Mercal store than one that is completely opposed to him. Oddly, in this case we find that the control variable that should most matter according to government claims—the level of poverty (*sewer*)—has the exact opposite association that we would expect with the number of Mercal stores. The relationship is statistically significant but in the wrong direction; in fact, the wealthiest municipalities are actually about 10–15 percent more likely to have a Mercal store than the poorest ones. This finding may be a result of the fact that our dataset covers only one aspect of the Mercal program, the Type I stores, and excludes a significant portion of the program that may be used more in certain urban zones, in particular the open-air markets. Perhaps a larger sampling of all the Mercal programs would have a clearer, more sensible relationship to indicators of need.

Notes

We thank the BYU David M. Kennedy Center for International Studies; the BYU College of Family, Home, and Social Sciences; and the Weidenbaum Center at Washington University for grants supporting this research. Special thanks also to our former research assistants: David Hansen, Laurie Evans, David Jackson, and Aaron Russell at BYU, and Jacob Gerber at Washington University. Finally, we thank our colleagues Brian Crisp, Jay Goodliffe, Michael Penfold-Becerra, Dan Hellinger, and David Smilde for their insights. The conclusions are the responsibility of the authors.

    1. The website for *Aló Presidente* is http://www.alopresidente.gob.ve.

    2. At the beginning of each interview, we explicitly informed participants that their responses were voluntary and confidential, and we took care never to ask for identifying information. Site-level interviews were always conducted individually and out of earshot of other aid recipients and program directors or facilitators. In contrast, ministerial-level interviewees were not guaranteed confidentiality.

    3. Misión Robinson n.d.; Omar Calzadilla (national coordinator of Misión Robinson), interview with the authors, Caracas, July 14, 2005; and Michael Jáuregui (National Co-

ordinator of La Sala Situacional Nacional, Misión Ribas), interview with the authors Caracas, June 27, 2005.

4. *Aló Presidente* No. 227, July 3, 2005.

5. Omar Calzadilla (national coordinator of Misión Robinson), interview with the authors, Caracas, July 14, 2005.

6. Ibid.

7. *Aló Presidente* No. 227, July 3, 2005.

8. Omar Calzadilla (national coordinator of Misión Robinson), interview with the authors, Caracas, July 14, 2005.

9. Information was provided by the Sala Situacional Nacional of Misión Ribas in 2005 (document in possession of the authors).

10. Michael Jáuregui (national coordinator of La Sala Situacional Nacional, Misión Ribas), interview with the authors, Caracas, June 27, 2005.

11. Paulina Campos (national coordinator of Misión Sucre), personal communication with the authors, February 1, 2006.

12. Sol Santander (coordinator for Academic Planning, Misión Sucre), interview with the authors, Caracas, June 30, 2005.

13. Campos, personal communication.

14. Here a comparison between Sucre and Mercal, our two randomly sampled programs, is illustrative. While about 64 percent of Sucre workers indicated that they were salaried (rather than volunteers or recipients of stipends) and only 27 percent indicated that this was their principal employment, 91 percent of Mercal employees said they were salaried and that this was their principal employment. Mercal employees were generally also less well off than the workers in the educational misiones. When asked about the type of housing they live in, about 17 percent of the Mercal workers reported living in the top two of the four possible categories, while 50 percent of the volunteers in Sucre reported the same. The figures for Barrio Adentro, which do not reflect a random sample, typically lie somewhere between these two extremes, but closer to Mercal, as 82 percent of the workers and coordinators that we interviewed in Barrio Adentro indicated that their work was their main employment, but only 33 percent said they were salaried and 21 percent indicated they lived in the top two categories of housing.

15. This information was taken from the website for the program (http://www.mercal.gov.ve) in February 2006.

16. *Aló Presidente* No. 242, December 12, 2005.

17. *Aló Presidente* No. 243, January 8, 2006.

18. In Spanish: *"¿Participan muchos de sus compañeros aquí en las organizaciones populares de su comunidad, como por ejemplo los Círculos Bolivarianos, los Comités de Tierra Urbana, los Comités de Agua, las Asociaciones de Vecinos, las juntas vecinales, o algún ONG? . . . ¿En cuáles? . . . ¿Y Ud es un miembro activo/a en (organización)?"*

19. José Alvarez, interview with the authors, Caracas, June 15, 2005.

20. Omar Calzadilla (national coordinator of Misión Robinson), interview with the authors, Caracas, July 14, 2005; Michael Jáuregui (national coordinator of La Sala Situacional Nacional, Misión Ribas), interview with the authors, Caracas, June 27, 2005; and José Alvarez, interview with the authors, Caracas, June 15, 2005.

21. We hasten to emphasize that teachers working full-time in public schools did not normally receive a stipend for participating as facilitators in the educational misiones. This voluntary work—in the sense of being both noncompulsory *and* unpaid—is re-markable and again highlights the greater autonomy manifest in the educational mi-siones.

22. In our study, the most common Chavista organization mentioned was the Comité de Salud. Fourteen of our workers mentioned belonging to this kind of organization, of which seven also mentioned working in a Barrio Adentro clinic. This seems to con-trast with the findings of García-Guadilla in this volume, who notes that the Comités de Tierra Urbana (CTU) have significant ties to misiones. We found that this was the second-most mentioned organization, with seven respondents (four from Mercal, three from Sucre). However, we did not study the misiones (such as Habitat) that seem more likely to have this kind of association.

23. We downloaded this data from the website of the National Electoral Commission, www.cne.gov.ve.

24. This is based on the assumption that education levels are a likely indicator of Sucre enrollment. We think this is a reasonable assumption, given that education levels are associated with Ribas enrollment.

25. We tested for the possibility that this outcome was simply the result of the educa-tional requirements for these two misiones. That is, if at least a grade-school education is required for Ribas (and a high-school one for Sucre), it is possible that these misiones are located predominantly in middle-income neighborhoods. These neighborhoods are also more likely to be only moderate supporters of Chávez. However, after including a squared term for poverty to capture this potential nonlinear effect, we still found little or no relationship between program allocations and our poverty indicator. See the ap-pendix for these results.

26. Levels of approval for Chávez did go up during the year after the recall election, from about 50 percent to a high of 60 percent in opinion polls (*Consultores 21*, 2006, quarterly survey on presidential approval; data in possession of author). However, this increase is too small to explain the very high levels of support for Chávez that we found in our onsite interviews. In the presidential election of summer 2000, when presidential approval also hovered around 60 percent, Chávez won only 63–68 percent of the vote in the areas we surveyed.

27. We asked this question "gently," toward the middle of the survey and after a set of less controversial questions about the basic structure of the misión. Several forms of the question were possible, depending on how the conversation went, but generally the interviewer asked, "It's evident that the misión offers very valuable services. From what you know, are program recipients required to support the government? For example, do students/recipients have to participate in marches and campaigns?" If answers were unclear or evasive, the interviewer returned to the topic again with follow-up questions of their own design.

28. Omar Calzadilla (national coordinator of Misión Robinson), interview with the authors, Caracas, July 14, 2005.

29. Our interviewee also insisted that any professors that tried to "propagandize"

for the opposition would be fired. We took this to mean that pro-Chávez campaigning during previous elections was not seen as partisan but representative of a legitimate people's movement, of a whole system rather than a narrow set of interests. Names of this and the following interviewee have been deleted to provide anonymity, but notes from these interviews are available on request.

30. The population figures in these preliminary reports are accurate for the major urban municipalities, but population counts in the more rural municipalities seem to suffer from minor non-systematic measurement error. Using this indicator surely biases our parameter estimates downward, that is, toward finding less of an effect.

31. Mean and standard deviation of log scholarships are 5.15 and 0.92.

32. Mean and standard deviation of *Mercal stores* are 0.62 and 2.20. However, *Mercal* lacks a presence in 254 out of 335 municipalities. Of the 208 Mercal locales in Venezuela, 31 are located in Libertador (Caracas) and 16 in Maracaibo; the municipalities of Girardot, Caroní, Iribarren, Sucre (Miranda), Sucre (Sucre), Vargas, and San Francisco each have at least 5 Mercal locations. It is obvious that Mercal stores are distributed mostly in urban centers, and therefore population size is the best predictor of Mercal presence.

33. We re-ran the model for Ribas enrollment with a squared term for *pct college*, assuming that this might account for the curvilinear effect of poverty, but the results were not statistically significant.

CHAPTER EIGHT

Defying the Iron Law of Oligarchy II

Debating Democracy Online in Venezuela

Daniel Hellinger

Shortly after the polls closed on December 2, 2007, Venezuelans learned that for the first time since the presidential election of 1998, a period covering ten national elections, their charismatic president, Hugo Chávez Frías, had suffered an electoral defeat. Two packages of constitutional reforms that he put forth (after discussion and some alteration in the National Assembly) had failed to pass by less than a percentage point. But the defeat was made more palpable by opposition majorities in Chavista strongholds in poor urban barrios and by a very low turnout. On December 3, Chávez seemed to accept responsibility for the outcome, just as he had after the failed coup of 1992, saying, "I was mistaken in choosing the moment to propose the reform."[1] He also mused, "Perhaps we are not mature enough to begin a socialist project without fear. We are still not ready to launch a socialist government."[2]

For the most part, the official government media, especially *La Hojilla*, the nightly program devoted to deconstructing opposition discourse through satire and ridicule, followed the president's line. Many prominent Chavista politicians highlighted the effectiveness of the opposition campaign, implying that the people had been deceived about the true content of the reform packages. However, in a different media arena, the Internet, a much more profound debate was taking place about the meaning of the vote. On blogs and discussion forums, grassroots activists, officials on the lower rungs of the political hierarchy, intellectuals, and others were carrying on a rich discussion. They offered differing and often complex diagnoses of the defeat of the reform package. Some offered analyses similar to those on the *oficialista* media, but many others dared to question the desirability of the reform package itself and even to question the leadership of Chávez.

The tenor of the discussion reflects in many respects the kind of political interaction envisioned by Michael Hardt and Antonio Negri in *The Multitude* (2004). "The Multitude," they say, is the emerging global force for socialist emancipation, a heterogeneous "living alternative that grows with Empire" that opens the possibility for "democracy on a global scale for the very first time." The Multitude's heterogeneity, say Hardt and Negri, requires its parts to discover through discourse "the common that allows them to communicate and act together." It organizes itself in a way distinct "from centralized forms of revolutionary dictatorship and command." The "main commonality" is the desire for democracy in social and economic spheres, not just in the political sphere. These spheres "become increasingly indistinct from politics, hence socialist" (xiii–xvi).

One review of *The Multitude* summarized Hardt and Negri's thesis in this way: "The network struggles of the multitude . . . are more effective and democratic than earlier models of popular or guerilla warfare. The Multitude, for example, can organize itself horizontally, siphon support for Empire, and strike proficiently using the Internet" (Tampio 2005). Hardt and Negri themselves contend, "A distributed network such as the Internet is a good initial image or model for the Multitude because, first, the various nodes remain different but are all connected in the Web, and, second, the external boundaries of the network are open such that new modes and new relationships can always be added" (2004, xv).

Hardt and Negri's conception of revolutionary socialist politics is certainly problematic. Can all points of view and priorities be encompassed within a movement for revolutionary change? How are conflicts about goals and strategies to be resolved without a more formal institutional context than a "network"? Will disputes ultimately resolve themselves through communication? Is there a place for a political party in organizing the Multitude, and if so, what kind? Does this vision of a revolutionary social force underestimate the importance and potential of the "proletariat" defined in more classically Marxist terms?

In this examination of Bolivarian democracy on the net, we shall see that forging commonality and overcoming tendencies toward verticalism and personalism are extraordinarily challenging, even on the Internet. On the other hand, the character of the Internet makes it very difficult for a government to isolate and dismiss criticism within its own ranks. Points of view and discussion rarely heard in either private and state media find expression and elicit debate in this arena. In this respect, participation on the Internet in Bolivarian Venezuela resembles in some ways that of community media, as other chapters in this book explore.

The search for democratic communality engages Venezuelans in the creative activity of re-imagining democracy, a theme explored through the survey research presented in "Defying the Iron Law of Oligarchy I" (chapter 1, this volume), where I suggested that this task involves overcoming Michel's Iron Law of Oligarchy. Were Venezuelans to accomplish this task, even imperfectly, they would be making history, much in the way that the founders of the American (U.S.) Republic did in experimenting with constitutional forms in the late eighteenth century. The prospects for success in forging genuine and innovative democratic institutions in Venezuela in the end may depend not so much on the quality of President Chávez's leadership as on the determination of Venezuelans engaged in political activism to reconcile the competing principles of participation and representation.

In this chapter we examine popular conceptions of the roles of participation and representation through the analysis of debate on the Net regarding Chávez's attempt to accelerate revolution after December 2006. Our research will focus on Aporrea.org, an electronic space combining news reports, blogs, and forums, which has become the most utilized site on the Web for discussion among dedicated grassroots leaders, public officials, and intellectuals in Venezuela. In this way I hope to make three contributions to the theme of this book:

— To contribute an additional study of an area of experimentation with popular participation, the Internet.
— To ascertain the degree of consensus and debate among middle-level Chavista cadres and activists.
— To evaluate the degree to which conceptions of democracy, especially of the relative weight accorded representation and participation, coincide with attitudes we uncovered in our survey of residents of barrios with a history and reputation for a high degree of popular organization.

Working in poor barrios and underserved rural areas, many Bolivarian cadre are certainly not regular users of the Internet, yet thousands of them have gone online to discuss the issues and exchange experiences.

On the Internet, however, the tensions between the representative and participatory principles in the constitution are highlighted both in the nature of the issues and in the discourse itself. For example, after his landslide reelection in 2006, President Chávez announced that Venezuela would pursue twenty-first-century socialism by forming a United Socialist Party of Venezuela (PSUV), accelerating programs of "endogenous development," and authorizing another constitutional assembly to reshape the constitution. The subsequent defeat of these constitutional reforms in a December 2007 referendum unleashed a broader debate that had been somewhat attenuated until that time.

The analysis here will focus on discourse about democracy. This focus allows us to draw some comparisons between the attitudes of grassroots leaders with that of the broader Chavista social base explored in "Defying the Iron Law of Oligarchy I."

Internet Discourse, Autonomy, and Participation

Asamblea Popular Revolucionaria (Aporrea.org) was founded in May 2002 expressly to serve as a forum for discussion and advancement of participatory democracy. *Aporrea* loosely translates as "the beat." The organization's birth followed hard upon the short-lived coup of April 2002, when popular radio, cell phone, and Internet communications were crucial in rallying popular defense of the Chávez regime (L. Gómez 2003). Aporrea says it seeks "to divulge socio-economic news and opinion, identifying with the process of revolutionary and democratic transformation of Venezuela" as "a popular alternative news agency, [and] open digital bulletin board interactive with the movement of people and workers."

Aporrea's founding team was Trotskyite, but they were quickly joined by a variety of other tendencies within the broader Bolivarian movement.[3] Occasionally the editors of the page have denied access to someone claiming to criticize the Chavista project within the bounds of Bolivarian ideology. However, unlike the official media, Aporrea provides a forum for some very harsh criticism, all the more biting in that it comes from within, sometimes from individuals whom the president's most ardent followers regard as apostates.

Such was the case with Orlando Chirino, leader of the Classist, Unified Revolutionary and Autonomous Front (C-Cura) of the National Workers Union (UNT), who opposed the constitutional amendments, criticized certain aspects of the endogenous development policies, and in January 2008 was fired from his job in the state oil company (his job was eventually restored). In 2007 Chirino and his supporters were able to fully air their views about the constitutional reform package on Aporrea. At times they were targets of bitter denunciations, but they were afforded full access to the readership. A posting by Chirino on November 23 complained of dirty tactics by other Chavista factions and disputed another posting on Aporrea that equated his opposition to the reforms as a vote for Bush. Many who criticized Chirino still interpreted his firing as an attack on the autonomy of the labor movement in general, and he elicited for the most part messages of support from leaders of other tendencies in the UNT.

Occasionally, a contributor has been banned for engaging in inflammatory rhetoric and highly personal accusations. For example, Jorge Mier Hoffman, a frequent contributor, found himself exiled from Aporrea. In a salutary message, Mier complained that the editors placed the thought of Marx ahead of that of Bolívar, whom he regarded as a more faithful exponent of humanist socialism. A review of Mier's writings showed considerably more incendiary assertions, such as a claim that Marxism could be equated with fascism.[4] Of course Mier could not be banned from the Internet; his own blog had 575 registered users in 2007.[5]

There is no mistaking the pro-Chávez tenor of discussion on Aporrea, which sometimes borders on sycophantic. However, even among the most ardent supporters of Chávez there seems to be a commitment to maintaining Aporrea's autonomy. The attitude of its coordinators seems to be cut from the same cloth as that which animates community broadcasters, as described by Fernandes and by Schiller in this book. As David Smilde points out in the introduction, the liberal conception of civil society is inadequate for locating such groups that seek autonomy but not necessarily separation from the state. In the context of a highly polarized society in which mass leadership has been entrusted, at least for the present time, to a highly charismatic leader, a political missionary, the question arises whether autonomy can, in fact, be maintained. Pancho Tosta, an opposition blogger in the United States, claims (without offering evidence) that the entire operation is funded by the Venezuelan government.[6]

Aporrea in 2006 was registered to one of its editors, Martin Sánchez, a former student in the United States, living in Caracas at the time (later to return to the United States for graduate school in California). According to a WHOIS search by Domain Tools, Aporrea had changed its host five times by December 2006, when it was being hosted on a dedicated server provided by Atjeu L.L.C. in Glendale, Arizona. Atjeu has no apparent political mission or connection to the Venezuelan government. The minimum monthly fee listed on Atjeu's busness site in 2007 was US$129 per month. On Aporrea, Sánchez says that the forum is entirely maintained by voluntary labor.

The coordinators leave ambiguous the question of whether they accept government support. They invite noncommercial advertising from the private sector, government, and social movements but say they seek "autonomy without submitting ourselves to the logic of capital."[7] However, "financing through donations is insufficient because the pockets of the people are limited, as we do not receive contributions from the rich, not because we don't want money, but because we won't sell out and want to remain free of all suspicion." What then of state funding?

Nor is it easy to seek help though the social policies of the state, a terrain on which the people have obtained important conquests in the present revolutionary process, because there remains the inertia of capitalist state institutions. . . . Our political independence, our editing and critical work, is neither comfortable to nor controllable by bureaucratic strata that demand silence or draw limits, that compromise resources, make deals, or distill sectarianism. . . . Fortunately, we have also found some help, still very limited but welcome without conditions contrary to our principles, where there are broader and clearer visions, where it is better understood what it means to break the media blockade and open new channels for the revolution.

It is difficult to gauge how many readers and posters participate on Aporrea. Some indication comes from the statistics on visits tracked at the bottom of each posting and from the number of replies generated. Early in the day (December 15, 2006) that Chávez launched his call for a united PSUV, anticipating the announcement, a contributor named "Bombom" posted a call: "My wish, *comandante*, [is] that you form without delay a grand party of the Venezuelan left." By January 30, 2007, the posting had been read over 4,700 times and generated 186 responses. This discussion still fell far short of the record. The category "Obras del gobierno—todos a contribuir" (Government achievements—everyone contribute), initiated on June 14, 2006, had generated 792 responses and 48,891 visits by January 30, 2007 (though it is difficult to know how many discrete visitors there were). Another topic, "Poesía y revolución," opened on October 15, 2006, had generated 132 responses and over 2,600 readers. Aporrea promises potential advertisers (*colaboradores*) that ads and notices will reach "tens of thousands of viewers" daily.

According to Internet World Stats for 2006, approximately three million of Venezuela's twenty-six million people were Internet users. This amounts to an Internet penetration of 11.8 percent, considerably lower than countries in the Southern Cone (e.g., Argentina is at 34 percent and Chile at 42.4 percent), and slightly below the rate of use in Brazil (13.9 percent). These estimates, compiled from data gathered from Nielsen ratings and the International Telecommunications Union, may underestimate the full extent of Internet usage. Computer access is widely shared in apartments and neighborhoods in Venezuela, and several low-cost Internet cafés can be found in towns of any size. Thailand had a similar score (12.5 percent) in 2006 as well as a similarly extensive distribution of low-cost cafés. Brazil and Venezuela both ranked in the top fifteen countries for average hours per visitor to major sites in a survey done by Direct

Marketing News on May 12, 2006, also suggesting much higher usage than surveys uncover.[8]

Aporrea offers a forum for contributors, a blog, and news taken mostly from the publications sympathetic to the government. It frequently reprints editorials and analyses from print sources, such as editorials by Eleazar Díaz Rangel, editor of *Ultimas Noticias*, the highest circulation newspaper in the country, and it re-posts video clips made by community media organizations, Vive TV (a cable and Internet channel affiliated with the National Assembly) and the state television network (VTV). Many clips are taken from VTV's *La Hojilla*. Its host, Mario Silva, was elected to a high leadership position in the PSUV in 2008. But Silva and his program periodically come under criticism from those who feel it is intolerant or too much influenced by the government.[9]

A sense of Aporrea's independence can be gleaned from an incident illustrating the limits of official media in Venezuela. On September 15, 2005, President Chávez called *La Hojilla* to urge Silva to cease defending Walter Martínez, a journalist on VTV, who claimed that "false revolutionaries" were in control of the station and of some government positions. The next day, Martínez and his program were gone, provoking much debate. On September 21, Julio Mosquera, after first recognizing Martínez's skills as a journalist, defended the firing on Aporrea with a critique of Martínez's program, *Dossier*. "*Dossier* presents a Eurocentric (or Anglo-centric) view of the world. The greater part of the program is dedicated to events, generally military, happening in the Northern Hemisphere." However, Mosquera was alone that day in opposing the tide of criticism; ten other postings on Aporrea called for the program's reinstatement (which did not occur). One contributor wrote, "I, Zulay Farías M., feel vindicated, respected, and full of hope because of the courage of Walter Martínez; his cry was mine" (September 19). After Silva's election to the national committee of the PSUV, a number of posters raised questions about a conflict of interest. For example, after praising Silva's revolutionary credentials and work on *La Hojilla*, Anderson G. Salas suggested on May 14, 2008, that because of the new position someone else should take his place in the media. Salas also worried that Silva would use his media advantage to challenge the incumbent governor of the state of Carabobo, Aragua, "un verdadero gobernador socialista" (a true socialist governor).

The participants on Aporrea come mainly from two groups. One group consists of grassroots leaders who self-consciously distinguish themselves from the professional political class that occupies bureaucratic posts and elected positions. Many of this corps of thousands are ordinary Venezuelans who have joined enthusiastically in the work of missions, communal councils, grassroots committees, popular radio stations, women's circles, radical union movements, and Electoral Battle Units (community teams dedicated to getting out the Chavista vote). The second group consists of the professional politicians, government officials, and traditional intellectuals (professors, poets, etc.) who have aligned themselves with Bolivarianism, if not with Chávez himself.

The first category of contributors to Aporrea may come closest in the Bolivarian Revolution to formation of what Antonio Gramsci regarded as "organic intellectuals." Gramsci insisted that such intellectuals "work incessantly to raise the intellectual level of ever-growing strata of the populace, in other words, to give a personality to the amorphous mass element. This means working to produce intellectuals of a new type which arise directly out of the masses, but remain in contact with them to become, as it were, the whalebone in the corset" (1978, 340). Although some intellectuals, in the sense of specialist workers in culture, might become organic intellectuals, for Gramsci the revolution cannot be successful unless the exploited class can produce its own.

Shall We Party? The Debate about the PSUV and Accelerating Revolution

In this section, I offer a summary of the debate that took place in Aporrea during the six weeks (December 15, 2006, to January 31, 2007, unless otherwise indicated) after the president's call for formation of a unified party; for a new enabling law (*ley habilitante*—essentially an authorization to make law by decree, subject to review by the Assembly, in limited areas for a defined time); and for reform of the 1999 Constitution. The discussion took place in the context of several other presidential initiatives, including the re-nationalization of telecommunications and other previously privatized enterprises; elimination of the political autonomy of the Central Bank (a measure intended to ease the transfer of oil-export earnings into governmental programs); the allotment of 43 percent of the 2007 budget to projects authorized by local communal councils; a call to adjust salaries so that no official would earn more than three million bolívares (approximately US$1400) per month; an instruction to all cabinet ministers (many of whom were new) that they were to work no more than three days in their office and were to spend the rest of their time in the field; measures to exploit majority state ownership of heavy oil in the Orinoco region; and the first increase in domestic gasoline prices in twelve years.

Most of these matters evoked little dissent among the contributors to Aporrea. The recovery of majority ownership in oil, reduction of Central Bank authority, and re-nationalizations were viewed in general as long overdue reversals of neoliberal policies. The gas-price increase, potentially a sensitive issue because it was an immediate catalyst for the Caracazo in 1989, evoked postings that were mostly critical of opposition attempts to take advantage of the move. Several contributors pointed out that the increase would hit those who could afford gas-guzzling SUVs the most. Others pointed out that merchants had already raised prices, using the gas hike as an excuse.

Denunciations of corruption and bureaucratic ineptitude are frequent subjects of discussion. Chávez argued that his pack of constitutional amendments was needed to address these problems. However, toward the end of January, several contributors began to call instead for use of existing mechanisms to hold officials responsible. Leaders of the Movimiento Electoral del Pueblo (MEP) called for use of the *revocatorio* mechanism on January 30, which was endorsed by several posters. (The Bolivarian Constitution permits recall of elected officials when they pass the midpoint of their terms.) Other opinions placed more stress on strengthening existing popular organizations to supervise elected officials. For example, one poster (Miguel Maregatti, January 26) issued a call to form Juntas de Abastemcimiento Popular (Popular Supply Councils) linked to communal councils to combat corruption in the Mercal program.

Corruption and inefficiency are often associated with the Punto Fijo regime, but many contributors see too much continuity between current practices and those of that era. A typical complaint was registered on December 31 by Tamara Lías on behalf of artisan workers in Aragua state. Complaining that a promising law to promote the artisan economy had been corrupted by clientelism, she wrote, "Well known among us are the names and faces of those pseudo-artisans and artisans that were 'installed' on the State Council of Artisans of Aragua and that 'represent us' in any regional, national, or international event, at the same time earning credits, support, subsidies, institutional help, etc."[10] Lías pointed to an exposition cancelled at the last moment after organizers had already spent millions of bolívares. Rather than being treated as cultural workers, artisans are more typically regarded as producing commercial objects or products for tourists, she said. Before 1998 a complaint of this nature would have been phrased in the context of demand for more authentic representation. Lías, typical of Bolivarian cadres, demanded not more honest representation but rapid and effective implementation of direct participation of artisans through their own councils.

These discussions took place in the context of a broader debate about how to pursue "socialism of the twenty-first century," about the president's call for revision of the constitution to revise the "geometry of power," and about his call for all parties in his coalition to disband and for their members to join the new PSUV. Many contributors immediately backed the president's call for the PSUV without qualification. "Those who have doubts about socialism of the twenty-first century and the necessity of constructing the PSUV should leave the process, because to doubt at this moment is to lose valuable historic time for the construction of real socialism," wrote Carlos Omar Fernándea of the Frente Único Revolucionario Simón Bolívar (Simón Bolívar unified revolutionary front) on January 15, condemning leaders of the parties in the Bolivarian alliance for failing to "understand the importance of putting aside their particular interests." The Frente announced on January 25 its decision to dissolve itself into the PSUV "without conditions and without asking conditions from anyone."

The topic "EL PSUV: El Partido Socialista de Venezuela" (The PSUV: Venezuela's Socialist Party) generated 187 postings and over 4,800 visits in the six weeks after the president's announcement. The vast majority of postings were enthusiastic, but much of the enthusiasm was generated by the hope that the new, unified party would replace the MVR with a more democratic revolutionary organization. Daniela Saidman, a journalist from eastern Bolívar state and member of a popular movement formed initially to resist the coup of April 13, 2002, expressed hope that the PSUV would give voice to "millions of Venezuelans who aim for revolutionary transformation." Saidman went on, however, to say, "What we are not capable of accommodating is imposition of leaders. The unified party is the possibility of constructing an authentic democracy, without tricks, where the popular voice will be the standard-bearer for all the social conquests to come" (January 4, 2007).

A somewhat triumphalist tone characterized the arguments of many who endorsed the call to form the PSUV. However, it was not the anti-Chávez opposition that they saw as losers but the Chavista political establishment, whose practices they frequently associated with those of the Punto Fijo era. The PSUV would finally put these politicians in their place! Their solution to the bureaucratization and corruption of the revolution was not seen merely to construct a party more representative of the people, but to create one more organically linked to the people through participation. Hopes for the future were often embedded in a more general assertion that the solution to the corruption and clientelism was the elimination of a class of professional politicians entirely — a theme closely linked to replacing representative democracy with participatory democracy. In this respect, the reorganization of the revolutionary movement was regarded as part and parcel of Chávez's announcement of impending constitutional and legal reforms intended to produce a new "geography of the state" and to strengthen the role of communal councils.

However, a significant number of contributors questioned the wisdom of forming a single party as well as the manner in which the president was demanding disciplined acceptance and the haste with which the party was to be founded. Of particular importance was a critique, widely circulated in various electronic and print journals, by Edgardo Lander, an influential leftist professor with a family history closely entwined with the history of the left in Venezuela.[11] Lander wrote on December 26, 2006, that the rush to form a single party of the left had overtaken the need, endorsed by Chávez himself, to study the fate of "twentieth-century socialism" and develop a vision allowing for more pluralism. Referring to the proposal to meld all parties into the PSUV, Lander wrote, "In this case, what has been enunciated, far from contributing to clarify ideas, can only help conceal the absence of collective reflection and the construction of a false notion of consensus, a consensus not to debate a matter so critical to the future of the country." Lander called for the reservations expressed by the smaller parties in the government coalition (e.g., over the internal organization of the party and its ideology) to be taken seriously and not dismissed as mere postures to hold onto power and access to patronage.

Reaction was mixed. Some posters greeted his critique with a polemic decrying any suggestion to resist Chávez's call for unity. Omar Marcano, a Communist Party member of the National Assembly, for example, responded, "Because people who believe in the process require short-term results, the people are not disposed to tolerate sterile debates that only waste time. The debate should be oriented to construct participatory democracy . . . , not to merely mark off territory" (December 27). José Zamora, identifying himself with the Revolutionary Socialist Front, endorsed the need for a single leftist party but rebuked Marcano for denigrating Lander's warning about the failure to truly analyze the failures of twentieth-century socialism (January 9).

Suspicion about professional politicians in the Chávez coalition in many instances reaches the point of outright cynicism. Few were more vitriolic than José Sant Roz, a novelist and mathematics professor at the University of the Andes in Mérida. His posting on December 6, 2007—which was visited over 1,740 times in the four months following the referendum—painted a portrait of Chavista officials celebrating the defeat of the referendum:

> At the moment that the results were made known, the headquarters of the MVR in Mérida were occupied by those barons who function (and still function) to perfection under the command of Don Corleone Luis Miquilena.[12] A parade of luxury cars [arrived] as though we were in front of a five star hotel on the French Riviera. Here were the entrepreneurs

and contractors waiting to toast the results, come what may. What does it matter; they always win. The fattest fish said, "We've already lost; they're [the anti-Chávez opposition] ahead by 8 points. . . ." A deputy of the National Assembly interrupted him: "The PSUV isn't worth crap, and something more, comrades: Let's celebrate anyway." A high representative of the judiciary intervened: "By all means, I read this entire Reform and it's a disaster. It's not worth approval. Come on, let's toast." . . . Like many fellow citizens I awoke [the next morning] thinking, what do we do now, and I was overcome by a sense of horror. Nine years have passed and in grand measure we are still governed by *adecos* [supporters of AD]. . . . I swear that almost all the officials of Mérida on the government payroll voted in favor of NO, and they did it because of the immense and anti-communal indifference that the sheiks of government showed in regard to the Reform campaign. Grey, sluggish, and languid were officials of the governorship and mayoralty in regard to Bolivarian Project.

Those most enthusiastically in support of the PSUV initiative often refer to Chávez as *comandante*, reflecting a (male) gendered notion of political struggle. One of many such communications was posted by *voceros* (spokespersons) for the Collectivos Comutarios of the 23 de Enero barrio in the city of Maracay, who called on "Comandante Hugo Chávez" to advance the formation and empowerment of communal councils. At the same time, however, the voceros appealed to "our maximum leader" to intervene and help them resist the local municipal council's adjudication of land sales in violation, they claimed, of urban land reform statutes. As in many postings about local conflicts, writers linked formation of the PSUV and reform of the state with a hope that these actions would remove corrupt or inefficient politicians blocking the democratic will of the community.

While contributors to Aporrea usually praise the leadership of President Chávez enthusiastically, many also disagreed openly with the president, even before the December 2007 referendum defeat, when criticism exploded (as discussed below). Aura M. Rodríguez bluntly entitled her posting in December 2006, "Chávez is wrong," and predicted that a Chavista opposition would eventually emerge. She also argued that there were large sectors of the middle class who were not *esquálidos,* who also should be considered part of the popular sector and not excluded from participation in government. Edmundo Iribarren wrote on December 26, "This discussion [about the PSUV] does not form a part of the day-to-day experience in the life of the people. For example, it is not a central focus of the activity of communal councils, defined as the embryonic cell of the new society, nor among the many conglomerations of missions nor among workers and peasants, fundamental protagonists of socialist construction; nor in buses and *por puestos* [vans or small buses]." Iribarren held out the possibility of a more promising result: "The Venezuelan people have demonstrated to the utmost that they are prepared for more complicated tasks, to be truly protagonists in their history, constructing a party of revolution from the roots, which is the only form in which we should discuss a party of the revolution. A party has to be capable in a given case of saying 'no' to its own *comandante*."

Saying no to the *comandante* can be difficult, but Jesús Puerta, referring to a series of earlier efforts by Chávez to create a political organization devoid of the vices of the past, diagnosed the problem as one that goes beyond the president himself on December 20, 2007: "This rapid succession of political organizations is symptomatic of the tension between the Chávez style of leadership and any form of permanent political organization, but also is a characteristic of our process: an extreme 'fluidity' of the 'revolutionary subject,' whose only 'fixed' factor . . . is the leadership of Hugo Chávez." He went on, "We can say that there are three acerbic criticisms directed at the parties: their political inefficiency, their parasitism regarding the political capital of Chávez, and the demonstrated capacity of the masses to act politically without unnecessary 'intermediaries.'" However, Puerta still supported the formation of a single party of the left in the quest to find an organizational form that goes beyond effective representation, one that integrates participation and representation more effectively.

For many grassroots Chavistas, the parties in the oficialista coalition, including the MVR, had no right to interpret the results of the December 3, 2006, landslide for Chávez as any type of mandate for their own political aspirations. "If the members of the Miranda Command [the name given to the Chávez campaign structure in 2006] are the new leaders of the PSUV," wrote Saidman, "we'll be right back where we started. It was the middle level leaders of the MVR who had responsibility for re-legitimating *compañero presidente*. It wasn't the Miranda command that gave the votes to Chávez; it was more [due] to his leadership that hasn't lost brilliance in these eight years of government. Everyone knows this" (January 3, 2007). Rosalia del Prado noted on January 3, 2007, that Chávez's call for the PSUV was not the first time that he sought to reinvigorate his movement after an electoral triumph. She warned that real victory belonged to the people; that just as in the 2004 recall campaign, it was the local "patrols" and UBEs (Electoral Battle Units) that won the day, not the politicians given command posts.

Nicmer Evans, a political scientist from the Bolivarian University, an institution founded by Chávez to advance revolutionary and popular higher education, called for the PSUV to be built upon social movements, defined as "all
organized social sectors that have as their goal defense of fundamental principles or human rights through actions that pressure centers of power," and
community organizations, defined as "social structures that encourage action
for betterment of the quality of life in their home regions" (January 3, 2007).
Amado Rivero, a frequent contributor, community activist, and vocero for integral security of the communal council of Las Acacias, in the state of Lara, insisted that communal government must replace the "representative structure
of the Fourth Republic" (January 16, 2007). Similarly, Rivero exhorted readers
to insist that the PSUV itself be composed of members elected as *delegates* (n.b.,
not *representatives*) of communities in order to avoid professional politicians
from controlling the party.

Not all posters are enchanted by the notion of horizontal networks. The
drive for discipline and unity underlay some of the support for creation of the
PSUV. Some contributors advocated that party membership be limited to militants advancing the revolution through work in the missions and popular organizations. Pedro Figueroa identified himself without apology as a state leader
of the MVR and veteran of several education missions and promotion of cooperatives. As a result of his experience with many communal councils, said
Figueroa (January 26, 2007), he had concluded, "We are several years away
from a true transition, but the time for transitions is past. For this reason I believe in the idea that a party ought to be controlled, at least in its first stage,
while we dismantle the destructive values of capitalism." Appealing to Lenin-
ist thought on formation of a revolutionary party, he made clear that control
ought to be in the hands of those admitted to party membership by fulfilling
requirements of a certain profile.

Yet another view, somewhat of a synthesis between the vanguardist and
post-modern views of the party, was expressed by William E. Izarra, a former
air force officer heading the quasi-governmental Ideological Education Center.
He argued that the conflict between discipline and democracy persists under
reformism but would be resolved in revolutionary Venezuela through an "assembly method" in which "the community will not require intermediation of
any sort alien from its own structures" (December 28, 2006). The communal
councils will respond to these assemblies and eliminate those representative
functions of parties that lead to clientelism. The old party role "was to *carneti-
zar* [make access to the state dependent on having a party membership] everything that they could exploit to their benefit, which depended on how many
votes they could total up at election time. . . . Now this role ought no longer

to exist. . . . The political party will be the electoral instrument to take power, transfer it to the people, and train the community to exercise it."

Horizontal Governance

Despite the generally negative tone of postings about government officials, several of the latter are frequent contributors to Aporrea. David E. Monroy, an official in the Ministry of Planning, put forth on January 12, 2007, an agenda for discussion, including the need "to decide if the *deepening of democracy* implies, among other things, elimination of representative democracy, to be totally and definitively replaced by *direct democracy*, as well as [discussion of] all matters related to proportional representation of minorities" (his emphasis). Monroy could not be accused of simply following the Chávez line as he asserted that the ley habilitante was "at least needless given the political correlation of the National Assembly." He urged the Assembly not to wait for decrees to legislate on social security, health, public administration, and other matters. Attached to his posting was a form that listed each ministry with a blank space where readers could mail back suggestions regarding how popular power could be implemented in each case.

Rivero, the vocero from the state of Lara, suggested (January 14, 2007) that society would be much more democratic if the system of electing municipal officials were replaced by a network of communal councils. This "model would arise from the community and replace the parish councils [sub-municipal units of government]. Councilmen and the figure of the mayor, and the municipal council, a den where the only thing generated is the parasitism of bureaucracy, would disappear. [In its place would be] established a new figure and organ of municipal popular power by an assembly of voceros of communal councils." Nicmer Evans, a Bolivarian University professor, had proposed (in an article read over 3,400 times) that networks of communal councils be incorporated in the constitution and integrated into a revised system of municipal power (August 19, 2005).

Though translated here as "spokespersons," the term *voceros* has a deeper meaning in the discourse about popular power. Much as evangelicals might want to eliminate the clergy as intermediaries between God and believers (see Smilde in this volume), Rivero would eliminate mediators between the people and the sovereign. The figure of vocero was formally contemplated in the law (of 2002) creating communal councils, which mandates that resources be allocated to them and that, under penalty of a fine, mayors must consult with them through the institution of a planning council. The choice of *vocero* rather than *representante* to designate council members is indicative of how the new constitution and accompanying laws attempted to articulate two distinct branches of government—one representative and one participatory.

In these postings, we often find echoes of Hardt and Negri's neo-Marxist theories of empire and the multitude (2000, 2004), which advance the notion of horizontal networks, enabled by the changes in the mode of production fostered by information technology, serving as a revolutionary organization. Gustavo Fernández Colón, a professor at the University of Carabobo, argued on December 12, "In a few words, the political party is inscribed fundamentally in the moribund system of representative democracy and, in this same respect, is one of the great obstacles to the organic maturation of participation and protagonism of popular communities." Colón argued on December 17 that political organization sought to approximate "a confederation of communities, or a network of diverse social organizations, with distinctive interests and ideologies . . . It ought to privilege *horizonalidad* and permanent dialogue as the primary orientation for construction of a new state, not *verticalidad* and ideological homogenization." A revolutionary party "structured on the basis of functional differentiation between leadership cadre and mass militants, between representatives and the represented" only "brings 'benefits' when evaluated using the parameters of modernity."[13]

Aporrea has hosted vigorous debate over the character, style, and contributions of Chávez as a leader. "The caesarist revolutionary style of leadership of the process of transformation has much impeded the development of a collective leadership," wrote Javier Biardeu, a socialist at the Central University of Venezuela (UCV), warning that the PSUV might end up ultra-centrist in its organization and produce populist authoritarianism (January 17, 2007). Colón, on the other hand, was more sanguine about the need for strong leadership (December 12, 2007): "The effectiveness of emerging revolutionary leaders, such as Hugo Chávez and Evo Morales, is due basically to their ability to act as direct interlocutors with popular communities, their aptitude to dialogue with the excluded from the point of view of their (the 'excludeds') own language and vision of the world." Okrim Al Qasal, a Venezuelan blogger often re-posted on Aporrea, admonished other posters to take some responsibility for the tendency of people to regard Chávez as a mortal god: "We must make a mental and verbal effort, because Chávez is mortal, one day he will leave this earth . . . and then what? The communal councils, greater participation, delegation of rights—and more important, of responsibilities—to the people, all this points down the same road: that it should be *the persons* and not *the person* (Chávez) that takes Venezuela where it deserves" (January 22, 2007).

Postings about participation frequently reflect concerns about the levels presently achieved but optimism about potential. Alfredo Mourad Naime, affiliated with the Bolivarian Foundation for Education and Participatory Democracy, cast doubt on the preparedness of the people to exercise a high level of participatory democracy: "Real popular participation by the people in the administration and shaping of the country has been little. An example of this is that the people wait desperately for *comandante* Chávez in order to present petitions to satisfy elemental necessities, such as housing, health and work" (January 20, 2007). Still, Naime claimed, the people were ready for a prolonged and serious discussion about constitutional reform, which should not be entrusted to experts and intellectuals alone.

Overwhelmingly posters favored horizontal over vertical ties. Del Prado expressed optimism that this time the president would succeed in institutionalizing popular democracy though the PSUV because "unlike earlier processes, now the spaces for discussion, organization, political work [and] mobilization exist all over" (January 1, 2008). She cited the growth of neighborhood councils, barrio assemblies, collectives, urban land committees, health committees, voluntary work in missions, and other organizations of working men and women. This should lead to socialism, she argued, because "that person in the community begins to resolve problems and becomes part of the process of taking power in the community . . . , when he or she goes to their place of work, their factory, the enterprise where they work, he or she is also victim of the violence exercised by capital that operates as though no changes were taking place in Venezuela" (January 1, 2007).

The way to avoid the Iron Law of Oligarchy, supporters of radical constitutional reform seem to imply, is to develop networks in place of hierarchy. In his post on December 12 (discussed above), Jesús Puerta came close to addressing Michel's famous dictum directly:

> Has it not been a historical constant that political parties have devolved into an oligarchy? This happens when political organizations fall into established routines, become formalized and hierarchical. In general terms, this happened in the USSR and other pseudo-socialist countries of the twentieth century, and in the representative democracies as well. Effectively, the proposal for a unified party carries the risk of bureaucratization and oligarchization.

However, according to Puerta, the need to develop the organizational capacity to contest the bourgeoisie for hegemony justified creation of the PSUV as a new form of party that could transcend the obsolescence of the old style of party.

The dangers would be mitigated by the continued existence of the very opposition that the PSUV will contest and by the level of mobilization of the masses.

Endogenous Development and Democracy

Representative democracy, like neoliberalism, is identified in the minds of many militants with an economic model responsible for social and political exclusion. Rafael Pompillo Santeliz, in a widely distributed posting, cited intellectuals such as the Mexican Enrique Dussel and the Italian Antonio Negri in arguing that the excluded, or the "multitude," are the social force that will play the role of the proletariat in Venezuela's socialist revolution (January 4, 2007). Many Aporrea contributors regarded the creation of participatory institutions as absolutely essential to achieving inclusion of the informal ("marginalized," in older parlance) sector, which had perhaps doubled in Venezuela between 1980 and 2000.

Bolivarian ideology stresses "endogenous development" as key not only to improving the material conditions of life but also to the foundation of a solidaristic sector of the economy that will be necessary to sustain popular hegemony and twenty-first-century socialism. However, on Aporrea one finds considerable dissent about many aspects of endogenous development. Especially divided is the Bolivarian labor movement, the UNT (National Union of Workers). Cooperatives, say some UNT leaders, operate on the principles of capitalism and inadequately take into account the broader needs of the community. Other contributors argue that the co-management schemes and cooperatives are used by PDVSA and other firms to deny workers basic unionization rights under the labor code. A group of workers affiliated with several unions in the eastern oil regions demanded on January 27, 2007, that the government move more quickly on nationalization, but not because they sought participation in running the company. They were motivated mainly by the refusal of the existing company, a mixed enterprise with a majority of private shares in the hands of foreign investors, to recognize their union.

To other radical activists, the problem with endogenous development and co-management has less to do with compromising labor rights. Their view is that the "communal state" is being developed alongside the more typical bourgeois economic and state structures. Collectivo Invedecor, a popular education movement, said that comanagement schemes—which usually involve workers and the state sharing ownership of nationalized enterprises, with the state retaining majority control—will only erect barriers to revolution. The Collectivo predicted that "the mediations of 'state capitalism' will block completely a genuine revolutionary strategy in this field" (January 23, 2007). Luis E. Rangel, a journalist, warned that cooperatives are not necessarily socialist in outlook: "The majority of transport lines are cooperatives in the purest style of savage capitalism" (January 29, 2007). Francisco Sierra Corrales, posting in response to President Chavez's visit to a ranching cooperative in the state of Cojedes, broadcast on *Aló Presidente* on January 29, complained that the president failed to see how the nearby community was excluded from the economic benefits of the prosperous enterprise. The village residents continued living in acute poverty, while "the cooperative is a model of capitalist production because it seeks profit, and private property is exercised over the means of production."

Disputes over organization of the labor movement make evident issues that will almost inevitably arise in organizing the PSUV. Some UNT factions call for direct elections of the leadership by the base, while others see such elections as a formula for disunity and alienation of leaders from the base. Francisco Sierra Corrales, a lawyer, lamented (January 3, 2007) that the debate over the PSUV had distracted labor leaders from the immediate task of overhauling the nation's labor laws: "It is a shame how labor leaders at this time are speaking in such a distant and mechanical way about the unified party, constitutional reform, and, of course, about twenty-first-century socialism . . . but not the social security law and reform of the current labor law. This is patronizing and more like the Fourth Republic." Another labor activist, Scarlet De Yesi, president of an educators' union, complained on January 16, 2007, that too many labor leaders continued in the fashion of the Fourth Republic to play the role of boss and union leader: "Enough with excuses! The workers of this country want elections now!" By contrast, Luis Primo, a member of the UNT national coordinating council, said, "The problem within the UNT is not electoral; it is a problem of leading workers to transform the society and produce socialism. Struggles over material issues are important as long as they always are subordinated to the general struggle for socialism" (January 29, 2007).

A group of labor activists, Movimiento 21, in the aluminum industry claimed that the appointment of Carlos Lanz, a former guerrilla known for his involvement in a notorious kidnapping case of a foreign businessman, had inspired hope of revolutionary advances, but, the group complained, Lanz was really only seeking confrontation with truly revolutionary forces (January 12, 2007). It would be difficult to measure the size or influence of Movimiento 21, but it is notable that the article had been read over 1,600 times by February 1, 2008, on Aporrea alone.[14] Lanz, at the time president of the second largest aluminum company in Venezuela, is a frequent contributor to Aporrea. He never responded directly to Movimiento 21 but made clear his view that co-management could achieve the goal of "overcoming the slavery of wage labor" in a posting (Jan. 21, 2007) read 415 times.

Asamblea Socialista, a coalition of activists and at least twenty-four different unions in the state of Zulia, insisted that the PSUV not reproduce the clientelist structures of the past. This was a common call, but in this posting ensuring the democratic character of the PSUV was linked to their endorsement of comanagement and self-management schemes—including a call for work governance over the state oil company, PDVSA. As we saw in "Defying the Iron Law of Oligarchy I," there seems to be little support for this proposition in the pro-Chávez barrios. The lengthy (and ultimately unsuccessful) occupation of a bathroom fixture factory, Sanatarios de Maracay, was discussed extensively on Aporrea and generated sympathetic coverage reproduced from Vive TV. Similarly, the lengthy and bitter strikes at the SIDOR steel factory in Bolívar state generated much criticism of the government's labor policies and demands for nationalization—ultimately achieved in 2008.

Robert Sánchez, a coordinator of Aporrea, intervened in the debate on December 21, 2006, with a warning (read over thirty-six hundred times) that the PSUV "could provoke a profound political crisis with Chavismo." For Sánchez, such a crisis was not to be feared, but welcomed:

> A unified clientelist party . . . cannot fit within a system that seeks to overtake the model of representative democracy proper to bourgeois liberalism. Participatory and protagonistic democracy implies disappearance of political professionals as a category inherent in the bourgeois model of doing politics. Protagonistic democracy supposes a citizenry capable of exercising politics directly, without intermediaries; all citizens exercise their rights and do not delegate them to "representatives." Upon professional politicians disappearing, the traditional parties (those of the opposition but also of Chavismo), made up of these professional politicians . . . will no longer exist in this form, since all citizens ought to be capable and have the right to exercise any responsibility of popular representation, also subject to social control, to rendering accounts, to a specific mandate, and be subject to the right of recall at any moment.

Such radical perspectives might seem utopian, but they have real-world implications when those with power hold them. At the same time (December 2006) that he announced his dramatic measures to accelerate the revolution, President Chávez replaced many stalwarts in his cabinet with relatively younger politicians, often from outside his own political establishment. For example, he designated a member of the Communist Party, David Velásquez, to be the new minister for participation and social development, charged with developing the plan for strengthening communal councils and designing the new geography of the state. When José Ramón Rivero, the new minister of labor appointed at the same time, informed Chávez that he is a Trotskyist, Chávez responded, "Well, what is the problem? I'm also a Trotskyist! I follow Trotsky's line, that of permanent revolution."

After the Referendum Defeat

There is not much doubt that the period after the defeat of the package of constitutional amendments spurred the richest debate among Chavistas, something that becomes evident in comparing postings before and after the referendum of December 2007. Many, perhaps a majority of contributions in this period running up to the referendum staunchly defended the party line, frequently following several patterns. The tendency to see in opponents the opposite characteristics of one's self frequently occurred in a kind of demonology or "mirror imaging." Given the record of intervention, one can hardly dispute the calls for vigilance against el imperio (the empire), but often demonology substituted for analysis of the power and limits on power of the United States. Domestic and international opponents were often lumped together, so that el imperio became the combined forces of the U.S. government, translation corporations, Globovisión (the opposition TV station), Colombia, neoliberalism and their allies in the Venezuelan elite. Support for Chávez not only took the form of approval of his policies and the reform, but was often highly personal, written as poems or letters. Many posts in favor of the reforms took on a triumphalist tone—anticipating victory, ridiculing the opposition, and taking for granted another landslide victory for Chávez.

Not that criticism of the constitutional reforms was absent. In contrast to Canal 8, the state television network, where programs slavishly supported the reforms and ridiculed critics both inside and outside the Chavista camp, Aporrea gave full voice to doubts. At times, after enthusiastic supporters of the president attacked critics, other supporters of the reforms would intervene to contest treatment of critics as outcasts, as was the case with the postings by Edgardo Lander. When General Raul Baduel announced his opposition to the reform package on November 8, 2007, a blow made more severe by Baduel's important role in mobilizing sectors of the military loyal to Chávez against the coup of April 11, 2002, several posters were harshly critical in intensely per-

sonal ways about his "betrayal." But several other posters warned against ostra-
cizing Baduel or substituting vitriol for reason in responding. A letter posted
November 8, 2007, by Gilo Muirragui, a contributor living in the United States,
warned, "To say that during these years of the Bolivarian Revolution he has
done nothing is like trying to convince everyone that the world is flat. To disavow the accomplishments of [Baduel] is like denying that people in Caracas
eat *arepas*," referring to the popular corn-cake sandwiches.

After the referendum on constitutional reform went down to defeat on
December 2, the tone of triumphalism was replaced by one of regret and often
self-criticism. A number of postings took note of the swagger and uncritical
tenor of most postings before the election, in some cases citing this attitude
as a reason for a high rate of abstention. The day after the vote, the historian
Arnulfo Poyer Márquez wrote, "We have been triumphalist, and we showed
it in this campaign. I can only speak of Mérida where I was during this time.
There was more concern on the official side about mounting the celebratory
campaign than diffusing and responding to the lies of the opposition with acute
analysis."

From the referendum defeat through the early months of 2008, posters repeatedly called attention to corruption, inept local figures, and more. In the
months before the referendum, one found daily perhaps five or six such posts
that were sharply critical of Hugo Chávez; in the weeks afterward it was not
unusual to find forty to fifty such posts—the number falling only during periods of intense crisis with Colombia. The tone of criticism grew more strident,
unapologetic, and urgent. Besides doubts about the sincerity of professional
politicians, some were willing to find the president negligent, if not culpable,
for failures of governance—to deal with bureaucratic inefficiency, crime, and
corruption. The criticism moved much closer to the presidential palace, with
more warnings about the shortcomings of advisors and ministers. Criticism was
often aimed at the lack of institutions that could respond to popular grievances
and also at the exaggerated role of charisma and personalism in the leadership
of Chávez.

"Where in 2013 are we going to find a replacement for this president?"
asked José Sant Roz (December 5, 2007). "I don't see it in the military. Will
it come from the Bolivarian students? I hope that wherever the next leadership emerges, we stop constructing him [*sic*] mainly in adversarial terms"—
that is, as the opposite of the Punto Fijo oligarchy. A similar frustration was
expressed by Erik Del Bufalo, who asserted, "Bolivarianism has ceased integrating new elements and is dangerously content with what it has achieved"
(February 24, 2007). Martín Zapata categorized several prominent leaders en-

trusted by Chávez with construction of the PSUV as nothing less than anointed by "the hand of God" and made the unflattering comparison of this group to the cabals that ran Acción Democrática and COPEI in the Punto Fijo era (February 23, 2007). He then criticized the president for dismissing even constructive criticism, as when a prominent talk show host on Canal 8 was forced, apparently by Chávez, to resign. Humberto Mendoz, a university rector highly sympathetic to Chávez, complained on February 24 that the president was doing little to forge a strategic political project. "It would be interesting to evaluate whether the revolutionary leadership over the last nine years has well interpreted the needs and aspirations of the exploited and excluded masses."

Conclusion

The organic intellectuals of Aporrea assume that they are giving voice to popular attitudes and aspirations, not merely analyzing or representing them. The actual degree of correspondence between their views and those for whom they speak is difficult to evaluate. However, even in comparison to respondents to our survey (see "Defying the Iron Law of Oligarchy I," chapter 1) in organized barrios, the cadres seem more radical in regard to nationalization and work-place democracy. On Aporrea the organic intellectuals of the Bolivarian movement exchange experiences and do collective thinking, often in dialogue with *intellectuals* in the more conventional sense of the term. Many from both groups seem exceptionally deferential to Chavista leadership, but the December 2007 defeat of constitutional reform seems to have deepened and widened, at least temporarily, criticism of the revolution and of Chávez himself. Most grassroots leaders seem to predicate loyalty to the *comandante* upon his promise to empower their communities. In many ways they form a revolutionary vanguard, but most reject consciously forming such a vanguard. Perhaps this is because, as we learned in "Defying the Iron Law of Oligarchy I," in organized communities of contemporary Venezuela, civil society seems relatively dense, and respect for democratic norms high.

The discussion on Aporrea is at times shrill and superficial, at other times tolerant and rich. Sometimes the discourse seems reduced to posturing about whose positions and attitudes are authentically "revolutionary." To some Chavistas, the latter is associated with eliminating professional politicians as a class and substituting direct democracy and mandated representatives (the voceros) in their place. The problems and shortcomings of direct democracy have received less attention. Many critics unhappy with an internal electoral result will simply blame co-optation with little reflection on the objective conditions. As we have seen, however, this is not always the case, and after the defeat of the constitutional reform package in the December 2007 referendum, more critical debate about deficiencies and leadership flowered.

At its best Aporrea facilitates the kind of horizontal networking that some intellectuals and community leaders say is needed to avoid the vices of bureaucratization and verticalism—i.e., to vitiate the Iron Law of Oligarchy. One also finds many contributors who defend theories and praxis on revolution associated with classical Marxist thought and modernism. The point here is not to argue the superiority of one view over another, but to note how the electronic bulletin board serves as yet another arena, like others mentioned in this book, for the percolation of democracy. Even where postings are the work of professional intellectuals (e.g., university professors), the audience is not other academics but organic intellectuals in the process of responding to the leadership of Chávez. Aporrea is not the antidote to the Iron Law of Oligarchy, but it facilitates resistance to its inevitability.

Notes

Tom Long, at the time a graduate student at American University, provided invaluable assistance in analyzing postings on Aporrea for this study, particularly postings immediately before and after the constitutional amendment referendum of December 2007. I directly quoted or paraphrased parts of his notes in that section, but I have done so selectively, so any errors are my own responsibility.

1. All translations of quotations from Aporrea or other news sources are my own.

2. *Presidente Chávez: Me equivoqué en la selección del momento para hacer la propuesta de Reforma* (video), Agencia Bolivariana de Noticias, December 3, 2007.

3. This information comes from an interview with Gonzalo Gómez, one of the founding members of Aporrea, entitled "En Venezuela el gobierno avanza y confronta al capital o la situación se congela y se pudre," published on the website for Prensa de Frente (Front Press), at http://www.prensadefrente.org. Data on Aporrea visitors are difficult to come by, but Quantcast.com, a site dedicated to analysis of traffic by Internet users in the United States, estimated that approximately nine thousand visitors (discrete users, not hits) per month consulted Aporrea, with users, compared to general use patterns, tending to be older (fifty-five to sixty-four most common), male, and either low or high (not middle) income.

4. One of Mier's complaints was found at http://www.elgusanodeluz.com on January 29, 2007, but the page is no longer available. For a critique of one of Mier's postings by the editors, see "Sr. Jorge Mier, me da usted pena . . ." posted by José Leonardo Zamora on October 13, 2005, at http://www.aporrea.org.

5. Mier's website is http://www.viejoblues.com. Opposition sectors turned early to the new medium of blogs, with a proliferation of highly critical English-language blogs produced both inside Venezuela and abroad. Probably the most evenhanded and informative blog, in Spanish, on the opposition side is Venezuela Analitica (at http://www.analitica.com). This site is not to be confused with the pro-Chavista website Venezuelanalysis (http://www.venezuelanalisis.com), which is not so much a blog as an edited site for news and opinion. Three pro-Chávez English language blogs are directly linked to it.

6. See http://www.conexionesonline.com/julhtm/nombres.htm.

7. See "Nosotros" link (equivalent of "Who are we?") on the home page.

8. The website for Direct Marketing News is http://www.dmn.ca.

9. For example, José Domingo Rojas critcizes La Hojillia's obsession with opposition news sources as superficial in a post to Aporrea titled "El programa más triste de La Hojilla," on February 28, 2008.

10. Translating forum posting poses something of a challenge, since much of the writing is free-form, not adhering strictly to rules of grammar and syntax. I have taken as few liberties as possible in punctuating or slightly editing statements, trying as best I can to maintain the emotional flavor, not just the literal meaning, of these messages.

11. I have attempted to identify group associations or the residence of each Aporrea poster cited here, but this has not always been possible.

12. Miquilena was a veteran leftist politician who managed Chávez's 1998 campaign and controlled the MVR in the style of the Punto Fijo regime until his resignation in protest at the president's proclamation of radical decree laws in November 2001.

13. Writing on behalf of the Colectivo Resistencia on January 10, 2007, José Angel Lucena and Luis Vargas expressed a similar perspective and warned against an intellectual division of labor.

14. Another worker committee at a small metallurgical factory called (January 16, 2007) for direct worker self-management (autogestión).

CHAPTER NINE

Venezuela's Telenovela

Polarization and Political Discourse in *Cosita Rica*

Carolina Acosta-Alzuru

From September 2003 to August 2004, two melodramas intertwined reality and fiction as they shared the heated Venezuelan stage: the rocky road to the recall referendum of President Hugo Chávez and the successful telenovela *Cosita Rica*, which garnered top ratings during those eleven months.[1] This show, a fascinating example of the world's most watched television genre (McAnany and La Pastina 1994), was inevitably linked to Venezuelan reality and became the epicenter in which media, culture, and society evidenced their complex interaction.[2] As *Cosita Rica* linked fiction to the country's sociopolitical crisis, it became a key ingredient in Venezuela's contemporary history.

Cosita Rica was more than the love story of its suffering protagonists—Paula C. and Diego. The telenovela was a careful mix of melodrama, chronicle, editorial, and humor. Its chemical formula included two isotopes of fiction—fiction that creates an illusion and fiction that evokes reality. The ingredients were the genre's usual: star-crossed love, intrigue, and misunderstandings. There was an important difference, though. These elements were soaked in the liquid—sometimes bubbly and refreshing, sometimes viscous and bitter—of Venezuelan reality.

In *Cosita Rica*, its author—the poet, columnist, and scriptwriter Leonardo Padrón—presents his personal vision of his country. The script suggests an author who opposes Chávez but who resists booby-trapping his telenovela with a Manichean view of Venezuela's political and socioeconomic crises. Therefore, even though he is open about his political position—"I declare myself openly, though not radically, opposed to Chávez" (Leonardo Padrón, June 18, 2003)—he writes characters and dialogues where "the depth of each side is never out of sight" (Beatriz Valdés, July 28, 2004).[3] *Cosita Rica* also reflects Padrón's uneasiness with the pernicious effects of political polarization. The telenovela shows the terrible consequences of Venezuelan lack of disposition in 2003–4 for real dialogue and generalized predisposition toward violence—a lethal mix that was pervasive in the country's political circles.

It is not easy to separate the political and the socioeconomic Venezuelas in *Cosita Rica*. Both are tightly linked through the characters and storylines. Both are represented using narrative, metaphor, and humor. In this chapter, however, I focus on the telenovela's political realm. Therefore, I center my attention on the characters that underpin *Cosita Rica*'s representation of political life: Olegario, La Chata, Juancho, and Tentación.

Theoretical Framework and Methods

Even though telenovelas are a key ingredient of Venezuelan everyday life, there are only a handful of books published in the country that focus exclusively on this media product (Acosta-Alzuru 2007; V. Alvarez 2007; Cabrujas 2002; Espada 2002; Guerra 2001; Rojas Vera 1993; A. Rondón 2006). There is also a small and influential body of literature comprising studies that reflect the stages and trends in mass-media research in Latin America and that have marked the examination of Venezuelan telenovelas (Acosta-Alzuru 2003a, 2003b, 2003c, 2003d, 2004; L. Barrios 1988a, 1988b; Coccato 1978, 1979a, 1979b; Colomina de Rivera 1974; Fernández 1995; Güerere 1994; Hyppolite 2000; Ishibashi 2003; Mendoza 1992, 1996). And to these voices, numbers, and interpretations, we must add the valuable reflections and analyses written by telenovela writers who shed even more light on this understudied television genre (Barrera Tyszka 2002; Cabrujas 1995a, 1995b, 1995c; Espada 2002; Garmendia, 2000; Martínez 2002, 2005; Padrón 1998, 2002; Policastro 2002).

This chapter, an examination of *Cosita Rica* as a locus of mediated political discourse in Venezuela's polarized Bolivarian democracy, contributes to this body of literature that is essential to the understanding of the television genre that is a key cultural ingredient in Venezuelans' daily diet. In the case of *Cosita Rica*, this genre established a dialogue between fiction and reality, and television and country. My analysis draws on the cultural studies insight that media and culture are inextricably linked since "culture is concerned with the production and the exchange of meanings—the 'giving and taking of meaning'—between the members of a society or group" (Hall 1997, 2). Recent cultural studies texts argue for an approach that examines processes of culture and communication from multiple perspectives using the "circuit of culture"

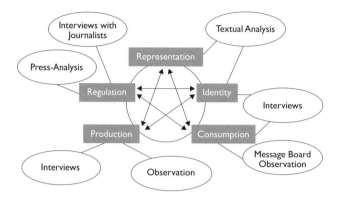

Figure 1 Theory and methods (based on "circuit of culture" from du Gay et al. 1997).

(du Gay et al. 1997). Meaning is produced and negotiated in each of the circuit's moments—*production, representation, identity, consumption,* and *regulation*. Each moment's individual study only gives us a partial view of how the meanings associated with a particular cultural product are produced, negotiated, and contested.

Telenovelas are a product of culture and media in which the articulations between the moments of the circuit are evidenced. Jesús Martín Barbero (1993) argues that the telenovela is a site of "mediations" between production, reception, and culture. There is constant negotiation between the writers, director, production team, actors, the audience, and the institutions that participate in the social formation. In addition, telenovelas are a perfect example of how production and consumption, traditionally represented as opposing forces, are deeply articulated (Quiroz 1993). In sum, the circuit of culture provides an organizational tool for this study—an attempt to understand the production, representation, consumption, and regulation of political discourse and polarization in the telenovela *Cosita Rica*.

I use a mix of qualitative methods for this complex case study (see figure 1).[4] *Representation* and *identity* were examined through textual analysis of the telenovela.[5] *Identity* was further studied, along with *consumption,* via individual and group interviews with audience members, open-ended e-mail questionnaires, and observation of Internet message boards devoted to *Cosita Rica*.[6] Individual interviews with the head writer, actors, directors, and producers, supplemented by participant observation in the telenovela's set and locations, allowed me to study the *production* aspects.[7] *Regulation* was examined through analysis of the extensive press coverage focused on *Cosita Rica* and individual interviews with entertainment reporters.[8]

Hola, Olegario

The Consorcio Luján, a cosmetics company, is a metaphor for Venezuela in *Cosita Rica*, presenting the country as corporation and enterprise. And just as recent Venezuelan history can be divided into before and after Hugo Chávez, the story of the Consorcio Luján is separated in two phases: before and after the ascent of Olegario Pérez to the presidency. Olegario is the illegitimate son of Nicomedes Luján, a wealthy and powerful businessman who never acknowledged Olegario as his offspring. Therefore, Olegario was raised in Margarita Island by his single mother, Concordia, an empanada seller. Olegario lacked the socioeconomic privileges abundant in his father's household. Resentment—fermented through a whole life waiting for the attention of his millionaire father—defines him and compels him to take what he feels has been denied to him: privilege, comfort, money, and, most of all, power. Olegario is also a charismatic man who is entertaining, witty, and talkative. This cocktail of charisma, resentment, and hunger for power defines the character.

The Consorcio Luján is a successful business that produces cosmetics and expensive perfumes. When Nicomedes dies of a heart attack, Olegario becomes president and introduces changes. He covers offices and hallways with large photos of himself and tries to divide the board of directors. Of an authoritarian nature and exaggerated personalism, Olegario is obsessed with power. He abuses it on a daily basis. His resentment toward those who led the Consorcio before him is immense. He knows they doubt his capacity to be president. But instead of trying to work with them he alienates and threatens them:

OLEGARIO: I know you see me as new, *negrito* and from the countryside. But, I will be a much better president than Nicomedes Luján! So, get ready! Because Olegario is here for a long time! (Episode 34)

He also establishes his power by insulting anyone who does not recognize him and his new position. Olegario is very sure of himself. He has no self-esteem problems. He surrounds himself with people who continuously flatter him; therefore, he never doubts his charisma and success. He is sure that being likeable is enough to be a good president:

OLEGARIO (to his mother): You have to see me when I'm in charge! I wave to everyone—the man in charge of the parking lot, the cleaning lady. They come to me and tell me about their needs, *Mamá*. People here adore me!!! (Episode 37)

Paradoxically, he is also paranoid. He is convinced that many in the Consorcio are conspiring to take him down. Hence, he orders that all conversations be secretly taped so he can listen to what his employees say about him and determine who is "against" him. These "opponents" are eventually fired as "traitors."

OLEGARIO: I'm the owner, president, and master of this Consorcio. If I want to bankrupt it, I will! If I want to fire someone, I will! Furthermore, I'm going to change the name of the corporation from Consorcio Luján to Consorcio Olegario Luján!

   . . .

OLEGARIO: It doesn't take a rocket scientist to understand what I mean. If you protest, you're fired! If you don't like my ways, go away! I'm the owner of everything and we do here whatever I want to do! (Episode 59)

Olegario is not a good administrator. During his tenure as president, Consorcio Luján goes from a successful enterprise to near bankruptcy. And even though he enjoys the perks of his position, his job bores him. What he enjoys most is Hola, Olegario, his weekly meetings with all his employees in which he offers to listen to them, but really never does. These meetings are presidential allocutions in which he talks for hours mixing business themes and personal anecdotes with jokes, songs, and poems:

OLEGARIO: I don't need this microphone! Without it I can be closer to my people. [*Facing his employees.*] I'm like you! And I sing really well! My mom, Concordia, used to say, 'This kid is going to be a singer!' When I was growing up we had this small record player, not a CD player, but a record player, and my mom would play records and I would sing. The first girlfriend I had, I wooed her when I sang, "Pero que chévere sería muy solitos los dos en Margarita, admirando sus playas tan bonitas y cantándole al mar una canción." (Employees clap as their president sings.) Ok, stop, stop! I didn't come here today to sing, but to talk about the future of our company. We are going to produce the first line of popular perfumes that will smell like patchouli and Vetiver! Refreshing aromas! I remember that my grandmother used to place Vetiver in her closet and mmm. . . . it smelled delicious![9] . . . I'm always surprised by my mom's system to prepare her empanadas. She's really quick and efficient. That's why I want to talk to you about pro-duc-ti-vi-ty. I checked our financial reports and . . . Because you need to know that I check those personally! . . . and I tell you: the party is over! [. . .] Green corduroys!! Can you imagine a handsome *morenazo* like me dressed in green corduroys? Hahaha! I looked like a steak topped with guacamole! But my girlfriend Isabelita didn't mind because love is blind, hahaha! (Episode 27)

Olegario is a president who talks a lot and does very little. He is a big spender with little planning. His lack of formal business education is obvious. He is a fisherman managing a corporation. Following the nouveau riche stereotype, Olegario firmly believes that money can buy good taste. He spends enormous amounts of money in tasteless business outfits that include tacky, colorful vests and ties, which he complements with thick rings on his fingers, heavy chains around his neck, and an eye-catching watch on his left wrist—all made of gold. His taste also shows the indelible mark of an exacerbated Venezuelan nationalism. His cellular phone's ringtone is the country's sentimental national anthem, "Alma Llanera." In his luxurious bedroom there is a traditional Venezuelan hammock—*chinchorro*—where he sleeps more comfortably than on his new fancy king-size bed. He feels secure and comfortable only among items of Venezuelan culture and cuisine.

Olegario is very Venezuelan, not only in his tastes but also in his mix of machismo, likeability, sense of humor, and charisma. He is extroverted, informal, and improvised. He never measures what he says or is careful about his actions, because he is convinced that money and power allow him to behave as he wishes. Throughout *Cosita Rica*, Olegario's tactless spontaneity is presented in hilarious fashion. He is a charismatic, humorous character who has the ability to inject comedy into almost any situation in the telenovela's plot.

In sum, Olegario is a president who lacks formal management training and experience, and is resentful and autocratic. And even though he defines himself as someone uninterested in politics—"I take care of business, not of politics. I don't care if there's communism, capitalism or slavery" (Episode 130)—his role as an opposition-tinted metaphor of Hugo Chávez is evident.[10]

The Production and Consumption of Olegario Pérez

From *Cosita Rica*'s inception, its writer was determined to "analyze power and its miseries" (Leonardo Padrón, June 18, 2003). The author develops his thesis through Olegario and his performance as president of Consorcio Luján. The character and his story are constructed so that they evoke Chávez's personality and history. But the plot is also an invitation to reflection. In a newspaper article, Padrón is quoted as saying, "Olegario is written as a reflection of power.

I've always thought that power, when exercised without lucidity, can vilify. . . .
I've written Olegario so that we figure out why we gave power to a man like
him" (Silva and Correia 2004). Padrón also said in an interview, "As a country,
we make the mistake of being enchanted by someone's personality, and not by
his or her abilities or talents. Deep down we have elected our destiny as if we
were electing a pop star or the most popular student in our class" (Leonardo
Padrón, May 8, 2004).

Olegario personifies Leonardo Padrón's viewpoint regarding Hugo Chávez
and his political success. Padrón is convinced that Chávez is in power because
of the profound identification that exists between the president and the average Venezuelan:

> Olegario is the archetype of the average Venezuelan male, with his most
> charming and most dangerous elements. That is, he is the exacerbation of
> the average Venezuelan's virtues and miseries. True, currently there is a
> noisy reference to that average Venezuelan: Chávez. I've always thought
> that the main reason Chávez is where he is now, is because he is a lot like
> the average Venezuelan. (Leonardo Padrón, May 8, 2004)

And the president's success isn't good news for Padrón, who sees Chávez as a
charismatic egocentric who happens to be an awful administrator: "This is our
greatest tragedy: we are governed by a loudmouth with an overdose of ego"
(quoted in Silva and Correia 2004, B8). Hence, "Olegario is improvised, rogue,
verbose, and conceited. He is a joker . . . and the joke is sadly on us." In this
way, Olegario is two representations in one character, two sides of the same
coin—Chávez and "the average Venezuelan":

DIÓMEDES (to Olegario): Why do you think everyone likes you? Because,
deep down, we're all like you. (Episode 64)

. . .

TIFFANY (to Olegario): Everyone has an Olegario inside. I don't know if it's
for better or worse, but that's the way it is. (Episode 64)

Sometimes the Olegario/Chávez metaphor works head-on and overtly. For instance, there are words in Olegario's mouth that are taken directly from Chávez:

OLEGARIO: Sometimes when I'm home, when I walk at night because I
can't sleep, I look around and I see so much luxury that I say to myself,
"*Cónchale*, Olegario, aren't you ashamed of being here while so many
children in this country went to bed in the streets and without anything
to eat?"

DIÓMEDES: Where have I heard that before? I'm not sure where, but I'm sure I've heard this before. (Episode 44)

Diómedes (and *Cosita Rica*'s viewers) are not mistaken—they have heard that before. On February 10, 1999, Chávez stated, "I declare that I'm socially mortified. And my anxiety increases when I arrive to La Casona, when I see its luxury.[11] When I'm there I can't sleep because I'm thinking of the children in the streets without any food" (quoted in La Rotta Morán 1999, 1–3).

More often, however, the metaphor is less direct since Olegario "is more satire than ridicule, more irony than reality, more reflection than denunciation" (Padrón 2004, 37). Throughout the telenovela there are parallelisms between the Consorcio Luján and Venezuela and its respective presidents. Under Olegario's management, Consorcio Luján almost goes bankrupt, while poverty in Venezuela increased 17.8 percent during the first five years of Chávez's government.[12] Both men speak of the past with resentment and scorn previous leadership. Chávez changed the country's name from "República de Venezuela" to "República Bolivariana de Venezuela." Olegario wants to change the company's name from "Consorcio Luján" to "Consorcio Olegario Luján." Venezuelan food provides comfort and security to Olegario; Chávez doesn't like foreign foods and cuisines, and always takes along his own chef wherever he goes (Marcano and Barrera Tyszka 2004, 125). Chávez inaugurates the *Escuelas Bolivarianas* (Bolivarian Schools), and Olegario wants *Guarderías Olegarianas* (Olegarian Daycares) in the Consorcio. Chávez requests "just a thousand million bolívares"—*un millardito*—from the Venezuelan Central Bank's international reserves (Rojas 2003), and Olegario demands un millardito from the Consorcio's board of directors. And, of course, both characters subject their audiences to unending allocutions in *Aló Presidente* and *Hola, Olegario*.

Carlos Cruz, a renowned Venezuelan actor, assumed the responsibility of portraying Olegario. And, even though Leonardo Padrón explained to him the allegorical relationship between Olegario and Venezuela's president, the actor decided not to focus on Chávez but on Olegario's "average Venezuelan" characteristics: "Wherever you go in Venezuela you will find an Olegario. Some are Olegarios because of their lack of manners, some because of their charisma and likeability, and some because of their womanizing and/or drinking habits. Olegario is a compendium of Venezuelans' psychological characteristics" (Carlos Cruz, May 4, 2004).

Olegario's mix of humor, lack of inhibition, and self-satisfaction made him one of the audience's favorite characters and inserted him into the Venezuelan imaginary. "I think this telenovela is Olegario" (MARIELBA, 35). "Olegario is the best character in *Cosita Rica*" (ROSALBA, 42). "I think Olegario is wonderful! I like him a lot! He spices the telenovela!" (IRENE, 57). There was no question about the character's success. The public enjoyed watching Olegario on their television screens and admired Carlos Cruz's performance: "He's fabulous! He deserves an Oscar!" (MIRNA, 77).

In a deeply polarized country like Venezuela, Olegario's success begged the questions: Why was the character liked? How did the audience read him? Which of Olegario's two facets—representing Chávez or the average Venezuelan—did the audience see in him? And, if they saw him as the president, why did Chavistas watch this satire of their leader? Those who participated in my study loved watching Olegario, but read him in two different ways. Opposition participants—anti-Chavistas—clearly saw Chávez in Olegario and enjoyed the critique of the president: "Olegario definitely represents Chávez, a resentful, angry man. He is an idealist at first, but with a thirst for vengeance. Once he has power and money he goes out of control, he's drugged by them" (MONICA, 46). "The character I enjoyed the most is Olegario Pérez. It may be because it's like mocking President Chávez" (AMELIA, 27).

In contrast, Chávez' supporters did not see their president in Olegario. "He's a man like so many around here" (MARIELBA, 35). Echoing actor Carlos Cruz's approach to the character as the average Venezuelan, ELENA (35) underscored that "this country is filled with Olegarios." Some Chavistas felt that Olegario represented "new money," "someone who had nothing and suddenly receives a fortune and goes crazy" (MARCOS, 26). And ERICA (45) added, "He isn't Chávez; he isn't the President."

My conversations with audience participants suggested a reception pattern. In a continuum between Chávez and the Average Venezuelan, anti-Chavistas' readings of Olegario could be placed toward the Chávez extreme; at the same time the Chavistas' interpretation was located toward the average Venezuelan extreme. Participants who defined themselves as politically neutral also fit the model, since they declared that Olegario was "sometimes Chávez and sometimes Olegario" (PATTY, 29). This pattern suggested a connection between the audience's political position and their reading of Olegario, a connection that resembled their perceptions of their president and their country.

Humor played a key role in Olegario's reception. The character provoked laughs in all publics—Chavista, neutral, and anti-Chavista. Some laughed *with* Olegario, while others laughed *at* Olegario. Chavistas enjoyed watching the *pícaro criollo*—the rogue Venezuelan male—exemplified by the character. They laughed *with* Olegario. Participants from the opposition, for whom Chávez is a constant irritant, took pleasure laughing *at* what they perceived as the president's shortcomings represented in Olegario. For them, Olegario is better than Chávez. They said, "I wish Chávez had Olegario's innocence" (MIGUEL, 20), and, "If only Chávez was as likeable as Olegario" (DANI, 27). Throughout the eleven months that *Cosita Rica* was on the air, the parallelisms between Chávez and Olegario and their respective appeals to the Venezuelan publics were remarkable. Just as Venezuelans of all political positions cannot take their eyes off their colorful president, *Cosita Rica*'s audience could not stop watching Olegario. In both characters' essences Venezuelans recognize a bit, or a lot, of themselves. And in that recognition there are elements of both rejection and acceptance.

Sí, No, and Viagra

Eventually, Olegario's story in the Consorcio Luján took a parallel route to Venezuela's political reality. In Episode 166 (May 10, 2004), a new character appeared in *Cosita Rica*: Tentación, Nicomedes Luján's wife, whom—in true telenovela fashion—everyone thought was dead. Since Nicomedes's widow was alive, Olegario's right to the presidency was questioned. Furthermore, Tentación was horrified at the Consorcio's economic crisis. After studying the company's financial reports and bylaws, she decided to activate a statute, written in by Olegario himself "so my workers love me even more," that allowed employees to participate in a referendum that could revoke the president. On July 1, 2004, four weeks after the CNE (National Council of Elections) activated the recall referendum of Hugo Chávez, the Consorcio Luján began the process of a similar consultation regarding Olegario's tenure as president.

Parallel paths lead to both referenda. Both Chávez and Olegario tried to impose the "NO" over the "SI."[13] While the opposition accused Chávez of implementing an illegal expedited citizenship process to add voters to his side (Meza 2004a; A. Reyes and Navarro 2004), Olegario brought to the Consorcio many of his friends from Margarita Island, where he grew up, and gave them "jobs" in the company, so that they had the right to vote (for him) in the upcoming company referendum. On June 18, Jimmy Carter mediated in a secret meeting between Chávez and then-opposition media mogul Gustavo Cisneros, owner of network Venevisión.[14] On July 21, Olegario and Tentación met secretly with a mediator to "negotiate." On July 11, the CNE warned Chávez he should stay away from political proselytism in his many *cadenas* (Meza 2004b).[15] On August 4, a Consorcio employee, acting as referee in the consultation process, scolded Olegario for campaigning in his weekly allocutions to his employees.

Fiction and reality, now on parallel paths, began to mix. One month before Chávez's referendum, the minister of information and communication met with Víctor Ferreres, president of Venevisión, and demanded that Olegario's referendum not happen on television before Chávez's took place in reality. The network complied and set up a self-censorship system in which their legal department carefully checked the telenovela's scripts. During *Cosita Rica*'s last month, Leonardo Padrón had to rewrite several dialogues and situations, and some scenes had to be retaped: "*Cosita Rica*'s situation during its last month was very delicate. The government lost its tolerance and pressured the network to carefully supervise the script. At that time Venevisión started censoring some dialogues and characters" (quoted in Torres Rivero 2005, 6).

Two weeks before Chávez's referendum, *Zeta*, a political magazine with a clear oppositional stance, veered from a thirty-year-old policy of not showing on its cover artists or entertainers, and displayed a picture of Olegario with the headline "'Olegario' tá cagao"—"'Olegario' is shitting his pants"—clearly referring to Chávez. On the day of the recall referendum, August 15, actor Carlos Cruz stood in line for many hours to vote. While he waited, people acted toward him as if he were Chávez: "We're going to revoke you!" "This is your last day in the presidency!" (Carlos Cruz, August 27, 2004). He was the target of so many similar comments that in his weekly column in the daily *Así es la Noticia*, the actor wrote:

> Never before had I received in such concentrated form the public's admiration and antipathy as consequences of playing a character. Becoming Olegario has been a tremendous learning experience for me. It hasn't been easy to go through the events preceding both recall referenda—the country's and the telenovela's. I've had to endure angry reactions from certain people and I've had to be very patient and understanding because I realize that they are confusing fiction and reality. I know that a lot of this is due to people's inability to express their sentiments directly to the character that they are relating Olegario to. But, let's use our common sense. Behind Olegario, the character, there is an actor and a human being. . . . Please understand that you should not unload your frustration on Olegario. He is fiction, and I just lend my body and soul so he can live. (2004)

Chávez won the recall referendum with 59.06 percent of the votes, and the opposition cried fraud.[16] On August 26, Olegario also won his referendum. Tentación—like the opposition—was not convinced of the adverse results. But, unlike the opposition, she did get the last word:

TENTACIÓN: You will have a great responsibility on your shoulders, Olegario. You will have to perform really well for the first time in your life because those who work under you will want to know if you're really capable of managing the company. So, if you really won, don't disappoint them!! And I will become your shadow. A shadow you will have to learn to respect!! (Episode 245)

In spite of his success in the company's referendum, Olegario was not totally happy. During the last two months of the telenovela, he suffered a condition that obsessed him and dampened his political success in the Consorcio: erectile dysfunction. Olegario tried everything to "fix the problem": aphrodisiacs, Viagra, bordellos, therapy, and even voodoo.[17] The storyline, soaked in humor, ridiculed Olegario. For instance, following the recommendation of his voodoo specialist, he carried a white duck everywhere with him, so that the duck would "absorb the bad influences." Given that in Venezuela the word for duck, *pato*, also means "gay," and the generalized Venezuelan *machista* view that homosexuals are not "real" men, Olegario and his duck generated numerous jokes and funny situations in *Cosita Rica*. His manhood was in question and that made the audience roar with laughter. In this way, the rogue Venezuelan male, *el pícaro criollo*, is punished on his most painful side. Several of my study's participants spontaneously asked me, "Do you think Chávez is impotent?" Many others commented on the parallelisms between Olegario and Chávez on this matter: "Personally, I don't care whether Olegario functions sexually, but I've already heard in the street that if Olegario has that problem, then Chávez must have it too" (GRACIELA, 43).

Olegario's erectile dysfunction counterbalances his referendum victory. In the final episode we find him, still the emblem of exacerbated nationalism, lying in a chinchorro by the side of a plastic pool where his duck swims happily surrounded by ducklings. Olegario ponders:

OLEGARIO: If you can't beat them, join them . . . Ah! It's wonderful to be President! Even if half of the employees don't talk to me, but . . . everything would be perfect if this little guy (*looks down towards his genitals*) would start working! (*with sadness*) *Cónchale*, Olegarito [using the diminutive form of his name to address his penis], stand up! What do I do with all this money if you're out of order? (Episode 245)

Study participants who are supportive of the president did not comment on Olegario's fate. When asked, they limited their answer to a numerical rating of how much they liked the story's ending (see figure 2). In contrast, opposition

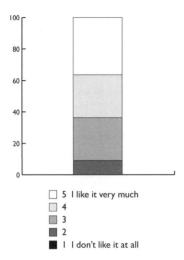

Figure 2 Audience perception of Olegario's storyline resolution (wins the recall referendum and suffers from erectile dysfunction).

This graph does not attempt to reflect the decoding patterns of the country's audience. It is only a visual representation of the participants' answers.

☐ 5 I like it very much
☐ 4
▨ 3
▨ 2
■ 1 I don't like it at all

participants had plenty to say about Olegario's winning his referendum. Some wrote explaining that this had "brought back bad memories of August 15."

Olegario's ending reflects writer Padrón's struggle to portray his view of Venezuela's political reality and, at the same time, punish Olegario's behavior. Two weeks before the referendum, Padrón wrote, "Suppose the NO option wins the referendum. I would have a dilemma. Because even if Venezuela decides not to sanction politically and morally the disaster we have become, I don't think I should reward Olegario. As a character, he deserves moral and administrative sanctions" (2004, 37).

And, at least one person in my study understood it that way, too:

I know that a lot of people wanted to kill Padrón for writing Olegario's ending that way. But, that was the country's reality, and the telenovela attempted to reflect it all the way. Therefore, he couldn't betray his story to give us the "happy end" that a lot of people would have liked to see for the country. His final reflection is significant, though. A referendum won amid doubts. A man who knows that half of his company doesn't want him, but doesn't care nevertheless. . . . I don't know if Chávez suffers erectile dysfunction, but it is pretty clear to me that he isn't a happy man. After all, he knows we don't like him and he doesn't care. (GRACIELA, 43)

Padrón had some bad experiences courtesy of the ending he wrote for Olegario. First, the network established stringent self-censorship after the government warned that Olegario's referendum should not be aired before the Chávez referendum took place (Leonardo Padrón, August 2, 2004).[18] Second, after the last

Figure 3 "You already know *Cosita Rica*'s ending. Mr. Cisneros also knows it. Don't watch *Venevisión*. *Venevisión* is an accomplice in the fraud" (my translation). E-mail message to Leonardo Padrón, from the dummy address olegario_sufragiocero@hotmail.com, August 17, 2004. Source: Leonardo Padrón.

episode aired, Padrón received anonymous text messages on his cell phone suggesting that he had been "co-opted" by Chavismo, and that he was "immoral" (Leonardo Padrón, August 31, 2004). In the view of these anti-Chavistas, the Cisneros family, owners of network Venevisión, had also been co-opted by the government after the Gustavo Cisneros-Chávez meeting mediated by Jimmy Carter two months before.[19] On August 17, two days after Chávez's referendum and before Padrón had written the final episode deciding Olegario's destiny, the writer received the following e-mail message from the dummy address olegario_sufragiocero@hotmail.com: "You already know *Cosita Rica*'s ending. Mr. Cisneros also knows it. Don't watch Venevisión. Venevisión is an accomplice in the fraud" (my translation; see figure 3).

Throughout the telenovela, anti-Chavistas had applauded the way Olegario's story was linked to Chávez's. However, after losing the recall referendum, they were upset when Olegario also won the fictional referendum. They felt that if in the past Olegario had been a satire of Chávez (and they liked that), now the character legitimized the president (and they did not like that). Just as they felt that international observers—the Carter Center and the OAS—had betrayed them by certifying the referendum results, now they believed that Padrón, *Cosita Rica*, and Venevisión had deserted them in their political battle against Hugo Chávez.

La Chata

Vehemence, personified in a woman of quick movements and aggressive speech, climbs the steep stairs that define el Barrio República, emblematic of the poorest neighborhoods in Caracas. Her name is Caridad Guaramato, but nobody remembers it. Everyone knows her as "La Chata," the neighbor who wants to be elected mayor.

The character evokes the well-known Chavista activist Lina Ron. They have the same appearance. Artificially colored, slightly unkempt, blonde hair tops her figure, which is always clad in jeans, a shirt knotted at the waist and her main identifier: a red baseball cap. It is the color of the Chavista revolution, in which La Chata is a full-time militant—Lina Ron and La Chata, reality and fiction, two women who distill radicalism and aggressiveness, as reflected in this statement from Ron: "[The revolution] is armed. Armed with weapons and the Constitution. Respect others so that you may be respected. They've called me a crook. Am I going to keep quiet? No way!! I will fight you and I will beat you too!!" (quoted in Salas 2003, 15).

La Chata is not far from similarly extreme positions. She detests everything she considers to be contrary to the revolution, and to defend her beloved "el que te conté,"[20] she is willing to fight even with her loved ones:

CHATA [speaking to her dear friend and business partner, Mamasanta]: Mamasanta, you've become a bit bourgeois. You prefer that I work at the bakery and not see the world's injustice. You prefer I sell bread while the coup mongers advance. (Episode 24)

Like her hero, La Chata has a simplistic, Manichean view of Venezuela, which she divides into poor and rich, good and bad, the people (*el pueblo*) and squalid coup mongers (*escuálidos golpistas*). Without any kind of reservation (*pudor*), she declares her hatred toward those who occupy the privileged echelons in the socioeconomic scale:

CHATA: Yes, I'm disgusted by the rich because they've always been disgusted by the poor, like us. But now they're screwed! Because while they were in power, nobody did anything for the poor. Now it's different. (Episode 12)

Behind her aggressive style, there is a high dose of idealism. Her actions are guided by her instincts and a genuine desire to have a better country. La Chata dreams of improving the lives of the people of her Barrio República. Hence, she wants to run for mayor. However, no pro-government party supports her. Therefore, she tries to organize her own political organization and campaign. Throughout this failed process, La Chata shows a great deal of naïveté that not only contrasts with her aggressiveness and radicalism, but also is an extension of her idealism. This mix of traits suggests a character who is in tune with the needs of those have no voice or privileges. At the same time, she has important shortcomings regarding her political and personal life. In consequence, she constantly makes mistakes. Humor and drama underline her errors in a critique to fundamentalism and violence.

Despite the physical and ideological coincidences between Lina Ron and La Chata, Leonardo Padrón emphasized that the character was "inspired, but only inspired, [by] Lina Ron." He further explained, "To write La Chata, I didn't do research on Lina Ron. What interested me is what she oozes: a sort of virulent radicalism, which is emblematic of political extremism" (Leonardo Padrón, May 8, 2004). Hence, for the writer, La Chata is not Lina Ron. Nor for Lourdes Valera, veteran actress who personified the character: "La Chata is a woman from a low socioeconomic level who believes in President Chávez's process. She's a violent woman. But she's also naïve. Above everything, she's a mother. She's also an honest woman, basic in her behavior, but honest. La Chata isn't Lina Ron. No, she's not!" (Lourdes Valera, April 29, 2004).

To be sure, it is in La Chata's private life where we find the elements that made her an endearing and unforgettable character even for anti-Chavistas who strongly reject the anxiety and discomfort that Lina Ron produces in them.

La Chata, the Woman

Like many Venezuelan women, La Chata is a single mother. The plot suggests that she left an abusive husband to become the head of a household where her eldest son, Rosendo, is an impenitent machista, and her youngest offspring, Cachito, is a petty thief. And, even though everyone in the barrio knows of Cachito's criminal activities, La Chata is steadfast in her refusal to believe those rumors and dreams that he will become a bank teller, more evidence of her naïve nature.

The development of La Chata's private realm saves her from being a Manichean, cartoonish character. At the same time, it facilitates one of the writer's messages in *Cosita Rica*: violence is never a solution. Throughout the telenovela, La Chata suffers terrible losses courtesy of senseless violence. Cachito dies when he attempts a bank robbery, and Rosendo is killed in a street protest turned violent. Rosendo's death evokes similar events in recent Venezuelan history: political protests that end in tragedy thanks to snipers and armed people who infiltrate them. No organization takes responsibility for this political violence, but both sides of the political polarization take advantage of it as they blame their opponents for it.

Like a Mother of Plaza de Mayo, La Chata grieves publicly. She hangs a picture of Rosendo on her chest and stands for endless days at the doorstep of the police headquarters waiting for an answer that nobody provides. There, she meets Juancho, an engineer and former employee of the state-owned oil corporation — PDVSA — who was fired for political reasons and now works as a cab driver. Like her, Juancho lost a son in a street protest that became violent. At first, La Chata resists the friendship and solidarity that Juancho offers her, simply because she considers him an *escuálido*. He reminds her that even though they are on opposite political sides, they are united by the absurd deaths of their sons. But the magnitude of their political differences is evident in their frequent arguments:

CHATA: I've never heard of a dictatorship in which every day people say bad things about the "dictator."

JUANCHO: Well, it's impossible that half of the country has decided, without reason, to say bad things about the government. Some of it must be right.

. . .

JUANCHO: You think that anyone who has some money is a thief and an exploiter. Have you ever thought that maybe that person has earned in an honest fashion each cent he or she has?

CHATA: No! Those people exploit their workers and cheat them. That is what we call savage neoliberalism [*neoliberalismo salvaje*]. (Episode 194)

Despite their endless political bickering, Juancho and La Chata fall in love. Their relationship is a power struggle between two formidable opposing forces: their love and their political differences. Leonardo Padrón's intention was to present "a conflict between love and political beliefs" (quoted in Silva 2004). Thanks to La Chata, Juancho visits a barrio for the first time in his life. Because of Juancho, La Chata is able to see the human side of the professional middle class who lost everything after the work stoppage of 2002–3. Finally, Juancho and La Chata accept their love and agree to disagree in politics. Ideologically, Juancho counterbalances La Chata. However, Juancho does not have the strident nature of the woman he loves. Therefore, *Cosita Rica* lacks a representation of the fundamentalist raucous behavior that also exists in some of Chávez's opponents. Moreover, Juancho's moderation further underscores La Chata's extremism.

Reading La Chata (and Lina Ron)

In the first six months of the telenovela, regardless of their political position, the audience's reading of La Chata was unanimous—she was Lina Ron. Even study participants who self-identified as Chavistas questioned her belligerent behavior: "I see Lina Ron in her. She's the typical politician who yells a lot and does very little. To be honest, I reject her" (MARCOS, 26). "La Chata is exactly like Lina Ron. The actress is doing a great job. I don't say this because I'm Chavista, but because Lina Ron is like that: loud, too loud" (MARIELBA, 35).

This reading of the character was gradually modified as the telenovela delved into the personal facets of La Chata. Both Chavistas and anti-Chavistas started perceiving La Chata as a woman who "isn't always" Lina Ron (ANA, 49). In their assessment, study participants clearly showed that their vision of Lina Ron did not include La Chata's family and personal elements. Hence, as *Cosita Rica*'s plot advanced, they liked La Chata more and more, while still disliking Lina Ron. "I don't know if Lina Ron could be as noble as La Chata is" (ELENA, 35). "There are moments in which I separate them completely because La Chata is more human and sympathetic than Lina Ron can ever be" (GRACIELA, 43).

In this way, study participants voiced their disbelief about the possibility that Lina Ron was more than the aggressive leader that they were used to watching on the political stage. Fiction and reality, however, were inextricably connected. Just as Olegario's erectile dysfunction elicited thoughts that Chávez may be suffering from the same condition, some of the study participants started considering the possibility that Lina Ron had a humane side: "Padrón made me think. I asked myself, what if Lina is like La Chata? Because if she is, then she's a good person" (DANI, 27).

Lina Ron never doubted that La Chata was an opposition-manufactured representation of her. When La Chata's son Rosendo died on *Cosita Rica*, Ron declared: "One of these evenings they killed one of my sons. I worry because it's a subliminal message and they may try to harm my son Humberto" (quoted in L. Castillo 2004). In the officialist web page Aporrea.org, Mario Silva García wrote in March 2004, "Lourdes Valera, a Lina Ron that we must try to understand because she's surrounded by shit. The kind of shit that's born in the cerro and that has no reflection in 'normal' society, the one that is promoted from Venevisión."[21] Francisco Diez, who represented the Carter Center during the negotiations between the government and the opposition in the years 2002–4, remembers that in the pre-referendum months the government complained several times about La Chata as a representation of Lina Ron. Diez does not recall similar complaints regarding Olegario as a metaphor of Chávez (personal communication with author, June 15, 2005).

During the time in which La Chata struggled to be a candidate for mayor, study participants from all political positions enjoyed the character. However, they did not want her to be triumphant in her political endeavors. Slowly, but surely, La Chata's personal and family issues became the dominant factors in the audience's readings of her. When *Cosita Rica* ended, the resolution of La Chata and Juancho's storyline was largely approved by study participants (see figure 4). Leonardo Padrón's antiviolence message was assimilated by the viewers who saw in La Chata one of *Cosita Rica*'s most important lessons: "We all

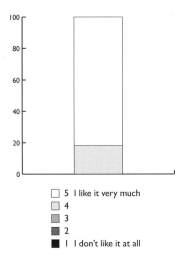

☐ 5 I like it very much
☐ 4
▨ 3
▨ 2
■ I I don't like it at all

Figure 4 Audience's perception of La Chata's storyline resolution.

have a space in this country! That is the great message of this couple. It isn't about not having disagreements, but about knowing how to handle them" (GRACIELA, 43). "It leaves us with a reflection: hatred and aggression never have good results . . . and she learned it through the deaths of her two sons. La Chata had to go through a process of reconciliation, with herself and with her country. And that's the great reflection this beautiful character leaves us with. She was one of the most important characters in the telenovela. One of those characters we, Venezuelans, will never forget" (MIGUEL, 20).

The Everyday Life of Politics and the Politics of Everyday Life: Representing and Consuming Political Venezuela

Keeping a balance among melodrama, humor, and metaphor, and evidencing his political position, Leonardo Padrón represents political Venezuela via *Cosita Rica*'s characters and storylines. The writer uses three different mechanisms to deliver his representation: fiction, editorialization, and re-creation.

With characters easily identifiable by the audience—maybe because they are allegories to political personalities, or they are women and men in which the public recognizes Venezuelans from their streets, schools, and workplaces—the writer creates fictitious situations and conversations that seem real because Venezuelans have witnessed them in the private and public domains of their everyday lives. In the same way that politics dominates Venezuela, fictional *Cosita Rica* was pervaded by the political. Viewers witness the intromission of politics in Venezuelan quotidian life as Olegario, La Chata, Juancho, and Tentación interact with the rest of the characters, highlighting the effects and perils of political polarization.

The telenovela also offers visions of Venezuela that are above its current political divisions:

BORIS: What side are you on?

MARIA SUSPIRO: I'm on my country's side. And that side's name is my mom, family, friends, and neighbors. My side is waking up in the morning and enjoying the view of the Ávila through my window.[22] And walking up to the creek where I like to bathe, and on my way greeting people of all ages and colors, and not being asked whether I'm a believer or not, or from the right or the left. I'm on the side of those who want to move forward. (Episode 109)

In this way, the telenovela editorializes at the same time it depicts reality. And even though that portrayal is also an opinion, editorializing is a more direct mechanism with simpler encoding that transmits the author's position in less ambiguous terms. For instance, when the country endured a week of opposition *guarimbas* (violent intifada-style street demonstrations), in *Cosita Rica* the teenager Nixon wrote in his journal:

NIXON [voiceover]: I'm very sad because of my country. My country used to resemble the word *happiness*. But now everything is different. There is fire in the streets. People are shooting each other. I can't feel the breeze from the Ávila because oxygen now stings, like eyes itch with tear gas. Some of my friends' parents have disappeared or are dead. Everyone has a stone in their hand . . . or in their minds. Everyone's angry. One of our teachers told us that this is the way wars begin. I'm very scared, even though my dictionary has words that could help us become the country we once were: *democracy, freedom, tolerance*. But, there's a word I've been searching for and I can't find: *peace*. I'm 15 years-old and I live in the country that grownups built. However, these days nobody is behaving like an adult. Instead, they act like rabid dogs. Is it possible that it's easier to kill ourselves than to respect each other? I'm 15 years-old and I want someone to give me back my country. Someone . . . or everyone . . . A country that resembles peace . . . peace . . . please. . . . (Episode 113)

In the same manner, the evening before Chávez's historic recall referendum, *Cosita Rica*'s episode ended with a collage of images of its characters as Nixon, once again, wrote in his journal:

NIXON [voiceover]: That day there was a lot of tension, not only in Barrio República, but throughout the country. The next day the nation's destiny would be determined and the decision was in our own hands. It was a huge responsibility! I kept thinking that the biggest responsibility we had was to make peace. That word, "peace," so short and, at the same time, so big. Once I read that "if you want to make peace, don't talk with your friends, talk with your enemies." Well, I'm just a kid and I don't have a vote on this yet. But, I certainly hope that grownups use their intelligence so that tomorrow we're all able to embrace our enemies so that this country which has been turned into anger and insult for a while now becomes peaceful again. Because the only victory that can unite us all is peace. (Episode 238)

Re-creation joins fiction and editorialization as tools used in the construction of the political Venezuela in *Cosita Rica*. Political demonstrations and violence in the streets are re-created in the telenovela with realism and precision. Such is the case of the Elinor Montes incident (February 27, 2004). Elinor Montes's abuse by government security forces was caught on tape and became the emblem of the opposition's accusations against the government's trampling of civil rights. On March 24, the incident was re-created in episode 129. Predictably, the re-creation was praised by the opposition media and severely criticized by the Chavista press.[23] The study participants were divided in their appreciation, and not by their political position. Some enjoyed watching the sequence, arguing that it "helped people comment what was happening in the country" (AMELIA, 27). Others thought it was "too much" (ANDREA, 35), and "too similar to the tragic events in the streets" (MONICA, 46).

Given the editorial nature of *Cosita Rica*, how did the study participants read the depiction of political Venezuela in this telenovela? In general, they approved it and acknowledged that it was one of the reasons they were hooked by the serial. "It was one of the aspects that caught my attention. The way it presented our political reality on the screen" (JAIME, 33). There was consensus among these audience members that *Cosita Rica* "shows what we're living every day." Almost half of the group (48 percent) defined the telenovela as slightly anti-Chavista (3 on the scale), while the other half was equally divided between those who considered it was neutral (4 on the scale) and those who considered it anti-Chavista (2 on the scale; see figure 5).[24] And, even though ROSALBA (42) believed that *Cosita Rica* was not a "radicalized" telenovela, both anti-Chavista GRACIELA (43) and Chavista MARCOS (26) were concerned about the lack of representation of the opposition's most radical sectors. In particular, MARCOS argued this could "instill even more division."

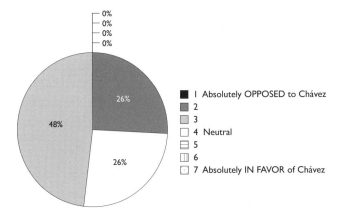

Figure 5 *Cosita Rica*'s political position, according to study participants.

These viewers, regardless of their political position, enjoyed *Cosita Rica*'s representation of the political situation, even in July 2004, one month before the telenovela ended, when both the public and writing team were showing signs of fatigue (see figure 6). It is impossible, however, to analyze here those audience members who stopped watching the telenovela, since everyone who participated in the study watched loyally until the final episode.

Padrón classified his telenovela as a 3 on the scale. From the inception of *Cosita Rica*, the writer had a thesis: the easing of polarization and the consequent reconciliation of Venezuelans from all political positions: "This is the fundamental premise of the telenovela. That every occasion which produces fractures and breakups merits a second opportunity: a reconciliation" (quoted in M. Reyes 2003, 12).

For the eleven months that *Cosita Rica* was on the air, the writer stuck to his premise. In our conversations and in press interviews, Padrón never veered from this line. One month before the final episode aired, when speculations about the post-referendum scenario pervaded Venezuela, the writer's goal was still to deliver a reconciliation message.

But, when the time came to write the final episode, he concluded it wasn't possible to write about political reconciliation: "We couldn't, we didn't know how to reconcile" (Leonardo Padrón, August, 19, 2004). Therefore, even though La Chata and Juancho—Chavismo and anti-Chavismo—end up together, they are not able to reconcile their political differences. *Cosita Rica*'s last reflection is, again, in the voice of teenager Nixon. "Diverse shots of the barrio's everyday life, with its purity and chaos, as an emblem of a country filled with doubts and hopes" (Episode 245, original script) are the images that foreground the

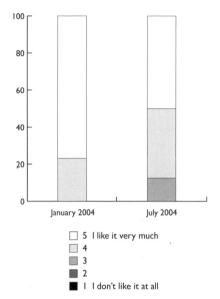

Figure 6 Audience perception of the depiction of Venezuela's political situation.

teenage narrator's last monologue. This time, however, the voice of Leonardo Padrón, himself, overlaps and substitutes for that of the young character. Blurring the line between reality and fiction until the very end, the writer delivers a message of hope as he sentences the impossibility of reconciliation:

NIXON [voiceover]: And this was the story of Barrio República. Or, better said, the story of a piece of this country, where anger and hope share the same streets, where our dreams are clad in the flag, a smile, and a maybe. Where everyone learns to fight for their ideas. A country that wants to resemble the word *reconciliation* . . . but, doesn't know yet how to achieve that. It seems that *reconciliation* has become the most difficult word in the dictionary. This is why I wanted to tell you these love stories. . . .

And the writer's voice overlaps Nixon's.

WRITER [voiceover]: Because the love between two people sometimes resembles war between two opposing sides. They say that everything's fair in love and war. But, the most important thing of both events is their ending. And there's nothing better than a happy ending . . . or a happy beginning . . . who knows? (Episode 245)

In this way, from beginning to end, *Cosita Rica* displays its author's version of political Venezuela. It is an interpretation tinted with the pre-Chávez social harmony illusion that is a key ingredient of the opposition's ideology. However, even though the telenovela has a clearly oppositional stance, it also includes many elements that foster reflection, encourage closing the gap between the two political extremes, and invite laughter so that viewers accepted it, regardless of their personal political posture.

For those who participated in this study, *Cosita Rica* was more than mere entertainment. It was "therapy" and "catharsis," a place where they recognized themselves and their circumstances in a reflective way, while they laughed and cried. Furthermore, the telenovela's tremendous success generated a huge number of news stories, as the press realized that the fictional *Cosita Rica* had become one more mechanism through which Venezuelans related to their reality. And both the government and the opposition reacted to the phenomenon and attempted to influence the representation of Hugo Chávez that Olegario was.

Why did a melodramatic television product elicit such commotion? Partly because of the uniqueness of the political moment that Venezuela was undergoing. But mostly because the "real" Hugo Chávez is a riddle Venezuelans are still trying to solve:

> Who is Hugo Chávez? At what point is he in the history of that boy who was raised by his grandmother in a house with a dirt floor? Is he a real revolutionary, or a pragmatic neopopulist? Where does his social sensibility end and his own vanity begin? Is he a democrat who is trying to build a country where there are no excluded people? Or is he an authoritarian *caudillo* [leader] who has appropriated the State and its institutions? Can he be both things at the same time? Who is this man who brandishes a cross while quoting Ché Guevara and Mao Tse Tung? When is he being himself? Which of many? Which of all the Chávezes that seemingly exist is the most authentic? (Marcano and Barrera Tyszka 2004, 388)

And Olegario provides possible clues to this brainteaser. The Hugo Chávez represented by Olegario Pérez is vain, self-important, paranoid, and an ineffective administrator. He is also an aggressive and charismatic communicator who knows well how to connect with "the people," when to break protocols to endear himself to them, and how to use victimization—his own and the people's—by his opponents and *el pasado* [the past] to promote his agenda. This Chávez is a proud and likeable machista. But, most importantly, he is drunk with power, addicted to it, and willing to do anything to have more and more of it.

We find more answers to the riddle of the "real" Chávez in the audience's reception of Olegario. Anti-Chavistas saw their president in Olegario's faults, but did not see him in the character's charisma, humor, and naïveté, wishing Chávez had those traits. In contrast, Chavistas did not recognize the president in Olegario, but saw the average Venezuelan in him. For them there was something very familiar about Olegario, something they liked, something that established a strong identification with Chávez's most endearing characteristics. In contrast, the audience's reading of La Chata breaks the logic of polarization, suggests a rejection to violence as a political means, and centers on the character's private sphere, implying that traditional gender views still dominate Venezuelan culture.

The analysis of *Cosita Rica*'s representations, and contexts of production and consumption, allows the examination of political discourse and formation of opinions outside of traditional political institutions—highlighting the need for this type of scholarship to understand the rejection of traditional institutions and the turn to charismatic populist leaders in countries like Venezuela, Ecuador, Bolivia, and Brazil. Hence, the study of *Cosita Rica* not only helps us better understand the conventions and dimensions of the electronic Scheherazade that every telenovela is, but also illuminates the links between media, culture, and society in the year in which telenovela, reality, and crisis worked together to write Venezuela's history, Venezuela's own telenovela.

Notes

1. Measurement of Venezuelan television audiences was provided in December 2004 by AGB de Venezuela on its website, at http://www.agb.com.ve. Since then, AGB Venezuela has merged with the Nielsen Company and has a new website, at http://www.agbnielsen.net.

2. With the notable exception of the 1992 telenovela *Por Estas Calles* (Hyppolite 2000; Márquez 1999), Venezuelan telenovelas have skirted the country's political context. There are, however, important differences between *Por Estas Calles* and *Cosita Rica*. *Por Estas Calles* became more chronicle than telenovela. Its main love story faded until it disappeared. *Cosita Rica* had less denunciation and more metaphor, poetry, and romance than *Por Estas Calles*.

3. A note about typographical conventions: throughout the chapter, the quotes by production participants (writers, actors, producers, and technical crew) will be identified parenthetically as participant's full name and full date of interview). Audience members' words will be noted by pseudonyms (in all caps) and their ages. All translations from Spanish to English are my own.

4. This chapter is only a section of my larger study of *Cosita Rica* and Venezuela (Acosta-Alzuru 2007).

5. *Cosita Rica* comprised 245 episodes.

6. Forty audience members participated in the study. They belong to all socioeconomic and educational levels, and represented all political positions in a self-definition scale of 1 to 7, with 1 being absolutely opposed to Chávez, 4 being neutral, and 7 being absolutely in favor of Chávez.

7. During the study I held over thirty hours of interviews with writer Leonardo Padrón, plus more than forty hours of interviews with actors, directors, and production team members.

8. I collected and analyzed 778 news stories about *Cosita Rica*. Although many of these were published in the entertainment pages of the country's major newspapers, a sizeable number of articles appeared in political and social commentary outlets.

9. In Venezuela, both patchouli and Vetiver are considered low-class fragrances.

10. As a signifier, Olegario has similarities and differences with his signified—Hugo Chávez. While Olegario has no formal education, Chávez was close to receiving his master's in political science from Universidad Simón Bolívar (Marcano and Barrera Tyszka 2004). Olegario almost bankrupts the Consorcio Luján, but Venezuela has seen economic growth in the Chávez era. However, it should be noted that the economy started growing after *Cosita Rica* ended in August 2004. While the telenovela was on the air, the economy was stagnant.

11. La Casona is Venezuela's official presidential residence.

12. Figure taken from the Instituto Nacional de Estadísticas, at http://www.ine.gov .ve/pobreza/menupobreza.asp.

13. The referendum question was whether the president should be revoked from his position.

14. See "Carter reunió a Chávez y a Cisneros," *El Nacional*, June 19, 2004. Since then, Cisneros and his network have moderated their political position and tone. Today, Venevisión's content can hardly be labeled as oppositional.

15. In a *cadena*, all nonsubscription media must broadcast the government's content live.

16. "Castillo Lara denuncia gigantesco fraude," *El Nacional*, August 17, 2004; "Mendoza: 'Vamos a demostrar que hubo fraude,'" *El Universal*, August 17, 2004; Lugo Galicia 2004; Mairena 2004.

17. Barbarita, a voodoo "specialist," also helps Olegario with the referendum results. That Chávez uses voodoo is among the many unconfirmed tales about him that make up the opposition's rumor mill. This is a favorite topic among bloggers; see for example, José Iglesias, "Reflexión del investigador José Iglesias para Hugo Chávez," at http:// www.tierradegracia.com/parahugo.html; and Kbulla, "De la pipa de Rómulo al escapulario de Chávez," at http://kbulla.blogspot.com/.

18. The network forced Padrón to eliminate a minor character before it aired—a district attorney whose last name was "Peterson"—because they determined that the character evoked controversial district attorney Danilo Anderson. Venevisión also modified

dialogues, re-taped some scenes, and eliminated the word *fraud* after Olegario's referendum.

19. It should be noted that up until the Chávez-Cisneros meeting, Venevisión was considered by both Chavistas and opponents as an opposition network. However, after that conversation, this perception has been modified. At the time of this writing (December 2007), the generalized view is that Venevisión is now pro-government. This widespread opinion was strengthened when the Chávez government renewed Venevisión's broadcast frequency concession and did not do the same for its competing network, RCTV, which never veered from its opposition line.

20. In *Cosita Rica*, Chávez is never mentioned by name. All references to him are "el que te conté" (the one I told you about).

21. The poorest of Caracas's barrios are located in the hills that surround the city. Hence, "*cerro* (hill) is sometimes used interchangeably with *barrio*. This quotation comes from the text of "La Hojilla," episode 41, which Mario Silva García posted to http://www.aporrea.org on March 26, 2004.

22. El Ávila is the name of the mountain that marks the North for those who live in Caracas. It is an important presence and an identifier of Venezuela's capital city.

23. For an opposition response, see Marlene Castillo, "Olla de grillos: Sala de espera," *El Mundo*, March 30, 2004; for a Chavista response, see Mario Silva García's posting to www.aporrea.org on March 26, 2004, cited above.

24. Using the same scale with which participants self-defined their political position: From 1 (absolutely opposed to Chávez) to 7 (absolutely in favor of Chávez).

CHAPTER TEN

The Color of Mobs

Racial Politics, Ethnopopulism, and Representation in the Chávez Era

Luis Duno Gottberg

Mediating the Streets

Contemporary political tensions in Venezuela suggest that the struggle for the streets not only occurs in public spaces but also in the private sphere, where citizens consume media messages. Streets are thus mediated. The evidence that supports interpretations of events, and hence future actions, circulates in the printed press and television: how many supporters each side has; who the acceptable political subject (so-called civil society) is; and who the violent, irrational mob is. The sociocultural process by which the notion of legitimate or illegitimate masses is produced, contested, and co-opted rests, therefore, not only on the specific historicity of notions of what the people ought to be and how they ought to behave in the public sphere, but also, on the power of media mediation.[1]

Elsewhere I have studied representations of popular sectors allied with Chavismo disseminated by privately owned Venezuelan media (see Duno Gottberg 2003). Looking at journalism, press photography, and television, I analyzed the construction of an illegitimate political subject: "the crowd" or "the mob" (see figure 1). I suggested that those images equate to what I called, following Ranajit Guha's famous essay on subalternity, rebellion, and representation, "media counter-insurgent imaginary" (Duno Gottberg 2003). Such a process has had several consequences: first, it has created the image of an undesirable collective, a rebellious multitude whose political agency is—by definition—denied; and second, it has triggered the "moral panic" (Cohen 1980) that prompted certain sectors to build barricades (see figure 2) against the mob that may attack at any time.[2]

In what follows, I concentrate on one aspect of this process that I term "the

Circula de lunes a sábado en todo el país   **Bs. 300**

La violencia chavista se hizo sentir en todo el país

Hordas desatadas

Figure 1 "'Mobs' or Civil Society?" A newspaper headline published a few days before the coup in 2002 speaks to the ways in which representation produces political subjects *for* the public sphere while dismissing others as "pre-political." Source: *El País*, April 2002.

racialization of crowds." In other words, I discuss the stigmatized representation of the Chavista mass movement along racial lines, leading to the recurrent image of a dark-skinned mob that overtakes the streets. I also analyze a complementary aspect of this phenomenon—what I understand as a particular strategy of populist interpellation, that is, racialized discourses generated by Chavismo.

The processes of representation discussed in these pages, and more specifically, the racialization of crowds, are among the many devices deployed in the general struggle for hegemony that permeates the Venezuelan political arena today. Racialization is one result of the contradictions within a national project that maintains legacies of colonialism, that is, racism, racial discrimination, and the degradation of labor.[3] It is misleading to read the current proliferation of racist language as an isolated or passing event; it is connected to the history of racial formations in the country, as well as the more immediate confrontation of today's heterogeneous political forces. It is within the concep-

Figure 2 In the eastern part of the city, middle-class neighborhoods prepared for "mobs" that would allegedly descend from the slums to loot their houses. Source: Caracas 2002 (http://www .urru.org/11A/Fotos.htm).

tual framework of coloniality and the struggles over hegemony that one must understand the diverse processes of the racialization of crowds in contemporary Venezuela.

As a whole, this chapter seeks to provide an understanding of the racialization of politics in the Chávez era, but most importantly, it suggests that this phenomenon cannot be evaluated as the mere invention of a "belligerent populist leader." I would suggest that the intensity of the current exchange speaks to the depth of the contradictions revealed by the loss of elite hegemony, which has unleashed social forces that had been previously contained within the framework of an oligarchic democracy and the myth of racial harmony.

Venezuelan Racial Politics and the Culture of Ethnopopulism

It is difficult even to discuss the subject of racism in Venezuela. Convinced we are a *mestizo* nation (which is true in terms of mixing), we Venezuelans pride ourselves on our lack of racial discrimination (which is true only in comparison to the United States or Europe). We see ourselves as a *café con leche* people that have integrated black and white into a distinctive and harmonious mixture. Similar to Cubans, for example, we consider ourselves strangers to the kind of prejudice common in *other* countries. Since the issue is theoretically resolved, not only do we refuse to talk about it but we react defensively to any attempt to re-think our "racial democracy."[4]

The discourses of racial democracy—transculturation or *mestizaje*—have been key elements in the construction of a politics that ignored racial prejudice by assuming the resolution of ethnic conflict in a homogeneous nation of mixed-race people. As such, they are part of the multiple strategies and negotiations implemented in the construction of "the people," and what I am calling ethnopopulism.[5]

These ideas might help us understand some of the strategies employed to deny any racial tension in the *patria café con leche* as well as the strategies deployed by Chavismo and the opposition in order to achieve hegemony. The erasure of social conflict, the co-optation of popular will, and also radical popular mobilizations are all possible within this strategy. Here I depart from Ernesto Laclau's famous concept of populism (1977), in which

> what transforms an ideological discourse into a populist one is a *peculiar form of articulation* of the popular-democratic interpellations in it. . . .

populism consists in the presentation of popular-democratic interpellations as a synthetic-antagonistic complex with respect to the dominant ideology. . . . Populism starts at the point where popular-democratic elements are presented as an antagonistic option against the ideology of the dominant bloc. (172–73; emphasis in the original)

Extending Laclau's well-known formulation, I propose that we understand ethnopopulism as a particular articulation of popular-democratic interpellations centered on the production of a unified subject along ethnic or racial lines, through an appeal that rests on cultural or biological formations. Such discourse essentializes the identity of the people, inventing its past and predicting its future as a cohesive whole sustained by a common race or ethnicity.

This concept can be related to Etienne Balibar's notion of "fictive ethnicity." The author explains that this idea doesn't suggest a mere illusion without historical effects, but that it should be understood in a similar manner as the *persona ficta* in the juridical tradition, in that those included are represented as a natural community, with shared origin, culture, and interests. In turn, fictive ethnicity is closely connected to crucial mechanisms of nation building:

Fictive ethnicity is not purely and simply identical with the ideal nation which is the object of patriotism, but it is indispensable to it, for, without it, the nation would appear precisely only as an idea or an arbitrary abstraction: patriotism's appeal would be addressed to no one. It is fictive ethnicity which makes it possible for the expression of a preexisting unity to be seen in the state, and continually to measure the state against its "historic mission" in the service of the nation and, as a consequence, to idealize politics. By constituting the people as a fictively ethnic unity against the background of a universalistic representation which attributes to each individual one—and only one—ethnic identity and which thus divides up the whole of humanity between different ethnic groups corresponding potentially to so many nations, national ideology does much more than justify the strategies employed by the state to control populations. It inscribes their demands in advance in a sense of belonging in the double sense of the term—both what it is that makes one belong to oneself and also what makes one belong to other fellow human beings. Which means that one can be interpellated, as an individual, *in the name of* the collectivity whose name one bears. The naturalization of belonging and the sublimation of the ideal nation are two aspects of the same process. (Balibar, quoted in Williams 2002, 36; emphasis in original)

In a more recent discussion, Laclau explains that two crucial elements precede the articulation of populism: first, the separation between the people and power; second, the possibility of identifying and satisfying a series of popular demands (2005, 99). For the sake of our argument, this conceptualization can be understood in terms of *demands of integration and assimilation* into a national project (through mestizaje) or *recognition of difference* (through identity politics). These opposing demands and strategies of representation are the basis of two different practices of ethnopopulism that nevertheless coincide in the construction of the people. In the first, ethnicity is paradoxically erased by the process of assimilation: "Somos todos la misma gente; todos mestizos" (We are all the same; all mestizo). It is possible that such practice may lead to forms of civic nationalism, where belonging is determined by the adherence of the individual (citizens) to the law, culture, and territory, more than by his or her particular origin or blood.

The second possibility emphasizes difference and seems more closely related to ethnic nationalism. As I will explain later, this articulation has become visible during Hugo Chávez's government, although co-existing with the more widely seen expression of civic nationalism. The uses of racialized markers to describe the opposition, as well as the explicit constitutional recognition of indigenous people's rights, and the attempt to include similar legislation for Afro-Venezuelans in the package of constitutional reforms of 2007 (defeated by referendum) may speak to this.

In his study of ethnic nationalism, Anthony D. Smith calls the "Janus-faced posture" of this ideology both "integrative and divisive" (1983, 256). This characterization is particularly productive for our concept of ethnopopulism, as we may argue that such a Janus-faced feature satisfies the strategy of antagonism deployed by populism in "the presentation of popular-democratic interpellations as a synthetic-antagonistic complex with respect to the dominant ideology" (Laclau 2005, 99). Within this dynamic of *antagonism* and *demand*, popular forces could be absorbed and channeled by elites seeking to establish hegemony, but we should not ignore the possibilities of radical mobilization generated by such phenomena, which are frequently dismissed in narrow conceptions of popular or populist politics. We must keep in mind that populism can be articulated by the elites as a way to unify and co-opt a heterogeneous collective within a process of modernization, but it can also be articulated from within certain oppressed groups as a political strategy of mobilization that allows the creation of a community of resistance.[6] I would like to call this second expression of populism the *popular ethnic* to emphasize its subaltern articulation as well as its counter-hegemonic impulse. The tension between these two co-existing possibilities should play a fundamental role in our understanding of the dynamics of populism. I would also like to suggest that this idea must inform our approach to national projects characterized by "soft racism" or "discrimination without violence," as Mauricio Solaún and Sidney Kronus (1973) have explained for the case of Colombia.

Most of the racial discourses analyzed in this chapter function within what Ángel Rama called "the lettered city" (1996, 4), and what we may term "the mediatic city"—that is, discourses generated by a creole intellectual elite that interpellates national collectives as a unified national subject and, fundamentally, *as a means of dissolving any antagonistic impulse*. As Laclau has warned, "populism is [not] always *revolutionary*. It is sufficient for a class or class fraction to need a substantial transformation in the power bloc in order to assert its hegemony, for a populist experience to be possible" (1977, 172–73; emphasis in original).

These kinds of discourses have long been articulated at the intersection of Venezuelan culture and politics, much before they began to manifest themselves in the Chávez era in contradictions generated by current representations of the racialized crowd. In a now-famous anecdote, Andrés Eloy Blanco, a well-known Venezuelan poet and founding member of Acción Democrática, compared the racial composition of Venezuela with "café con leche" in an article in *El País* on April 25, 1944. The article was a response to a letter from a friend who told him that the Brazilian government was thinking of resolving "the Negro problem" by offering whites a stipend if they married Afro-Brazilian people. As Winthrop Wright relates, the poet thought the proposal offensive and unrealistic, particularly for his compatriots who had reached a "racial balance" after several centuries of mestizaje (1990, 391).

Eloy Blanco then recalls a conversation with a North American professor, to whom he said, "You have never worked out how to make coffee or how to treat the Negroes. Your coffee is too light and your Negroes too black. . . . If America has to be white, I prefer our method of making coffee. And our form of making café con leche, which will be a bit slower, but better" (1944). With these words, Blanco, a founding member of a party that had a number of Afro-Venezuelans in its lower posts, articulated the old notions of "whitening" and cultural assimilation within a putatively non-racist discourse. African components are here assimilated to the nation, but only insofar as they are on their way to becoming "white" or "whiter."

In consideration of these ideas, it is interesting to look at a novel such as *Pobre Negro* (1937), which recounts the nineteenth-century wars known as the "Federal Wars," where racial conflict was notoriously present. The author, Rómulo Gallegos, is another founding member of Acción Democrática and was elected president in 1948. In *Pobre Negro*, the freeing of the slaves is seen to produce conflict if not accompanied by complete integration, or assimilation: "That very freedom had complicated his life, promising him a narrow road that promptly led to the *impasse* of tyrannical necessity," the narrator says (1937, 117; my translation, emphasis in original).

Racial conflict, however, is attenuated toward the end of the novel. The rebellion of the main character, Pedro Miguel, wanes under the influence of Luisana's mestizo love. The foundational romance thus confirms the whitening of a nation where the races have found their natural balance—*in theory*. Gallegos writes: "No longer a battlefield between irreconcilable races, as he previously came to fear, but quite the opposite, the constructive harmony of a nation which will face its future with decisiveness and courage, accepting in full consciousness the *fait accompli* of *mestizaje*" (89; my translation, emphasis in original). As explored by John Beverley (1999), Julie Skurski (1994), Javier Lasarte Valcárcel (1992, 1995) and Raquel Rivas-Rojas (2001), this discourse of reconciliation is a fundamental element in Gallego's populist literary representations, and I would suggest it must be seen as an instrumental aspect of his interventions in Venezuela's political arena.

We see then that two of the founders of Venezuela's most important populist party, Gallegos and Blanco, celebrate the synthesis of the nation based on the erasure of the black subject as such. This discourse was instrumental to a recasting of Venezuela's national project that took place between 1935 and 1948 and from 1958 to 1989 as one of popular democratic modernization. Nevertheless, the synthesis of what it is to be Venezuelan, our condition as *café con leche* subjects, makes any discussion about racism seem absurd given the mestizo reality of a country that guaranteed the participation of all Venezuelans in national affairs. Racial democracy coexists in this manner with racial exclusion, which brings us once again to Laclau's comment about non-revolutionary articulations of populism.

East/West: The Civil Society versus the Crowd

The tension between racial democracy and racial exclusion is present almost every day in news reporting, as exemplified in the following quotations drawn from government and opposition sources alike:

Múltiples lesiones sufrió José Espinoza, técnico de Globovisión, al ser "confundido" con un chavista en plaza Altamira." ("José Espinoza, a Globovisión technician, suffered multiple injuries as a result of being mistaken to be a Chavista at the Plaza Altamira; quoted on the Chavista website, www.aporrea.org.)

Un grupo de simpatizantes del presidente Hugo Chávez intentó secuestrar a un español que tomaba fotografías de una trifulca en la caraqueña Plaza Bolívar. (A group of sympathizers of President Hugo Chávez attempted to kidnap a Spaniard who was taking photos of a disturbance in the Plaza Bolívar.) (Quoted on the opposition website, www.libertaddigital.com.)

There is an imaginary geography of political confrontation in Venezuela which brings with it very real, tangible consequences, namely today's racialization of crowds. This geography is well symbolized by two urban spaces in Caracas: Plaza Altamira on the east versus Plaza Bolívar on the west. On one side is the opposition, which seeks to remove elected president Hugo Chávez from office; on the other are the Chavistas who support him. On one side, several wealthy neighborhoods are sites of the fiercest rejection of the government. On the other, not far from where shantytowns have been growing for over fifty years, Chavistas organize their demonstrations. Although the actual spatial arrangement of politics is more fluid in practice, the political imaginary on both sides retains this rather stark contrast. In May of 2003, the opposition organized a mobilization to achieve popular support among the people from the west; the event was called "the re-conquest of the west."[7]

Keeping in mind the political implications of this kind of mapping, let us consider how this geography was present in an episode of a TV program that is extremely popular among the opposition, significantly titled *Aló Ciudadano* (Hello citizen; on Globovisión) to invite comparison with Chávez's *Aló Presidente*. The episode in question was screened in January of 2002, and demonstrates the representation of two contrasting political subjects: on one side, civil society; on the other side, the "other" or mob. The host, Leopoldo Castillo, compares the gatherings of the opposition in Plaza Altamira and that of the Chavistas, who moved eastward and settled in front of the offices of the state-owned oil company.

The first sequence in the Globovisión report portrays, without any comments, the concentration of an opposition in Plaza Altamira and prompts no qualifiers about the characteristics of people in the gatherings. By contrast, when the report shifts to the second sequence regarding a pro-government group, Castillo treats the Chavistas as an ignorant, lazy, and violent crowd. The host says that people are talking in small groups, as if conspiring to do something illegal. They gather under trees, they gamble, they obstruct traffic; in short, they monopolize a public space that does not belong to them. One man has a backpack on his shoulder, which is immediately read by Castillo as a sign of potential violence: "What do they have in those bags?"[8] Even the vests used by journalists become suspicious when used by Chavistas: "What do they keep in all those big pockets?" The commentator insists that he is not making judgments as to whether these characteristics are good or bad, he is simply describing them. Nor does he have to say anything negative, because a commentator sitting next to him draws the conclusion that the Plaza Altamira and the Chavista gatherings have "cultural differences."

This audiovisual message belongs to a series of discourses about the presence of "certain kinds of people" on the streets and constitutes an attempt to construct subjectivities, interpellating certain collectives as organized political subjects or as dangerous masses. Such coded representation is not isolated, nor is it exclusive to television. A blatant example was published in an editorial in *El Nacional* when a Chavista demonstration was criticized in the following terms: "The response of the President and his entourage to the concerns of Venezuelan society about the grave crisis we are experiencing. . . . consisted of bringing the usual lumpen in from the interior once again, bussing them in with their pieces of bread and bottle of rum."[9]

Another example of this media construction of social subjects in exclusionary terms is apparent in a headline of *El Nacional*. On the front page we read, "Civil Society Bangs Its Pots and Pans" (October 2002). The headline refers to a group opposed to the Chávez government that has expressed their discontent on this occasion by banging their pots and pans in the streets. However, some readers were irritated by what they perceived as an attempt to define civil society in restricted terms, given that the headline appeared to take for granted that government sympathizers were part of the so-called third sector. The response of the newspaper was even more symptomatic, defending itself from criticism with the argument that it was increasingly difficult to work out who was part of civil society. This reply suggests that what is really problematic is the visibility of a new social subject: the mob, whose political action is unrepresentable or inconceivable in terms of a legitimate project (see Coronil and Skurski 1991).

This contempt for popular sectors aligned with Chavismo reveals one of the motives for their emergence as a new political factor previously subsumed in a now dismantled hegemonic order. It is the new visibility of these sectors in public and institutional spaces that likely triggered anxiety among some of those who maintained such order. In that sense, the comments of Napoleon Bravo, the moderator of a TV program for RCTV, are quite revealing. He talks about *los marginales* (the disenfranchised) and what happens when they come into power: "With the disenfranchised the situation is really bad. When they make a mistake they blame others. *Can you believe how democratic this country is that even the disenfranchised are in power?*" (24, aired in February 2002, Channel 4; my emphasis).

As we will see, those *marginales* who took over the presidential palace are racialized. Humberto Celi, a prominent leader of Acción Democrática, described the crowd that gathered to listen to the victory speech at the presidential palace thus, "When I saw Chávez triumphant on the 'People's Balcony,' greeting the multitude, and the TV cameras focused on those delirious faces, I said to myself, 'My God, those are the *negritos* of Acción Democrática'" (quoted in Hellinger 2003, 42). This phrase is of great importance for understanding the complexities of racial politics in contemporary Venezuela. If the statement "the negritos of Acción Democrática" is to be read as an expression of a creole elite's desire to absorb and control a particular social force, then we can see the origins of the anxiety produced by the rearrangement of hegemony that Chavismo has brought about, as well as how such a rearrangement is connected to racialized discourses. The "negritos" were always there, but the problem seems to arise when such subjects are no longer docile—when they are no longer *their* "negritos." This hypothesis is reinforced by the discursive strategies deployed by the opposition during the 2006 electoral campaign, when such racial markers were a fundamental feature of advertisement of a faction that wanted to prove its popular appeal.

On the other hand, after the reversal of 2002's coup d'état against Chávez, there took place a significant expansion of alternative media as well as state-controlled media (see chapter 4, "Catia Sees You," by Schiller, and chapter 5, "Radio Bemba in an Age of Electronic Media," by Fernandes). In most of these, we have also witnessed the emergence of an illegitimate political subject: *el escuálido* (the squalid or languid), a term used to describe the opposition to Chávez. The rhetoric that produces such a subject is based on a disqualification justified by what Chavistas perceive to be the elites' political condition (whether they are seen as fascists or oligarchs) or based on xenophobic reactions, as it is frequent to hear that those who oppose the government are non-Venezuelan. In this sense, Chavismo also articulates the rhetoric of ethno-populism when the struggle is defined in terms of an antagonism between the *national-popular-of-color* and the *white-foreign*.

The responses to Manuel Rosales's electoral campaign of 2006 are quite telling in this regard. One of Rosales's electoral promises was the direct distribution of oil revenue through a debit card (figure 3) that would allow the purchase of services (health, education, etc.) now delivered by the state. This promise was often paired with another theme—the claim that programs offering discounts and favorable finance terms for oil purchases by poor countries (e.g., Petrosur and Petrocaribe) are give-aways of the national patrimony (figure 4). The rationale for the debit card system is anchored—not without contradictions—in the neo-liberal credo which suggests that the private sector is more efficient and reliable than the state, and that to become a consumer is to empower the citizen. Another interesting element of the campaign was the multiple values appropriated to the color "black." It was obviously a reference to "oil," but it is also related to "the people," as in the case of Gladys Ascaño (see figure 5), the woman who served as "the face" of the campaign.[10] The message condenses in this manner the reference to a double source of capital: the economic (the mineral) and political (a racialized popular constituency).

Figure 3 A supporter of Manuel Rosales displays a copy of "Mi negra" during the electoral campaign of 2006. Mr. Rosales's campaign chief, Jose Vicente Carrasquero, told the BBC that this important element of his electoral campaign consisted of "a black plastic debit card," which, he said, they "propose[d] to hand out to some two million poor families: "Each month we intend to transfer up to $450 to the card, depending on the current oil price, so the families can go out and buy food or save the money to set up a small business" ("New Life for Venezuela Opposition?" October 3, 2006, BBC News, http://news .bbc.co.uk/2/hi/americas/5389460.stm).

Figure 4 This still of an ad from the Rosales campaign suggests that Chávez is giving away oil revenue to foreign countries. Rosales promised in contrast to devote these resources to the people of Venezuela, but through direct transfers and privatization of state programs, transforming citizens into small entrepreneurs and consumers of services.

Figure 5 As in this example of campaign propaganda, the campaign slogan of "Mi negra" often appeared with a photo of Gladys Ascaño. Oil and race thereby came together in Rosales's own brand of populism.

Figure 6 This image was one of several circulated by *chavistas* to counter the Rosales campaign. Condolezza Rice and George W. Bush appear side-by-side with Manuel Rosales, indicating that "Mi negra" represents U.S. imperialism and is therefore anti-national. In a classic populist strategy of interpellation, *race* is rearticulated within a nationalist framework to suggest that not all blackness represents the best interest of Venezuelan people.

Many Chavistas were offended by the use of a racialized discourse and eventually reacted by insinuating that the woman in the picture was not Venezuelan, or that she represented Condoleezza Rice (figure 6). The implication was that she could not be an Afro-*Venezuelan* if she supported the opposition. This is a good example of the connections of ethnopopulism to the discourse of the nationalism, as discussed above.

The Color of Crowds

The racialized depiction of historical conflict within the Federal War (1859–63) in Gallegos's *Pobre Negro* is often on display in more crude form in popular culture. A prime example is the treatment of Ezequiel Zamora, a nineteenth-century mulatto general on the Liberal side of the war. In the war, the confrontation between liberals and conservatives dovetailed with a racial struggle dating back to Independence. Chávez's embrace of Zamora as a heroic champion of the masses has stimulated profound interest and heated debate in scholarly representations of the past as well. Just as Chavistas have embraced the image of Zamora, the opposition has seized upon the contradictory and complex words and actions of this historical figure.

Daniel Hellinger has addressed Chavista hermeneutics of history in detail, explaining how national heroes and public holidays are part of the current debate (2001). He identifies Ezequiel Zamora as one of the main historical figures used in the rhetoric of the Bolivarian movement—the other two being Simón Bolívar and Simón Rodríguez. The gesture is not new, as the figure was previously celebrated during the 1960s by certain leftist groups; but his reappearance in the new political arena is particularly intense and debated. Chávez has cleverly played upon the symbolic power of this widely known figure, who happens to be from the same region of Barinas as Chávez. In fact, Chávez and his co-conspirators named their military rebellion of February 4, 1992, after the popular Liberal *caudillo*. Also, Hellinger writes, "Like Zamora, Chávez employs an egalitarian discourse that is often vague on specifics, laced with racial overtones, evocative of the resentments of the masses, and threatening to elites" (2001, 5–6).[11]

Elías Pino Iturrieta, a fierce critic of Chávez, has written extensively about the issue, stating that the reinvention of Zamora occludes not only the true contradictions of this historical figure, but more significantly, the contradictions and deficiencies of the current government.

Certainly Zamora led a peasant uprising and proposed redistribution of
land in the beginning of his political life. But also it is clear that afterward he forgot his liberation slogans after marrying well and obtaining
haciendas, in order to polish his image in [the] bosom of high society, to
enjoy the fruits of the sweat of his slaves and support the dictatorship of
José Tadeo Monagas, one of the most lamentable of the nineteenth century. What about these episodes of social ascent and complicity with personalism? What about this man that quit being the *caudillo* of the poor
to transform himself into the hereditary landowner and friend of a corrupt president? They cannot publically air this dirty linen whose tawdry
nature doubtlessly no revolutionary would respect. One must overlook
these welts that deface the image of the *catire* [slang for blonde hair] of
the humble. One must choose only that which can fool the unwary. Thus
we have Zamora without apologies, presented to society by the *comandante*. A "revolution" that does little to change life needs to look to appropriate for itself distant and exaggerated glories that it cannot find on its
own to offer. The distortion of the past not only opens space for maneuvering, it also engages an enemy that limits transformations. This facilitates a discourse that characterizes those opposed to the comandante
as "oligarchs." For this reason it is necessary to intone again the songs
of the federal army. For this reason begins the creation of an Ezequiel
Zamora that is and is not, but is at the service of the patriots in their
battle against the bad children of the nation. And the memory of society,
the storehouse of everything that illuminates the past of everyone, the
beacon thanks to which society does not become a congregation of idiots,
can go to hell. (2001)

An episode of the popular comedy program *Radio Rochela*, broadcast by the
opposition television network RCTV, demonstrates how this intellectual debate takes popular form. It is worth transcribing the exchange between the
two creoles that participate in the scene. Their discussion is revealing of the
complex relationship in which elites both desire and disavow a relationship
with "the people," especially in relationship to the stereotyped image of Afro-
Venezuelans.

MORALES (CREOLE MAN 1): The Federals are destroying all good looking
  people . . . And I desired Eza Mora so much . . .[12]
CREOLE MAN 2: Morales, I think that such love is impossible at this moment.
  You should look for a woman like Irene Sáez.
MORALES: I don't know what's up with that Mora that makes me fall in love.

Until when . . . until when will we have to stand this dictatorship of the ugly? Look at this. [*He shows the picture of an Afro-Venezuelan man.*] Look well at him. He looks like. . . . He looks like a portrait . . . the portrait of an orangutan. [*In anger, he throws the picture on the floor.*]

CREOLE MAN 2: Morales, you have done a lot of things to deserve the love of that woman. You have gone out without brushing your teeth, without shaving, without even showering. You have put on masks of ugly men. You should calm yourself.

MORALES: You are right, my friend, you are right. If there is anything I could do . . . anything so that Mora would look at me as a Federal.

CREOLE MAN 2: Why don't you crash against a wall and disfigure your face? Why don't you let Tyson tear off your ears?

MORALES: No, no. Whatever we do, we'll do with creativity.

CREOLE MAN 2: Morales, do you believe in reincarnation?

MORALES: Yes, some. Why?

CREOLE MAN 2: Maybe you should wait to live another life, so you can have surgery and make yourself look ugly.

In the sketch, a creole male tries to court "Eza Mora" (phonetically similar to "Ezequel Zamora"), a feminine figure that represents the people (Humberto Celi's negritos), assumed to be dark-skinned and poor. To seduce her, this upper class man must resemble the people, which for him means not to shower, brush his teeth, or dress neatly. Another character, a friend, advises him to pursue the love of someone different, like Venezuelan Irene Sáez, a white, blond-haired winner of the Miss Universe contest. Nevertheless, the creole complains that his populist transvestism is not working, and that the "dictatorship of the ugly" is therefore succeeding. While it is fair to assume that nineteenth-century creole elites differentiated themselves from the poor partly on the basis of a discourse of hygiene, what is interesting for our purposes, assuming the program is indeed representative of widely held attitudes, is that *they continue to do so*, thereby affirming their continuity with the past in the face of Chavista rupture, which, we argue, is imaginary as well as real (González-Stephan 1999).

The clip is revealing of certain perceptions of "the populace" among elites in Venezuela. Moreover, it is revealing of a double articulation of desire and rejection generated within the appeal to "el pueblo." It is therefore a good example of a co-opted expression of ethnopopulism, this form of transvestism which occludes racial discrimination by subtle forms of assimilation. Crucial to this linkage is the assertion of a subtler sort of masculine sexual desire; in this context, recourse to overt, aggressive domination, the kind we associate with the

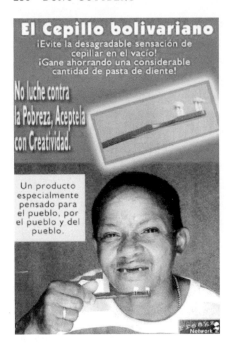

El Cepillo bolivariano
¡Evite la desagradable sensación de
cepillar en el vacío!
¡Gane ahorrando una considerable
cantidad de pasta de diente!

No luche contra
la Pobreza, Aceptela
con Creatividad.

Un producto
especialmente
pensado para
el pueblo, por
el pueblo y del
pueblo.

Figure 7 This violent image carries the
racist implication that poverty, Chavismo,
and the people are all connected. Source:
The opposition blog Resistencia Bucare-
Caracas (http://resistenciabucarecaracas
.blogspot.com), 2003.

U.S. South, is not an option. Unlike the violent exclusion that followed slavery
in the United States, blacks in Venezuela are to be subject to a benign paternalistic inclusion in the nation through heterosexual union.

In response to public complaints about discrimination as presented on television, the owners of TV channels aligned with the opposition to Chavez's
government have argued a lack of understanding of the Venezuelan sense of
humour.[13] More examples demonstrate that this defence is a way of masking the
profound contradictions of the discourse of racial democracy in Venezuela. The
following picture (figure 7), using a racial slant to bind together poverty, Chavismo, and "el pueblo," was circulated in opposition web pages and presents a
profoundly aggressive and insulting image of the Chavista constituency.

Another example of this kind of racialized construction of subjects appeared
in the form of a cartoon showing three well-known journalists opposed to the
Chávez government, who are disguised as members of a "mob" (figure 8). In
the drawing, these professionals appear as rag dolls, painted black so as to pass
unnoticed by those violently opposed to them.

The text contains a pun on the meaning of *mono* (monkey), which in Venezuela also designates a humble person of color. In this string of meanings, it is
suggested that the permanent use of disguise means that the characters must

Figure 8 Another example of a racialized construction of popular subjects, this cartoon showed three well-known journalists opposed to the Chávez government disguised as members of a "mob." In the drawing, these professionals appear as rag dolls, painted black so as to pass unnoticed by "those violently opposed to them." Source: *El Camalón*, October 2002.

start to smell like animals. Another visual image associating Chavistas with monkeys (figure 9) circulated among the opposition. In it, a monkey holds Venezuela's constitution.

Another powerful example was presented by the TV program *Today's Headlines*, whose anchorperson, Orlando Urdaneta, on one broadcast during a period of high political tension (the oil industry work stoppage of December 2002 to March 2003) gave a long disquisition on what he called "ugly people." The populist gesture of the discourse of mestizaje was followed by a series of subsequent comments that were openly racist: "Why, aah? A country full of beautiful black women and men, of impressive indigenous men and women, of people of mixed blood, proud of the best master brewer, for the quality of that marvellous mix, ahh, the best European produce with that creole magic, *why then so many ugly people*? Where do they get them from? It's like a Fellini film, but without the Italian's talent" (*Today's Headlines*, December 19, 2002, Globovisión, emphasis in original). In this first part we can identify ideas associated with what I have called ethnopopulist discourse, building on mestizaje to provide acceptability to the ethnic factors that flow into a homogeneous national subject. The responsibility for mixing falls upon the "master brewer" who joins "the best produce of Europe" with "creole magic"; again, we see the presence of creole masculine desire as the driving, shaping force of the nation. Urda-

Figure 9 The image implies that *los monos* ("monkeys," the lower classes of color) are now in charge of constitutional matters. Source: The opposition blog, Resistencia Bucare-Caracas (http://resistenciabucarecaracas.blogspot.com), 2003.

neta does not refer to the violent processes of assimilation to which blacks and natives were subjected, but only to something incidental to mestizaje, charmingly characterized as magical. Note that it is the master who does the mixing; that the power of his sexuality is magic; that to join the Venezuelan nation, black and indigenous people are to be acted on—penetrated—by the master. If this reading is correct, it would show, in effect, that elites continue to imagine their rule in republican Venezuela through metaphors of power and control taken from a time when the country was still an Atlantic slave colony.

Another fragment of Urdaneta's discourse clearly shows how this paternalist rhetorical gesture becomes an overtly aggressive posture. Referring to Aristóbulo Istúriz, a prominent Afro-Venezuelan politician then serving as Minister of Education, he comments,

> Aristóbulo, for example . . . Remember when he was working here? Didn't he look better? Now this is really pronounced [pointing to his mouth]. He looks like he's suffering from gorilla jaw. Now that I've said gorilla, haven't you analysed the gestures of the other guy? There's some Cro-Magnon influence, Neanderthal, "monastic" then, almost at the level of

banana.[14] If you don't believe me, try and watch *Vale TV*, that every once in a while has really interesting documentaries on these jewels of the animal world. (*Today's Headlines*, December 19, 2002, Globovisión)

What these clips, pictures, and cartoons have in common is the attempt to chastise certain sectors of the Venezuelan population that align themselves with Chavismo in search of participation in public affairs and the making of state policy. They intertwine rhetoric about the violence of the Other and the dichotomy of civilization versus barbarism with diverse racial slurs that appear under the sign of laughter.

These examples suggest that to understand political polarization in Venezuela we should consider the possibility that these representations are directly connected to the presence in the streets and in the institutional spaces of power of popular sectors that were previously organized and unified under a populist regime to which they had alienated their political agency. Although the dangers of the re-production of such co-optative, discriminatory politics exist within Chavismo, certain differences may exist.

Chavismo between Ethnopopulism and the Popular Ethnic

The century-old debate about the iconography of Simón Bolívar has been renewed in the Chávez Era. It is foreseeable that a symbol that seems to incarnate the body of the nation would be subjected to numerous rewritings, to countless projections of contending political agendas. In a recent unpublished essay, Javier Guerrero (2006) discusses the debate surrounding the queering of "El Gran Varón de la Patria," recounting the debate prompted by Venezuela's financing of a float for the 2006 Carnival of Rio (see figure 10). The theme was, of course, Simón Bolívar. Without ignoring the fascinating issues advanced by Guerrero about sexuality and politics in Venezuela, I would like to focus on the dispute about the hero's racial identity, for it clearly represents the contradictions we have identified in racial democracy as well as in the complexities of ethnopopulism.

In response to the *carioca* representation of Bolívar, Venezuelan journalist Marianela Salazar complains that the hero has been disfigured with the complicity of Chavéz's government. In her article "La comparsa carnavalesca," she writes, "The chubby scarecrow with flat nose and arched eyebrows reduced Bolivar's figure to a carnivalesque nonsense, adding elements that characterize drag queens. . . . PDVSA [the state-owned oil company], sponsoring such

Figure 10 The School of Samba Villa Isabel parades a *carioca* and *zambo* Bolívar in Rio de Janeiro. The event was later the subject of debate between Chavistas and the opposition. Picture courtesy of J. Guerrero.

an aberration—a parade of naked *garotas* [show girls], feathered and winged mulattos, samba players happy in excess—allowed the image of the Liberator to be disfigured, caricaturized and degraded" (*El Nacional*, March 1, 2006).

The references to the "flat nose" and the recourse later in the text to old documents that demonstrate Bolívar actually had an aquiline nose, are part of a not-so-subtle racialized discourse. The complaint continues, indicating that the underlying project behind the Chavistas' appropriation of the nineteenth-century figure is to achieve identification with the current president: "There have been numerous descriptions of Bolívar by those who meet him, and none show a single feature that resembles Chávez," writes Salazar (*El Nacional*, March 1, 2006).

The problem of Chávez's mimetic appeal to Bolívar is only one aspect of a more complex chain of identifications that must be seen as a whole to understand the political imaginary of the country today, for this chain also expands to incorporate "el pueblo." Moreover, the identification process flows between the leader and the people in a dynamic way, posing a significant problem for any political articulation that is built upon derogatory approaches to the racial identity of the president. It is possible to speculate that while the body of the nation imagined and summarized in the non-white identity of Bolívar allows projections of "the people" in the figure of the national hero as well as in the image of the president, the construction in terms of a white identity would work in the opposite way. It is in this manner that identification would play a dominant role in the mechanics of ethnopopulism, and what critics have failed to understand is that it is precisely because of the failures of racial democracy that such articulation is not only possible, but also tremendously successful in the Chávez Era.

Significantly enough, Hugo Chávez also responded to and capitalized on the polemic generated by Bolívar's parade in the carnival of Rio in his weekly program *Aló Presidente*, reinforcing the image of a non-white Simón Bolívar:

> It was 3:30 a.m. when Villa Isabel [the school of samba] entered the Sambódromo of Rio de Janeiro and thousands, hundreds of thousands of people stood up to cheer. . . . at the rhythm of samba, at the rhythm of love, at the rhythm of joy, of utopia, or the new times that have come to this land. And look at the majestic figure of our Simón Bolívar, plus his black features, that seem so right to me. Because the Venezuelan oligarchy whitened Bolívar. I don't have anything against whites, but Bolívar wasn't white. . . . Bolívar was born among blacks. His hair was curly. He didn't have green eyes. And you see some portraits where he has green eyes, yellowing hair and [a] white face. Bolívar was small and they make him big. No, Bolívar was small, with [a] penetrating voice, and he was zambo. (*Aló Presidente* No. 248)

Thus Chávez specifically celebrates and emphasizes the non-white traits of Bolívar that others reject. It is true that this gesture would play a role in the identification of the people with the charismatic leader seen in many articulations of populist discourses; at the same time, the recourse allows a sense of restitution among those who have felt excluded within a supposedly color-blind society.

To understand this interplay of race, identification, and restitution as a mere demagogic mechanism that seeks to co-opt popular will is to ignore the complexities of populism. Such reductionism has its precedents in the psychology of crowds from the nineteenth century, when the masses were seen as falling into a hypnotic trance under the spell of leaders. Laclau has suggested a different approach in his analysis of the process of identification. Building from a careful reading of Freud, he conceives a relationship with the leader that does not abolish a collective rationality and reminds us of the multiple variables that exist within hegemony, generated between coercion and consensus (2005, 82–84). In terms of Venezuelan racial politics in the Chávez era, this idea is instrumental to understanding the relationship established between indigenous and Afro-Venezuelan movements with the state.

It is by now obvious that the racialization process generated within Chavismo has its own peculiarities and articulates *different versions* of what I call ethnopopulism. One of these versions we may term the "popular ethnic" to signal the agency among Afro-Venezuelans and indigenous communities negotiating their political projects for self-government within the context of the current government, which they tend to support against the opposition.

Contradictions are not scarce, nevertheless. Some expressions of racialized discourse are reminiscent of Acción Democrática's historical use of racial politics. For example, on a trip to Mexico, Chávez visited the Basilica de la Virgin of Guadalupe, and his discourse was reminiscent of the ideology of mestizaje: "The brown-skinned Virgin is not only part of the Mexican soul, but of all the peoples in this brown America. That's why she is brown, because she is like us. . . . Let's open the horizon for the brown American utopia."[15] It is possible that this articulation of the discourse of mestizaje is closer to the notion of the people conceived by José Martí in Cuba than to the tradition of assimilation represented by the cosmic race of Vasconcelos in Mexico. By this I mean that "the brown American utopia" represents a form of popular democratic interpellation generated within a radical populist project more than a project engineered by a creole elite.

Another strategy of racialization that can be identified within Chavismo seems closer to liberal multiculturalism. While Acción Democrática created the image of Juan Bimba, a raceless subject that represented a synthesis of Venezuelaness, Chavismo seems to acknowledge a heterogeneous popular subject that exists along the lines of black, indigenous, and mestizo identities. We could argue, with Balibar and Wallerstein (1991) and Wade (1997), that this is a key element in a national discourse that stresses unity along with difference. It is possible that this might lead to the co-opting of subaltern groups functioning as monadic units within the nation, but we should not ignore the emergence of an important Afro-Venezuelan and indigenous movement that reconfigures racial discourse—and political practice—within and beyond the Bolivarian nation.[16]

It is important to recognize that, like popular movements that led to the transformation of Venezuelan politics after the late eighties, ethnic mobilization precedes Chávez. Several cultural and political groups pushed for the recognition of indigenous and Afro-Venezuelan traits of national identity, independently or within some form of agreement with the state. In the seventies, for example, the Ministry of Education supported Pensamiento, Acción Social e Identidad Nacional (PASIN), a group that advanced—rather unsuccessfully— an ambitious project to reform the teaching of Venezuelan history. Other projects flourished in an autonomous manner, such as Teatro Negro de Barlovento or the vibrant groups for El Barrio Marín, from which certain leaders of the current Afro-Venezuelan movement would emerge. In the nineties, Claudio Fermín (AD) and the aforementioned Aristóbulo Istúriz (Causa R), both dark-skinned, also signaled a transformation of Venezuelan racial politics.[17] These precedents are important in order to think about the autonomy of the different movements that pursue identity politics in Venezuela today.

Another more problematic form of racialization that emerged during 2001–2 has lead to what we may term *expatriation*. Such discourse described the factions opposing Chavismo as white foreigners, helping to fan xenophobia.[18] This can be read as a strategy of antagonism that portrays the group that previously held power as a racist/classist power bloc, which must be confronted by the reinforcement of black and indigenous identities. The discourses generated from within certain sectors of the opposition have frequently precipitated the polarizing, exclusionary reaction among the "popular ethnic." Likewise, such discourses also provided ammunition for more traditional forms of ethnopopulist appeals to the people—*morenos, negros, indígeneas* or *mestizos*—against the racist Other.

Conclusion

Chávez defines himself as *mestizo, zambo, negro,* and *indio*, recasting his ethnic identity in strategic ways to address his constituency. In turn, mestizos, zambos, negros, and inidios often identify with him in ways that replicate the classic relation of the populist charismatic leader to "the people." Nevertheless, if we focus too narrowly on the traditional criticism of populism, we overlook fundamental problems. For example, what social forces create and respond to "popular ethnic" discourse, and what levels of autonomy might they achieve?[19] Finally, what happens when the factions that held power until recently repudiate the non-white, non-creole identity of a president that mirrors the people? If populism functions here as the articulation of a multi-ethnic and multi-class front that is politically antagonistic to the former ruling bloc, it is necessary to understand that the production of a new regime of racial representation is crucial in the consolidation of popular support.

The comments that circulated in the media about the "ugliness of the president" and about his "lack of class" reinforce the notion that the political forces opposing Chavismo also oppose the idea of the people as an active political subject. Here it is worth recalling Humberto Celli's comment about "sus negritos" and Hellinger's assertion that "such rueful comment on *negritos* evokes the manner in which class and racial identity are intertwined in Venezuelan political culture, something Chávez has effectively appropriated to advantage" (Hellinger 2003, 49).

The topic is complex, and racial representations have been modified on each side of the struggle, especially since the coup of 2002. Each side seeks to redefine its identity in more inclusive terms while carefully monitoring the language and the visual discourse it produces. As explained earlier, the recent use of racial discourses by the opposition, specifically within the electoral campaign of Manuel Rosales, is a good example of this.[20]

It is obvious that recent transformations in racial discourses do not represent the overcoming of contradiction in Venezuela's racial politics, but rather its re-casting; they could lead to the reinforcement of one of the most negative aspects of ethnopopulism by co-opting popular demands. Nevertheless, it is also possible that within the multiple redefinitions of this racialized context, new social movements might emerge, with political agendas that go beyond discussions of Chavismo versus opposition.

The comforting discourse on Venezuelan mestizaje, articulated through what I call the "ethnopopulist imaginary," needs to be dismantled. The study of current media representation-production of crowds suggests that contemporary political conflicts undergo subtle and not-so-subtle forms of racialization, and that the consensus that preceded the Chavista government was based on the occlusion of prejudices that underlie the design of the nation. Venezuela was not so much color blind as it was blind to racial conflict due to the ethnopopulist approach to such tensions.

Notes

1. The bibliography on the construction of the public sphere and media strategies of legitimating social subjects is vast. For some references, consult Bel et al. 2005; Dahlgren 1995; Darby and MacGinty 2003; Downing 2001; Eber and Neal 2001; Korzenny, Ting-Toomey, and Schiff 1992; Ruben and Lievrouw 1990; Scannell, Schlesinger, and Sparks 1992; Thompson 1994. On Venezuelan media and politics, see J. Barreto 1995; Bisbal 1994; Britto García 2003; Roldán 1990.

2. The concept of moral panic was advanced by Stanley Cohen (1980) in his study of youth disturbances in Britain during the 1960s. He defined the concept as follows: "A condition, episode, person, or group of persons emerges to become defined as a threat to societal values and interests; its nature is presented in a stylized and stereotypical fashion by the mass media; the moral barricades are manned by editors, bishops, politicians and other right thinking people; socially accredited experts pronounce their diagnoses and solutions; ways of coping are evolved or . . . resorted to; the condition then disappears, submerges or deteriorates and becomes more visible" (9).

3. Aníbal Quijano (1995) has explored the colonial origins of the idea of race and its long-lasting effects after colonialism disappears. He writes, "Coloniality has not ceased to be the central character of today's social power. . . . With the formation of the Americas a new social category was established. This is the idea of 'race.' . . . Since then, in the intersubjective relations and in the social practices of power, there emerged, on the one hand, the idea that non-Europeans have a biological structure not only different from Europeans; but, above all, belonging to an 'inferior' level or type. On the other hand, the idea that cultural differences are associated to such biological inequalities. . . . *These ideas have configured a deep and persistent cultural formation, a matrix of ideas, images, values, attitudes, and social practices, that do not cease to be implicated in relationships among people, even when colonial political relations have been eradicated* (167–69; my emphasis).

4. On racial democracy in Latin America see: Twine 1998, Domínguez 1994, Wade 1997, Wright 1990, De la Fuente 1999 and 2001, Duno Gottberg 2003.

5. This reflection is part of ongoing research titled "The Color of the People: Ethnopopulism and the Politics of Culture in Venezuela." The notion of ethnopopulism presented here is a working concept, and a further discussion will be offered in aforementioned work.

6. In a crucial study of this matter, Gareth Williams (2002) has addressed the interrelation of these concepts suggesting that "developmentalist populism and . . . the discourse of transculturation [share] their ability to produce and articulate the people as an effective means of transcending the neocolonial oligarchic state apparatus and of integrating the disenfranchised sectors into modern (national) socioeconomic configurations (34).

7. "La reconquista del oeste," *Panorama*, Maracaibo daily, 24 May 2003.

8. Transcription by author from files maintained by the Ministry of Culture, Caracas.

9. "La respusta del gobierno," *El Nacional*, October 14, 2002.

10. Gladys Ascaño is a member of COPEI (Partido Socialcristiano), and is known to have been active in popular organizations within her community, a slum named "Julián Blanco" in Petare. An interview with Gladys Ascaño can be found on the website for Gentiuno, at http://www.gentiuno.com/articulo.asp?articulo=4777.

11. Richard Gott (2005) has devoted a chapter to the relationship of Ezequiel Zamora and the ideological project of Hugo Chávez.

12. I transcribe "Esa Mora" as "Eza Mora" to make the allusion to the nineteenth-century leader clear.

13. After a formal complaint from the Ambassadors for several African nations, Alberto Feredico Ravell, General Director of Globovisión, declared that his critics didn't understand Venezuela's sense of humor. The complaint was raised after a program aired on 28 February 2004, when the gathering of the president of Zimbabwe and other diplomats from Africa was compared with the movie *The Planet of the Apes*.

14. Aristóbulo Istúriz formerly hosted a show on that channel. The joke is about the minister's looks, a consequence of his being Afro-Venezuelan. Then he refers to Chávez, who is made fun of for being a *zambo* (a mix of African and indigenous people). We can see another allusion to *mono* (monkey), with the joke word *monastic*, which properly refers to "monastery," but is turned by the presenter's fury into an allusion to apes.

15. "Acude Hugo Chávez a la Basílica de Guadalupe," *El Universal*, May 27, 2004.

16. To disregard such a fact is also ignoring the agency of social groups that effectively maneuver within the framework of populist politics. The work of Jesús "Chucho" García—the intellectual, activist, and leader of the Network of Afro-Venezuelan Organizations and Strategic Alliance of Afro-descendants in Latin America—provides an excellent example of complex and fructiferous negotiations of some social movements with the Bolivarian State. In personal conversations, García has repeatedly reiterated that he is neither a *Chavista*, nor a *Bolivariano*, but a *Revolucionario*. Nevertheless, such affirmations are usually followed by his support of *el proceso*—understood as a larger phenomenon generated by the coming of Hugo Chávez into power, along with the struggles of different social groups that precede and transcend him.

It is worth recalling that in 1999, during the discussions of the new constitution sponsored by the National Assembly, García was extremely critical of the lack of support for the long-due recognition of an Afro-Venezuelan constituency. In that moment, the Unión de Mujeres Negras and the Fundación Afroamérica decided to unite into the Network of Afro-Venezuelan Organizations to pressure the state: "Cuando sentimos el rechazo gubernamental se nos presentó la disyuntiva de optar entre la confrontación y la persuasión. Acordamos encarar un proceso de persuasión, de *realfabetización* del gobierno chavista." ("When we felt the governmental rejection we were presented with the options of confrontation and persuasion. We agreed to pursue a process of persuasion, of *realphabetizing* the Chavista government.") For a very good exposition of the political project of Network of Afro-Venezuelan Organizations, see also García's interview with María Gabriela Mata Carnevali (2008).

In the case of Venezuela's indigenous movement, more immediate results emerged from the discussions of the 1999 National Assembly, which lead to parliamentary representation and increasing involvement in the national affairs (see Van Cott 2002).

Both movements, the Afro-Venezuelan and Indigenous, have not only managed to move forward diverse projects of infrastructure, health, and education in the Amazon, Guajira, and Barlovento regions, but they have also developed networks that go well beyond the national borders, organizing conferences, seminars, and, in the case of Wayuu directors like David Hernández-Palmar, co-productions with other indigenous communities from Brazil.

17. For an excellent study of racial politics in this period and the significance of Claudio Fermín's presence in Venezuelan national politics, see Alejandro Velasco, "The Hidden Injuries of Race" (2002).

18. On July 17, 2003, Mario Silva García posted "El Odio a Chávez o la Herencia del Inmigrante" to the web portal Aporrea.org (http://www.aporrea.org/actualidad/a3888 .html). In it, he writes, "Wherefore so much hatred toward Hugo Chávez? In all of the opposition demonstrations, not only can we see lots of hate directed at the popular policy of Comandante Hugo Chávez, we also see the same middle class faces with their distinctly defined features. White, almost all of European descent and of a Spanish, Portuguese, and Italian profile in the majority" (my translation).

19. See González-Stephan 1999.

20. I suggest that the articulation of ethnopopulism within the electoral campaign of Rosales is based on a neo-liberal appeal to the people as consumers. Rosales understands the importance of a racialized convocation of the people within a project that seeks to redistribute the oil revenue, creating consumers of social services that otherwise would be delivered by the state. See Duno Gottberg 2006.

CHAPTER ELEVEN

Taking Possession of Public Discourse

Women and the Practice of Political Poetry in Venezuela

Elizabeth Gackstetter Nichols

Pero la poesía no es una pistola; no sirve . . . para eliminar un enemigo
o para seducir al público. No es instrumento útil de poder. Sirve para abrir
pequeños espacios de libertad donde pueden entreverse los misterios
del mundo y de la propia conciencia.

Yolanda Pantin and Verónica Jaffé, "El bárbaro y las trampas de la poesía"

In her study of democratic women's organizing in Venezuela, Elisabeth Friedman states that one of the "broad concerns facing scholars and practitioners of
democratization" in Latin America is how to integrate those members of civil
society who exist outside the centers of political power and influence (2000,
10–11). Friedman also states that the most urgent question in the transition remains, "What mechanisms—formal or informal—will allow all citizens to pursue full citizenship and adequate representation of their interests?" (11). In the
past twenty-five years, one answer to this question in Venezuela has been the
publication of literature and women's participation in the literary arena.

In Venezuela, the danger of the woman who knows too much is found in the
image of successful women not only in academic circles but in business as well.
As Venezuelan poet María Auxiliadora Alvarez observes, "The image of the successful, solitary executive woman is emblematic of the twentieth century because the mark of maternal success is the only possible way to balance the supposed moral failure of this indocile woman" (2003, 5; my translation). Women
cannot be allowed success through their intellectual or organizational powers
in public as well as domestic and familial success. To maintain the boundaries
of the archetypical compound women must be confined to one or the other.

However, in the Chávez era, these boundaries have been more difficult to maintain. Because so many of the grassroots programs (*misiones*) have targeted the poorest sectors of the population, our attention might automatically gravitate toward these activist communities that support the government. More often, the more familiar faces of women in Venezuelan politics would include figures such as Lina Ron and Iris Varela, the highly controversial and outspoken Chavista members of the National Assembly; Nora Castaneda, who has toured the world promoting the work of the Women's Development Bank; or María Corina Machado, the very visible leader of the opposition group, SUMATE ("join up"). This chapter looks at women's literary and poetic voice, a less visible but persistent feminine presence in politics, one that has severely criticized the old regime but has moved into opposition to Chavismo as well.

The progress toward more adequate representation of women's interests and experience has been striking, especially as more women are able to publish poetry. As Julio Miranda's research shows, the number of titles published by women has increased in each decade: twenty-five works in the 1970s, fifty-seven in the 1980s and sixty-three in the period 1990–95 alone. As Miranda also indicates, these thirty years seem to show the beginnings of a "normalización" or "profesionalización" (1995, 12) of women's writing. This becomes even clearer when we examine "activities parallel to the poetry of our authors—university professors, journalists, narrators, essayists, dramatists, filmmakers, editors, cultural functionaries, etc.—parallel to their poetry" (7). The texts themselves form a part of a complex of literary and intellectual activity for women entering more forcefully into public dialogue.

While not all women in contemporary Venezuela are afforded the same opportunities for self-expression or access to public dialogue, a segment of the female population has taken up the task of creating an authentic voice for women, using that voice to participate in the conversations that shape the community. Using the particular opportunities that have opened to them as poets in the literary arena, in the past twenty-five years women who had previously been deprived of voice and agency in the public sphere have broken the barriers erected to their freedom of expression, opening "small spaces of liberty," where they might find their own distinctive, public voice.

Women, Decency, and Participation in the Public Arena

Latin American women seeking to re-imagine themselves face a twofold task: they must reject the descriptions that have been created and perpetuated by the

guardians of discourse, and they must find a way for their new vision of themselves to enter the public sphere. These two problems are inextricably linked.
Latin American society demands that a "decent" woman be private, humble,
self-sacrificing, and chaste. To achieve this, women are tied to the home and
enclosed in it. As Debra Castillo explains, culture has traditionally supported
"the privatized and inward-looking Hispanic house and . . . the virtual confinement of married women to the home" in order to maintain the chastity
and purity of "women of good family" (1992, 11). In fact, the old-fashioned but
widely used term *mujer pública* in Latin America may still be understood as a
euphemism for a prostitute. The implication is clear: a woman who leaves the
home and enters the public arena is not a decent woman.

In her chapter "Venezuela's Telenovela," Carolina Acosta-Alzuru discusses
the generally negative impression that viewers have of the public figure Lina
Ron and her soap-opera doppelgänger, "La Chata," in the 2004 telenovela
Cosita Rica. La Chata, as described by Acosta-Alzuru, is portrayed as "vehemence, personified in a woman of quick movements and aggressive speech."
In this she is evocative of the real-life figure of Ron, antagonistic political organizer and Chávez supporter. Together the two women, says Acosta-Alzuru,
"distill radicalism and aggressiveness," operating within the show "without any
type of *pudor*"—a word that can be translated as "reservation" or "shame."

In the drama, La Chata is both a mother and a presumptive mayoral candidate. Indeed, the first story line written for the character followed her political campaign. Acosta-Alzuru finds, however, that this type of female figure is
perceived as belligerent, politically active, and without any modesty—a purely
negative image. In interviews with Venezuelan citizens of a cross-section of
society (though mostly women), Acosta-Alzuru finds consensus in the rejection
of this type of female participation. Perception of the character of La Chata
changed only when the plot and script began to focus more on the character's
family and love life, and less on her political goals. Those interviewed express
a specific preference for the more passive Chata over the more aggressive version evocative of the loud Lina Ron. In Acosta-Alzuru's study, the story lines
dealing with La Chata's romantic story scored much higher than those dealing
with her run for political office. For many, both La Chata's and Lina Ron's versions of political discourse are inappropriate.

We see, then, the underlying difficulties for women as they seek to enter
public discourse. In contemporary Venezuela, it is not a matter of simply physically leaving their homes but ideologically rejecting the *pudor* and *recato* that
have traditionally limited their voice.[1] These two terms represent the expectations inherent in the archetypes mentioned above. *Pudor* refers to the idea

of a woman's proper decorum, modesty, purity, and humility. *Recato* is the expectation of prudence, caution, and shyness. While progress has been made in Venezuela on women's issues, Acosta-Alzuru's study of *Cosita Rica* reveals the underlying social prejudices against women being too *gritona*—speaking out too much, or being too aggressive.

Jean Franco explores this struggle by considering more obvious examples of women entering into public discourse: the women's movements of the 1970s in Central America and the Southern Cone of Chile and Argentina that began as resistance movements to brutal authoritarian regimes. Franco categorizes these activities as "survival movements" in the sense that they "come into being when the state can no longer deal with the day-to-day survival of its citizens" (1992, 68). Women participated in political protests, organized soup kitchens, and occupied land for housing. In all of these activities, they "went public," leaving the confinement of the home to enter political and social struggles. While this may be seen as removed from the type of intellectual struggle that poets undertake, it is of the same root.

In Venezuela, women on both sides of the highly polarized political environment have gone public in this way. Just as the young women described in Sujatha Fernandes's chapter on local radio explore issues of community and barrio identity in their public radio programs (see "Radio Bemba in an Age of Electronic Media," chapter 5, this volume), writers broadcast their ideas about identity through poetry and Internet publication. In the case of contemporary women in Venezuela, political and social struggles force women out into the streets in protest, but in the current context, the streets are not only roadways and sidewalks; they are electronic in the form of radio airwaves and computer linkages. As they march on both kinds of streets women are searching for their "specific and authentic voice" as Susana Reisz puts it (1996, 36).

For well-educated women of the middle and upper class, the main subjects of this chapter, there is a more accepted avenue for public discussion of politics and social issues: poetry and literary circles. Indeed, for years literature has proved an effective way for some women to enter public dialogue because of the uniquely privileged position that writers have traditionally held in Latin America. Sylvia Molloy reminds us of the long history that equates literary ability with general intellectual authority in society:

> Since the time of the writer-statesman, that frequent nineteenth-century figure, the image of the Latin American writer as one invested with an authoritative voice and engaged in the affairs of the polis, although more subtly formulated now than it was one hundred years ago, is still

in effect. In this context then, to speak of a woman writer is in a way to postulate an antinomy: a subject, traditionally perceived as being "private" and devoid of authority, appears endowed with intellectual power within the public sphere. (1991, 108)

While Molloy is discussing the difficulties this antinomy creates for the patriarchal intelligentsia, we can see how contemporary women authors make use of the traditionally imbued authority today. The power ceded to poets by the institution of the writer-statesmen profitably challenges the archetypical expectation of feminine *pudor* and *recato*, providing an avenue through which women's discourse may legitimately egress into the public arena.

Literary Agency in Venezuela since 1980

The use of lyric poetry to communicate social commentary by women authors in Venezuela may be traced as far back as Enriqueta Arvelo Larriva in the 1920s, who urged women, "Entremos en lo bárbaro con el paso sin miedo" ("We should enter into barbarism, advancing without fear"; Pantin and Torres 2003, 143–44). It is not until the end of the twentieth century, however, that this project comes to fruition. Authors such as Arvelo Larriva, María Calcaño, Enriqueta Terán, and Miyó Vestrini were under-appreciated in their time for their efforts in this area. In more recent decades, however, barbarous poetic voices have had more impact.

Lo bárbaro in Venezuela takes on additional significance as the country's national identity has long been identified with synthesizing the noble but savage character of its Afro-indigenous population with the civilizing impulse of the European, as expressed in Rómulo Gallegos's *Doña Barbara* (1929). It is the female antagonist, Doña Barbara, who must be subjugated by Santos Luzardo, the mestizo educated at the Central University, who would reclaim his father's land from the female usurper. So what does Larriva mean by "entremos en lo bárbaro"? Confront it or adopt it?

Venezuela over the last twenty-five years has provided two types of examples of how women use this literary agency to enter into dialogue on issues of national interest. First, we can see how women use the text of poetry itself to challenge the status quo, questioning both the state of contemporary gender relations and the economic stratification within the nation. In addition, we may see how women in Venezuela make use of the literary community and the opportunities for extra-poetic communication it affords to share their message.

Perhaps the most famous, or infamous, text that seeks to call attention to the plight of women and the poor in modern Venezuela is the collection *Cuerpo*, written in 1985, by María Auxiliadora Alvarez (1993). Alvarez relates that she wrote the poems collected in *Cuerpo* as a direct response and protest to the Venezuelan government after her experience in giving birth in a public hospital (M. Alvarez 2003). Describing the collection in later years, Alvarez asserts, "The intention of this book was to transcend personal circumstances and pronounce the social reflecting, poeticizing the underprivileged situation of women in the multiple concomitant spaces impacted by the experience of maternity and childbirth" (9; my translation). Indeed, Alvarez used the work to challenge the official indifference of the state to the situation of an underprivileged and underserved class of women who suffered terribly in the public hospitals of the nation. As such, the work represents a commentary on the circumstances of both women and the poor.

The collection represents a type of testimonial poetry where the poet speaks for "the homeless and the tortured" registering "a new class of participants in the public sphere" (Franco 1992, 70–71). A child of privileged upbringing, Alvarez recounts that she was horrified by her experience, a full immersion in the lives of lower-class women: "In 1981, I gave birth to the second of my three children in a public hospital of Caracas . . . The public hospitals of my country are not arenas [*recintos*] of health but of illness and death" (2003, 10; my translation). Because of this experience, Alvarez was moved to write poetry that described her newfound comprehension of class differences and of the plight of all women. The poet relates, "I was horrified to become aware of the total vulnerability of women and the masculine system of power, including doctors, the government, military leaders, and heads of families, circumstances that aggravate indigence. Overall, illiterate or poor women reproduce alone in subhuman conditions" (11).

The poems in *Cuerpo* are not for the faint of heart. They contain unflinching imagery of the suffering inherent in the process of giving birth, suffering here exacerbated by the indifference and malice of the men in control. The triumvirate of power mentioned in her remarks appears in Alvarez's work as "doctor/cárdinal/teniente coronel [lieutenant colonel]" (1993, 17), a collection of men who assign women numbers instead of names, functionally treating them all the same, despite any difference in life experience, education, or social class. Indeed one can see how even a woman of a middle-to-upper-class upbringing would find herself subject to the powers represented by these figures: the government, the church and the military. The process of childbirth, and masculine control of that process, is indeed one of the practical concerns that can be seen to link women of different social classes.

The poems in *Cuerpo* speak from a generalized female perspective, here a "yo" (I) who identifies herself only as "[la] vagina que soy / . . . herida inteligente" (vagina that I am / . . . intelligently wounded). The poetic voice describes herself first by the feminine body parts that seem most important to the men around her and also as the animal they treat her like "hembra inteligente / . . . / reptil de espaldas" (intelligent female / . . . / reptilian back; 18). In this way she communicates her solidarity with the women who surround her: fellow numbers, body parts, animalized creatures without souls.

This poetic "yo," then, always speaks to a generalized interlocutor identified only as "Ud." or "Uds." This person or persons is unswervingly male in nature. The poem "usted nunca ha parido (you've never given birth), for example, is directed to a faceless doctor, undeniably male in his lack of personal experience with childbirth yet also indisputably in a position of hierarchical power above the speaker in his position as doctor. In this way the poetic voice speaks from a universalized female subject position to a more powerful and morally corrupt collection of men, linking the experience of reproduction to the collective powerlessness of women as they lay on the birthing table. This imagery is more graphic than the more abstract scenes of domestic desperation created by poets such as Yolanda Pantin, but is perhaps even more communicative of the precarious nature of female existence because it pulls no punches. These poems truly and literally describe the battle of these women between life and death.

Jean Franco contends that women in Latin America, like indigenous groups or blacks in the region, all necessarily write in the margins of society, removed and isolated from the dominant ideological and intellectual discourse (1988, 505–6). This marginal position, however, offers the initial protection of official disdain and neglect. Within this alienated space, women can write freely on topics that would be immediately ejected from the mainstream of intellectual discourse. As Debra Castillo explains in her consideration of Franco's idea,

> Ambiguously visible and invisible at the same time, negated and neglected by indifference, what Franco calls the "regions of refuge" of the marginalized could be turned into a political tool, could become central once the center turned its eye on them. Pragmatically then, one of the jobs of the woman writer is to probe delicately at the edges of this official indifference, to force the dominant culture to recognize these regions, to unleash their dormant power, to impinge upon official consciousness. (1992, 58)

This is precisely what we see in Alvarez's poetry and the poetry of the Venezuelan women who follow: the use of the marginalized popular discourse allowed

them to test the fences of the patriarchal compound. Women will use this limited agency in informal and journalistic circles to force official recognition.
Women's voices have been marginalized within a patriarchical society, but in
contemporary Venezuelan poetry, oppositional voices are confronting a state
that expressly defines its goal as incorporation of the marginal.

Assuming the Voice of the "Writer-Stateswoman": Poetry and Political Discourse

The quotation that begins this paper comes from a different type of text. The
poets Verónica Jaffé and Yolanda Pantin, taking advantage of their positions
as writers, used their voices to participate in a different type of protest movement, one directed at the political establishment and the administration of
President Hugo Chávez. The power of poetry to draw the attention of both the
elite and the common, the powerful and the marginalized, explains its continued centrality in the discourse of the nation. This clarifies why President
Chávez and his administration would choose continually to justify themselves
using poetry, as Chávez often does in speeches and radio addresses. This idea
then also explains the agency that was afforded to other poets such as Yolanda
Pantin and Verónica Jaffé as they entered the arena of political dialogue. These
women use their position as writers to speak out with a public voice on issues
of contemporary politics in verse, but also in other literary venues.

Pantin and Jaffé founded the publishing house Pequeña Venecia with the
poets Blanca Strepponi and Antonio López Ortega in 1989. Choosing the name
"Little Venice" for the house was, for the creators, an ironic recognition of
Venezuela's colonial heritage and its struggle to create a new identity free of
the original representation of a diminutive version of somewhere else.[2] An
additional intention of the authors was to create "a non-profit civil association
and a private option that seeks to create a non-official space for the publication of poetry," according to their website.[3] Let us focus on the second portion
of that mission statement, as it reveals important information about the social
consciousness of the authors. All four writers felt that the two main publishing
houses in Venezuela did not allow enough freedom of artistic and political expression because they were funded by the government.

The formation of a publishing house for poetry, independent of the state, allowed for the creation of a new space and a new public forum for the communication of artistic and socially important ideas. Indeed later editions of poetry
from the same website, Pequeña Venecia, came with a note at the end that read,

Pequeña Venecia is an editorial project that seeks to open new space for the poetry of our country. In these times there are not a few obstacles that both authors and readers confront when they wish to see their work or discontent reflected. Venezuelans or foreigners, young writers or those who have already achieved recognition, essayists and translators, will have access by merely proposing to give or recognize diverse artistic manifestations and thought that give witness to and nurture that which is contemporaneous in our culture. (My translation)

As this quotation shows, there is a real desire here to create a space where a specific type of public, the world of educated "Venezuelans and foreigners, young writers and established authors, essayists and translators," can get together to discuss thoughts on contemporary life and culture. The publisher and its web presence, of course, represented a very specific community: an elite set of authors, academics, scholars, and students who have cultivated their skills and talents through the resources of economic privilege. In this way, we should remember that while the publishing house was independent of the state, it cannot be considered independent of the economic forces of private capital. From this perspective, it served as a clearing house and vehicle for discussion through the physical publication of the poetry series and through the house's web presence at www.pequenhavenecia.com, which lived on the internet from February 2001 until February of 2005.

One clear example of the website's use as a forum for political discourse is the open letter "A message from Venezuelan writers, artists, and academics to their colleagues all over the world," which appeared on the website on March 17, 2004. This letter, signed by some 220 Venezuelan writers and scholars, appeared in the midst of extreme political polarization and the controversies swirling around the invalidation by the National Electoral Council of signatures on petitions to force a recall election. It denounced President Hugo Chávez and his administration in strong terms. The text appeared in Spanish, English, and French, and declared clearly that:

Instead of trying to achieve a national consensus, Chávez has used a poisonous speech, promoting violence, hate between social classes and the exclusion of vast sectors of middle class people branding them as oligarchs. His aggressive, insolent and offensive speech, unfitted of a true head of state, aimed at disqualifying middle class values, has hampered their initial support, and now they constitute, together with a large low-income population, an opposition close to 70 percent which is trying to revoke his mandate by the recall vote, a sacred right of the Constitution.

The content of this message is less important for our purposes here than its intended audience: "colleagues all over the world." By publishing the text on the website, in three languages, this group of Venezuelan intellectuals clearly opened the conversation on Venezuelan politics to a wide, international public that they knew was listening in, virtually, across the borders. What is represented by such essays, as well as the poetry published by *Pequeña Venecia*, is dialogue within a reading, writing, and debating public of international scholars, artists, writers, academics, and students. In effect, it served as a counterpart to the Chavista forum, Aporrea.org, discussed by Hellinger in "Defying the Iron Law of Oligarchy II" (chapter 8, this volume). It should not be lost on us in our discussion here that three of the founders of this worldwide town hall were women. While remaining active as editors, Yolanda Pantin, Blanca Strepponi, and Verónica Jaffé took advantage of their opportunity and published literary works within *Pequeña Venecia*. In addition, Pantin and Jaffé used the web presence to publish social and political essays—a mixing of literary and public discourse common in Venezuela. One key essay that speaks directly to the power of poetry and the poetic to offer women agency in public discourse is the text, "El bárbaro y las trampas de la poesía," authored by Pantin and Jaffé (2003) and published on the website on March 17, 2004.

In the essay, cited at the beginning of this chapter, Pantin and Jaffé chastise Hugo Chávez for using poetry as an instrument of propaganda in his radio addresses, in public speeches, and in official documents. It is indeed quite common for both Chávez and members of his government to cite literature in their speeches, following the tradition of literature in public discourse. The two women decry both the misuse of others' work and the manipulation of *palabrería* (verbiage) and *seudo lenguaje poético* (pseudo poetic language). They accuse Chávez of a "uso perverso de la palabra" (perverse use of words), arguing, "Es necesario saber que en Venezuela estamos sometidos a la autoridad de la mentira y que la poesía es utilizada para hacer daño" ("It is necessary to know that in Venezuela we are subject to the authority of lies, and poetry is used to do harm"; 2003, 1).

Pantin and Jaffé go on to argue that this attempt at repression through poetic verse will always be ultimately ineffective. Indeed, the "trampa [trap] de la poesía" for the "barbarian" in question (i.e., Chávez) is that by trying to manipulate others through poetry, he reveals himself through his words: "La palabrería, pues acaba por revelar la verdad de que la pronuncia" ("His vulgar discourse thus ends up revealing the truth of what he pronounces"). In the view of Pantin and Jaffé, poetry may never be successfully used as an instrument of repression for this reason. The essay describes how Chávez has used (or rather misused) the poetry of Vicente Huidobro, César Vallejo, Mario Benedetti, and others in an attempt to "refrendar su discurso falaz" (give weight to his deceptive discourse; 2003, 2). It is these poets' intention to deconstruct Chávez's reading of the poetry he hopes to use to prove his point. Perhaps more clearly stated, the poets do not believe that Chávez has engaged in a critical reading of the poetry at all. Their point here is that Chávez wields the poems he uses in his addresses like blunt objects, swinging the words around without appreciating the fine edge, and finer meaning, that each possesses.

In doing this, Pantin and Jaffé argue that Chávez's own ignorance of the more subtle meanings of the poetry he uses lays open his underlying intentions: to create false dichotomies intended to subjugate the Venezuelan people. This interpretation would certainly be challenged by other analysts, such as Duno Gottberg in "The Color of Mobs" (chapter 10, this volume), who see underlying racism in portrayals of Chávez as uncivilized and his followers as *turbas* (mobs). Although Chávez and his followers hold a firm grip on state power, they see themselves in a larger context as struggling against the cultural and economic hegemony of those they have displaced. Rather than "subjugating" they see themselves as "liberating" the Venezuelan people. It is this notion that the opposition poets here desire to undermine or subvert.

Perhaps because of its subtlety, poetry is, for Pantin and Jaffé, necessarily subversive in nature. The poets describe this view of poetry as a method of communication more appropriate for challenging structures of power than for supporting the ideology of a repressive government. They assert,

> But poetry is not a pistol; it does not serve, as the adviser and his patron think, to eliminate an enemy and to seduce the public. It is not a convenient instrument of power. It serves to open small spaces of freedom where the mysteries of the world and our own consciousness can intermingle, but never [can it be used] as a servile and inoffensive medium to manipulate passions and minds. A known example [is] . . . the insidious relationship between power and poetry that we not bear, the broken link between Breton and César Moro due to the orthodoxy of the surrealist revolution, or the dissonance of [Cuban poet] Heberto Padilla from the Cuban Revolution, which landed him in jail and exile. (2003, 2; my translation)

Fully aware of the power of poetry and its authors to publicly express opposing ideas, Pantin and Jaffé underline the capacity of poetry to open "small spaces" of public dialogue where dissident thought can be expressed and interchanged. It is no accident that they invoke "el caso Padilla"[4] in this venue to remind the readers of how literary actors can bring international attention to issues of local political importance.

For these particular women in Venezuela then, poetry, and the spaces surrounding the production of poetry are exactly the locations in which they may persuade others to adopt their goals by expressing themselves, much as Alvarez undertook to do before Chávez in *Cuerpo*. Looking beyond the constraints of femininity imposed upon them by traditional society, and seeking answers to the problems plaguing the nation, women look to the future. They may do this in new and socially subversive ways, observing the present, as did Alvarez, or by seeking guidance from figures of the past, as Yolanda Pantin does in the poem "El hueso pélvico" (The pelvic bone; 2002).

The Power of the Pelvic Bone: Searching for an Image, Reaching for a Voice

The poem "The pelvic bone" is a long meditation on the goddess, the nation, the nature of human origins, and the daily struggles and politics of Venezuela. The poem, published in book form earlier, appeared on the Pequeña Venecia website beginning in August of 2002.[5] On the web page, it was accompanied by two photographs of Alejandro Colina's statue of the goddess María Lionza, which has stood for fifty years on the median of the Autopista del Este in Caracas. The poem provides an example of both the use of poetry for political commentary and the writers' recognition of the use of the Internet to gain access to an international forum.

The poetic voice of the poem begins by recounting a car trip into the center of "the city" on her way to a demonstration or protest. In the car, the speaker sees the statue of María Lionza, and begins a contemplation of that image, and especially of the most notable feature, the pelvic bone held high in the air. The presence of the photos of the Colina statue on the web page immediately identifies the image in the poem, and therefore, we may assume that "the city" is Caracas. In addition, the date of the poem, December of 2001, indicates that the protest mentioned would be one of the early marches against President Chávez at the beginning of the civil unrest that has marked his presidency.[6]

The poem uses the figure of María Lionza to represent a symbolic mother of the nation. The goddess "Carga la ciudad / Sobre la espalda" (Carries the city / On her back) as she sits "Al centro / De su artería / Fluvial" (In the middle / Of its fluvial / artery; 2002, 3). The poetic voice here makes clear that she does not believe in the divinity of the goddess but still views her as symbolic of the origins of the nation. Speaking directly to the statue, to María Lionza, the speaker says,

Salve reina	[All hail the queen
Que estás en las aguas	you who are in the waters
Digo esta oración	I speak this prayer
Ante tu estatua	before your statue
—mas tú no existes,	—even though you don't exist
sino en el hueso materno.	except in the maternal bone] (2)

Here the poetic voice uses the informal *tú* in her address, indicating a level of affection and intimacy. The speaker's position is ambivalent, nonbelieving but still drawn to the figure of María Lionza, seeing the pelvic bone as representative of childbirth, in this case the birth of the nation. Indeed, while the poetic voice does at times speak from the first-person singular, the majority of commentary to the goddess is addressed from a collective position through the pronoun *nosotros*. This use of the first-person plural indicates the speaker's belief that she speaks for all in the nation, male and female, as they consider her. María Lionza is represented as "our" goddess for the Venezuelans.

In Pantin's poem, the nation is in turmoil, searching for guidance and for identity. In this struggle, María Lionza represents a symbol of hope, as seen through the "haz de luz blanca" (ray of white light; 2002, 2) seen shining through the pelvic bone, illuminating the distressed and angry citizens as they go to join the protest. Her poetic voice considers the statue as representing both spiritual power and the subjugation of women and indigenous peoples in Venezuela. The goddess can in fact be seen to represent marginalization in three distinct ways: through her position as woman; through her representation (in most versions of the legend, despite the very obvious problem that she is named "María") as indigenous; and in her position as representing a "Third World" nation, one still struggling to overcome or incorporate its colonial heritage.

María Lionza however, in her position as goddess, also represents power in her persistence, in her strength, in her ability to carry the city and the nation on her back, not bowed over with resignation, but defiantly upright, thrusting the pelvic bone into the air. The goddess is "algo que no [es] autoderogativo, como acostumbra serlo / nuestro forcejeo cotidiano" (something that [is] not self-derogative, as our daily struggle / is accustomed to being; Pantín 2002, 1). She fights the national malaise with her pride and her presence. She gives a specific national identity to a colonized nation, a country named with a diminutive: "Nombrado con ánimo de sojuzgarlo, peyorativo, / Porque uno es el nombre que lleva" (Named with a motive to diminish it, pejoratively / Because one is the name one carries; 1).

Pantin is not the first poet to use the goddess in this way. In the 1990s *Editorial Pomaire* began a series of poetry works titled *Colección LA DIOSA de la poesía.*[7] All of the works in the publisher's Goddess of Poetry collection appeared with that title and a silhouetted image of the statue of María Lionza on the cover. On the inside flap, the *Editorial* describes the intent of the collection, and justifies the title in the following way:

> The myth of an aboriginal goddess surrounds the deepest psychology of the Venezuelan being, and her metaphor—a queen, naked, exuberant, who roams the countryside mounted on a tapir or anteater, and who in the rivers rides an anaconda—has the highest believability. "A human society cannot survive for long unless its members are psychologically contained by a living central myth that gives each individual a reason for being," says Edgard F. Endinger. Every culture is an amalgamation of symbols that constitutes the origins of thought. Every culture, therefore, is mythic in origin, a-temporal, simultaneous. María Lionza is an authentic myth that takes us back to our origins, and reconnects us to a mystery. (Padrón 1994; my translation)

Pantin, in her poem, takes advantage of that position of the goddess as central, yet marginalized to represent the power of the people, the power of women and the power of poetry to give hope to the nation. In the poem, María Lionza combines the possibility of mercy of the Virgin with the power of the supernatural and wild nature in Venezuelan society. The fact that this mercy may be extended even to an unbeliever, such as that represented by the poetic voice, only highlights the power and grace of the goddess in her relation to the Venezuelan people.

As Daisy Barreto observes in her study of the intersection of religion and politics in Venezuela, citizens find in religion "consolation and relief from despair" (2007, 2) in times of political turmoil. While most poor Venezuelans might have believed democracy was strengthening as Chávez gained more power, this was not true for many members of the middle class. For them, says Barreto, especially after the first few years of the Chávez administration, the credibility of "political institutions and the authority of leaders had eroded" (2). In older days in Venezuela, a return to religion for many people might have meant a turn to traditional Roman Catholicism. However, as Barreto also argues, the Catholic Church in Venezuela was co-opted by the wealthy opposition to the Chávez government, and its symbols were ever more strongly identified with middle and upper classes (4). In this way, to profess devout Catholic faith has become to effectively "take a side" in the political struggle.

Another strong religious force in Venezuela, the evangelical Protestant and Pentecostal church, offers another religious perspective. These faith traditions, however, have found much less resonance among the middle-class Venezuelans than among the poor, for reasons that Smilde and Pagan explore in "Christianity and Politics in Venezuela's Bolivarian Democracy." Not surprisingly, then, Venezuelan middle-class poets seeking a profound and authentic national faith from which to draw metaphors and conceits turn to the Goddess, who offers the only truly Venezuelan religion, a "genuine historical-cultural and religious tradition, and a symbolic prototype of the national identity" (Barreto 2007, 1; my translation). When Pantin seeks to embrace María Lionza, it can be seen as a wider attempt to reject the forces of colonization, which she associates with evangelicals, and seek independence for the nation.

Barreto criticizes intellectuals in Venezuela who "do not hesitate to show ambiguous and ambivalent positions that bring them closer to recognizing the figure of María Lionza and, at the same time, to rejection and exclusion from the cult" (2007, 10; my translation). Her work shows that practical support for the public practice of the faith has indeed eroded despite constitutional protections. However, if those on the margins of political discourse, such as women intellectuals, can find the inspiration they seek in María Lionza, perhaps this will lead back to more practical political support for the cult's rights.

Pantin's poem is optimistic, hoping to gain something from her search for the authentic Venezuelan belief, not only for herself but for the nation as a whole. Pantin, like other women authors in Venezuela, seeks the latent power possible in María Lionza. When Pantin address the statue of María Lionza as "Queen" in her poem, she summons the goddess in her incarnation as leader. As she prays for help in solving the problems of the state, she looks to María Lionza as protector of Venezuela, the strong and powerful woman who grips the tapir with muscular legs. And while Pantin expresses the ambiguity of her own faith in the goddess, she pins her hopes for the future on María Lionza, as spirit and soul of the nation. She urges her readers to believe: "Cree, cree en algo / que no sea corrupción" (Believe, believe in something / that is not corruption). She urges readers to place their faith in the symbolic center that is María Lionza, who carries the nation on her back.

When the Colina statue of María Lionza broke in two in June of 2004, many in Venezuela saw it as an attempt by the goddess to warn the nation of the danger of the deep divisions plaguing the politically polarized state. Pantin's "El hueso pélvico" shows how poetry may be used to enter the conversation on the transition, as it seeks to describe that turmoil, working around a nationally formed, unique, and original symbol of femininity. The poem reaches out to the power and comfort offered by the national symbol to unify the nation. Like the essays of the Pequeña Venecia editorial, published in a forum founded by a trio of female poets, the poem represents the potential of the practice of writing in Venezuela.

Conclusions

It will always be true, of course, that those women who have both the education and the opportunity to write poetry will come from the more privileged classes of Venezuelan society. Any consideration of women in Venezuela must, of course, recognize differences in life experience. It would be a false assumption, however, to claim that the interests of elite women have no connection to the interests of the women in the barrios surrounding Caracas. The Venezuelan feminist Márgara Russotto agrees with this idea, stating that the definition of "woman" for purposes of academic study can reveal

> . . . an interpretation of women, as an "anomalous" social group, that annuls or at least lends the divisions of class in their traditional sense, in honor of a single impossibility that unifies them: that of not being able to get ahead in any of the hierarchies that organize society, not in the military, civil or religious hierarchies; not even in the extremely formalized world of science nor in the desolate dispersion of their lives. (1997, 26)

While it may be that women poets speak from a different level of society, the issues that they speak to are the same for all women. The reconstruction of identity, the need to subvert the established hierarchies and speak truth to power are the same whether the means provided to achieve that goal is local radio or published verse.

Notes

1. My discussion of these two terms is indebted to Debra Castillo's work on this topic (see D. Castillo 1992, 16–17).
2. The name *Venezuela*, or "Little Venice," was originally given to the area by Italian cartographer Amerigo Vespucci upon his arrival to Lake Maracaibo in 1499. Discover-

ing the homes of the indigenous people there, constructed over the water, Vespucci was reminded of Venice in his native country.

3. My translation. *Pequeña Venecia*'s website (www.pequenhavenecia.com/quienes somos) has subsequently gone offline.

4. "El caso Padilla," as it has come to be known, refers to the case of the dissident Cuban poet Heberto Padilla, who in 1968 published a collection of poetry mildly critical of Castro's revolution. Padilla was imprisoned, forced to sign a confession, and later exiled from the island. The case brought international attention to the repressive policies of the Castro government and provoked an outcry among writers, academics, and intellectuals. An international group, including Sartre, Beauvoir, Sontag, Cortázar, Vargas Llosa, and Paz published a series of essays decrying the Castro government's repression of free speech and creating a great deal of ill will and bad publicity for the Castro administration.

5. The website is no longer active, but interested readers may find the poem in Pantin's *Poesía Reunida 1981–2002* (2004).

6. The poem is dated simply "December 2001." As such it may refer specifically to a 12-hour general strike that was called by the business group *Fedecamaras* on December 10, 2001. On that day, the nation effectively shut down, and thousands of people took to the streets in protest marches such as the ones alluded to in the poems. Whether or not the protests mentioned in the poem specifically refer to the December 10 events, opposition to Chavez in general had reached a critical point by December of that year.

7. The title of the collection and quotations about its purpose are taken from one of the works to appear in it—Leonardo Padrón's *Colección LA DIOSA de la poesía* (1994).

CHAPTER TWELVE

Christianity and Politics in Venezuela's Bolivarian Democracy
Catholics, Evangelicals, and Political Polarization

David Smilde and Coraly Pagan

Somewhat unexpectedly, religion has become one of the primary media of conflict in Venezuela during the tumultuous decade of Hugo Chávez's presidency. Given the crisis of Venezuela's traditional political parties the Catholic Church has been one of the few institutions with enough credibility to counter the Chávez administration and has done so virtually from the first days of the government. At almost every turn—from the National Constitutional Assembly to the April 2002 coup, from the 1998 elections to the 2004 recall referendum— the Catholic Church has been intimately involved or actively vocal. The Chávez administration, in turn, has aggressively sought, from 1999, to confront the monopoly of the Catholic Church in order to increase social and political space for other social actors more conducive to the government's agenda. One of the main media of this effort has been support for evangelical Protestant churches. The Chávez government has repeatedly attempted to form an alliance with evangelical Protestants as a way of channeling new social and political actors into its participatory democracy. The reaction of evangelicals has been mixed, with most churches remaining officially apolitical but with several becoming open and outspoken allies of President Chávez (Smilde 2004a, 2004b).

This entry of religious institutions and practice into the political fray is surprising given their traditionally cautious approach to politics in Venezuela. First, despite being instrumental in overthrowing the dictatorship of Marcos Pérez Jiménez, the Catholic Church did not have a strong public political role during the forty-year Punto Fijo democracy. Traditionally weak, and heavily dependent on state subsidies, it has historically been cautious, focusing its energies on education (Daniel Levine 1981). The evangelical movement is not particularly strong either, by regional standards. While Venezuela was home to one of the most successful attempts at an evangelical political party—the Organización de Renovación Auténtica (ORA; see Smilde 2004a)—this party never enjoyed widespread support among evangelicals, and politics was not an important focus among evangelical leaders and congregants. Increased political participation has not been without cost as it has brought to public light clear divisions within both the Catholic Church and the evangelical movement. While the Catholic hierarchy has vigorously opposed the Chávez government, several bishops and priests, as well as grassroots Catholic communities, have publicly expressed their sympathies to the government's revolutionary project and openly rejected the hierarchy's oppositional stance. And while some neo-Pentecostal evangelical groups have openly supported the government and taken part in government initiatives, others have expressed a principled apoliticism while occasionally criticizing the government.

The stances of Catholic and evangelical leaders do not seem to conform to any sort of straightforward analysis of institutional interests. For example, while it makes sense for the Catholic Church to oppose the Chávez administration given that the base of Catholic devotion and the focus of the church's attention has long been the upper-middle class, the church receives massive subsidies from the executive branch of the Venezuelan government (Smilde 2000). The hierarchy's fervent opposition, then, is not clearly in its self-interests, as it puts these subsidies in danger. Similarly, while one might think that there is a natural affinity between evangelicals and the Chávez movement based on class, the most strongly pro-Chávez evangelicals are not actually the poorest, but those "neo-Pentecostal" churches that derive their membership from the middle classes. In other words, looking closely at Catholic and evangelical political positions seems to point toward an irreducible impact of ideological commitments. The Catholic Church is seemingly motivated to some degree by a commitment to liberal democracy, economic globalization, and human rights. Pro-Chávez evangelicals, on the other hand, appear to be motivated by a brand of theocratic thought that easily grafts onto nationalism (Smilde 2004b). There is precedent for such differing political engagements of Catholics and evangelicals—Sandinista Nicaragua being the clearest. There the Catholic Church became divided between the hierarchy's critical stance toward the Sandinistas and the "popular" church's open support and participation in the Sandinista government (see Dodson 1986; Crahan 1989; P. Williams 1989). And the evangelical movement became divided between criticism of the Sandinistas articulated by the U.S. Christian Right and collaboration with the Sandinista government or international nongovernmental agencies by progressive evangelicals (see C. Smith and Haas 1997).

In this chapter we focus on the entry of religion into Venezuela's current political conflict, focusing on local political dynamics—most concretely on the attempt by the Chávez movement and government to bring religious organizations into the Bolivarian Revolution, as well as the efforts of religious leaders to navigate the new sociopolitical context. Examining these processes will not only give us entrée into the nature of Venezuela's Bolivarian democracy but also will provide us with a case study of the nature of political cleavage in a larger regional transition (Roberts 2002; Hechter 2004).

Christianity in Venezuela

The nineteenth-century revolution and civil wars seriously diminished the social presence and importance of the Catholic Church in Venezuela. Indeed the role of the Catholic Church in society and politics was one of the main issues that led Venezuelan liberals to secede from La Gran Colombia led by Bolívar. It was also an issue at the heart of the civil wars that followed, throughout most of the nineteenth century. As a result, by the beginning of the twentieth century, the Catholic Church had been socially diminished and was seriously weakened—despite still enjoying official privileges. Through the twentieth century, it slowly built up its social presence, primarily by focusing on education and servicing the religious needs of the upper-middle and upper classes. However, it came to be highly dependent on foreign clergy—close to two-thirds are foreign born—as well as state funding for its social and educational programs. The Catholic Church receives state money from a complicated variety of sources including directly from the executive branch of the federal government through ministries, as well as from state and municipal governments, for its social and educational programs, and for the maintenance of churches and cathedrals.

The main national organization of Venezuela's Catholic Church is the Venezuelan Episcopal Conference (hereafter referred to as the VEC) that brings together the bishops and archbishops of all the different dioceses and archdioceses in the national territory. This seemingly clear and discrete national structure is complicated by a couple of realities of the Venezuelan church. First, there is a large presence of clergy belonging to religious orders that do not report to the VEC. Second, there are many foreign clergy on loan to the Venezuelan Episcopate that really answer to their home dioceses. Finally, the VEC's independence vis-à-vis the state is complicated by the 1964 modus vivendi between the Venezuelan government and the Catholic Church, which makes the Catholic Church the official Church of Venezuela but requires all bishops and archbishops to be Venezuelan, and gives the government veto power over the designation of bishops. The executive branch of the government also provides financial resources for Catholic education and other social programs, as well as the upkeep of churches and temples, giving it considerable power over the Church. Nevertheless, the Catholic Church is the largest and most respected civil organization in the country.

In Venezuela, as in most Latin American countries, the great majority of the population is Catholic, but only in a nominal sense. They identify themselves as Catholic but do not regularly participate other than in rituals that mark rights of passage—baptism, first communion, marriage, and death—or moments of crisis. At such times, religious symbols, practices, and professionals are employed in processes of reflection and reaffirmation, and long periods of inactivity may be followed by bursts of religious practice. Nevertheless, in the upper social strata, consistent participation is common, with numerous forms of small groups gaining devotion in recent decades. The theology of these groups is increasingly similar to Protestant theology. While there is still an important emphasis on the Virgin Mary, there is also an increasing emphasis on Jesus Christ. And while there is still a reverence for the authority of priests and bishops, there is increasingly a tendency to form small groups of laity that discuss and practice together. There remains a strong tendency to emphasize the role of the Catholic Church as the guardian of a moral society in which authority and tradition are respected.

Politically, the Catholic Church has traditionally exercised a cautious role—although this role was key in the overthrow of the dictator Marcos Pérez Jiménez. Through the 1980s and 1990s, during the process of the institutional decline of the Venezuelan State, the Catholic Church became one of the most respected institutions in Venezuelan society as well as one of its main repositories of intellectual capital. The Venezuelan Church traditionally steered away from confessional politics, but it was able to rely on the Social Christian party COPEI to come to its defense vis-à-vis the state (Daniel Levine 1981).

Protestants have existed in Venezuela virtually since the founding of the republic and their presence has occasionally become a political issue. In an episode foreshadowing the efforts of the Chávez government, in the late nineteenth century, anti-clerical Venezuelan president Antonio Gúzman Blanco officially encouraged Protestant immigration as a means to counter the Catho-

lic Church's power and facilitate modernization of the populace. Nevertheless, growth of non-Catholic Christianity really only began with the period of
urbanization after the middle of the twentieth century, and that growth was
modest given the relative peace and prosperity accompanying Venezuela's process of urbanization. Indeed, up until the end of the 1980s, Venezuela provided
relatively infertile ground for evangelical growth compared to other Latin
American countries. Since then, the growth has been dramatic, as the percentage of population that considers itself evangelical roughly doubled in the decade of the 1990s. Evangelicals constitute a little less than ten percent of the
population and are evenly distributed among social classes. The image of evangelicals as largely a lower-class phenomenon is both correct and misleading as
it is generally used. Members do predominantly come from the lower sectors,
however, not disproportionately so. Evangelicalism is predominantly a lower-
class phenomenon because Venezuelans are predominantly lower class.

While the Catholic Church traditionally aims at a significant institutional
presence that dispenses God's grace universally, evangelicals generally see
their institutions as means to the end of evangelization and facilitation of Christian lifestyles and not as permanent ends in themselves. Thus while Catholic
churches have traditionally built up institutions that compete with state institutions and have to create a policy toward them—usually some mixture of competition, collaboration, and resistance—evangelical churches tend to develop
less substantial institutions that are concerned with the state only in a negative
sense—trying to ensure themselves an autonomous social space in which they
can focus on their religious practice and evangelization.

Evangelicals make reference to the primitive church portrayed in the Christian New Testament and use it as a reference to criticize the Catholic Church's
institutional role in society. Given this traditional lack of interest in institution
building, evangelical social presence has not necessarily translated into a significant political presence. Nevertheless, one of the most well-known experiments with an evangelical party in Latin America occurred in Venezuela with
ORA, headed by a Baptist chemistry professor, Godofredo Marín. ORA participated in the last three electoral cycles of the Punto Fijo era, each time gaining
one or two seats in the Congress. Such was ORA's success in the 1988 elections
that French historian Jean Pierre Bastian wrote that the "mechanisms of electoral manipulation" used by ORA provided a model for the new "confessional
politics" of Latin American evangelicals (Bastian 1994, 273). That year Marín
attracted almost one percent of the presidential vote, and ORA gained two
seats in the Congress.

Evangelical pastors generally saw Marín as an important ally in the Congress and permitted him to campaign in their churches. They rallied around him in 1988 and contributed strong support from the pulpit. They gave the party official, if somewhat less enthusiastic, support again in 1993. ORA was always less attractive to the grassroots evangelicals of the lower and lower-middle classes that tend toward Pentecostalism. These evangelicals were generally more anti-establishment and less conservative than Marín and ORA. The party's strength came from the minority of evangelicals among the middle and upper-middle classes that tend toward Baptist and neo-Pentecostal churches, among whom his conservative politics resonated and his willingness to collaborate with traditional parties seemed reasonable. Below we will see how these differences played out in the 1998 elections (Smilde 2004a).

A more influential evangelical voice today is provided by the two main organizations in Venezuela, the Evangelical Council of Venezuela (hereafter referred to as the ECV) and the Pentecostal Evangelical Council of Venezuela (PECV). They are not mutually exclusive, and many Pentecostal churches belong to both. They have traditionally shied away from politics not having to do with issues of religious freedom. Beyond this institutional presence Venezuela's evangelical Protestants have an important informal social presence due to their mobilization in public space (Smilde 2004c). In entire areas of Venezuelan society, such as the horrific prisons and the barrios, they are often the only manifestation of civil society present. Furthermore, given evangelical attendance norms and inadequate coverage of Catholic churches, it seems safe to say that on any given day of the year, more people attend evangelical than Catholic religious services.

Mobilization, Campaign, and the Search for Political Allies

While the entry of religion into the political fray is clearly a manifestation of increasing religious dynamism as well as the diversification of the political field, the most tangible proximate cause of religion's entry into politics was the mobilizing efforts of Hugo Chávez and other leaders of the Movimiento Bolivariano Revolucionario 200 (MBR-200). In an attempt to gain allies in their fight against the existing democratic regime they sought the support of religious leaders, movements, and institutions. During the two years they served in jail as a result of the failed 1992 coup attempt, leaders of the MBR-200 worked on plans to transform their military movement into a civilian political movement. Key to their strategy was the idea of gaining a base among new social actors and movements.

In documents from this period, the leaders of the movement called for a national dialogue between the MBR-200 and what they called "new social and political forces" that exhibited the desire, capacity, "recognized honesty and public morality" to promote changes in Venezuela. The first two forces mentioned in one key statement were the Catholic Church and "the Evangelical Community" (MBR-200, n.d.). Another document, written after the pardon of Chávez and other MBR-200 leaders by President Rafael Caldera in March 1994, argued that "the Movement must have a policy of alliances with the most advanced and revolutionary forces of our society, a policy of allies is vital for the achievement of historical objectives and strategies of the movement." Among the seven potential allies listed were "Christian and evangelical churches with a progressive orientation" (MBR-200 1994). This was in part because of the strategy of tapping into sectors of civil society that were already organized but not incorporated into the party-state apparatus, and partly because of the guiding emphasis on the "moral regeneration" of Venezuelan society.

During this mobilization period and up through the presidential campaign of 1998 Chávez frequently used biblical imagery in combination with war terminology and nationalistic slogans from Bolívar and other founding fathers. These morally charged metaphors clearly provided impetus to the movement, framing its efforts as a historic struggle for the salvation of Venezuela. This discourse struck a nerve in a Venezuelan population disillusioned by a two-decade political and economic downward spiral and has been one important source of his continuing popularity. However, such religious metaphors also succeed in polarizing political opinion inasmuch as even mild criticism falls on the opposing side of a Manichaean divide between supporters and opponents. Throughout this period, Chávez also consistently made mention of evangelicals whenever he spoke of new actors in civil society. This should not be interpreted necessarily as favoritism toward them since he simultaneously reached out to the Catholic Church. Rather, it should be seen as an attempt to gain a foothold among social actors without strong political affiliations or networks.

Among both Catholics and evangelicals this outreach by candidate Chávez received a mixed reception—not clearly positive or negative but cautiously open. The level of discontent in the populace was such that members of the Catholic Church hierarchy were open to the idea of profound change. High-profile clergy such as Monsignor Mario Moronta and Luis Ugalde, rector of the Universidad Católica Ándres Bello, spoke of a constitutional assembly as necessary.[1] In general, the Catholic Church was open and friendly but cautious with respect to Chávez's candidacy. In October of 1998 the bishops and archbishops of Venezuela released a document in which they criticize existing Venezuelan democracy as well as the existing candidates for speaking half truths and being vague.[2] They asked the media to be objective and the armed forces to be the guarantors of the constitution, not participants in the elections. In that document and through interviews with the mass media in October and early November of 1998, members of the hierarchy expressed their concern for tendencies toward authoritarianism in the electoral process.[3] They weren't only worried about Chávez; his main electoral opponent, Governor Henrique Salas Romer, had also made declarations that he would not tolerate a strongly opposed Congress—suggesting the possibility an *autogolpe* (coup) such as the one carried out by Alberto Fujimori in Peru.

Chávez never met with evangelical leaders, although he frequently referred to evangelicals in his campaign. These mentions were enormously popular among everyday evangelicals and some came to believe that Chávez was himself becoming evangelical (Smilde 2004a). Godofredo Marín, on the other hand, initially declared his candidacy in the 1998 process; however, seeing his chances for regaining his congressional seat as slim, he renounced his candidacy and threw his support behind Social Democratic Candidate Luis Alfaro Ucero. In doing so he caused an uproar in the evangelical community, which felt insulted. Marín regained his congressional seat out of the deal, but lost the little evangelical support he still retained (Smilde 2004a). He largely dropped out of public life after the Congress was abolished by the constitutional assembly.

Constitutional Assembly and the First Years of Government, 1999–2000

In the first three years of the Chávez administration the outreach to organized Christianity diverged into a complex favoritism for evangelicals and an antagonistic relationship with the Catholic Church. At the beginning of January 1999, Chávez met with members of the Catholic hierarchy who had expressed their willingness to mediate conflicts that might arise surrounding the constitutional assembly.[4] Chávez was well received by the VEC. Afterward Chávez said he hoped that members of the Catholic Church would participate in the government and even run in congressional elections and participate in the constitutional assembly. Baltazar Porras, Bishop of Merida, said the Catholic Church would be a "critical instance."[5] True to this statement, the Catholic Church raised its voice regarding articles on religious freedom, state control of education, and abortion, as well as on the process and President Chávez's involvement.

The Catholic Church criticized the expansion of the freedom of religion to include not only confession but practice. The 1961 Constitution allowed freedom of confession but charged the state with the responsibility of monitoring religious practice to make sure it is compatible with "morality and good custom." This provision had become a thorn in the side of new religious movements and had been actively defended by the Catholic hierarchy. In response to the change, Monsignor Hernán Sánchez Porras argued that sectarian religions would be able to carry out all sorts of human right abuses without official recourse. The 1999 constitution also reinforces the conception of the state as having the primary responsibility for education. Since the 1970s, private institutions have gained a large percentage of the education market in Venezuela, and have gained the upper hand in quality. The Catholic Church, as well as other sectors, was hoping for a more open recognition of this role. This, as well as the reinforcement of the state's obligation to provide health care, led to criticisms, on the part of members of the hierarchy, of the constitution as "backward and statist."

But by far the most pointed conflict between the Catholic Church and the National Constitutional Assembly (ANC) came over the question of abortion. Venezuela's 1961 Constitution provided a tenuous but not implausible basis for Venezuela's anti-abortion laws in Article 74, by which the state is required to provide "integral protection" to a child "from the moment of conception." The Catholic Church hoped to solidify the constitutional basis by adding the latter phrase to the article on the right to life. When it was not added, the Catholic Church worked behind the scenes with sympathetic members of the Constitutional Commission to have the phrase introduced after debate on the articles had concluded. When this maneuver came to light it caused a scandal within the ANC and led to an agreement to debate the clause again. A quick debate struck the phrase from the text upon the rationale that it would prohibit therapeutic abortions and would best be left for lower-level legal debate. As a result, the 1999 constitution neither supports nor precludes anti-abortion laws—the phrase "from the moment of conception" was left in the article about maternity, but purposefully excluded from the article providing "integral protection" to children. Thus, originally hoping to gain ground, the Catholic Church and other opponents of abortion found themselves confronted with a net loss. The Catholic Church mobilized substantial marches in several large cities but eventually lost the battle.

In addition to these topics of special interest, the Catholic Church also raised its voice regarding the democratic character of the process—urging the Constitutional Assembly to take into account nonmajoritarian opinions. It also criticized as anti-democratic what it considered Chávez's "Lone Ranger style" of supporting the new constitution, his demonization of critics, and his use of apocalyptic images to predict what would happen if the new constitution was not approved.[6]

The Constitutional Assembly was not the only sequence of events that troubled the relationship between the Catholic Church and the government. There were also a series of moves threatening the Catholic Church's government subsidy. While it is difficult to know exactly how much the Catholic Church receives in total, upper estimates put its subsidy at more than 150 million dollars a year. However, in July 1999, the Chávez administration announced that it would be cutting the subsidy by 80 percent as part of across-the-board budget cuts. Nonetheless, negotiations were carried out in a cordial atmosphere, and the size of the cut was reduced to 50 percent.

The Chávez government made a couple of other unilateral policy moves that shored up evangelicals' place in Venezuelan society. It appointed as head of the Directorate of Religion of the Ministry of Justice—the government organ responsible for monitoring religious activity in Venezuela—a lawyer who, while not himself evangelical, is a strong sympathizer and formerly represented them before the Directorate. In June 1999, newspapers reported that the Department of Education was ordering the fulfillment of an agreement that permitted and encouraged evangelical groups to give religious education in public schools—a roll formerly reserved for the Catholic Church. The agreement in question actually had been signed during the Caldera administration but had never been put into practice.

In contrast to the Catholic Church, evangelicals did put forward a dozen or so candidates for the Constitutional Assembly. However, none of them were elected, as Chávez's candidates won over ninety percent of the assembly's seats. The favorable policy changes of 1999 were received with surprised delight, and while some evangelical leaders joined forces with Catholic leaders in the fight to include anti-abortion articles in the constitution, in December 1999 some evangelicals participated in the "Yes Commandos," which distributed copies of the proposed constitution and worked to get out the "yes" vote for the referendum.

Constitutional Assembly and the First Years of Government, 2000–2001

The two years following the Constitutional Assembly saw increasing attempts on the part of the government to reduce the social and institutional predominance of the Catholic Church in favor of new religious movements and an attempt to bring these latter within the government's project of change. From November 2000 to May 2001 the Office of Human Rights attempted to organize the Bolivarian Inter-religious Parliament (PIB) that would bring together representatives of all of the different religions in Venezuela with the goal of devolving governmental social projects and funds to them. The Catholic Church hierarchy criticized this initiative, calling it an attempt to "make the Church into an appendage of the government under the awning of social programs."[7] Cardinal Velasco declared that "the goal, we well know, is the creation of a 'Venezuelan Revolutionary Church'" (ACI Digital 2001).

The ECV and PECV, on the other hand, rejected the initiative largely because they distrusted the low-level administration officials—who misquoted several religious leaders in their glossy promotional brochures and were evasive about their origins and purpose—organizing the project and bristled at being lumped together with Afro-Venezuelan and New Age groups.[8] The initiative survived but has achieved little without the participation of Venezuela's main religious associations.

During 2001, the National Assembly also began to write and debate a bill for a new law on religious practice. The bill sought to place all religions on an equal footing with the Catholic Church. The president of the National Assembly, Willian Lara, said that the bill was not anti-Catholic but rather an attempt to put forth a law that would be consonant with the 1999 Constitution, which established the freedom of religion, and that the state should have equal relations with all religions without benefiting one over another. He said that the Catholic Church would lose some privileges, but "if it subsidizes a Catholic clerical elite then the state should pay similar attention to other churches and faiths." Baltazar Porras argued, in contrast, that "the fundamental objective of this proposal is to beat-up on the Catholic Church, not help out other religions."[9] The bill was never discussed because of the political crisis that began with the failed coup attempt of April 2002.

Period of Open Conflict, 2002–2004

While the first three years of the Chávez administration made clear the growing division between forms of Christianity in response to the Chávez administration, the period from 2002 to 2004 made clear the internal diversity within Catholicism and evangelicalism, as religious leaders increasingly confronted situations in which their traditionally cautious neutrality became difficult to maintain.

The April 2002 Coup

The Catholic Church gave its support to the oil workers' strike that preceded the coup attempt and apparently had prior knowledge of the April 2002 coup. Cardinal Ignacio Velasco received several visits from the conspiring generals in the days before the coup—although briefings from the U.S. Central Intelligence Agency suggest that the Catholic Church actually discouraged coup plans (Golinger 2005). Baltasar Porras, president of the VEC and Bishop José Luis Azuaje of Barquisimeto were present with the conspiring generals in Fuerte Tiuna in the early morning hours of April 12 to receive Chávez as he was escorted from the Miraflores Presidential Palace. And Cardinal Velasco also was present at the swearing-in of business-leader Pedro Carmona as interim president and signed the decree that abolished the National Assembly and Supreme Court. Velasco was later flown to Orchila Island to visit with Chávez during his brief exile. This intimate involvement permanently associated the Catholic Church with the coup and interim government.

However, diversity within the Catholic Church was revealed during this period among sectors that refused to tow the line of the interim government. The Society of Jesus religious order in Venezuela, and especially its leader Arturo Sosa S.J., has been strongly critical of the Chávez administration. However, the Jesuits also have a long history of independence from the Catholic Church hierarchy. In Venezuela their educational network, Fe y Alegría (Faith and joy), has become one of the most important insertions of the Catholic Church among marginalized classes and sectors, and they traditionally have a strong commitment to social justice and inclusion. Throughout the events of the April coup the Jesuits demonstrated their independence. For example, the Radio Fe y Alegría (RFA) network of stations refused to participate in the media blackout organized by the interim government. After Chávez was taken away from Miraflores in the early morning hours of April 12 and media reported that he had resigned, RFA broadcasts immediately cast doubt on the veracity of those reports. When the commercial media reported that Chávez administration cabinet members were unavailable because they were on the run, RFA interviewed them in their homes. When Attorney General Isaías Rodriguez held a press conference purportedly to present his resignation, but really to say that Chávez had not resigned and that Venezuela had suffered a coup d'état, the commercial media cut their coverage halfway through his declarations, but RFA covered the whole press conference. On April 13 the commercial media blacked-out coverage of resistance to the coup, showing instead cartoons, nature documentaries, and telenovelas. However, RFA continued its coverage interviewing people in the street and going to demonstrations (J. Barrios and Urdaneta Jayaro 2002).

Another notable turn of events came when the Jesuit priest and sociologist Mikel de Viana—a fierce critic from the beginning of the Chávez administration—wrote a letter to the interim president, Carmona. De Viana criticized the decision to dissolve the Assembly and local governments as a threat to the continuity of the constitution. "The price of the dissolution or destitution of [the Assembly and local governments] is the breaking of the constitutional thread in which case your government would become illegitimate right from the start." De Viana also complained that the interim government was unrepresentative of the opposition coalition "with an overrepresentation of conservative sectors and the well-off."[10]

One visible reaction from the evangelical movement came on April 12, just before the swearing-in of Carmona, when evangelical pastor and then-president of the ECV, Samuel Olson, participated in a televised service from the "Meritocracy Plaza" in front of PDVSA's Chuao offices, for those who had died and been injured in the violence the day before. Olson claims he participated in the service not to show support for the opposition but rather as a pastoral act of service during a moment of crisis. But the location of the service—PDVSA-Chuao was the most visible organizational location of the opposition movement—and the fact that television coverage went directly from that service to Pedro Carmona's swearing-in ceremony at the presidential palace gave the impression that Olson was giving his support to the new government. Godofredo Marín, the former congressman for ORA, was at the ceremony to show enthusiastic support and sign the decree. Together, these images gave the impression that the evangelical movement was unified in support of the new Carmona government.

However, such impressions of unity were irrevocably undermined when forces loyal to the Chávez government recovered the state television channel. Chávez officials made a call for religious leaders to come to the station to provide words of peace and reconciliation. One of the first to arrive was Bishop Jesús Pérez of the Renacer Church in downtown Caracas. He said that "by divine intervention, today we live in a free Venezuela that belongs to all Venezuelans."[11] Bishop Pérez has been an ardent government supporter and has a weekly program on state television. His church is consistent with a type of Christianity scholars have called *neo-Pentecostalism*, which focuses on messages of financial and entrepreneurial success. Indeed, his church runs an association called "entrepreneurs for Venezuela" that receives support from the government.

The government also received strong support from other neo-Pentecostal pastors. Apostle Elías Rincón participated in the dialogues in July 2002 and gave a speech in the closing ceremony in the name of the evangelical people. There he said that if Chávez really dedicates himself to pull Venezuela out of poverty and misery, "I assure you as an Apostle of Jesus Christ that he can count on the blessings, help, and support of God and also the unqualified support of those of us who know that God would be honored by such a mission" (2002).

While the violent events of 2002 made clear the diversity within both Catholicism and evangelicalism, it also revealed the spaces created for ecumenical collaboration. In May of 2002, a group calling itself the Christian Communities of Petare—Petare is a massive group of barrios at the eastern end of Caracas—published a document called "Letter to the Mass Media in Venezuela." In it they say, "We feel defrauded, deceived, manipulated and provoked by the violence that comes from the mass media. Several television channels and newspapers, as well as journalists, have had and continue to fulfill a terrible role in inciting rancor, bitterness, and hate" (Comunidades Cristianas de Petare 2002). The document was signed by thirty-two evangelical and Catholic churches or communities that had been brought together by the National Base Ecclesial Communities Coordinator of Venezuela.

The mainstream evangelicals represented by the ECV also participated in the National Reconciliation and Dialogue Roundtables organized by the government and which were boycotted by the National Federation of Chambers of Commerce (FEDECAMARAS), the Venezuelan Workers Federation (CTV), and the commercial mass media.[12] During this time the ECV also publicly called for the disarming of the Bolivarian circles and for the opposition to participate in the negotiations sponsored by the Carter Center in July of 2002.[13]

The General Strike, 2002–2003

After a period of uncertain and largely unsuccessful attempts at reconciliation in the aftermath of the April coup, in the second half of 2002 the conflict rekindled with the Supreme Court ruling that the events of April 2002 did not constitute a coup d'état. In October 2002, several of the officers absolved in this ruling declared the Plaza Francia in Altamira—an affluent area in the east of Caracas—to be a liberated zone. In early December, a general strike called by the opposition started slow but gained steam when PDVSA's merchant marine joined the strike and anchored their ships. The general strike lasted almost two months and included numerous marches, protests, and acts of violence.

The Catholic hierarchy was an integral part of this entire political process. While the bishops frequently made calls for non-violent solutions to the conflict, they also consistently criticized only one side of this conflict—the government—thereby implicitly supporting the opposition movement. In a document entitled "Avoiding Destruction, We Can Construct Reconciliation" released in the middle of the strike, the hierarchy called for quick action from the negotiations between the government and the opposition. But it also called for "sincere and effective decisions" from the government and warned that "this is no time for legalisms and political strategies that might appear to be a mockery."[14] During the same period, the Vatican representative Andre Dupuy suggested that the solution to the crisis did not have to be constitutional, arguing that "the Constitution was made for the people, not the people for the Constitution."[15] However, during this same month, a letter called "We, Christian Men and Women of Caracas, Also Exist!" was produced by eleven Catholic communities and organizations working in Caracas's barrios. The communiqué said, "We feel deeply hurt because the President of the Venezuelan Episcopal Conference, along with the Cardinal Archbishop of Caracas frequently speak and act in name of the Catholic Church without consulting us, and without taking into account, in any sense, the deepest sentiments of a good portion of its members." One of the authors, Father Bruno Renaud of Petare criticized the fact that the hierarchy seemed to have taken a partisan role in the conflict: "[CTV President Carlos] Ortega says that there is not going to be a Christmas, and as far as I know, no Bishop has reacted. You have to ask yourself what would have happened if that had come from President Chávez. The opposition delights in seeing how the country sinks, and in his Christmas message the President of the VEC dedicates itself to opposing Brazil or other country's providing the gasoline that we need."[16]

During the strike the ECV maintained a twenty-four-hour-a-day "prayer circle" in the same hotel in which the negotiations were taking place. They prayed for individual participants in the negotiations and handed out evangelical materials to "provide spiritual coverage." During the strike they also inaugurated what they called the Institute for Christian Social Studies, which sponsored talks and discussions in which members of the government and the opposition would discuss current events with the goal of reconciliation. About these events Pastor Samuel Olson said, "We have demonstrated our impartiality because the Evangelical people need to provide a Christian message of reconciliation."[17]

As happened with the April 2002 coup, the crisis solidified the support of some neo-Pentecostals. Apostle Raúl Ávila, director of the network of churches called the Christ for All Nations Center, increased his support for Chávez during this stage of open conflict. During the strike Ávila said that the resistance of the government was evidence that God had a special mission with Venezuela. "One thing we need to keep in mind is that no nation can endure fifteen days of a general strike. Argentina was shaken up in three days. Venezuela has already gone three weeks and it's still standing. You can see that God has a special purpose with this nation. What the opposition is doing is anti-human and anti-God" (Ávila 2002a). He later preached that God had spoken with him and told him to break down the "proud and stubborn spirit of Chávez."

The Referendum Process, 2003–2004

During the eighteen months after the general strike, the conflict centered around the opposition's attempt to unseat Chávez through the constitutionally-defined means of a recall referendum. Being tested for the first time, the entire process was open to interpretation and full of conflict. At the height of the conflict during the general strike, the opposition movement used the "liberated" Plaza Francia in Altamira as a place for strategic organization, rallies, and political speeches. But it also became a place in which everyday members sought to develop an alternative social space. Key to this was the Catholicization of the plaza. Images and statues of the Virgin as well as Bible verses were placed in key locations. The Catholic Church encouraged the process by having priests offer public masses from a stage. Regular patrollers took on the task of policing the plaza, seemingly working within the "civilization versus barbarism" dichotomy on which several other scholars have commented (e.g., Nichols's "Taking Possession of Public Discourse," chapter 11, this volume). Smilde personally witnessed a mob harassing a beggar with whistles and insults until he left the plaza after he unwittingly asked one of the people for some change. When Smilde asked what was going on, one of the women in the plaza explained to him that the patrols did not permit any crime, panhandling, or homelessness in this plaza. An implicit contrast was being made to most of the plazas in Caracas where these activities are common.

In turn, the Catholic Church and Catholicism became targets of unbridled hostility among supporters of President Chávez. When Cardinal Ignacio Velasco died in July 2003, Chávez supporters crashed the funeral in the Plaza Bolívar, throwing rocks and fireworks. During a march commemorating five years since the election of Hugo Chávez, on December 6, 2003, Chávez supporters decapitated a statue of the Virgin Mary in the Plaza Francia de Altamira. The Catholic Church publicly decried these acts, as charges were exchanged back and forth between Chavistas and the opposition. The ECV also publicly denounced the vandalism in the Plaza Francia.

In January 2004, the Catholic hierarchy released a document called "Let's Be Authentic Servants of the People." This was a tense period as the population waited for the National Electoral Council to render official results on whether sufficient signatures had been obtained. With clear reference to the Chávez administration, in a section called "Peace Threatened" it says, "We warn of the danger of changing our constitutional democracy for an exclusive and excluding revolutionary project, forcing a process of socioeconomic, political-juridical, cultural and even religious change, without the population's consent. As a consequence, the division between Venezuelans has deepened, generating a polarization without precedents" (VEC 2004a). When the CNE announced in February that approximately 1.5 million signatures were being put under observation because the signers' personal information had been written down by the same person, and that without these signatures there were not enough signatures for the recall referendum, several days of violent street protests ensued. In the midst of the crisis the VEC emitted a document criticizing the CNE's ruling, accusing it of failing to guarantee and facilitate the citizenry's voice. Its "flip flopping, contradictions and at will modifications of the regulations and rules of the game" were said by the VEC to be worsening the crisis and playing with violence. This time, on the other hand, the VEC also criticized the violent protests of the opposition: "The anarchy promoted or unleashed, as well as the disproportional repression, is totally reproachable; they serve no cause and produce nothing but pain and death" (VEC 2004b).

In June of 2004 the National Electoral Council ruled that the opposition had obtained sufficient signatures for the recall referendum and the electoral process was on for mid-August, with each side moving for advantage and consolidating allies. In the opening statement to the annual bishop's conference in July of 2004, Cardinal Rosalio José Castillo Lara called for Catholics to participate in the referendum: "We need to ask ourselves which future we want to elect, one with a closed society or one with a plural society" (VEC 2004c). At the end of the conference the bishops released a declaration, "Referendum, Conscience and Responsibility," urging Catholics to vote and suggesting that they remember that "the solutions to big and serious problems cannot be improvised, do not happen by chance, nor do they come from political messianism. The country demands authentic, responsible and forward-looking leadership" (VEC 2004d). Members of the Chávez government pointed to these documents as evidence of the Catholic Church's partiality toward the opposition. MVR Congresswoman Cilia Flores argued that these proclamations "show their partiality toward the opposition, and they drift ever further away from religious principles."[18] Vice President José Vicente Rangel urged the Catholic Church to stay out of politics, citing the Pope's injunction for the Church to refrain from "circumstantial politics." Rangel argued that the Venezuelan Church is broad and diverse and that the hierarchy needs to respect that: "The Pope has been categorical with respect to this. He has clearly demarcated the necessity for the Church not to get involved in daily, contingent politics, because the Church is not just the hierarchy. All of us form the flock."[19]

During the referendum period internal differences among evangelicals erupted into public conflict. At the end of July, two weeks before the referendum, there were multiple acts of support from different social sectors in favor of the government. Two of these events—the "Clamor for Venezuela" and the "Million Prayers for Peace" meetings—involved neo-Pentecostal groups. These groups threw their support behind the Chávez government, speaking in the name of the entire evangelical movement. In probably the clearest public demonstration of division within the evangelical movement, the ECV released a statement in which it rejected the attempt of these neo-Pentecostal churches to speak for all evangelicals and argued that they were officially apolitical. President Samuel Olson argued that these churches had forgotten the "healthy separation of Church and State." Elías Rincón, president of Unicristiana, which had organized the meetings, argued that the ECV only represented a small percentage of the evangelical population and had no more right to speak in the name of evangelicals than he did. Speaking directly to Samuel Olson, Rincón argued, "The times we are living are different from those in which you and I were formed as Christians. It is not true that the Church is completely apolitical; it never has been. I know this from the sixty-one years I've been part of her and from the forty-three years I've been in the ministry" (ALC 2004).

Politics and Christianity in Bolivarian Democracy—Four Tendencies

Out of this narrative of the role of Christianity in Venezuela's political conflict from 1998–2004 we can distill four distinct tendencies. Within Catholicism we can see, on the one hand, opposition to the Chávez administration concentrated in the hierarchy and upper- and upper-middle-class laity. On the other hand we can see support or neutrality among religious professionals and organizations that are relatively more distanced from the main institutions of the Catholic Church. Within the evangelical movement we can see, on the one hand, neutrality and reserve among traditional evangelical sectors. On the other hand we can see enthusiastic pro-government stances among neo-Pentecostal churches.

The Catholic Opposition: Hierarchy and Laity

In a regional perspective the fact that the Catholic Church hierarchy has taken such an antagonistic role should not be surprising, as the Church was a vocal opponent to similar revolutionary, leftist governments in the past, such as Nicaragua and Cuba. However, from the perspective of Venezuela, such a vocal role is a departure from the norm. In his comprehensive analyses of the Venezuelan Catholic Church, Daniel Levine (1981, 1992) portrays the Venezuelan Church as poor, weak, and only having a minor role in Venezuelan society. It has traditionally avoided political leadership of any kind, prided itself on being nobody's enemy, and distinguished itself by its ability to coexist with parties of the left. Furthermore, the Catholic Church traditionally receives vast subsidies totaling tens of millions of dollars from the central government for their educational institutions and bishops' salaries, as well as for the maintenance of cathedrals and churches.

However, as Levine argues, the Catholic Church is not inherently quietist. Given certain organizational dynamics and political conjunctures, it can turn against established political authorities. And its religious perspectives cannot be reduced to something else. Religious ideas have an irreducible impact that varies in significance. If we reflect on the particular development of the Catholic Church, its engagement in society, and the particular perspectives of the bishops and some of the laity, we can make sense of its oppositional stance.

From the middle of the twentieth century, the Venezuelan Church set out to strengthen itself in two ways: by focusing on education among elite sectors of the population, not only in primary and secondary schools, but through a Catholic University in Caracas; and through apostolic and pietistic organizations among elite sectors. By the 1960s this educational focus was also extended to the popular sectors by organizations formally independent of the hierarchy (Daniel Levine 1981, 234). On the one hand, it was thought that this focus on elite sectors would help develop a national leadership. On the other hand, the focus on education and strictly religious groups made sense given the social engagement and programs carried out by the social Christian party COPEI. Thus dominant Catholic institutions have long been mostly engaged and mostly in tune with the urban middle and upper classes, precisely the strongholds of the Chávez opposition. It makes sense, therefore, that they would reflect the perspectives of these classes. Furthermore, one of the reasons that the hierarchy has suddenly gained an important political voice is the implosion of COPEI as a viable political party. The Catholic Church can no longer count on its perspective being brought into public debate by COPEI politicians and now must do so for itself.

Venezuelan bishops tend to receive abstract theological and philosophical training that emphasizes an unchanging, hierarchical order in which everything has a place. Anything that upsets this order is generally seen in negative terms as disorder and instability (Daniel Levine 1981, 104). Thus their discomfort with the "democratic revolution" is to be expected. One of the main motivations on the mind of bishops is always the well-being and unity of the institution (201). In their criticisms of the Chávez government they tend to focus on threats they perceive to central aspects of liberal democracy, such as the freedom of association and expression, and individual liberties. Their traditional anti-communism is also reflected in their criticisms of the state-centered economic policies of the Chávez government. They have clearly left behind their former position that they do not have anything to contribute to the political sphere. From the beginning of the Chávez administration they have promised to be a "critical instance" and have repeatedly stated that they see the social and political life of Venezuela as part of their mission.[20] And we cannot forget that when we talk about Catholicism and the opposition to the Chávez government, we need to speak not only about the hierarchy but also about lay followers among middle- and upper-income sectors. Among them, devotion to the Virgin Mary provides a sense of righteousness and power—indeed there were widespread rumors among the opposition that Chávez was afraid of the Virgin.[21]

Alternative Catholicism

One of the main changes in Latin American Catholicism in recent decades is precisely the fact that there is less unity around the hierarchy and leadership of the bishops and greater independence among popular groups (Daniel Levine 1992, 8). And this is exactly what we have seen in the case of Venezuela. Not all members of the Catholic Church have agreed with the active oppositional stance developed by the church hierarchy. When we refer to an "alternative" Catholic sector, we do not mean that they are necessarily pro-Chávez. Rather they claim to be non-political and therefore against the politicization of the Church. Nevertheless, they often speak through a discourse of peace, justice, and popular mobilization that bears an elective affinity to the discourse of the Chávez government.

While the hierarchy portrays "the Church" as a unified ecclesiastical structure guided by an authoritative doctrine, popular groups tend to see it as a historical community of believers, emphasizing multiple sources of authority, shared experience, and solidarity (Daniel Levine 1992, 9). However, we must be careful not to assume that all popular groups dissent from the hierarchy's stance—groups such as the Grupo Social CESAP are clearly aligned with the opposition. Those who tend to have this critical stance tend to themselves live in the popular barrios and be relatively more independent of diocese and other ecclesiastical structures (87). Most of them are small groups headed by foreign clergy, which makes them less relevant to the bishops as they do not have a future in the upper echelons of the hierarchy (Daniel Levine 1981, 217).

The popular groups we see dissenting from the official stance of the hierarchy reflect an outlook similar to the one Daniel Levine has called "sociocultural transformation." Open political confrontation and partisanship is played down in favor of community organization and religious values. They tend not to struggle through the church organization but rather through parallel proclamations and actions, such as the work done by the journalists of RFA or the letters written by the Christian communities of Petare. In a retrospective written by two RFA journalists, this perspective is made clear—rather than endorse Chavismo they aim for equanimity and therefore resist some of the excesses of the opposition. In their conclusion the communities affirm that "in spite of the fear, values of citizenship and Christianity came to the fore in the conduct and behavior of RFA journalists, who worked to make sure the country was not left without information and opinion" (J. Barrios and Urdaneta Jayaro 2002).

Traditional Evangelical Church

The perspective of the Evangelical Council of Venezuela with respect to the Chávez administration is best described as one of reserve. This grouping contains a great diversity of churches including long-established Baptist and Presbyterian churches concentrated among the middle classes as well as traditional Pentecostal churches hailing from the lower classes. This makes their relationship to the Chávez administration a complex one fraught with the potential to divide their constituency since most of the traditional middle-class evangelicals are anti-Chávez, while most of the lower-class Pentecostals are pro-Chávez. In addition, evangelicals' traditional stance against revolutionary rhetoric and concern for corporatist politics has been tempered by the numerous policy decisions and moves in favor of evangelicals. Samuel Olson, president of the ECV, explained to us that while under the Chávez administration the Directorate of Religion has been consistently supportive of evangelicals; evangelical lawyers were consulted regarding a new law on the freedom of religion; and evangelicals have been given positions in the government—Olson and other evangelical leaders find out about these initiatives after the fact, "The openness of this government has been helpful in certain ways. . . . But we have never been brought into any type of conversation with the Executive [branch of the government]. We have never met with the President of the Nation. So we have no way of knowing his reason for being open—or apparently being open—to the Evangelical Church."[22]

Olson and other ECV leaders maintained an independent position vis-à-vis government initiatives. While they resisted participation in the Bolivarian Religious Parliament, members of the ECV participated in the independent commission that selected new members of the National Electoral Council in June of 2000 (Olson 2001). They participated in the dialogues sponsored by the government after the April 2002 coup and maintained friendly and collaborative relations with the neo-Pentecostal churches that are not part of the ECV. However, that relationship became strained in the referendum period as their very different perspectives on their proper relationship to politics and the state came to the fore.

Neo-Pentecostalism

The neo-Pentecostal perspective is probably the most unexpected and surprising of the four perspectives revealed here. We think it can be best understood by looking at their religious ideas. The neo-Pentecostal perspective is what would be called "dominion theology," a perspective we can gain entry into by looking at the titles used by neo-Pentecostal leaders. Traditional Venezuelan evangelicals are so anti-authoritarian that they avoid using the title "reverend," preferring instead "pastor." In contrast, "bishop," used by Jesus Pérez, denotes hierarchy and authority. The title of "apostle" used by Elías Rincón y Raúl Ávila has traditionally been rejected by evangelicals since apostolic succession—the idea that there is a continuous succession of authority from the Apostle Paul to the current Pope—is the basis of the Roman Catholic Church's claim to legitimacy. Apostle Rincón knows this but argues that among evangelical groups rejection of papal authority has become a rejection of all forms of authority, which can be dysfunctional. He seeks to organize the evangelical movement into a coherent group, hence the title of apostle. While the role of a pastor is to lead a particular congregation, the role of an apostle is broader: "The apostle watches over the nation and has the capacity to appreciate God's revelation at particular moments" (Rincón, quoted in Quintero 2003). Rincón leads an organization called Unicristiana, which seeks this unity among evangelicals.

The name of Raul Ávila's federation—the Christ for all Nations Center—is similarly revealing. It demonstrates an aspiration to bring the secular structures of the nation-state under the dominion of Christianity. The basis of the perspective presented by Rincón and Ávila is the example of Nebuchadnezzar, the king of Babylon who conquered and enslaved the people of Israel. Even though he was "impious," the prophets of the Old Testament present him as an instrument that God used to punish, purify, and reform Israel. Rincón, for example, argues that the revelation of God did not end during the biblical period but continues today in Venezuela. "Chávez is part of God's plan. Sometimes we forget that God used Cyrus and Nebuchadnezzar as part of his plans" (Rincón, quoted in Quintero 2003). In December of 2002, during the opposition general strike, Raúl Ávila preached a message in which he told of twelve years of prophecies he had received about the conflict that would occur in Venezuela. These prophecies revealed that God had a special "unction" with Venezuela, and that a "judgment day" would come to Venezuela in order to prepare it to serve as "a beacon of liberty for Latin America" (Ávila 2002b).

These neo-Pentecostal churches have collaborated with numerous government initiatives and received financial support for a number of their social programs. Their dominion theology easily grafts onto the revolutionary nationalism of the Chávez movement and government.

Conclusion

We can see a number of fundamental motors driving this entry of religion into the public sphere in Venezuela's Bolivarian democracy. On the one hand, we can see that the MBR-200 and the Chávez administration sought from the beginning to involve religious groups in the political process in their attempt to break down the existing democratic regime. At first, religious movements mainly reacted to the government. However, we see a gradual transition of these movements and groups toward becoming political actors themselves. Neo-Pentecostal groups have seized the opportunity and developed a close collaboration with the government. The Catholic Church has become an aggressive participant not only because its traditional privileges have been threatened but because it cannot count on political allies to defend its interests and voice its perspective. The middle and upper social strata that form the core members of the opposition movement are likewise without traditional political representation and have increasingly moved toward other forms of associational life and ways of making meaning. Devotion to the Virgin and other aspects of Catholic practice have provided orientation and a discourse through which they address their complex new environment.

This entry of religion into the democratic debate and discourse is part of a larger tendency in which symbolic constructions other than the modernization-development discourse are used to frame political mobilization (Hechter 2004). In Venezuela and elsewhere, this tendency provides a moral charge to political conflict that, on the one hand, can reduce the possibility of dialogue and tolerance. On the other hand, it provides a means through which overt political interests can be superseded and reconciliation can be sought.

Notes

1. "Piden constituyente sin bichos," *El Universal*, July 11, 1998.

2. "Instan a no guiarse por la irracionalidad. Obispos exhortan al voto y al respet," *El Universal*, October 24, 1998.

3. "Cada uno de los miembros de la Iglesia tiene su candidato," *El Universal*, November 1, 1998.

4. "Obispos analizarán cómo participar," *El Universal*, January 7, 1999.

5. "Presidente electo solicito a la Iglesia mantener el dialogo abierto y franco," *El Universal*, January 11, 1999.

6. "Iglesia rechaza espíritu de 'llanero solitario' de Chávez," *El Universal*, December 10, 1999.

7. "Entrevista con Mnsr. Baltasar Porras: Desde el inicio este gobierno ha querido controlar a la Iglesia," *El Universal*, December 22, 2003.

8. "Denuncian presiones en remoción de directora de cultos," *El Nacional*, May 13, 2001; Olson 2001.

9. "Venezuela discute ley de culto," BBC Online, February 5, 2002; http://news.bbc.co.uk/hi/spanish/latin_america/newsid_1802000/1802434.stm.

10. "DeViana alerto sobre el final de Carmona," *El Universal*, April 15, 2002.

11. "Chávez: presidente nuevamente," *Chile Hoy*, February 14, 2002.

12. "Sin Fedecamaras ni la CTV instalaron las mesas de dialogo," *El Nacional Online*, May 5, 2002.

13. "Iglesias Evangélicas apoyan desarme de grupos civiles," *El Universal Digital*, July 9, 2002.

14. "Obispos reclaman 'propuestas concretas' a negociadores," *El Universal Digital*, December 14, 2002.

15. "Nuncio propone salida mas alla de la Constitución," *El Universal Digital*, December 9, 2002.

16. Aliana González, "Ortega clausuró la Navidad y los obispos no dijeron nada," *Tal Cual*, January 13, 2003.

17. Samuel Olson, phone interview with David Smilde, February 11, 2004.

18. "Cilia Flores: Conferencia Episcopal esta parcializada con la posición," *El Universal*, July 13, 2004.

19. "Rangel advierte sobre 'porrismo' en la Iglesia que perturba el dialogo," *El Universal*, July 9, 2004.

20. "Obispos analizarán cómo participar," *El Universal*, January 7, 1999.

21. "Chávez desmiente temerle a la Virgen," *El Universal Digital*, January 11, 2004.

22. Samuel Olson, interview with David Smilde, Caracas, December 26, 2001.

Chavismo and Venezuelan Democracy in a New Decade

Daniel Hellinger

In his introduction to this co-edited volume, David Smilde points out that "an overwhelming focus on the central institutions of the democratic state and organized political actors such as parties and unions" in the vast majority of English-language literature on Venezuela from the twentieth-century "left scholars and journalists under-appreciative of the extent of discontent and the burgeoning forms of alternative participation growing within Venezuelan society." With a handful of exceptions, the same criticism could be made of contemporary scholarship on Venezuela.

The highly polarized political situation in Venezuela attracts attention to familiar aspects of politics in a pluralist democracy. Newspaper headlines abroad continue to emphasize the words and actions of Hugo Chávez. Critics and supporters argue about Venezuela's membership in the Organization of American States or Mercosur. Experts analyze state oil policies and Venezuela's positions in OPEC. What ordinary Venezuelans think and what they are doing remains largely obscured, visible only occasionally in reports about presidential approval ratings or in analyses sifting through the entrails after the most recent of seemingly incessant electoral campaigns. In this book, we have tried to look beyond the headlines and the most visible forms of politics in Venezuela, to put more emphasis on praxis and the politics of everyday life in the Chávez era.

No single volume can possibly explore all of the participatory forms that have sprung up in Venezuela in recent decades, but the ones documented in this book show the myriad ways that the Bolivarian Revolution has engendered civic engagement and practices—some overtly political and familiar, some innovative and novel. The new forms of civic engagement and experimentation documented throughout this book continue to occur in communal councils, cultural activities, discussions about popular programs, Internet blogs, community media, and numerous other forums.

We recognize that this surge of grassroots participation that has characterized Venezuelan politics in the Chávez era has yet to become institutionalized. When we say *institutionalized* we refer less to notions of taming participation than to mechanisms linking the state and civil society in ways that guarantee democratic governance. Liberal theorists usually think of the proper relationship between civil society and the state as one that runs "one way" from the former to the latter. Civil society should have an impact on the state but not vice versa.

Concerns raised about the clientelism, personalism, and concentrated executive authority in Venezuela might best be addressed by imagining alternative ways to institutionalize a democratic relationship between the state and civil society, one that enhances popular, democratic governance by permitting social movements and groups to participate actively and collaborate with the bureaucracy and elected officials. To put it in the parlance of the Bolivarian Constitution of 1999, this institutionalized relationship should provide for a "protagonistic" role for social movements and groups. Chávez clearly regards the spread of communal councils and the establishment of the PSUV as steps toward institutionalizing such a protagonistic role for civil society, but both of these Chavista innovations remain in gestation. Reacting to the highly co-optive system of Punto Fijo and the general distrust of political parties in Venezuela, the young PSUV began formulating statutes and ideological principles to further the process of institutionalizing such a relationship.

The studies in this book demonstrate that the task is not impossible, but formidable obstacles remain to be overcome. On the one hand, Venezuelans have accumulated over the last decade (if not over a longer period, as Velasco shows in his chapter) significant experience with new forms of social organization and participatory governance, but the central government retains most of the classic features of the petrostate, truly a leviathan with strong cultural and material proclivities toward top-down corporatism. Many grassroots Chavistas continue to decry the irregularities and allege manipulation of internal processes by bureaucrats and politicians. Most of our contributors validate their concerns, but too often criticism seizes on these shortcomings to dismiss the Bolivarian experience as nothing more than a new episode in a familiar story of populism and clientelism, failing to recognize a much more nuanced and complex process at work.

The PSUV held primaries in 2008 to choose candidates for the November

2008 regional elections and will also hold primaries in 2010 for the National Assembly elections scheduled for September, a signal accomplishment in a country where democratic nomination processes are more often promised than delivered. However, the PSUV, despite President Chávez's initial threats to expel any other leftist parties from the revolutionary process, is not the only party of influence in the Venezuelan Left, and the process of coalition building cannot always be reconciled with full empowerment of the rank and file.

If we look more closely at what is happening in the public sphere in Venezuela, we find that the opposition faces some issues that run parallel to those bedeviling the Chavistas. For example, a mass student movement emerged in reaction to the government's decision not to renew the broadcast license of RCTV in 2007, an opposition television network that, like other private outlets, played a significant role in supporting the coup that ousted Chávez briefly in 2002. (We would be remiss not to mention that there is also a large pro-government student movement supportive of the government.) Opposition parties immediately seized upon the movement, and not long afterward a sector among the students began warning of the dangers of co-optation and the need to develop a broader project with appeal to previously excluded parts of the population.

What our collection of studies suggests is that we err if we continue to focus only upon elections, legislative battles, and conventional news and public affairs programs. Regardless of how the September 2010 legislative elections or the presidential election scheduled for late 2012 turn out, tensions will continue to be generated between the low politics going on in neighborhoods, literature circles, soup kitchens, school rooms, motorcycle clubs, and so on and the high politics involved in political campaigns and international quid pro quo. Venezuelan politics and popular participation will bear the imprint of the experiences of the last few years. If social scientists and journalists keep their eyes fixed only upon conventional arenas of politics, they will fail to fully comprehend Venezuela not only now but in the post-Chávez era, whenever that may come.

References

Abu-Lughod, Lila. 2005. *Dramas of Nationhood*. Chicago: University of Chicago Press.

ACI Digital. 2001. "Iglesia en Venezuela rechaza controvertido proyecto de ley de Cultos." Agencia Católica de Informaciones en América Latina. http://www.aciprensa.com.

Acosta-Alzuru, Carolina. 2003a. "Fraught with Contradictions: The Production, Depiction, and Consumption of Women in a Venezuelan Telenovela." *Global Media Journal* 2 (2). http://lass.calumet.purdue.edu/cca/gmj/gmj_pastissues.htm.

———. 2003b. "'I'm Not a Feminist . . . I Only Defend Women as Human Beings': The Production, Representation, and Consumption of Feminism in a Telenovela." *Critical Studies in Media Communication* 20 (3): 269–94.

———. 2003c. "Tackling the Issues: Meaning Making in a Telenovela." *Popular Communication* 1 (4): 193–215.

———. 2003d. "Tackling the Issues: Meaning Making in a Telenovela." *Popular Communication* 1 (4): 193–215.

———. 2004. "Producing Telenovelas in a Time of Crisis: The Venezuelan Case." Paper presented at the Association for Education in Journalism and Mass Communication meeting, Toronto, July.

———. 2007. *Venezuela es una telenovela*. Colección Homo Videns. Caracas: Alfa.

Alayón Monserat, Rubén. 2005. "Barrio adentro: Combatir la exclusión profundizando la democracia." *Revista Venezolana de Economía y Ciencias Sociales* 11 (3): 219–44.

ALC (Agencia Latinoamericana y Caribeña de Comunicación). 2004. "Secuela del referendo: Polémica entre evangélicos." August 18. http://www.cristianos.com.

Alcántara Sáez, Manuel. 2002. "Experimentos de democracia interna: Las primarias de partidos en América Latina." Working Paper 293, Kellogg Institute for International Studies, University of Notre Dame, Notre Dame, Ind., April.

Alexander, Robert J. 1969. *The Communist Party of Venezuela*. Stanford, Calif.: Hoover Institution Press.

Almandoz, Arturo. 1999. "Transfer of Urban Ideas: The Emergence of Venezuelan Urbanism in the Proposals for 1930s Caracas." *International Planning Studies* 4 (1): 79–95.

Almond, Gabriel A., and Sidney Verba. 1963. *The Civic Culture: Political Attitudes and Democracy in Five Nations*. Princeton: Princeton University Press.

Alvarez, Coromoto. 1978a. "De 'maniáticos del desorden' califica Mantilla a quienes participan en sabotajes en Caracas." *Ultimas Noticias*, October 7.

———. 1978b. "Sucesos como los del 23 de enero hacen más graves deficiencias existentes en los servicios públicos." *Ultimas Noticias*, October 7.

———. 1982. "Primer refinanciamiento de deuda del INAVI por 2.408 millones logró Ugueto en el exterior." *Ultimas Noticias*, October 22.

Alvarez, María Auxiliadora. 1993. *Cuerpo/Ca(z)a*. Caracas: Fundarte.

———. 2003. "La esfinge (des)honrada o la metáfora de la maternidad." Presentation given on Theme Day, Drury University, Springfield, Mo., February 2.

Alvarez, Sonia, Evelina Dagnino, and Arturo Escobar. 1998a. "Introduction: The Cultural and the Political in Latin American Social Movements." In *Cultures of Politics, Politics of Cultures: Re-visioning Latin American Social Movements*, edited by Sonia Alvarez, Evelina Dagnino, and Arturo Escobar, 1–29. Boulder, Colo.: Westview.

———, eds. 1998b. *Cultures of Politics, Politics of Cultures: Re-visioning Latin American Social Movements*. Boulder, Colo.: Westview.

Alvarez, Valentina. 2007. *Lágrimas a pedido: Así se escribe una telenovela*. Caracas: Alfa.

Amaral, Santos. 1982. "Secuestrados otros 3 vehículos y van once por protesta de habitants del 23 de enero." *Ultimas Noticias*, January 18.

Ang, Ien. 1991. *Desperately Seeking the Audience*. London: Routledge.

Antillano, Andrés. 2005. "La lucha por el reconocimiento y la inclusión en los barrios populares: La experiencia de los Comités de Tierras Urbanas." *Revista Venezolana de Economía y Ciencias Sociales* 11 (3): 205–18.

Aporrea. 2006. "Denuncia: trabajadores de SIDEROCA, víctimas de 'guarimba' de politiqueos disfrazados de 'chavistas.'" May 2. http://www.aporrea.org.

Arconada Rodríguez, Santiago. 2005. "Seis años después: mesas técnicas y consejos comunitarios de aguas." *Revista Venezolana de Economía y Ciencias Sociales* 11 (3): 187–203.

Arendt, Hannah. 1963. *On Revolution*. New York: Penguin.

Argotte, Daisy. 1981. "La ira presidencial sacudió las voluntades: Una 'Operación Cayapa' dejo limpio al 23 de enero." *Diario de Caracas*, December 24.

Asamblea Metropolitana de Comités de Tierra Urbana de Caracas. 2004. *Democratización de la ciudad y transformación urbana: Propuesta de los CTU a la Misión Vivienda*. Caracas: Vicepresidencia de la República, Oficina Técnica Nacional para la Regularización de la Tenencia de la Tierra.

Aufderheide, Patricia. 2000. "Grassroots Video in Latin America." In *Visible Nations: Latin American Cinema and Video*, edited by Chon A. Noriega, 219–38. Minneapolis: University of Minnesota Press.

Auyero, Javier. 1999. "From the Client's Point(s) of View: How do Poor People Perceive and Evaluate Political Clientelism." *Theory and Society* 28:297–334.

———. 2000. *Poor People Politics: Peronist Survival Networks and the Legacy of Evita*. Durham: Duke University Press.

Auyero, Javier, and Débora Alejandra Swistun. 2009. *Flammable: Environmental Suffering in an Argentine Shantytown*. New York: Oxford University Press.

Ávila, Raúl. 2002a. "El Señor, Dios de las naciones." Sermon presented at Centro de Cristo de las Naciones, Caracas.

———. 2002b. "¿Centro de Cristo para las naciones: Posición política o palabra profética?" Sermon delivered at the Centro de Cristo de las Naciones, Caracas.

Baiocchi, Gianpaolo. 2005. *Militants and Citizens: The Politics of Participatory Democracy in Porto Alegre*. Stanford, Calif.: Stanford University Press.

Baldó, Josefina. 2002. "La política de vivienda para Venezuela." In *Venezuela en perspectiva*, edited by C. Genatios, 348–54. Caracas: Fondo Editorial Cuestión.

Balibar, Etienne, and Immanuel Wallerstein. 1991. *Race, Nation, Class: Ambiguous Identities*. Translated by Chris Turner. London: Verso.

Banco Obrero. 1951. *La batalla contra el rancho: Urdaneta y Pedro Camejo, un nuevo para los obreros venezolanos*. Caracas: Banco Obrero.

———. 1954. *El problema de los cerros en el área metropolitana: Informe preliminar sobre el cerro piloto presentado por el Banco Obrero y la gobernación del distrito federal*. Caracas: Sección de Investigaciones Social, Económica, y Tecnológica, Banco Obrero.

———. 1956. *Actas del Banco Obrero*. Vol. 44. Caracas: Banco Obrero.

———. 1957. *Actas del Banco Obrero*. Vol. 47. Caracas: Banco Obrero.

Barrera Tyszka, Alberto. 2002. "Desde las tripas de un culebrón." *Revista Bigott*, no. 61 (September–December): 62–65.

Barreto, Daisy. 2007. María Lionza: Polarización religiosa y política en la Venezuela contemporánea. Unpublished manuscript, Caracas: Escuela de Antropología/ Universidad Central de Venezuela.

Barreto, Juan. 1995. *Los medios de los medios: Campos culturales y dispositivos mass-mediáticos de subjetividad en la crisis de lo político*. Caracas: Editorial Planeta, Universidad Católica Andrés Bello, and Fundación Carlos Eduardo Frías.

Barrios, Javier, and Belkis Urdaneta Jayaro. 2002. "Desenredando los nudos del silencio." Radio Fe y Alegría, June. http://www.feyalegria.org.

Barrios, Leoncio. 1988a. "Television, Telenovelas, and Family Life in Venezuela." In *World Families Watch Television*, edited by J. Lull, 49–79. Newbury Park, Calif.: Sage.

———. 1988b. "Television, telenovelas y vida cotidiana en el contexto de la familia." *Apuntes* 3:1–52.

Bastian, Jean Pierre. 1994. *Protestantismos y modernidad latinoamericana: Historia de unas minorías religiosas activas en América Latina*. Mexico: Fondo de Cultura Económica.

Battaglini, Oscar. 1993. *Legitimación del poder y lucha política en Venezuela, 1936–1941*. Caracas: Universidad Central de Venezuela.

Bel, Bernard, Jan Brouwer, Biswajit Das, Vibodh Parthsarathi, and Guy Poitevin, eds. 2005. *Media and Mediation*. Thousand Oaks, Calif.: Sage.

Bennett, W. Lance, and Robert M. Entman. 2001. "Mediated Politics: An Introduction." In *Mediated Politics: Communications in the Future of Democracy*, edited by W. Lance Bennett and Robert M. Entman, 1–32. Cambridge: Cambridge University Press.

Betancourt, Rómulo. 1959. *Mensaje del ciudadano Rómulo Betancourt, presidente de la república, dirigido a los trabajadores en la noche del 30 de abril de 1959, con motivo de la celebración del 1ro de mayo.* Caracas: Presidencia de la República.

Beverley, John. 1999. *Subalternity and Representation: Arguments in Cultural Theory.* Durham: Duke University Press.

Binder, Amy. 2002. *Contentious Curricula: Afrocentrism and Creationism in American Public Schools.* Princeton: Princeton University Press.

Bisbal, Marcelino. 1994. *La mirada comunicacional.* Caracas: Ediciones Alfadil.

Blee, Kathleen. 2002. *Inside Organized Racism: Women in the Hate Movement.* Berkeley: University of California Press.

Borja, Jordi. 2003. *La ciudad conquistada.* Madrid: Alianza Editorial.

Brando, Jesús Eduardo. 1977. "Muerto a tiros dos menores en manifestación de protesta falta de agua." *El Nacional,* November 4.

Briceño, J. H. 1973. "Caracas alcanzó ayer 2.615,484 habitantes pero no nos alegremos, porque el 44.9 por ciento de esa población vive en la marginalidad." *El Nacional,* November 4.

Britto García, Luis. 2003. *Venezuela: Investigación de unos medios por encima de toda sospecha.* Caracas: Fondo Editorial Questión.

Burgwal, Gerrit. 1995. *Struggle of the Poor: Neighborhood Organization and Clientelist Practice in a Quito Squatter Settlement.* Amsterdam: CEDLA.

Buxton, Julia. 2008. "Venezuela's Bolivarian Revolution." *Global Dialogue* 10 (Summer–Autumn): xxviii. http://www.worlddialogue.org/content.php?id=424.

Cabrujas, José Ignacio. 1995a. De cómo la televisión se planteó ser menos estúpida. *El Nacional,* April 29.

———. 1995b. "Mala suerte: Pérez veía Rafaela." *El Nacional,* May 6.

———. 1995c. "Materia fecal." *El Nacional,* April 22.

———. 2002. *Y Latinoamérica inventó la telenovela.* Caracas: Alfadil.

Cardoso, Fernando Enrique, and Enzo Faletto. 1978. *Dependencia y desarrollo en América Latina: Ensayo de interpretación sociológica.* Mexico: Siglo Veintiuno Editores.

Cariola, Cecilia, and Miguel Lacabana. 2005. "Los bordes de la esperanza: Nuevas formas de participación popular y gobiernos locales en la periferia de Caracas." *Revista Venezolana de Economía y Ciencias Sociales* 11 (1): 21–41.

Cariola, Cecilia, M. Lacabana, L. Bethencourt, G. Darwich, B. Fernandez, and A. T. Gutiérrez. 1989. *Crisis, sobrevivencia y sector informal.* Caracas: Editorial Nueva Sociedad.

Carlson, Eric, ed. 1961. *Proyecto de evaluación de los superbloques.* Caracas: Banco Obrero.

Cartaya, Vanessa, and Yolanda D'Elia. 1991. *Pobreza en Venezuela: Realidad y políticas.* Caracas: Cesap-Cisor.

Castells, Manuel. 1997. *The Power of Identity: Economy, Society, and Culture.* Cambridge: Blackwell.

Castillo, Debra A. 1992. *Talking Back: Toward a Latin American Feminist Literary Criticism.* Ithaca, N.Y.: Cornell University Press.

Castillo, L. H. 2004. "Declaro la guerra frontal al chavismo sin Chávez." *El Nacional*, May 9.

Castillo, Marlene. 2004. "Olla de grillos: Sala de espera." *El Mundo*, March 30.

Coccato, Mabel. 1978. "La telenovela venezolana desde 1953 a 1961." *Videoforum* 1:105–32.

———. 1979a. "Apuntes para una historia de la telenovela venezolana: Segunda parte, desde 1962 hasta 1970." *Videoforum* 3:87–113.

———. 1979b. "Apuntes para una historia de la telenovela venezolana: Tercera parte, desde 1971 hasta 1979." *Videoforum* 3:87–113.

Cohen, Jean L., and Andrew Arato. 1992. *Civil Society and Political Theory*. Cambridge: MIT Press.

Cohen, Stanley. 1980. *Folk Devils and Moral Panics: The Creation of the Mods and Rockers*. New York: St. Martin's.

Coleman, David. 2003. "Venezuela's Chávez Hands Over Land Deeds to Caracas Slum Dwellers." *BBC Worldwide Monitoring*, May 12. http://www.monitor.bbc.co.uk.

Colomina de Rivera, Marta. 1974. *El huésped alienante: Un estudio sobre audiencia y efectos de las radio-telenovelas en Venezuela*. Maracaibo: Universidad del Zulia.

Comunidades Cristianas de Petare. 2002. "Carta a los medios de comunicación social de Venezuela." Caracas, June 4.

Consejo Supremo Electoral (CSE). 1983. *Las cuatro primeras fuerzas políticas en Venezuela a nivel municipal, 1958–1978*. Caracas.

Constitución de la República Bolivariana de Venezuela. See CRBV.

Contreras, V. 2005. *Informe de Pasantías Cortas: Proyecto de regularización de la tenencia de la tierra, sector Toro Muerto*. Caracas. Universidad Simón Bolívar.

———. 2006. "Los retos de la planificación estratégica: Formulación del plan especial participativo, equitativo y solidario del sector Toro Muerto, Municipio Caroní; Informe de pasantía intermedia para optar al título de 'Urbanista.'" Manuscript, Universidad Simón Bolívar, Caracas.

Corney, Frederick. 2004. *Telling October: Memory and the Making of the Bolshevik Revolution*. Ithaca, N.Y.: Cornell University Press.

Coronil, Fernando. 1997. *The Magical State: Nature, Money, and Modernity in Venezuela*. Chicago: University of Chicago Press.

Coronil, Fernando, and Julie Skurski. 1991. "Dismembering and Remembering the Nation: The Semantics of Political Violence in Venezuela." *Studies in Comparative Society and History* 33 (2): 288–337.

Corrales, Javier. 2006. "Explaining Chavismo: The Unexpected Alliance of Radical Leftists and Generals in Venezuela since the Late 1990s." Paper presented at the Second Conference on Venezuelan Economic Growth, 1970–2005, Harvard University, April 28–29.

Corrales, Javier, and Michael Penfold. 2007. "Venezuela: Crowding Out the Opposition." *Journal of Democracy* 18 (2): 99–113.

Crahan, Margaret E. 1989. "Religion and Politics in Revolutionary Nicaragua." In *The Progressive Church in Latin America*, edited by Scott Mainwaring and Alexander Wilde, 41–63. Notre Dame, Ind.: University of Notre Dame Press.

CRBV (Constitución de la República Bolivariana de Venezuela). 1999. *Gaceta Oficial número 36.860*. Caracas, December 30.

———. 2000. *Versión definitiva con corrección de erratas; Gaceta Oficial extraordinaria número 5.453*. Caracas, March 24.

Crisp, Brian F., Daniel H. Levine, and Juan Carlos Rey. 1995. "The Legitimacy Problem." In *Venezuelan Democracy Under Stress*, edited by Jennifer McCoy, Andrés Serbin, William C. Smith, and Andrés Stambouli, 139–70. Miami, Fla.: University of Miami North-South Center.

Cruz, Carlos. 2004. "Cara y cruz: Ficción y realidad." *Así es la Noticia*, August 23.

CSB (Coordinadora Simón Bolívar). 2004. *Propuesta para la participación popular por la base*, October 7. http://www.aporrea.org/a10001.html.

Dagnino, Evelina. 1998. "Culture, Citizenship, and Democracy: Changing Discourses and Practices of the Latin American Left." In *Cultures of Politics/Politics of Cultures: Re-visioning Latin American Social Movements*, edited by Sonia Alvarez, Arturo Escobar, and Evelina Dagnino, 33–63. Boulder, Colo.: Westview.

Dahl, Robert A. 1971. *Polyarchy: Participation and Opposition*. New Haven: Yale University Press.

Dahlberg, Matz, and Eva Johannson. 2002. "On the Vote Purchasing Behavior of Incumbent Governments." *American Political Science Review* 96 (1): 27–40.

Dahlgren, Peter. 1995. *Television and the Public Sphere: Citizenship, Democracy, and the Media*. Thousand Oaks, Calif.: Sage.

Darby, John, and Roger MacGinty. 2003. *Contemporary Peacemaking: Conflict, Violence, and Peace Processes*. New York: Palgrave Macmillan, 2003.

Datanalisis. 2008a. *Informe de Encuesta Nacional Ómnibus*. Caracas, Venezuela. February.

———. 2008b. *Informe de Encuesta Nacional Ómnibus*. Caracas, Venezuela. April.

de Blay, M. Louisa. 1959. *Treinta años de Banco Obrero*. Caracas: Banco Obrero.

de la Fuente, Alejandro. 1999. "Myths of Racial Democracy: Cuba, 1900–1912." *Latin American Research Review* 34 (3): 39–73.

———. 2001. *A Nation for All: Race, Inequality, and Politics in Twentieth-Century Cuba*. Chapel Hill: University of North Carolina Press.

de la Torre, Carlos. 2000. *Populist Seduction in Latin America: The Ecuadorian Experience*. Athens: Ohio University Center for International Studies.

D'Elia, Yolanda (Coordinadora). 2006. *Las misiones sociales en Venezuela: Una aproximación a su comprensión y análisis*. Caracas: Instituto Latinoamericano de Investigaciones Sociales.

Diamond, Larry. 2008. "The Democratic Rollback: The Resurgence of the Predatory State." *Foreign Affairs* (March/April), 36–48.

Diamond, Larry, Andreas Schedler, and Marc F. Plattner, eds. 1999. *The Self-Restraining State: Power and Accountability in New Democracies*. Boulder, Colo.: Lynne Rienner.

Dietrich, Heinz. 1996. *Socialismo del Siglo XXI*.

D'Imperio, Ocarina Castillo. 1990. *Los años del buldozer: Ideología y política, 1948–1958*. Caracas: Fondo Editorial Tropykos.

Dirlik, Arif. 2001. "Place-Based Imagination: Globalism and the Politics of Place." In *Places and Politics in an Age of Globalization*, edited by Roxann Prazniak and Arif Dirlik, 15–51. Lanham, Md.: Rowman and Littlefield.

Di Tella, Torcuato S. 1965. "Populism and Reform in Latin America." In *Obstacles to Change in Latin America*, edited by Claudio Veliz, 47–74. London: Oxford University Press.

Dixit, Avanish, and John Londregan. 1996. "The Determinants of Success of Special Interests in Redistributive Politics." *Journal of Politics* 58 (November): 1132–55.

Dodson, Michael. 1986. "Nicaragua: The Struggle for the Church." In *Religion and Political Conflict in Latin America*, edited by Daniel Levine, 79–105. Chapel Hill: University of North Carolina Press.

Domínguez, Jorge. 1994. *Race and Ethnicity in Latin America*. New York: Garland.

Dominguez, Jorge, and Anthony Jones, eds. 2007. *The Construction of Democracy: Lessons from Practice and Research*. Baltimore: Johns Hopkins University Press.

Dornbusch, Rudiger, and Sebastian Edwards, eds. 1991. *The Macroeconomics of Populism in Latin America*. Chicago: University of Chicago Press.

Downing, John. 2001. *Radical Media: Rebellious Communication and Social Movements*. Thousand Oaks, Calif.: Sage.

du Gay, Paul, Stuart Hall, Linda Janes, Hugh MacKay, and Keith Negus. 1997. *Doing Cultural Studies: The Story of the Sony Walkman*. London: Sage.

Duno Gottberg, Luis. 2003. *Solventar las diferencias: La ideología del mestizaje en Cuba*. Frankfurt: Vervuert—Iberoamericana.

———. 2004. "Mob Outrages: Reflections on the Media Construction of the Masses in Venezuela (April 2000–January 2003)." *Journal of Latin American Cultural Studies* 13 (1): 115–35.

———. "Las tropelías de la turba: construcción mediática de las masas en Venezuela," *La Cultura Venezolana del siglo XX*. Caracas: Universidad Simón Bolívar—Fundación Cultural Bigott—Fundación Mercantil.

Duverger, Maurice. 1968. *Party Politics and Pressure Groups: A Comparative Introduction*. New York: Thomas Y. Crowell.

Eber, Dena Elisabeth, and Arthur G. Neal. 2001. *Memory and Representation: Constructed Truths and Competing Realities*. Bowling Green, Ohio: Bowling Green State University Popular Press.

Ellner, Steve. 1988. *Venezuela's Movimiento al Socialismo: From Guerrilla Defeat to Innovative Politics*. Durham: Duke University Press.

———. 2003. "Introduction: The Search for Explanations." In *Venezuelan Politics in the Chavez Era: Class, Polarization and Conflict*, edited by Steve Ellner and Daniel Hellinger, 7–26. Boulder, Colo.: Lynne Rienner.

———. 2005. "Revolutionary and Non-Revolutionary Paths of Radical Populism: Directions of the *Chavista* Movement in Venezuela." *Science and Society* 69 (2): 160–90.

———. 2008. *Rethinking Venezuelan Politics: Class, Conflict, and the Chavez Phenomenon*. Boulder, Colo.: Lynne Rienner.

Ellner, Steve, and Daniel Hellinger. 2003. "Conclusion: The Democratic and Authoritarian Directions of the Chavista Movement." In *Venezuelan Politics in the Chavez Era*, edited by Steve Ellner and Daniel Hellinger, 215–26. Boulder, Colo.: Lynne Rienner.

Ellner, Steve, and Miguel Tinker Salas, eds. 2007. *Venezuela: Hugo Chavez and the Decline of an Exceptional Democracy*. Lanham, Md.: Rowman and Littlefield.

Escobar, Arturo. 2001. "Place, Economy, and Culture in a Post-Development Era." In *Places and Politics in an Age of Globalization*, edited by Roxann Prazniak and Arif Dirlik, 193–217. Lanham, Md.: Rowman and Littlefield.

Espada, Carolina. 2002. "El candor de Cabrujas." *Revista Bigott*, no. 61 (September–December): 66–69.

Febres, Carlos Eduardo. 2005. "Misiones: ¿Estrategia para la inclusión social?" Reported in *El Universal*, Forum Caracas, July 8, 2008.

Ferguson, James. 2004. "Power Topographies." In *A Companion to the Anthropology of Politics*, edited by David Nugent and Joan Vincent, 383–99. Malden, Mass.: Blackwell.

Ferguson, James, and Akhil Gupta. 2002. "Spatializing States: Toward an Ethnography of Neoliberal Governmentality." *American Ethnologist* 29 (4): 981–1002.

Fernandes, Sujatha. 2006. *Cuba Represent! Cuban Arts, State Power, and the Making of New Revolutionary Cultures*. Durham: Duke University Press.

Fernández, H. 1995. "Evaluación de las telenovelas en la TV venezolana." *Anuario ININCO* (7):97–112.

Fernandez Kelly, Patricia, and Jon Shefner, eds. 2006. *Out of the Shadows: Political Action and the Informal Economy in Latin America*. University Park: Pennsylvania State University Press.

Fishman, Robert M. 2004. *Democracy's Voices: Social Ties and the Quality of Public Life in Spain*. Ithaca, N.Y.: Cornell University Press.

Forment, Carlos. 2003. *Democracy in Latin America, 1760–1900: Volume 1, Civic Selfhood and Public Life in Mexico and Peru*. Chicago: University of Chicago Press.

Foucault, Michel. 1978. *The History of Sexuality: An Introduction*. New York: Vintage.

———. 1984. "What is Enlightenment?" In *The Foucault Reader*, edited by Paul Rabinow, 32–50. New York: Pantheon.

Fox, Jonathan A. 1997. "The Difficult Transition from Clientelism to Citizenship: Lessons from Mexico." In *The New Politics of Inequality in Latin America*, edited by David A. Chalmers, Carlos M. Vilas, Katherine Hite, Scott Martin, Kerianne Piester, and Monique Segarra, 391–420. Oxford: Oxford University Press.

Franco, Jean. 1988. "Beyond Ethnocentrism: Gender, Power and the Third-World Intelligentsia." In *Marxism and the Interpretation of Culture*, edited by Cary Nelson and Lawrence Goldberg, 503–15. Urbana: University of Illinois Press.

Franco, Jean. 1992. "Going Public: Reinhabiting the Private." In *On Edge: The Crisis of Contemporary Latin American Culture*, edited by George Yudice, Jean Franco, and Juan Flores, 65–83. Minneapolis: University of Minnesota Press.

Frechilla, Juan José Martín. 1994. *Planos, planes, y proyectos para Venezuela:*

1908–1958 (Apuntes para una historia de la construcción del país). Caracas: Universidad Central de Venezuela.

Friedman, Elisabeth J. 2000. *Unfinished Transitions: Women and the Gendered Development of Democracy in Venezuela, 1936–1996*. University Park: Pennsylvania State University Press.

Gallegos, Rómulo. 1929. *Doña Barbara*. Caracas: Araluce.

———. 1937. *Pobre Negro*. Caracas: La asociación venezolana de escritores.

García Canclini, Nestor. 2001. *Consumers and Citizens: Globalization and Multicultural Conflicts*. Translated by George Yúdice. Minneapolis: University of Minnesota Press.

García-Guadilla, Maria Pilar. 2002. "Democracy, Decentralization and Clientelism: New Relationships and Old Practices." *Latin American Perspectives* 29 (5): 90–109.

———. 2003. "Civil Society: Institutionalization, Fragmentation, Autonomy." In *Venezuelan Politics in the Chavez Era: Class, Polarization and Conflict*, edited by Steve Ellner and Daniel Hellinger, 179–96. Boulder, Colo.: Lynne Rienner.

———. 2005. "The Democratization of Democracy and Social Organizations of the Opposition: Theoretical Certainties, Myths, and Praxis." *Latin American Perspectives* 32 (2): 109–23.

———. 2008. "La praxis de los consejos comunales en Venezuela: ¿Poder popular o instancia clientelar?" *Revista Venezolana de Economía y Ciencias Sociales* 14 (1): 125–51.

García Ponce, Guillermo. 1977. *Relatos de la lucha armada: 1960–67*. Valencia: Vadell Hermanos.

Garmendia, Salvador. 2000. "Ibsen gana el juego." *El Nacional*, October 23.

Gaudichaud, Frank. 2006. "An Interview with Orlando Chirino, National Coordinator of the New Venezuelan Workers Union, UNT." Axis of Logic, April 2. http://www .axisoflogic.com.

GAUS-USB (Laboratorio de Investigación en Gestión Ambiental, Urbana, y Sociopolítica). 2006, 2009. "Nuevas organizaciones socials bolivarianas: Comités de tierra urbanos y consejos comunales en Venezuela." Manuscript (research project in progress), Interdisciplinary Research Laboratory on Environmental, Urban, and Sociopolitical Conflict Resolution, Universidad Simón Bolívar, Caracas.

Gay, Robert. 1998. "Rethinking Clientelism: Demands, Discourses and Practices in Contemporary Brazil." *European Review of Latin American and Caribbean Studies* 65:7–24.

———. 2006. "The Even More Difficult Transition from Clientelism to Citizenship: Lessons from Brazil." In *Out of the Shadows: Political Action and the Informal Economy in Latin America*, edited by Patricia Fernandez-Kelly and Jon Shefner, 195–218. University Park: Pennsylvania State University Press.

Gellner, Ernest. 1977. "Patrons and Clients." In *Patrons and Clients in Mediterranean Societies*, edited by Ernest Gellner and John Waterbury, 1–6. London: Gerald Duckworth.

Germani, Gino. 1978. *Authoritarianism, Fascism, and National Populism*. New Brunswick, N.J.: Transaction.

Giddens, Anthony. 1998. *The Third Way: Renewal of Social Democracy*. Cambridge: Polity.

Ginsburg, Faye. 1991. "Indigenous Media: Faustian Contract or Global Village?" *Cultural Anthropology* 6:92–112.

———. 1994. "Culture/Media: A (Mild) Polemic." *Anthropology Today* 10 (2): 5–15.

Golinger, Eva. 2005. *El código Chávez: Descifrando la intervención de los Estados Unidos en Venezuela*. La Habana: Editorial de Ciencias Sociales.

Gómez, F. 1978. "Murió el otro joven herido durante disturbios en 23 de enero." *Ultimas Noticias*, October 8.

Gómez, Luis. 2003. "The New Voice of the Venezuelan People: An Interview with the Aporrea.org Collective." *NarcoNews* 29: part 1, April 21; part 2, April 23. http://www.narconews.com.

González-Stephan, Beatriz. 1999. "Cuerpos de la nación: Cartografías disciplinarias." *Anale* 2:71–106.

Gott, Richard. 2000. *Hugo Chávez and the Bolivarian Revolution*. London: Verso.

———. 2005. *Hugo Chávez and the Bolivarian Revolution*. New York: Verso.

Gramsci, Antonio. 1978. *Selections from the Prison Notebooks*. Edited and translated by Quinton Hoare and Geoffrey Nowell Smith. New York: International.

Güerere, Abdel. 1994. *Producción de telenovelas*. Caracas: IESA.

Guerra, Ibrahim. 2001. *Telenovela y consumo comercial en América Latina: Desde "El derecho de nacer" hasta "Betty La Fea."* Caracas: Comala.com Edición X demanda.

Guerreero, Javier. 2006. "El gran varón: Disputas del cuerponacional en tiempos de revolución." Paper presented at the symposium Reinventing Venezuela: A Symposium on Culture, Memory and Power, November 17, University of California, Berkeley.

Guiffrida, Laura, and María Salcedo, 2005. "Análisis y comprobación de los cambios de la dinámica urbana en las comunidades de Víctor Baptista, el Calvario, Rómulo Gallegos, y el Naranjal, con la introducción de los Comités de Tierra Urbanos; Comparación entre los casos de estudio y el modelo formal." Manuscript, Universidad Simón Bolívar-GAUS, Caracas.

Guillén, Maryluz. 2002. *Democracia y ciudadanía: Organizaciones de derechos humanos en Venezuela, 1989–2000*. Master's thesis, Universidad Simón Bolívar, Caracas.

Guillén, Maryluz, and María Pilar García-Guadilla. 2006. "Las organizaciones de derechos humanos y el proceso constituyente: Alcance y limitaciones de la constitucionalización de la inclusión en Venezuela." *Cuadernos del Cendes* 23 (61): 69–98.

Gupta, Akhil. 1995. "Blurred Boundaries: The Discourse of Corruption, the Culture of Politics, and the Imagined State." *American Ethnologist* 22 (2): 375–402.

Habermas, Jurgen. 1989. *The Structural Transformation of the Public Sphere: An Inquiry into a Category of Bourgeois Society*. Cambridge: MIT Press.

Hall, Stuart. 1997. "The Work of Representation." In *Representation: Cultural Representations and Signifying Practices*, edited by Stuart Hall, 13–74. London: Sage.

Haller, Dieter, and Chris Shore. 2005. "Sharp Practice: Anthropology and the Study of Corruption." In *Corruption: Anthropological Perspectives*, edited by Chris Shore and Dieter Haller, 1–28. London: Pluto.

Hansen, Thomas Blom, and Finn Stepputat. 2001. Introduction to *States of Imagination: Ethnographic Explorations of the Postcolonial State*, edited by Thomas Blom Hansen and Finn Stepputat, 1–38. Durham: Duke University Press.

Hanson, James. 1977. "Cycles of Economic Growth and Structural Change since 1950." In *Venezuela: The Democratic Experience*, edited by John Martz and David Myers, 93–112. New York: Praeger.

Hardt, Michael, and Antonio Negri. 2000. *Empire*. Cambridge: Harvard University Press.

———. 2004. *Multitude: War and Democracy in the Age of Empire*. New York: Penguin.

Harnecker, Marta. 2005. *Understanding the Venezuelan Revolution*. New York: Monthly Review.

Hawkins, Kirk A. 2003. "Populism in Venezuela: The Rise of *Chavismo*." *Third World Quarterly* 24 (6): 1137–80.

———. 2009. "Is Chávez Populist? Measuring Populist Discourse in Comparative Perspective." *Comparative Political Studies* 42 (8): 1040–67.

Hawkins, Kirk A., and David R. Hansen. 2006. "Dependent Civil Society: The Círculos Bolivarianos in Venezuela." *Latin American Research Review* 41 (1): 102–32.

Hawkins, Kirk A., and Guillermo Rosas. 2006. "Social Spending in Chávez's Venezuela." Paper presented at the annual meeting of the Southern Political Science Association, Atlanta, Ga., January 5–7.

Hayden, Tom. 2004. *Street Wars: Gangs and the Future of Violence*. New York: New Press.

Hechter, Michael. 2004. "From Class to Culture." *American Journal of Sociology* 110 (2): 400–445.

Hellinger, Daniel. 1984. "Venezuela: From Populism to Neoliberalism." *Latin America Perspectives* 43 (Fall): 33–59.

———. 1991. *Venezuela: Tarnished Democracy*. Boulder, Colo.: Westview Press.

———. 2001. "Chávez, Globalization, and *Tercermundialismo*." Paper presented at the Congress of the Latin American Studies Association, Washington, D.C., September 2–8.

———. 2003. "Political Overview: The Breakdown of Puntfijismo and the Rise of Chavismo." In *Venezuelan Politics in the Chávez Era: Class, Polarization, and Conflict*, edited by Steven Ellner and Daniel Hellinger, 27–54. Boulder, Colo.: Lynne Rienner.

———. 2005. "Venezuela en el siglo veinte: La formación de la sociedad civil." In *Los projectos y las realidades: América Latina en el siglo veinte*, edited by Eduardo Cavieres, 159–82. Valparaíso, Chile: Ediciones Universitarias de Valparaíso.

Hernández, Juan Antonio. 2004. "Against the Comedy of Civil Society: Posthegemony, Media, and the 2002 Coup d'etat in Venezuela." *Journal of Latin American Cultural Studies* 13 (1): 137–45.

Hernández, M. 1982. "Habitantes del 23 de enero comprometieron a organismos a solucionarles sus problemas." *Ultimas Noticias*, January 21.

Holloway, John. 2002. *Changing the World without Taking Power: The Meaning of Revolution Today*. London: Pluto.

Hopenhayn, Martin. 2000. "Nuevas formas de ser ciudadano: ¿La diferencia hace la diferencia?" *Revista RELEA* 11:109–22.

Huntemann, Nina. 2003. "A Promise Diminished: The Politics of Low-Power Radio." In *Communities of the Air: Radio Century, Radio Culture*, edited by Susan Merrill, 76–92. Durham: Duke University Press.

Huntington, Samuel. 1968. *Political Order in Changing Societies*. New Haven: Yale University Press.

Hyppolite, Nelson. 2000. "Por Estas Calles." Paper presented at International Communication Association meeting, Acapulco, Mexico, June 15.

Ianni, Octavio. 1975. *La formación del estado populista en América Latina*. Mexico: Ediciones Era.

Ikegami, Eiko. 2005. *Bonds of Civility: Aesthetic Networks and the Political Origins of Japanese Culture*. New York: Cambridge University Press.

Ishibashi, Jun. 2003. "Hacia una apertura del debate sobre el racismo en Venezuela: Exclusión e inclusión estereotipada de personas 'negras' en los medios de comunicación." In *Políticas de identidades y diferencias sociales en tiempos de globalización*, edited by D. Mato, 33–61. Caracas: FACES-UCV.

Izarra, William. 2004. "La UBE es poder popular." *Aporrea*, July 12. http://www.aporrea.org/actualidad/a8899.html.

James, Daniel. 1988. *Resistance and Integration: Peronism and the Argentine Working Class, 1946–1976*. Cambridge: Cambridge University Press.

Jelin, Elisabeth. 1999. "Toward a Culture of Participation and Citizenship: Challenges for a More Equitable World." In *Cultures of Politics/Politics of Cultures: Re-visioning Latin American Social Movements*, edited by Sonia Alvarez, Arturo Escobar, and Evelina Dagnino, 405–14. Boulder, Colo.: Westview.

Joseph, Gilbert, and Daniel Nugent. 1994. "Popular Culture and State Formation in Revolutionary Mexico." In *Everyday Forms of State Formation*, edited by Gilbert Joseph and Daniel Nugent, 3–23. Durham: Duke University Press.

Karl, Terry Lynn. 1986. "Petroleum and Political Pacts: The Transition to "Democracy in Venezuela." In *Transition from Authoritarian Rule: Latin America*, edited by Guillermo O'Donnell, Philippe C. Schmitter, and Laurence Whitehead, 196–219. Baltimore: Johns Hopkins Press.

———. 1995. "The Venezuelan Petro-State and the Crisis of 'Its' Democracy." In *Venezuelan Democracy under Stress*, edited by Jennifer McCoy, Andrés Serbin, William C. Smith, and Andrés Stambouli, 33–55. Miami: University of Miami North-South Center.

———. 1997. *The Paradox of Plenty: Oil Booms and Petro-States*. Berkeley: University of California Press.

Katsiaficas, G. 2007. "El significado de la autonomía." Caosmosis biblioweb, November 9. http//caosmosis.acracia.net/wp2pdf/texto_de_caosmosis.pdf.

Kitschelt, Herbert. 2000. "Linkages between Citizens and Politicians in Democratic Polities." *Comparative Political Studies* 33 (6–7): 845–79.

Kitschelt, Herbert, and Steven I. Wilkinson, eds. 2006. *Patrons, Clients, and Policies: Patterns of Democratic Accountability and Political Competition*. New York: Cambridge University Press.

Korzenny, Felipe, Stella Ting-Toomey, and Elizabeth Schiff. 1992. *Mass Media Effects across Cultures*. London: Sage, Speech Communication Association International and Intercultural Communication Division.

Lacabana, Miguel, and Cecelia Cariola. 2005. "Construyendo la participación popular y una nueva cultura del agua en Venezuela." *Cuadernos del CENDES* 22 (59): 111–36.

Laclau, Ernesto. 1977. *Politics and Ideology in Marxist Theory: Capitalism, Fascism, Populism*. London: New Left.

———. 1978. "Hacia una teoría del populismo." In *Política e ideología en la teoría marxista: Capitalismo, fascismo, populismo*, edited by Ernesto Laclau, 165–233. México: Siglo Veintiuno Editores.

———. 1985. "Tesis acerca de la forma hegemónica de la política." In *Hegemonía y alternativas políticas en América Latina*, edited by Julio Labastida and Martín del Campo, 19–44. Mexico: Siglo Veintiuno Editores.

———. 2005. *La razón populista*. México: Fondo de Cultura Económica.

Lander, Edgardo. 1995. *Neoliberalismo, sociedad civil y democracia: Ensayos sobre América Latina y Venezuela*. Caracas: Universidad Central de Venezuela.

———. 2004. "El campo político de fuerzas y alianzas: Actores, tensiones y poder." Paper presented at the national seminar Política social: ¿Un nuevo paradigma? Escuela de Gerencia Social, Universidad Central de Venezuela, Caracas.

———. 2007. "El referéndum sobre la reforma constitucional." Editorial, Transnational Institute, December 24. http://www.tni.org/detail_page.phtml?act_id=17740.

Lander, Luis E., and Margarita López Maya. 2005. "Referendo revocatorio y elecciones regionales en Venezuela: Geografía electoral de la polarización." *Revista Venezolana de Economía y Ciencias Sociales* 11 (1): 33–58.

La Rotta Morán, Alicia. 1999. "Le tengo el ojo puesto a La Casona." *El Universal*, February 10.

Lasarte Valcárcel, Javier. 1992. *Sobre literatura venezolana*. Caracas: Ediciones La Casa de Bello.

———. 1995. *Juego y nacio: Postmodernismo y vanguardia en Venezuela*. Caracas: FUNDARTE/Alcaldía de Caracas.

Lawson, Kay. 1980. "Political parties and linkage." In *Political Parties and Linkage: A Comparative Perspective*, edited by Kay Lawson, 3–24. New Haven: Yale University Press.

Lazar, Sian. 2004. "Personalist Politics, Clientelism, and Citizenship: Local Elections in El Alto, Bolivia." *Bulletin of Latin American Research* 23 (2): 228–43.

Lebowitz, Michael. 2003. "Venezuela National Union of Workers." *ZNET*, April 2. http://www.zmag.org.

Legler, Thomas, Sharon Lean, and Dexter S. Boniface, eds. 2007. *Promoting Democracy in the Americas*. Baltimore: Johns Hopkins University Press.

Levine, Daniel H. 1973. *Conflict and Political Change in Venezuela*. Princeton: Princeton University Press.

———. 1981. *Religion and Politics in Latin America: The Catholic Church in Venezuela and Colombia*. Princeton: Princeton University Press.

———. 1990. "How Not to Understand Liberation Theology, Nicaragua, or Both." *Journal of Interamerican Studies and World Affairs* 32 (3): 229–45.

———. 1992. *Popular Voices in Latin American Catholicism*. Princeton: Princeton University Press.

———. 2002. "The Decline and Fall of Democracy in Venezuela: Ten Theses." *Bulletin of Latin American Research* 21 (2): 248–69.

Levine, Donald N. 1995. *Visions of the Sociological Tradition*. Chicago: University of Chicago Press.

Leyton, Tulio. 1976. "Falta de agua cobra características dramáticas en barrios y urbanizaciones." *Ultimas Noticias*, October 4.

Lichterman, Paul. 2005. *Elusive Togetherness: Church Groups Trying to Bridge America's Divisions*. Princeton: Princeton University Press.

Lindbeck, Assar, and Jorgen W. Weibull. 1987. "Balanced budget redistribution as the outcome of political competition." *Public Choice* 52 (3): 273–97.

Líneas generales del plan de desarrollo económico y social de la nación. 2001–2007. Caracas: Ministerio del Poder Popular de Planificación y Finanzas.

Linz, Juan, and Alfred Stepan, eds. 1996. *Problems of Democratic Transition and Consolidation: Southern Europe, South American, and Post-Communist Europe*. Baltimore: Johns Hopkins University Press.

Lombardi, Maria Laura. 1982. "Se justifica el secuestro de un camión?" *El Nacional*, January 21.

Lomnitz, Larisa Adler. 1988. "Informal Exchange Networks in Formal Systems: A Theoretical Model." *American Anthropologist* 90:42–55.

Lomnitz-Adler, Claudio. 1992. *Exits from the Labyrinth*. Berkeley: University of California Press.

López, Ramón. 2005. Interview with Alejandro Velasco.

López Maya, Margarita. 1997. "El repertorio de la protesta popular en Venezuela, 1989–1994," *Cuadernos del CENDES* 14 (36): 109–30.

———. 1999. "Venezuela: la rebellion popular del 27 de febrero de 1989." *Revista Venezolana de Economía y Ciencias Sociales* 5 (2–3): 177–200.

———. 2000. "Refounding the Republic: The Political Project of *Chavismo*." *NACLA Report on the Americas* 33 (6): 22–28.

———. 2003. "Hugo Chávez Frias: His Movement and His Presidency." In *Venezuelan Politics in the Chavez Era: Class, Polarization, and Conflict*, edited by Steve Ellner and Daniel Hellinger, 73–92. Boulder, Colo.: Lynne Rienner.

———. 2005. *Del Viernes Negro al Referendo Revocatorio*. Caracas: Alfadil.

———, ed. 2006. *El bravo pueblo*. CD-ROM database. Caracas: Universidad Central de Venezuela-Consejo de Desarrollo Científico y Humanístico.

———. 2008. "Caracas: Estado, sujeto popular y cómo hacer para que las cosas funcionen." Unpublished manuscript, Universidad Central de Venezuela, Caracas.

López Maya, Margarita, and Luis E. Lander. 2006. "Venezuela: Las elecciones presidenciales de 2006 ¿Hacia el socialismo del siglo veintiuno?" Paper presented at the seminar América Latina 2006: Balance de un año de elecciones 2 (CEPC), Madrid, December.

López Maya, Margarita, David Smilde, and Keta Stephany. 2002. *Protesta y cultura en Venezuela: Los marcos de acción colectiva en 1999*. Caracas: FACES-UCV/CENDES/FONACIT.

López Villa, M. A. 1986. "La arquitectura del 2 de diciembre." *Boletín del Centro de Investigaciones Históricas y Estéticas* 27:148–72.

López Villa, M. A. 1994. "Gestión urbanística, revolución democrática y dictadura militar en Venezuela (1945–1958)." *Urbana* 14–15:103–19.

Lugo Galicia, Hermán. 2004. "Partidos políticos de oposición consideran ilegítimo al gobierno." *El Nacional*, August 17.

MacRae, Donald. 1969. "Populism as Ideology." In *Populism: Its Meaning and National Characteristics*, edited by Ghita Ionesco and Ernest Gellner, 153–65. New York: Macmillan.

Magallanes, Rodolfo. 2005. "La igualdad en la República Bolivariana de Venezuela (1999–2004)." *Revista Venezolana de Economía y Ciencias Sociales* 11 (2): 71–99.

Mainwaring, Scott P. 1999. *Rethinking Party Systems in the Third Wave of Democratization: The Case of Brazil*. Stanford, Calif.: Stanford University Press.

Mairena, María José. 2004. "Coordinadora democrática intentará impugnación para repetir el revocatorio." *El Nacional*, August 17.

Manaure, Mateo. 1982. "El 23 De Enero: Un Bravo Pueblo." *El Nacional*, January 23.

Mankekar, Purnima. 1999. *Screening Culture, Viewing Politics: An Ethnography of Television, Womanhood, and Nation in Postcolonial India*. Durham: Duke University Press.

Marcano, Cristina, and Alberto Barrera Tyszka. 2004. *Hugo Chávez sin uniforme: Una historia personal*. Caracas: Editorial Debate.

———. 2007. *Hugo Chávez: The Definitive Biography of Venezuela's Controversial President*. New York: Random House.

Marcus, John T. 1961. "Transcendence and Charisma." *Western Political Quarterly* 14 (March): 236–41.

Márquez, Patricia. 1999. *The Street is My Home: Youth and Violence in Caracas*. Stanford, Calif.: Stanford University Press.

Martín Barbero, Jesús. 1993. *Communication, Culture and Hegemony: From the Media to Mediations*. London: Sage.

Martínez, Ibsen. 2002. "Cordial abominación de la TV." *Revista Bigott*, no. 61 (September–December): 70–75.

———. 2005. "Romancing the Globe." *Foreign Policy* 151:48–56.

Martz, John D., and Enrique Baloyra. 1979. *Political Attitudes in Venezuela: Societal Cleavages and Public Opinion*. Austin: University of Texas Press.

Martz, John D., and David J. Myers, eds. 1977. *Venezuela: The Democratic Experience*. New York: Praeger.

Mata Carnevali, María Gabriela. 2008. "Diálogo con Jesús 'Chucho' García. Red de Organizaciones Afrovenezolanas: Balance y perspectivas. Entre la confrontación y la persuasión." *Humania del Sur: Revista de estudios Latinoamericanos, Africanos y Asiáticos* 3 (5): 139–46.

Mayer, Arno J. 2000. *The Furies: Violence and Terror in the French and Russian Revolutions*. Princeton: Princeton University Press.

McAnany, Emile G., and Antonio La Pastina. 1994. "Telenovela Audiences: A Review and Methodological Critique of Latin American Research." *Communication Research* 21 (6): 828–49.

McClintoch, Cynthia. 2001. "Peru's Sendero Luminoso Rebellion: Origins and Trajectory." In *Power and Popular Protest: Latin American Social Movements*, edited by Susan Eckstein, 61–101. Berkeley: University of California Press.

McCoy, Jennifer, Andrés Serbin, William C. Smith and Andrés Stambouli, eds. 1995. *Venezuelan Democracy under Stress*. Miami, Fla.: University of Miami North-South Center.

McCoy, Jennifer L., and David Myers. 2004. Introduction to *The Unraveling of Representative Democracy in Venezuela*, edited by Jennifer L. McCoy and David J. Myers, 1–10. Baltimore: Johns Hopkins University Press.

Medina, Jesus Petit. 1969a. "Barricadas y disparos: tomado el 23 de enero por sus habitantes como protesta por llevar 3 dias sin agua." *Ultimas Noticias*, May 5.

———. 1969b. "Tomaron habitantes Calle de Propatria en protesta por aguas negras en plena via." *Ultimas Noticias*, May 18.

Mendoza, María Inés. 1992. *La telenovela latinoamericana en la década del 80*. Madrid: Universidad Complutense.

———. 1996. "La telenovela venezolana: De artesanal a industrial." *Diálogos de la comunicación* 44:37–50.

Meza, Alfredo. 2004a. "Battaglini descarta impedir inscripción de cedulados de la Misión Identidad." *El Nacional*, June 21.

———. 2004b. "Rodríguez exhorta a Hugo Chávez a no hacer proselitismo en cadenas." *El Nacional*, June 11.

Michels, Robert. 1915. *The Iron Law of Oligarchy: A Sociological Study of the Oligarchical Tendencies of Modern Democracy*. New York: Free Press.

Ministerio de Comunicación e Información. 2005. *Misión Sucre*. Document in possession of authors.

Miranda, Julio. 1995. *Poesía en el espejo: Estudio y antología de la nueva lírica femenina venezolana (1970–1994)*. Caracas: Fundarte.

Mische, Ann. 2008. *Partisan Publics: Communication and Contention across Brazilian Youth Activist Networks*. Princeton: Princeton University Press.

Misión Ribas. n.d.a. *Formación de la ciudadanía en el marco de la refundación de la República*. Pamphlet. Caracas: Misión Ribas.

———. n.d.b. *Orientaciones generales para la facilitación*. Pamphlet. Caracas: Misión Ribas.

———. n.d.c. *Política educativa de la Misión José Félix Ribas: Nueva etapa*. Pamphlet. Caracas: Misión Ribas.

Misión Robinson. n.d. *Una sola misión: Tercer taller nacional Misión Robinson*. Caracas: Misión Robinson, Comisión Presidencial.

Mitchell, Timothy. 1991. "The Limits of the State: Beyond Statist Approaches and their Critics." *American Political Science Review* 85 (1): 77–96.

———. 1999. "Society, Economy, and the State Effect." In *State/Culture: State-*

Formation after the Cultural Turn, edited by George Steinmetz, 76–97. Ithaca, N.Y.: Cornell University Press.

Molina, José E. 2004. "The Unraveling of Venezuela's Party System: From Party Rule to Personalistic Politics and Deinstitutionalization." In *The Unraveling of Representative Democracy in Venezuela*, edited by Jennifer L. McCoy and David J. Meyers, 152–78. Baltimore: Johns Hopkins University Press.

Molloy, Sylvia. 1991. Introduction in *Women's Writing in Latin America: An Anthology*, edited by Sara Castro-Klaren, Sylvia Molloy, and Beatriz Sarlo, 107–24. Boulder, Colo.: Westview.

Moreno, C. 1982. "No ceden habitantes de Monte Piedad y mantienen retenidos 10 vehículos." *Ultimas Noticias*, January 19.

Movimiento Bolivariano Revolucionario 200. n.d. (ca. 1992 or 1993). ¿Y como salir de este laberinto? Propuesta Bolivariana. 12 pages. Library of the Centro de Estudios de Desarrollo, Universidad Central de Venezuela, Caracas.

———. 1994. *Conferencia de organización*. 15 pages. Caracas: Coordinadora Nacional del Movimiento Bolivariano Revolucionario 200.

Mudde, Cas. 2004. "The Populist Zeitgeist." *Government and Opposition* 39 (Fall): 541–63.

Múnera, Leopoldo. 1998. *Rupturas y continuidades: Poder y movimiento popular*. Bogotá: Universidad Nacional, Lepri-Cerec.

Muñoz, Agustín Blanco. 1998. *Habla el Comandante*. Caracas: Universidad Central de Venezuela.

Nader, Laura. 1972. "Up the Anthropologist: Perspectives Gained from Studying Up." In *Reinventing Anthropology*, edited by D. Hymes, 284–311. New York: Pantheon.

Navarro, Juan Carlos. 1995. "In Search of the Lost Pact: Consensus Lost in the 1980s and 1990s." In *Venezuelan Democracy under Stress*, edited by Jennifer McCoy, Andres Serbín, William C. Smith, and Andres Stambouli, 13–31. New Brunswick, N.J.: Transaction.

Neuhouser, Kevin. 1992. "Democratic Stability in Venezuela: Elite Consensus or Class Compromise?" *American Sociological Review* 57:117–35.

Newman, Kathy. 2003. "The Forgotten Fifteen Million: Black Radio, Radicalism, and the Construction of the 'Negro Market.'" In *Communities of the Air: Radio Century, Radio Culture*, edited by Susan Merrill Squier, 109–33. Durham: Duke University Press.

Norden, Deborah L. 2003. "Democracy in Uniform: Chavez and the Venezuelan Armed Forces." In *Venezuelan Politics in the Chavez Era: Class, Polarization and Conflict*, edited by Steve Ellner and Daniel Hellinger, 93–112. Boulder, Colo.: Lynne Rienner.

Nuijten, Monique. 2003. *Power, Community, and the State: The Political Anthropology of Organisation in Mexico*. London: Pluto.

Ocampo, José Antonio, and Juan Martín, eds. 2003. *A Decade of Light and Shadow: Latin America and the Caribbean in the 1990s*. Santiago, Chile: Economic Commission for Latin America and the Caribbean.

O'Donnell, Guillermo. 1999. "Polyarchies and the (Un)Rule of Law in Latin America: A Partial Conclusion." In *The (Un)Rule of Law and the Underprivileged in Latin America*, edited by Juan E. Méndez, Guillermo O'Donnell, and Paulo Sérgio Pinheiro, 303–37. Notre Dame, Ind.: University of Notre Dame Press.

Oficina Técnica Municipal Caracas. 2005. "Democratización de la ciudad y transformación urbana: propuesta de los CTU a la Misión Hábitat." Caracas.

Oficina Técnica Municipal Coroní. 2004. "Comités de Tierras Urbanas (CTU)," Etado Bolívar, Municipio Caroní.

Olivera, Oscar (with Tom Lewis). 2004. *Cochabamba: Water War in Bolivia*. Boston: South End.

Orellana de García-Maldonado, Angelina. 1989. *Sesenta años de experiencia en desarrollos urbanísticos de bajo costo en Venezuela*. Caracas: Instituto Nacional de la Vivienda.

Ottaway, Marina. 2003. *Democracy Challenged: The Rise of Semi-authoritarianism*. Washington: Carnegie Endowment for International Peace.

Pacheco, Milvia, Elba Ramos A., and Mirian Rangel R. 1987. "Aproximación al estudio de la parroquia 23 de Enero de Caracas." Dissertation, Universidad Central de Venezuela, Caracas.

Padrón, Leonardo. 1994. *Colección LA DIOSA de la poesía*. Caracas: Editorial Pomaire.

———. 1998. "La mal querida: Apuntes para odiarla mejor." Cátedra de Literatura "José Antonio Ramos Sucre," Universidad de Salamanca.

———. 2002. "La telenovela: ¿Género literario del siglo vientiuno?" *Revista Bigott*, no. 61 (September–December): 44–54.

———. 2004. "Bajo la lupa de Leonardo Padrón." *Zeta*, July 30, 37.

Panizza, Francisco. 2005. "Introduction: Populism and the Mirror of Democracy." In *Populism and the Mirror of Democracy*, edited by Francisco Panizza, 1–31. London: Verso.

Pantin, Yolanda. 2002. "El hueso pélvico." Pequeña Venecia. http://www.poiesologia.com/poema.php?codigo=1116.

———. 2004. *Poesía Reunida*. Caracas: Otero Ediciones.

Pantin, Yolanda, and Verónica Jaffé. 2003. "El bárbaro y las trampas de la poesía." Pequeña Venecia.

Pantin, Yolanda, and Ana Teresa Torres, eds. 2003. *El hilo de la voz: Antología crítica de escritoras venezolanas del siglo viente*. Caracas: Fundación Polar.

Parenti, Christian. 2005. "Hugo Chávez and Petro-Populism." *The Nation*, April 11, 15–21.

Pásara, Luis. 1991. *La otra cara de la luna: Nuevos actores sociales en el Perú*. Buenos Aires: Centro de Estudios de Democracia y Sociedad.

Peattie, Lisa Redfield. 1968. *The View from the Barrio*. Ann Arbor: University of Michigan Press.

Penfold-Bencerra, Michael. 2007. "Clientelism and Social Funds: Empirical Evidence from Chávez's Misiones Programs." *Latin American Politics and Society* 49 (4): 63–84.

Pérez, José Manuel. 1978. "Bochiches en el 23 de enero por falta de agua con partici-
pacion de encapuchados con armas largas." *Ultimas Noticias*, October 6.

Pérez, Lyon. 1976. "Betancourt arremete contra el M.A.S. por su crecimiento, re-
sponde Eloy Torres." *Ultimas Noticias*, September 15.

Pérez Jiménez, Marcos. 1954. "Presidencia de la República, Decreto No. 115." *Gaceta
Oficial de la República de Venezuela, Año 82—Mes 8* (24.462), 1–3.

———. 1955. "Copia textual del discurso pronunciado por el Presidente de la República, General Marcos Pérez Jiménez a la nación." *El Nacional*, December 3.

Petkoff, Teodoro. 1970. *Socialismo para Venezuela?* Caracas: Editorial Domingo
Fuentes.

———. 1976. *Proceso a la izquierda, O de la falsa conducta revolucionaria*. Barcelona:
Editorial Planeta.

———. 2005. *Las dos izquierdas*. Caracas: Alfadil.

Pino Iturrieta, Elías. 2001. "La lectura tendenciosa de la historia. Zamora como
invento partidario." http://www.ucab.edu.ve/tl_files/sala_de_prensa/recursos/
ucabista/feb-2001/p30.htm.

Policastro, Cristina. 2002. "TV en clave amistosa." *Revista Bigott*, no. 61 (September–December): 56–61.

PROVEA (Programa Venezolano de Educación-Acción en Derechos Humanos). 1999,
2004, 2005, 2006, 2007. *Situación de los derechos humanos en Venezuela: Informe
anual octubre/septiembre*. Caracas: PROVEA.

Putnam, Robert. 2000. *Bowling Alone: The Collapse and Revival of American Community*. New York: Simon and Schuster.

Quijano, Aníbal. 1995. "Raza, etnia y nación: Cuestiones abiertas." In *José Carlos
Mariategui y Europa*, edited by Roland Forgues, 167–88. Lima: Editorial Amauta.

Quintero, Manuel. 2003. "La Iglesia no puede ser neutral." Agencia Latinoamericana y
Caribeña de Comunicación (ALC), December 24. http://www.alcnoticias.org.

Quiroz, María Teresa. 1993. "La telenovela en el Perú." In *Serial Fiction in TV: The
Latin American Telenovelas*, edited by Anamaria Faduli, 33–46. Sao Paulo: Universidad de Sao Paulo.

Rama, Ángel. 1996. *The Lettered City (Post-Contemporary Interventions)*. Durham:
Duke University Press.

Ramos Rollon, María Luisa. 1995. *De las protestas a las propuestas: Identidad, acción y
relevancia política del movimiento vecinal en Venezuela*. Caracas: Nueva Sociedad.

Rangel, Domingo Alberto. 1990. "Nuestras guerrillas de los años sesenta fracasaron
porque eran solo un detonante para un golpe." *Ultimas Noticias*, August 26.

Rangel, Domingo Alberto, and Agustín Blanco Muñoz. 1981. *La lucha armada: La
izquierda revolucionaria insurge*. Caracas: Universidad Central de Venezuela-FACES.

Ray, Talton. 1969. *Politics of the Barrios of Venezuela*. Berkeley: University of California
Press.

Reich, Otto. 2005. "Latin America's Terrible Two: Fidel Castro and Hugo Chávez Constitute an Axis of Evil." *National Review Digital*, April 11. http://nrd.nationalreview
.com.

Reid, Michael. 2007. *Forgotten Continent: The Battle for Latin America's Soul.* New Haven: Yale University Press.

Reisz, Susana. 1996. *Voces sexuadas: Género y poesía en Hispanoamérica.* Lleida: Ediciones de la Universitat de Lleida.

Relea, F. 2005. "23 de Enero, bastión del chavismo." *El País* (Madrid), December 3.

Remedi, Gustavo. 1997. "The Production of Local Public Spheres: Community Radio Stations." In *Latin American Cultural Studies: A Reader,* edited by Ana Del Sarto, Alicia Ríos, and Abril Trigo, 513–34. Durham: Duke University Press.

Reyes, Asención, and Ramón Navarro. 2004. "Oposición solicita al CNE controlar gastos de campaña presidencial." *El Nacional,* June 8.

Reyes, María Alejandra. 2003. "Una Cosita Rica nos atrapa cada noche." *Revista Paréntesis (magazine of the El Carabobeño, Valencia),* October 12.

Riley, Dylan. 2005. "Civic Associations and Authoritarian Regimes in the Interwar Period: Italy and Spain in Comparative Perspective." *American Sociological Review* 70:288–310.

Riley, Dylan, and Juan J. Fernandez. 2006. "The Authoritarian Foundations of Civic Culture: Spain and Italy in Comparative Perspective." Working Paper No. 135–06, Institute for Research on Labor and Employment Working Paper Series, University of California, Berkeley.

Rincón, Elías. 2002. "Acta de entrega de los primeros informes de la comisión presidencial para el Diálogo." Speech presented at public event, Teatro Teresa Carreño, Caracas, August 14.

Rivas, M. 2004. "El problema de los barrios." *Revista SIC* 665:211–21.

Rivas-Rojas, Raquel. 2001. *The Venezuelan Identity Tale (1935–1941) from Criollismo to Populist Regionalism.* London: University of London Press.

Roberts, Kenneth. 1998. *Deepening Democracy? The Modern Left and Social Movements in Chile and Peru.* Stanford, Calif.: Stanford University Press.

———. 2001. "Party-Society Linkages and Democratic Representation in Latin America." Paper presented at the 23rd International Congress of the Latin American Studies Association, Washington, D.C., September 6–8.

———. 2002. "Social Inequalities without Class Cleavages in Latin America's Neoliberal Era." *Studies in Comparative International Development* 36:3–33.

———. 2003. "Social Polarization and the Populist Resurgence in Venezuela." In *Venezuelan Politics in the Chavez Era: Class, Polarization, and Conflict,* edited by Steve Ellner and Daniel Hellinger, 55–72. Boulder, Colo.: Lynne Rienner.

Rodriguez, Francisco. 2008. "An Empty Revolution: The Unfulfilled Promises of Hugo Chávez." *Foreign Affairs* 87 (2): 49–62.

Rohter, Larry. 2000. "Officials Say Chavez Wins In Venezuela." *New York Times,* July 31.

Rojas, Alberto. 2002. "Gobierno negó apoyo armado." *El Universal,* August 6.

———. 2003. "Exigen al BCV 'un millardito' de las reservas internacionales." *El Universal,* November 10.

Rojas Vera, L. R. 1993. *La telenovela venezolana: El éxito de un negocio comunicacional.* Maracaibo: Imprenta de Mérida.

Roldán, Esteva Grillet. 1990. *Medios de comunicación y lucha ideológica en la Venezuela del boom petrolero: Cuatro ensayos y un prólogo desechable*. Caracas: Ediciones Metropolitanas.

Rondón, Alí E. 2006. *Medio siglo de besos y querellas: La telenovela nuestra de cada día, Trópicos*. Caracas: Alfa.

Ruben, Brent, and Leah A. Lievrouw. 1990. *Mediation, Information, and Communication*. New Brunswick, N.J.: Transaction.

Rubin, Jeffrey W. 1997. *Decentering the Regime: Ethnicity, Radicalism and Democracy in Juchitán, Mexico*. Durham: Duke University Press.

———. 2004. "Meanings and Mobilizations: A Cultural Politics Approach to Social Movements and States." *Latin American Research Review* 39 (3): 106–42.

———. 2006. "In the Streets or in the Institutions?" *LASAForum* 37 (1): 26–29.

Russotto, Márgara. 1997. *Bárbaras e ilustrados: Las máscaras de género en la periferia moderna. Caracas*: Fondo Editorial Tropykos.

Salamanca, Luis. 1997. *Crisis de la modernización y crisis de la democracia en Venezuela*. Caracas: Universidad Central de Venezuela.

———. 2004. "Civil Society: Late Bloomers." In *The Unraveling of Representative Democracy in Venezuela*, edited by Jennifer L. McCoy and David J. Meyers, 93–114. Baltimore: Johns Hopkins University Press.

Salas, Marcos. 2003. "Lina Ron, 'Voy camino a la santidad.'" *Tal Cual*, September 10.

Salas, Yolanda. 1987. *Bolívar y la história en la conciencia popular*. Caracas: Universidad Simón Bolívar.

Salazar, Carolina. 2003. "Los Comités de Tierra Urbana: ¿Un nuevo movimiento social?" Manuscript. Caracas: Universidad Simón Bolívar.

Sarli, Alfredo Cilento. 1996. "La visión estratégica del Banco Obrero en el período 1959–1969." In *Leopoldo Martínez Olavarria: Desarrollo urbano, vivienda y estado*, edited by Alberto Lovera. Caracas: Fondo Editorial Alemo.

Scannell, Paddy, Philip Schlesinger, and Colin Sparks. 1992. *Culture and Power: A Media, Culture, and Society Reader*. Newbury Park, Calif.: Sage.

Scott, James C. 1977. *The Moral Economy of the Peasant: Rebellion and Subsistence in Southeast Asia*. New Haven: Yale University Press.

———. 1998. *Seeing Like a State: How Certain Schemes to Improve the Human Condition Have Failed*. New Haven: Yale University Press.

Seligman, Mitchell. 1992. *The Idea of Civil Society*. New York: Free Press.

Sharma, Aradhana, and Akhil Gupta. 2006. "Introduction: Rethinking the State in the Age of Globalization." In *The Anthropology of the State: A Reader*, edited by Aradhana Sharma and Akhil Gupta, 10–40. Malden, Mass.: Blackwell.

Shefner, Jon. 2008. *The Illusion of Civil Society: Democratization and Community Mobilization in Low-Income Mexico*. University Park: Pennsylvania State University Press.

Shifter, Michael. 2007. "Slouching Toward Authoritarianism." *Foreign Affairs*, November 7.

Silva, Katiuska. 2004. "Verdades y turbulencias se aproximan a Cosita Rica." *El Nacional*, April 27.

Silva, Katiuska, and Alexis Correia. 2004. "El humor es la única inteligencia que ejercemos unánimemente." *El Nacional*, January 19.

Silverman, Sydel. 1977. "Patronage as Myth." In *Patrons and Clients in Mediterranean Societies*, edited by Ernest Gellner and John Waterbury, 7–19. London: Gerald Duckworth.

Skocpol, Theda, and Morris P. Fiorina, eds. 1999. *Civic Engagement in American Democracy*. Washington: Brookings Institution Press; New York: Russell Sage Foundation.

Skurski, Julie. 1994. "The Ambiguities of Authenticity in Latin America: *Doña Barbara* and the Construction of National Identity." *Poetics Today* 15 (4): 605–42.

Smilde, David. 2000. "Evangelicals Bring Chávez's Message to the People." *Oxford Analytica*, January 28.

———. 2004a. "Contradiction without Paradox: Evangelical Political Culture in the 1998 Venezuelan Elections." *Latin American Politics and Society* 46 (1): 75–102.

———. 2004b. "Los evangélicos y la polarización: La moralización de la política y la politización de la religión." *Revista Venezolana de Economía y Ciencias Sociales* 2 (2): 163–79.

———. 2004c. "Popular Publics: Street Protest and Plaza Preachers in Caracas." *International Review of Social History*. Supplement 49:179–95.

———. 2007. *Reason to Believe: Cultural Agency in Latin American Evangelicalism*. Berkeley: University of California Press.

———. 2008. "The Social Structure of Hugo Chávez." *Contexts* 7 (1): 38–42.

Smith, Anthony D. 1983. *Theories of Nationalism*. 2nd ed. Teaneck, N.J.: Holmes and Meier.

Smith, Christian, and Liesl Ann Haas. 1997. "Revolutionary Evangelicals in Nicaragua: Political Opportunity, Class Interests, and Religious Identity." *Journal of the Scientific Study of Religion* 36 (3): 440–54.

Snodgrass Godoy, Angelina. 2006. *Popular Injustice, Violence, Community, and Law in Latin America*. Stanford, Calif.: Stanford University Press.

Solaún, Mauricio, and Sidney Kronum. 1973. *Discrimination without Violence: Miscegenation and Racial Conflict in Latin America*. New York: Wiley.

Statistical Abstract of Latin America. Reference series (1955–2001). Los Angeles: University of California, Los Angeles Latin American Center.

Steinmetz, George. 1999. Introduction to *State/Culture: State Formation after the Cultural Turn*, edited by George Steinmetz, 1–50. Ithaca, N.Y.: Cornell University Press.

Stokes, Susan. 1995. *Cultures in Conflict: Social Movements and the State in Peru*. Berkeley: University of California Press.

———. 2005. "Perverse Accountability: A Formal Model of Machine Politics with Evidence from Argentina." *American Political Science Review* 99 (3): 315–25.

Sylvia, R., and C. Danopoulos. 2003. "The Chavez Phenomenon: Political Change in Venezuela." *Third World Quarterly* 24 (1): 63–76.

Tampio, Nicholas. 2005. "Can Multitude Save the Left?" *Theory and Event* 8(2). http://muse.jhu.edu/journals/theory_and_event/v008/8.2tampio.html.

Tanner Hawkins, Eliza. 2006. "Community Media in Venezuela." Paper presented at the annual meeting of the Latin American Studies Association, San Juan, Puerto Rico.

Taussig, Michael T. 1993. "*Maleficium*: State Fetishism." In *Fetishism as Cultural Discourse*, edited by Emily Apter and William Pietz, 152–85. Ithaca, N.Y.: Cornell University Press.

———. 1997. *The Magic of the State*. New York: Routledge.

Taylor, Charles. 1995. *Philosophical Arguments*. Cambridge: Harvard University Press.

Thompson, John B. 1994. "Communication and the Mediation of Social Worlds: Social Theory and the Media." In *Communication Theory Today*, edited by D. J. Crowley and David Mitchell, 1–26. Stanford, Calif.: Stanford University Press.

Tocqueville, Alexis de. 1835–39. *Democracy in America*. New York: Knopf, 1945.

Torres Rivero, Solmar. 2005. "Con la ley resorte la TV es más fatua." *Tal Cual*, August 18.

Trinkunas, Harold A. 2004. "The Military: From Marginalization to Center Stage." In *The Unraveling of Representative Democracy in Venezuela*, edited by Jennifer L. McCoy and David J. Meyers, 50–70. Baltimore: Johns Hopkins University Press.

Trouillot, Michel-Rolph. 2001. "The Anthropology of the State in the Age of Globalization." *Current Anthropology* 42 (1): 125–38.

Turner, Terrence. 1991. "Representing, Resisting, Rethinking: Historical Transformations of Kayapo Culture and Consciousness." In *Colonial Situations: Essays on the Contextualization of Ethnographic Knowledge*, edited by George W. Stocking, 285–313. Madison: University of Wisconsin Press.

Twine, France Winddance. 1998. *Racism in a Racial Democracy: The Maintenance of White Supremacy in Brazil*. New Brunswick, N.J.: Rutgers University Press.

Ugalde, Luis, Luis Pedro España, Carmen Scotto, Anabel Castillo, Tulio Hernández, Néstor Luis Luengo, Marcelinao Bisbal, and María Gabriela Ponce. 1994. *La Violencia en Venezuela*. Caracas: Monte Avila Editores Latinoamericana.

United Nations. 2010. *Report on the World Situation 2010*. New York: Department of Ecnomic and Social Affairs, Division for Social Policy and Development.

Urbina, Freddy. 1976. "Un joven muerto de balazo, otro herido, y numerosos intoxicados durante disturbios en el 23 de Enero." *Ultimas Noticias*, October 1.

———. 1978. "Murio uno de los niños heridos en tiroteo durante disturbios en sector del 23 de Enero." *Ultimas Noticias*, October 7.

Urla, Jacqueline. 1997. "Outlaw Language: Creating Alternative Public Spheres in Basque Free Radio." In *The Politics of Culture in the Shadow of Capital*, edited by Lisa Lowe and David Lloyd, 280–300. Durham: Duke University Press.

Valencia Ramirez, Cristobal. 2007. "Venezuela's Bolivarian Revolution: Who Are the Chavistas?" In *Venezuela: Hugo Chavez and the Decline of an Exceptional Democracy*, edited by Steve Ellner and Miguel Tinker Salas, 99–118. Lanham, Md.: Rowman and Littlefield.

Van Cott, Donna Lee. 2002. "Movimientos indígenas y transformación constitucional en Los Andes. Venezuela en perspectiva comparativa." *Revista venezolana de economía y ciencias sociales* 8 (3): 41–60.

VEC (Venezuelan Episcopal Conference). 2004a. "Seamos auténticos servidores del pueblo: Exhortación colectiva del Episcopado Venezolano." January 9. http://www.cev.org.ve.

———. 2004b. "Comunicado sobre decisión del CNE." March 3. http://www.cev.org.ve.

———. 2004c. "Palabras de Apertura 82 Asamblea." July 7. http://www.cev.org.ve.

———. 2004d. "Referendo, conciencia y responsabilidad." July 12. http://www.cev.org.ve.Velásquez, Ramón J. 1979. "Aspectos de la evolución política de Venezuela en el último medio siglo." In *Venezuela moderna: Medio siglo de historia, 1926–1976*, edited by Ramón J. Velasquez, 13–436. Caracas: Fundación Eugenio Mendoza.

Velasco, Alejandro. 2002. "The Hidden Injuries of Race: Democracy, Color, and Political Consciousness in Contemporary Venezuela." Masters thesis, Duke University.

Vila Planes, Enrique. 2003. "La economía social del proyecto bolivariano: Ideas controversiales." *Revista Venezolana de Economía y Ciencias Sociales* 9 (3): 111–43.

Villanueva, Carlos, and Carlos Celis Cepero. 1953. *La vivienda popular en Venezuela, 1928–1952*. Caracas: Banco Obrero.

Villanueva, Federico. 2008. "La política de vivienda para Venezuela." *Tecnología y Construcción* 24 (2): 79–82.

Viloria, C. 2002. "Grupo Carapaica disparó a la P.M." *El Universal*, August 5.

Wade, Peter. 1997. *Race and Ethnicity in Latin America*. London: Pluto Press.

Watters, Mary. 1933. *A History of the Church in Venezuela*. Chapel Hill: University of North Carolina Press.

Weber, Max. 1946. *From Max Weber: Essays in Sociology*. Translated, edited, and with an introduction by H. H. Gerth and C. Wright Mills. New York: Oxford University Press.

Wedeen, Lisa. 2008. *Peripheral Visions: Publics, Power, and Performance in Yemen*. Chicago: University of Chicago Press.

Weffort, Francisco. 1978. *O Populismo na política brasileira*. Rio de Janeiro: Paz e Terra.

Weyland, Kurt. 2001. "Clarifying a Contested Concept: Populism in the Study of Latin American Politics." *Comparative Politics* 34 (1): 1–22.

Weyland, Kurt. 2003a. "Economic Voting Reconsidered Crisis and Charisma in the Election of Hugo Chávez." *Comparative Political Studies* 36 (7): 822–48.

———. 2003b. "Venezuela's Worsening Political Crisis." *Foreign Affairs*, January–February. http://www.foreignaffairs.com.

Wiarda, Howard J. 2001a. *The Soul of Latin America*. New Haven: Yale University Press.

———. 2001b. "Venezuela Alert: Understanding Chávez." *Hemisphere Focus* 9(4), September 18. Washington: Center for Strategic and International Studies.

———. 2002. *Civil Society: The American Model and Third World Development*. Boulder, Colo.: Westview.

Wiesenfeld, Esther, and Euclides Sánchez, eds. 1995. *Psicología social comunitaria: Contribuciones Latinoamericanas*. Caracas: Fondo Editorial Tropykos.

Williams, Gareth. 2002. *The Other Side of the Popular: Neoliberalism and Subalternity*. Durham: Duke University Press.

Williams, Philip J. 1989. "The Catholic Church in the Nicaraguan Revolution: Differing Responses and New Challenges." In *The Progressive Church in Latin America*,
edited by Scott Mainwaring and Alexander Wilde, 64–102. Notre Dame, Ind.:
University of Notre Dame Press.

Winn, Peter. 1986. *Weavers of Revolution: The Yarur Workers and Chile's Road to Socialism*. New York: Oxford University Press.

Wortham, Erica Cusi. 2004. "Between the State and Indigenous Autonomy: Unpack-
ing Video Indígena in Mexico." *American Anthropologist* 106 (2): 363–69.

Wright, Winthrop. 1990. *Café con leche: Race, Class and National Image in Venezuela*.
Austin: University of Texas Press.

Zinn, Dorothy Louise, 2005. "Afterward: Anthropology and Corruption: The State
of the Art." In *Corruption: Anthropological Perspectives*, edited by D. Haller and
C. Shore, 229–42. London: Pluto.

Contributors

CAROLINA ACOSTA-ALZURU is associate professor in the Grady College of Journalism and Mass Communication at the University of Georgia. Her scholarship focuses on the links between media, culture, and society. She is the author of the book *Venezuela es una telenovela* (2007). Her research has been published in *Journalism and Mass Communication Monographs, Journal of Communication, Critical Studies in Media Communication, Popular Communication, Communication Review, Journal of Communication Inquiry*, and *Mass Communication and Society*, among others.

JULIA BUXTON is senior research fellow in the Centre for International Co-operation and Security at the University of Bradford, UK. She has published extensively on the social, economic, and political changes under way in Venezuela and is a specialist on the narcotic drugs trade, democratization programming, and post-conflict reconstruction. Recent publications include *The Politics of Narcotic Drugs* (Routledge, 2010) and numerous articles on Venezuela in anthologies and journals.

LUIS DUNO GOTTBERG is associate professor of Caribbean studies and film at Rice University. His current research for an upcoming book, "Dangerous People: Hegemony, Representation and Culture in Contemporary Venezuela," explores the relationship between popular mobilization, radical politics, and culture. He is the author of *Miradas al margen* (Fundación Cinemateca Nacional, 2008), *Solventando las diferencias: La ideología del mestizaje en Cuba* (Iberoamericana/Vervuer, 2003), *Imagen y subalternidad: El cine de Víctor Gaviria* (Cinemateca Nacional de Venezuela, 2003), and *Cultura e identidad racial en América Latina: Revista Estudios* (Universidad Simón Bolívar, 2002).

SUJATHA FERNANDES is an assistant professor of sociology at Queens College and the Graduate Center of the City University of New York. She is the author of *Cuba Represent! Cuban Arts, State Power, and the Making of New Revolutionary Cultures* (Duke, 2006) and *Who Can Stop the Drums? Urban Social Movements in Chávez's Venezuela* (Duke, 2010).

MARÍA PILAR GARCÍA-GUADILLA is professor of urban planning and political sciences at the Universidad Simón Bolívar, Venezuela. She is director of the Interdisciplinary Research Laboratory on Environmental, Urban, and Socio-political Conflict Resolution (GAUS-USB) and has more than 120 academic publications in books and scientific journals, including three edited books on social movements. Currently, she is researching New Bolivarian social organizations and working on a book about the post-constitutional conflicts in polarized Venezuela.

KIRK A. HAWKINS is assistant professor of political science at Brigham Young University. He is the author of *Venezuela's Chavismo and Populism in Comparative Perspective* (Cambridge, 2010). He studies Venezuelan politics and populism, as well as political parties and the politics of economic development. He has published articles in *Comparative Political Studies, Latin American Politics and Society, Latin American Research Review,* and *Third World Quarterly.*

TIMOTHY GILL, who compiled the index, is a graduate student at the University of Georgia.

DANIEL HELLINGER is professor of political science at Webster University. He has published widely on Venezuelan politics, including (with co-editor Steve Ellner) *Venezuelan Politics in the Chávez Era* (Lynne Rienner, 2003). He is author most recently of *Comparative Politics of Latin America: Democracy at Last?* (Routledge, 2011).

MICHAEL E. JOHNSON is an attorney in Washington, D.C. He received a JD from Georgetown University Law Center, where he was a Global Law Scholar and the assistant submissions editor on the *Georgetown Journal of Law and Public Policy.* He has done research, humanitarian service, and legal work in Latin America.

LUIS E. LANDER is professor of the faculty of economic and social sciences at the Universidad Central de Venezuela. He has published over sixty articles and chapters in academic books and journals both nationally and internationally, including the book *Poder y petróleo en Venezuela* (editor). He is a member of the editorial board of the *Revista Venezolana de Economía y Ciencias Sociales* and was its director from 2004 to 2007. He is director of the electoral monitoring group Ojo Electoral.

MARGARITA LÓPEZ MAYA is professor in social sciences at the Center for Development Studies (CENDES) and the Universidad Central de Venezuela, where she is editor of the journal *Revista Venezolana de Economía y Ciencias Sociales.* Her publications include *Del Viernes Negro al Referendo Revocatorio* (2005) and (editor) *Protesta y cultura en Venezuela. Los marcos de acción colectiva en 1999* (2002). In 2008–9 she was a fellow at the Woodrow Wilson Center in Washington, D.C.

ELIZABETH GACKSTETTER NICHOLS is professor of Spanish language and literature and chair of the Department of Languages at Drury University. Nichols has published on Venezuelan poetry and women's studies both in the United States and in Venezuela in such journals as *Frontiers* and *Argos*. She is coauthor with Kimberly Morse of *Venezuela*, in the Latin America in Focus series (ABC-Clio, 2010).

CORALY PAGAN graduated with a bachelor of arts in sociology from the University of Georgia in 2007. She was a research associate at UGA's Latin American and Caribbean Institute from 2005 to 2006. She is currently working as an English and Spanish interpreter in Puerto Rico and studying bilingual early education.

GUILLERMO ROSAS is assistant professor of political science at Washington University in St. Louis and a fellow at the university's Center for Political Economy. He is the author of *Curbing Bailouts: Bank Crises and Democratic Accountability in Comparative Perspective* (Michigan, 2009). His research has been published in *American Journal of Political Science*, *Comparative Political Studies*, *International Organization*, and *Legislative Studies Quarterly*, among others.

NAOMI SCHILLER is an assistant professor in the Department of Anthropology at Temple University. During the period 2006–2007, she produced, with community media producers, several short films about community television production in Caracas. Her research and teaching focus on the anthropology of media, ethnographic film, the state, and social movements in Latin America.

DAVID SMILDE is associate professor of sociology at the University of Georgia and editor-in-chief of the journal *Qualitative Sociology*. He is the author of *Reason to Believe: Cultural Agency in Latin American Evangelicalism* (California, 2007); winner of the Distinguished Book Award, Sociology of Religion Section, American Sociological Association; and coauthor (with Margarita López Maya and Keta Stephany) of *Protesta y cultura en Venezuela: Los marcos de acción colectiva en 1999* (FACES-UCV, 2002).

ALEJANDRO VELASCO is assistant professor of Latin American studies at New York University's Gallatin School of Individualized Study. He is a recipient of a 2004–2005 SSRC International Dissertation Research Fellowship. His chapter in this volume draws from his dissertation, "'A Weapon as Powerful as the Vote': Street Protest and Electoral Politics in Caracas, Venezuela, before Hugo Chávez" (Duke University, 2009).

Index

Socialism, 21, 46–47, 59, 124, 167, 223, 228, 235, 237
Society of Jesus, 326–27
Solaún, Mauricio, 276
Stokes, Susan, 25
Strepponi, Blanca, 305
Southern Cone, 1, 7, 13, 58–59, 224, 301
Sucre en Comunidad (newspaper), 135, 146, 153–55
SUMATE, 299
SUNACOOP (National Superintendency for Cooperatives), 68, 79n6
Supreme Court, 166, 326, 328
Swistun, Débora Alejandra, 14

Táchira, 112
Teatro Negro de Barlovento, 293
Telenovelas. See *Cosita Rica*
Terán, Enriqueta, 302
El Tiempo de Caricuao (newspaper), 135, 143, 149
Tiro al Blanco, 164
Tiuna, 142
Tomando Perola, 140, 142, 144, 147
Torres, Eloy, 166–67
Transparency International, xi, xvi
Tribuna Popular (newspaper), 166–67
Twenty-first-century socialism, xxi, 11, 34–35, 47, 51, 56, 78, 221, 229, 236–37

UBES. See Electoral Battle Units
Ucero, Luis Alfaro, 322
Ugalde, Luis, 321
Ultimas Noticias (newspaper), 119, 130n6, 225
Unicristiana, 332, 337
Unified Socialist Party of Venezuela. See Partido Socialista Unico de Venezuela (PSUV)
United Autonomous Revolutionary Class, 46
United Nations, 63, 88
United States: Aporrea users in, 223, 240, 242n3; civil rights movement in, 189;

clientelism in, 106; foreign policy of, 1; government of, 29; hemispheric domination by, x, xii, xvii, xix; imperialism of, 139; liberal democracy in, xi; media ownership in, 129; racism in, 17, 143, 273, 286; welfare reform in, 18
Universidad Bolivariana de Venezuela, 195, 232–33
Universidad Católica Ándres Bello, 27n1, 321
Urban land committees. See Comités de Tierras Urbanas

Varela, Iris, 299
VEC. See Venezuelan Episcopal Conference (VEC)
Velasco, Cardinal Ignacio, 325–26, 330
VENEPAL, 47–48, 50
Venezolano de Televisión (VTV), 113, 115–16, 120, 126, 151
Venezuelan Episcopal Conference (VEC), 317–18, 326, 329, 331
Vila Planes, Enrique, 68
Villanueva, Carlos, 160–61
Vive TV, 115–16, 119–21, 151, 225, 238
VTV. See Venezolano de Televisión (VTV)

Williams, Gareth, 295n6
Winn, Peter, 159
Women's Development Bank, 299
Women's poetry, 23, 298–99; class in, 301–2, 313; history of, 302–5; "the pelvic bone" in, 309–13; political discourse in, 305–9
World Social Forum, 34
Wortham, Erica Cusi, 110
Wright, Winthrop, 276

Yaracuy, 61

Zambo, 290–91, 293, 296n14
Zamora, Ezequiel, 142, 283–85, 296n11
Zinn, Dorothy Louise, 107
Zulia, 49–53, 69, 238

David Smilde is associate professor of sociology,
University of Georgia.

Daniel Hellinger is professor of history, politics,
and international relations, Webster University.

Library of Congress Cataloging-in-Publication Data
Venezuela's Bolivarian democracy : participation,
politics, and culture under Chávez / David Smilde
and Daniel Hellinger, editors.
p. cm.
Includes bibliographical references and index.
ISBN 978-0-8223-5024-8 (cloth : alk. paper)
ISBN 978-0-8223-5041-5 (pbk. : alk. paper)
1. Chávez Frías, Hugo. 2. Democracy—Venezuela.
3. Venezuela—Politics and government—1999–
4. Representative government and representation—
Venezuela—History. 5. Political participation—
Venezuela—History. I. Smilde, David.
II. Hellinger, Daniel.
JL3881.V463 2011
320.987—dc22 2011006521